KING STEPHEN

KING STEPHEN

DONALD MATTHEW

Hambledon and London
London and New York

Hambledon and London
102 Gloucester Avenue
London, NW1 8HX

838 Broadway
New York
NY 10003–4812

First Published 2002

ISBN 1 85285 272 0

Typeset by Carnegie Publishing, Lancaster
Printed on acid-free paper and bound in
Great Britain by Cambridge University Press

Contents

Illustrations

Acknowledgements

The author and the publishers are grateful to the following for permission to reproduce illustrations: the Bodleian Library, Oxford, 4; the British Library, 3; Corpus Christi College, Cambridge, 1; the Pierpoint Morgan Library, New York, 2.

Abbreviations

AASS	*Acta Sanctorum*
AHR	*American Historical Review*
AM	*Annales Monastici*
ANS	*Anglo Norman Studies*
ASC	Anglo-Saxon Chronicle
BIHR	*Bulletin of the Institute of Historical Research*
BL	British Library
CDF	*Calendar of Documents Preserved in France*
CRSHR	Chronicles of the Reigns of Stephen, Henry II and Richard I
EEA	English Episcopal Acta
EHR	*English Historical Review*
GC	Gervase of Canterbury
GF	Gilbert Foliot, *Letters and Charters*
GS	*Gesta Stephani*
HSJ	*Haskins Society Journal*
HH	Henry of Huntingdon, *Historia Anglorum*
HN	*Historia Novella* of William of Malmesbury
HP	*Historia Pontificalis* of John of Salisbury
Jaffe	*Regesta Pontificum Romanorum*
JBBA	*Journal of the British Archaeological Association*
JH	John of Hexham
JMH	*Journal of Medieval History*
JW	John of Worcester
LE	Liber Eliensis
MGHSS	Monumenta Germaniae Historica, Scriptores
NMS	Nottingham Medieval Studies
OMT	Oxford Medieval Texts

OV	Orderic Vitalis
PBA	*Proceeedings of the British Academy*
PL	Patrologia Latina
PRS	Pipe Roll Society
RH	Richard of Hexham
RRAN	*Regesta Regum Anglo Normannorum*
RS	Rolls Series
SHF	Société de l'Histoire de France
SS	Surtees Society
TBGAS	*Transactions of the Bristol and Gloucester Archaeological Society*
VCH	*Victoria County History*

SPONSAE CARISSIMAE
OTII PRIMITIAS

Preface

Like many others, I was introduced to the reign of Stephen at an impressionable age. When I was nine, my father bought me fortnightly instalments of Walter Hutchinson's revamped *Story of the British Nation* and my eyes were caught by a picture illustrating the torments inflicted on prisoners in the course of the Anarchy. Childish interests in the period are inevitably unsophisticated, even crude. Some twelve years later, as an undergraduate, I was abruptly expected to discover how to study seriously a period described as chaotic. Within a few years, I found myself willy-nilly teaching History undergraduates a Special Subject on Stephen through original Latin sources. At that stage, I still had little appreciation of what was required and after a few years moved over to Special Subject studies of Louis IX of France and Henry II of England, rulers generally admired rather than censured. Yet, towards the end of my academic career, I reverted to Stephen. It was not only more manageable as a topic for undergraduate study; it never failed to attract a surprising number and variety of students, as Henry II did not.

For whatever reason Stephen initially arouses interest, as study of his problems obliges the historian to consider the difficulties facing any authority in dealing with those who persist in defiance of it. Can individual dissidents be bought off? Does this encourage others to hold out for more? Do negotiations with the recalcitrant discredit lawful authority? If governments resolve not to make concessions, can they be confident of getting their way by force? And what happens, if force proves inadequate or if the government's resolution falters? Does seeking compromise then amount to proof of good sense? Or to an admission of failure? English history has not lent itself to the study of such problems. Much of it is usually presented in terms of confrontation, as between rival teams of players, with historians expected to explain like sports writers why the winners beat the losers. The reign of Stephen cannot be fitted into this conception of the past. It offers the dispiriting spectacle of great efforts expended to no purpose. In national myth-making it has accordingly been treated as a period when 'government', vitiated by its origins in usurpation, lost its grip, with dire consequences for the nation. It is the main thrust of this book that this view needs reassessment.

After accumulating for over fifty years a great deal of information about the topic and discussing the problems with many generations of puzzled undergraduates, I felt sufficiently confident of what I knew and dissatisfied enough with much of what I had read to feel justified in airing some views of my own. My hope is that it may succeed in reintegrating Stephen and his times with the twelfth century.

Because I am confident that interest in Stephen extends outside the academic world, I have tried to write for a general readership and have kept the scholarly apparatus to a minimum. Annotation cannot be dispensed with altogether, but it has been deliberately limited to identification of the original sources of information; the temptation to engage in scholarly controversy has been generally resisted. What I owe to the erudition of previous writers is nonetheless manifest, even when my conclusions differ from theirs. What I owe to generations of Special Subject students is not so obvious, but deserves no less acknowledgement. Regular examination of the sources obliges everyone to recognise the difficulties of interpreting them and using them to try and grasp the nature of the actual situations they refer to. On his own, the historian will find this taxing enough; he may even be attracted to some eccentric ideas. In class, students are not disposed to let their teachers get away with very much. Moreover, discussion there throws up not only irreconcilable differences of opinion but unexpected insights. The study of history does not provide a foretaste of the day of judgement; it shows that disagreements are what the past is all about. Only a lifeless present can conceive of the past as dead.

Over the years, I have derived enlightenment and pleasure from talking about Stephen with a great many different friends and colleagues. My college tutor, Michael Wallace-Hadrill, commissioned my undergraduate efforts to come to terms with the topic; my first 'boss', Christopher Brooke, obliged me to engage with the original sources. I offer my thanks to those I consulted about specific problems, especially Cecil Slade, Mark Blackburn, Paul Harvey and Michael Kauffmann, who cannot, however, be held in any way responsible for the use I made of their counsels. Finally, I acknowledge what I owe to my publishers for encouraging me to write down something of what had been learnt in the last sixty years. Since the work has not involved research into manuscripts, these reflections from the classroom would not have been printed without the publishers' confidence in their potential interest to a wider audience.

1

Scene-Setting

In the context of England's long history, the mere nineteen years of King Stephen's reign have received a disproportionate amount of historical attention. In part this is because its dramatic events and reputation for blood and horror appeal to the popular imagination; everyone with a smattering of English history knows the story of the reign, at least in outline. It began with what seems like a daring adventure to seize the throne. When Stephen, count of Mortain, heard, probably at Boulogne (where he was also count in the right of his wife, the heiress Matilda) of the death of his uncle, King Henry I at Lions-la-Forêt in Normandy on 1 December 1135, he sailed immediately for England and within three weeks, without encountering any substantial opposition to his claims, had persuaded those responsible to recognise him as king and to crown him at Westminster.

Henry I's only legitimate son, William, had been drowned at sea in the ship-wreck of the White Ship (1120), but in 1135 William's older sister, Matilda, nursed expectations of succeeding her father. At the death of her first husband, the German Emperor Henry V, Matilda had returned to England after an absence of sixteen years and her father had required his barons to swear to defend Matilda's rights as his heir. Stephen had sworn along with others. In 1135, these oaths do not seem to have weighed very heavily on many consciences though according to Matilda's supporters, Stephen, by seizing the crown, had laid himself open to the charge that, as a perjurer, he was unfit to rule. At the beginning of Stephen's reign, however, Matilda herself had little room for manoeuvre. In 1128 she had been married to Geoffrey, count of Anjou, without general consultation in the kingdom. Geoffrey had never been received in England or recognised there as Henry's successor, as husband of his heiress. By the time Henry I died, Matilda had already borne Geoffrey two sons and was expecting a third child. On hearing of Henry's death, Geoffrey of Anjou duly made a show in Normandy of asserting his claims but was quickly expelled from the duchy. Without Normandy, Geoffrey was in no position to intervene in England. Even if Matilda had acknowleged the difficulties of securing the throne for her herself or her husband, she cannot have been expected to abandon the idea that her children had incontrovertible rights to the succession. In the immediate future, however, even the oldest, Henry, not three years of age, was clearly in no position to rule as king. An interim ruler was inevitable. In effect, it turned out that Stephen's coronation in England was sufficient to settle the matter even for Normandy. As soon as this was known, the lords of the duchy happily accepted Stephen as their ruler. By taking the crown, Stephen had stolen a march on Geoffrey.

Matilda herself did not come to England to dispute Stephen's title until nearly four years after his coronation. His resolve and ability were, however, challenged from the start by several different enemies, King David of Scotland in the north, Baldwin de Redvers, who seized Exeter castle and refused to accept Stephen as king, and by Welsh lords eager to take advantage of Henry I's death to reassert themselves in their own region. These various challenges may be interpreted as concerted and intended to promote Matilda's interests, but this cannot be certainly demonstrated. From the periphery, such attempts to topple Stephen not only failed to vindicate the 'legitimist' cause, but exposed its short comings. All Stephen's predecessors since 1066 had faced greater opposition at the start of their reigns, and Stephen weathered the first few years without serious embarrassment.

Most writers believe that it was only from the summer of 1139 that his luck began to run out. In June of that year, Stephen suspected three bishops, Roger of Salisbury, and his two nephews, Alexander of Lincoln and Nigel of Ely, of treachery. The king demanded the surrender of the bishops' powerful castles and, when they refused, arrested Salisbury and Lincoln; Ely escaped. In the uneasy situation that ensued, Matilda of Anjou arrived in England with her half-brother Robert, earl of Gloucester, a bastard son of Henry I who had been well provided by his father with lands in England, Wales and Normandy. Though Matilda herself was detained by the king's forces at Arundel, where she was allegedly only visiting her step-mother, Adeliza of Louvain, Henry I's second (and barren) queen, Gloucester slipped away to Bristol, the heart of his great estates, and began to work seriously for the disruption of Stephen's kingship. In a move that proved unwise, Stephen allowed Matilda of Anjou to be despatched into Gloucester's keeping. Almost immediately, the west country became unruly; despite Stephen's energetic reaction, Angevin partisans eventually prevailed in that region. Even so, real disaster did not strike until early in 1141, when Stephen became involved in a dispute with Gloucester's son-in-law, Ranulf, earl of Chester, over rights in Lincoln, on the other side of England. Ranulf appealed to Gloucester for support and a pitched battle was accordingly fought at Lincoln, in which, deserted by many supporters, Stephen was taken prisoner. The triumphant Gloucester was now apparently expected by Matilda to take advantage of the situation to make her ruler of England.

After negotiations lasting several weeks, the Angevin party was admitted to London where she anticipated formal coronation. Instead, within a few days, she was ignominiously chased out of the city, in a campaign master minded by Stephen's wife, Matilda of Boulogne, her own cousin, acting in alliance with Stephen's youngest brother, Henry, bishop of Winchester.

Queen Matilda consolidated this success three months later when her troops broke up the Angevin army at Winchester where it was besieging the bishop in his castle. In the rout which followed, Robert of Gloucester was himself taken prisoner. After protracted negotiations, an exchange of the two prisoners, Stephen and Robert, was agreed. At the end of this fateful year, 1141, Stephen therefore recovered his throne. In effect this openly confirmed the validity of his title but Gloucester refused to acknowledge the implications of this and despite Stephen's efforts, the king proved unable to bring the Angevins to heel: in England, most seriously, the west country continued for much of the reign to defy him. In the meantime Geoffrey took advantage of Stephen's pre-occupations in England to set about the conquest of Normandy.

The most easterly Angevin outpost was Oxford. Here, from the summer of 1142, Stephen besieged Matilda of Anjou in the castle. She managed to escape only at the end of the year, across the snow, in one of the most picturesque moments of English history. The conflict dragged on and disrespect for the king brought such unfamiliar conditions that the whole reign has usually been described quite simply as the 'Anarchy', or, in a phrase, quoted from its source in the vernacular chronicle, as the time 'when Christ and His saints slept'. The term anarchy implies such a sense of uncontrolled turmoil that any sign of Stephen exercising authority is commonly disregarded. Historians give the impression of waiting impatiently for the 'restoration' of the legitimate line and the reimposition of royal order. Yet towards the end of his reign, Stephen was confident enough of his own position to nominate his elder son, Eustace, as his successor in 1152. Even this has been interpreted not so much as a sign of his power but further evidence of his ineptitude. At the time, Geoffrey's son, Henry, who had been installed by his father as duke of Normandy in 1149, and succeeded him as count of Anjou in 1151, thought it expedient to come over and rekindle the Angevin cause in England. Welcomed in several parts of England, when he eventually arrived early in 1153, the young Henry still could not prevail by force of arms, proving that the Angevin succession did not command general support. Only the unexpected death of Eustace in August opened the way for a settlement. Stephen retained the throne for his lifetime and formally adopted Henry as his own lawful heir. Less than a year later, Stephen died and Henry of Anjou was accepted as

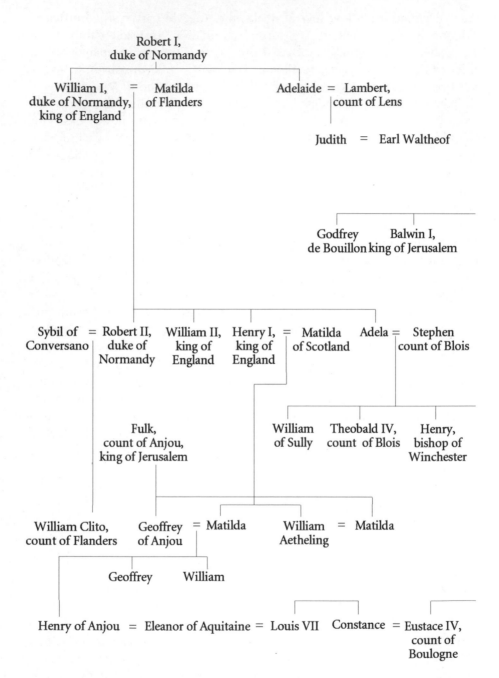

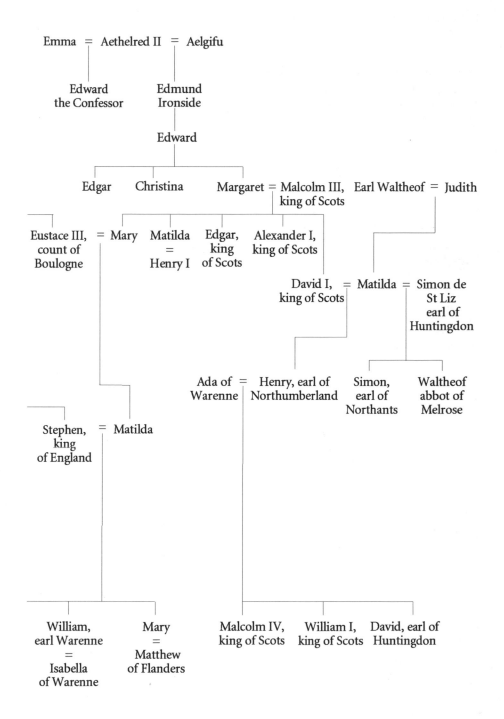

king in his place. The 'anarchic' interlude in England's long history of rule by strong kings was over.

The continuous activity and the unpredictability of the outcome to the very end may readily explain the fascination this reign has exerted over the popular imagination. For once, characters from medieval history emerge as personalities capable of still inspiring genuine interest. Stephen's easy going charm may have enabled him to acquire the crown without a battle; equally, it is believed to have rendered him incapable of ruthless government. The extraordinary daring of the 'empress' Matilda herself has few parallels. The drama of their confrontation depicted by historians surely echoes what contemporaries themselves saw: admirable protagonists in difficult situations, coping persistently with the vicissitudes of fortune.

The story-line apart, Stephen's reign has also been consistently interpreted as a tale with a moral. The king's misfortunes and the kingdom's misery have been presented as the terrible price Stephen, and England, were made to pay for his ambition. This interpretation obviously depends on a firm belief that wrong doing will in the long run be duly punished and on the confidence in a long-standing tradition that 'lessons' can be learned from reading about the past. The use of history for moral purposes cannot be mocked as 'old-fashioned', religious wishful-thinking. It goes back further than Christianity and has not yet been abandoned. The inclination not only to understand public affairs in terms of conflicts between the good and the bad, but to believe that the wicked should and can be punished for their evil deeds, if not by divine providence, then by the dedicated efforts of the righteous themselves still prevails, not least amongst popularist politicians. The determination to be proved right is so strong that even victory in war is no longer thought sufficient to resolve any doubts. It is now routine to have the moral worthiness of the cause and the war vindicated in the law-courts by securing convictions of the enemy for war crimes. In any dispute, it is assumed that human judgment can and should be employed to establish which party was in the right and which wrong. The historian is not expected to confine attention to elucidating, as precisely as possible, what happened when and why. 'History' itself is somehow supposed to weigh up the evidence and pronounce judgment. In some cases, the issue never seems to be in doubt. Stephen is a case in point. He has been consistently depicted as an opportunistic adventurer who infringed the legitimate rights of the 'empress'.

When Stephen declared his candidature for the kingship, it would have been difficult to name anyone more likely to be acceptable and successful. Though Matilda proved herself to be a formidable woman, she could not possibly have been expected in 1135 to have ruled in person. This would have amounted to an attempt to contradict current expectations by force of her personality alone. On account of her first marriage, she encouraged her supporters to address her with the title 'empress', but after her second marriage to Geoffrey, count of Anjou, several years her junior, her effective status was much less exalted. To think that Matilda's husband Geoffrey of Anjou, would in England have seemed preferable as king defies all common sense. Geoffrey, unlike Stephen, was quite unknown in England. Even on personal grounds, had his rights been admitted, there is no reason to suppose that he would have made a more successful ruler than Stephen. This makes it desirable to consider for what reasons some great men chose to defend the rights of Henry I's daughter, Countess Matilda, to the throne. In 1135 they were neither numerous, nor vocal, nor determined enough to carry much weight. Because they upheld what now seems the 'legitimist' position, their motives are generally assumed to be honourable and disinterested, but their contemporaries do not seem to have seen it like that: the 'moral' stance never made much impression. It is not therefore inappropriate to ask whether these barons did not expect to derive some advantage from opposing the new king in the name of the empress. They were not a very influential group. Only in 1141, with Stephen in prison and no alternative to him as ruler in sight but the empress, did the Angevin party ever achieve any wide degree of support. Within five months, even this began to melt away. If, after Stephen's release, his troubles were not over, the main reason for this was not any general wish throughout the kingdom to withdraw obedience, but the determination of Matilda herself to get vengeance on the king and keep the struggle going in the interests of her sons. In the end, she was in a sense vindicated. Her ultimate purpose was achieved when her son Henry of Anjou became king in 1154. Whether this outcome should be interpreted as proof of the triumph of right over wrong is another matter. Instead of accepting that from the beginning a civil war raged in defence of right against usurpation, a more realistic asseesment of the conflict is in order.

Whatever its merits as a tale with a moral, this view fails to explain some crucial elements of the story. Stephen did not gamble like an insouciant adolescent. In 1135 he was probably already in his mid forties; he had been a familiar figure in the kingdom for over twenty years, well known not only to the great men, but in the city of London. In person, he was affable and able to inspire loyalty. Even his enemies acknowledged his good qualities. In such a well-regulated kingdom as England was in the twelfth century, how could an ambitious baron have got away with being accepted as king in 1135, to the manifest detriment of the true heir? Not only this. Captured, imprisoned and humiliated for nine months, Stephen was restored to his throne, not properly deposed and ousted. Moreover, this supposedly incompetent ruler was then allowed to reign for another thirteen years. To assume that the kingdom was somehow duped in 1135 may be arguable; but it defies belief that the kingdom was prepared to readopt a king perceived as incompetent. The steady denigration of Stephen as a ruler intruded into another's seat has made the familiar tale into a kind of fairy-story.

Stephen was the only twelfth-century English king whose deeds (*gesta*) in England impressed a contemporary writer sufficiently to make it seem worth recording them in detail.[1] Stephen is presented as an exemplary figure, constantly exposed to fresh challenges, yet never wavering in valour. As a hero, his misfortunes are not attributed to weaknesses of character but invariably excused, either as a result of his virtuous respect for the advice given by others or because of adverse circumstances. The unknown author of the *Gesta* admired Stephen. One of the challenges facing modern inter-preters of the reign is how to make his point of view at least intelligible, if not totally convincing. The task is complicated by the fact that in some respects more is known about Stephen's nineteen years than about any comparable period in the whole century. Some of the finest chronicle writers of the age followed events closely; and none denied that Stephen possessed estimable qualifications for the kingly office. Although they were baffled to explain what went wrong, and made suggestions that inevitably reflect badly on the king's judgment, none of them suggested that Stephen himself neglected his responsibilities. They describe him ranging up and down the kingdom. They were aware of the very broad front of royal operations between Scotland and France. Their evidence indicates how little the king-dom had fallen apart with each neighbourhood shut in on itself. Local conditions were treated as though they were typical of what happened everywhere else: the 'national' outlook was shaped by local experience (as it often still is). What went on in every district cannot of course now be reconstructed in detail, but historians have put such exceptional efforts into trying to understand the local situations that for this reign they are now better known than for any other part of the twelfth century.

In periods of 'anarchy', historians might expect to find the situation too confused or the sequence of events too obscure for intelligent treatment. Anarchy, however, is not the appropriate word to describe King Stephen's England. That it is still regularly employed, in spite of many scholarly objections, tells us something significant about prevailing conceptions of English history. Attempts to weave it into the fabric of the English past have been made in various ways since the twelfth century, each according to the current preoccupations of the age. Fifty years after the death of King Stephen in 1154, a brief account of his reign was given by Gervase of Tilbury in a summary history of England, written as part of a more general work for the Emperor Otto IV, grandson of King Henry II.[2] According to Gervase, Stephen had been designated ruler by Henry I because his grandson Henry of Anjou was too young to govern for himself. Stephen's fine character is acknowledged. He was

> steadfast in faith, staunch in his promises, outstanding in warfare, of simple piety and free from all cupidity and greed. Bound by oath to care faithfully for the kingdom ... he was crowned, anointed and ruled his people successfully in the strength of his virtue, feared and loved by all, until misled by his simple good-nature and compassion for those deserving punishment and chastisement ... he forgot his oath and took it into head to disinherit the empress and her legitimate son, and to substitute in his place his own son, Count Eustace.

This is a surprisingly amiable picture of Stephen to have been current in Angevin circles, where a much more hostile view of Stephen's 'usurpation' might have been expected.[3] Instead, Stephen had been absorbed into an Angevin interpretation as the infant Henry's temporary guardian, who belatedly betrayed the trust put in him by a shameful, but understandable, attempt to hand on the crown to his own son. Like much else in this curious work, the account of Stephen bears little resemblance to what is now believed to be the true story of the king. Gervase is not be regarded as an 'authority' on the reign. Yet it is hardly possible to dismiss him as a pure fantasist, for he did not make it all up. The essence of his interpretation can be traced to chronicles written in northern France and Flanders in the time of Henry II himself.[4] These must reflect not mere fancy but what was believed about Stephen within a few years of his death in the parts of France geographically closest to England.

In the late twelfth century there were many men still alive with personal memories of both the times and the person of the king, not all of them unfavourable. The great knight, William Marshal, for example, who died only in 1219, probably often recounted his experiences as a boy when he was handed over to the king as a hostage for his father's good behaviour.[5] His father did not scruple to oppose the king and so put his son's life at risk, boasting that he had the wherewithal to make other sons if young William was killed, to Stephen's undisguised outrage. What William made of his father's willingness to sacrifice his own son the narrative does not indicate. As he remembered it, he had blithely enjoyed his opportunities as a boy in military camp to play soldiers with some of Stephen's great men and childish games with the king himself. By then in his late fifties, Stephen had taken a kindly interest in the bold lad and resolutely refused to think of taking vengeance on one whom his own father had so callously abandoned. The story of the boy's ordeal was not recalled to mock the king's weak reaction to his father's insolence but in respect for his unaffected and gentle character. Stephen was no brute, as William's father had been. The Marshal became prominent in the Angevin royal circle but did not forget what he himself owed to the old king.

There were probably many others with comparable memories. Stephen is almost universally recorded as a man of charming ways, not with hostility. One version of an early thirteenth-century 'feudal manual' of history refers to him without hesitation as *noble chevaler e debonere* and his burial at Faversham *noblement a grant honour*.[6] Some years after Gervase of Tilbury gave his version of history, Matthew Paris reported an even more strange distortion of the truth.[7] Here the familiar story of Stephen's rivalry with the Empress Matilda is turned on its head. Matilda becomes the intermediary between Stephen and her son Henry in 1153 by telling the king that Henry was the fruit of their own romance, when he had escorted her back to her husband in 1131. This made Henry his real son, not merely his adopted heir.[8] Again, it is less important to wonder how such an idea could come to pass as history, than to recognise that, had there been any general belief in their invincible antipathy, such a romantic story could never have arisen at all.

Whereas Stephen's adventure has generally been treated as a story of considerable human interest, modern historians have almost invariably taken a much more disapproving view of his rule. This is because they read the reign not for its picturesque possibilities but for what it contributed to the history of English medieval government. The Norman Conquest is believed to have been decisive for the development of monarchy. A generation later, Henry I devised new institutions of justice and fiscal management to enhance his authority. These were consolidated in the second half of the twelfth century by Henry II. In this scheme of historical growth, Stephen's reign contributed nothing. Rather, it is seen as retrograde, obliging Henry II in his early years to work for the recovery of royal powers Stephen had lost, before a royal programme of reform could be launched with renewed vigour.

Belief in the virtues of strong government, and even more in the duty of all governments to commit themselves to 'reform' of some kind, is unmistakably modern. Its values are purely secular, taking no account of such earlier principles about rulership as respect for the established customs of the realm, for God and for the church. No excuses for shirking the challenge of government are acceptable. Whereas medieval writers would have acknowledged that men, as inherently sinful, constantly thwart the most noble intentions and, as imperfectible, must fail to achieve their own ambitions in this life, modern confidence that rulers can do what they want and must be judged accordingly makes Stephen look inadequate for his office. Little attention has been given to establishing how much his subjects expected or required him to rule as his uncle had done. As a result, Stephen is bound to seem out of step, as though performing in a play without lines written for him. The first problem about Stephen's historical reputation is to establish how a character generally admired in his own day has been cast in such an unattractive role.

Until the last few months of his life, Stephen probably hoped that he would be succeeded after his death by one of his sons. Had this happened, his reputation would have been nurtured by his family. Instead, the succession of Henry of Anjou unavoidably prejudiced the long-term future of Stephen's good name. The Plantagenets not only established a line of kings for the next six or more generations; they committed English rulers to the defence of their extensive French lands and moulded expectations of English medieval government accordingly. To hold their place on the continent, English kings learnt how to obtain money and military forces from their English subjects, and to do this they had to persuade and coerce the kingdom in such wise as to make English kings incomparably strong. Over the generations, Stephen's reign looked more and more like a mere interlude which had contributed nothing to the shaping of such a kingdom.

In his own time, Stephen's subjects could have had no inkling of what was to come. Even his enemies had not by then formulated any vision of England's part in the dynastic ambitions of the counts of Anjou. The link with Aquitaine, which was to leave the most enduring legacy for English history, was not made until 1152, by Henry of Anjou's opportunistic marriage to Duchess Eleanor immediately after her divorce from King Louis VII of France. For most of Stephen's reign the implications of any English connection with the Angevins were not only unforeseen, but unforeseeable. In 1153, when Henry of Anjou was adopted as Stephen's heir, one of his attractions must have been not that he would revive royal authority but that he would be often absent, dealing with pressing affairs in his French lands. Who would have imagined in 1153 that Henry II would become the innovating government genius familiar from modern English history books? That Stephen became a nonentity in English historical legend has little to do with his reign as such. Before judging him in the light of history it is at least necessary to restore the real dimensions of his problems.

In the early thirteenth century it was still possible to treat Stephen without condescension. What passes for the traditional view is no more than a comparatively recent construction of a school of historical interpretation which stressed political development as the key to understanding the English past. Modern academic history has endorsed, but did not invent this tradition, which owes most to the intellectual influence on historical writing of

English common lawyers, with their interest in royal government, parliament and law-making, with the landlaw and the ruling classes; and their inveterate suspicion of the clergy, the pope, canon-law and indeed of the unruliness of the common people. Their values have dominated English writing about medieval history, and indeed still do, because of the consensus that the history of strong royal English government has been continuous at least since the Norman Conquest. The fortunes of the kingdom were tied to those of the monarchy itself, the only power then able to work for the 'nation'. Within this scheme of things, Stephen's reign has been used to provide an archetypal demonstration of the evils that befall the kingdom in the absence of strong rulership. Weak kings betray the hopes of their people for greatness and any faltering in their government becomes a disaster for the kingdom as a whole. Those who admire and seek to control central government are bound to regard any diminution of its powers of domination as an evil to be avoided at all costs. The consequences of Stephen's inadequacy have been grossly exaggerated to rub in the lesson more surely. The nineteen years when God and the saints slept have been treated as a fantastic self-contained episode, when anything was conceiveable and every disaster occurred. When it was over, real life resumed. Unlike other kingdoms, England has only once succumbed to such a fate in its millennial history and the lesson is never to be forgotten. Even the civil wars of the fifteenth and seventeeth centuries have not left such a negative mark on English history. Only one period has been singled out as the Anarchy. Some of the most recent historians of the subject do not blush to use the term still.

'Making sense' of English history has been attempted in almost every generation for the past nine hundred years. Certain features of the inter- pretation seem set in stone. Nevertheless, however much the story transmitted from one generation to another survives in a recognisable form, variations in emphasis have occurred, not usually because of fresh evidence coming to light but because of changing cultural expectations. This draws attention to the way present pre-occupations inevitably influence presenta- tion of events remote in time. Whatever the intrinsic interest of tracking these various assessments of Stephen down the centuries, it should not be allowed to seem like a minor branch of intellectual history. There can be no more convincing way of showing how the present always sets the agenda for writing about the past. Obviously, modern students of Stephen's reign bring to their reading an understanding of events and questions they think important, which modern historians have to address if they are to satisfy their readers. The revised views reflect the new values in circulation amongst both readers and writers of history. The process is not only unavoidable but indispensable. If views about the past were not 'updated', readers would find the old ones merely quaint. This should not, however, become an excuse for allowing present prejudices to get away with anachronistic judgments about the past. Historians, even of Stephen, may not be able to distance themselves completely from the preoccupations of their own age, but they must also try to observe the rules of their craft and test modern ideas against what the twelfth-century evidence clearly has to say about the reign. In other words, the sources must be coaxed into telling us what they really did witness, not tortured into confirming what we would like to believe.

2

Stephen's Historical Image

The earliest history of England to be widely distributed through the printing press was the Latin one Henry VII commissioned from the Italian scholar Polydore Vergil. This was not completed till 1533 when it was presented to Henry VIII.[1] Here already we have Stephen commended for his personal virtues and the principal cause of his troubles identified as violation of his oaths to Matilda and her heirs. Vergil is exceptional, however, for blaming Robert of Gloucester's obstinate attachment to Matilda's interests, rather than to those of the kingdom as a whole, when he rejected the barons' attempt to reach a general settlement in the autumn of 1141. Vergil makes a number of historical errors, sending Matilda to England in Stephen's sixth rather than fourth year, supposing her to be in Lincoln at the time of the battle in 1141, and still in England in 1153, taking part in the final negotiations for peace. Though he reports it only as a vulgar fiction, he nevertheless repeats the story about Stephen's liaison with Matilda, of which Henry of Anjou was the fruit. Likewise, he tells the familiar medieval story based on a textual misunderstanding about Matilda making her escape from Winchester in 1141 concealed in a coffin. Vergil obviously accepted that good stories deserved a place, however far-fetched. But he does not indulge in too much lachrymose description of the horrors of warfare, and he makes a genuine historical attempt to grasp the political realities of the situation in a manner that could have appealed to its intended readership. The barons or magnates of the twelfth century writers become 'heroes' in Vergil's Renaissance Latin, and they behave in this history as persons of consequence entitled to respect, rather than as pampered ruffians or the wicked 'feudalists' of modern myth. At the beginning of the reign, Stephen spontaneously allowed them to build castles at pleasure and only came to regret this later after Matilda arrived. The fault lay with his generosity and lack of foresight rather than with the innate unreliability of his nobles.

Vergil is particularly acute in linking events in England to the situation in France. Stephen's alliance with Louis VII is treated as crucial for his position. This is also said to have been what inspired Henry of Anjou's hatred of Louis and his marriage to Louis's divorced wife Eleanor, which in turn occasioned later warfare over Aquitaine. Similarly, Vergil sees that

Geoffrey seized his chance after Lincoln to occupy Normandy. His account of the attempt to reach a general settlement in the autumn of 1141, though based on William of Malmesbury, reveals his sensitivity to the political opportunities open at this juncture. According to him, Queen Matilda could not resist the temptation to treat her prisoner Gloucester as harshly as her husband had been treated, in order to illustrate the scriptural warning about being measured by the same means as are used to measure others. This is not what the sources report; it is what Vergil believed more likely.

Vergil also scatters a few homely proverbs through his text to ram home the kind of sense that some episodes of the story aptly demonstrated. His secular slant notably affects his assessment of the clergy in the reign. Henry Murdac, for example, who denounced William Fitz Herbert's election to the see of York election as vitiated, appears as a man of ambition, who tricked the pope into consecrating himself as archbishop. Henry, bishop of Winchester, perhaps because he was the king's brother, is specifically noticed in the final pages as one of the illustrious men of the age, though it seems strange to commend him for great constancy in all circumstances. The peace of 1153 duly came about when God willed it and inspired Stephen, whose ambitions had begun the troubles, to welcome the chance of peace. The death of Eustace, a young man of great promise, opened the way and deprived Stephen of the family relationship with Louis VII which had been so important politically. Stephen's comparative indifference to the rights of his second son, William, is explained by assuming that William was illegitimate. Of Stephen's government, Vergil comments that he made few if any financial demands on his subjects for his continuous wars, though he did take money from the bishops whose loyalty he suspected. The sole criticism Vergil could find of him was that, by seizing the crown, he violated justice. The emphasis on the hereditary right of monarchy is reinforced by reference to the evils that flow from disregarding them. There is nothing here about the evils of the feudal system or of an unruly nobility. Vergil's approach to the historical situation is above all shaped by the way he viewed the European politics of his own day. The past is brought to life by the present.

Ralph Holinshed, the most famous of English sixteenth-century historians, provided an exceptionally detailed account of Stephen.[2] In its way, it is also one of the most hostile, as its chapter heading, calling Stephen, 'earle of Bullongne', not 'king', immediately indicates: 'cause of all the trouble in having usurped another man's [a curious and significant error] right inheritance'. Not that Holinshed judged Stephen to be personally unsuited for kingship. 'Vices wherewith he should be noted, I find none, but that upon an ambitious desire to reign he break his oath which he made with the empress Maud', an echo of Polydore Vergil. Holinshed begins his account of the reign, however, by emphasising the role of the bishops in raising Stephen to the kingship, thinking that they

> should do God good service in providing for the wealth of the realm and the advancement of the church by their [own] perjury. For whereas the late king used himself not altogither for their purpose, they thought that if they might set up and create a king cheeflie by their especial means and authority, he would follow their council better and reform such things as they judged to be amisse.

For an assessment of Holinshed's views, his recognition that the origins of the ecclesiastical practice of appealing to Rome date from this reign is crucial. His disapproval of the bishops' initiatives, and of their plans of reform, stems from his Protestant dislike of papal interference. More insistently than Vergil, Holinshed saw Stephen's misfortunes as due to the direct intervention of God in punishing his perjury. This inevitably tended to diminish any concern for explaining in detail how things turned out. He is remarkably reticent about Matilda (or Maud as he calls her) and appears to be deliberately avoiding any discussion of her potential merits as a ruler. That oaths were sworn to recognise her as Henry I's heir is deemed sufficient to have made her rights unquestionable. Attempts to deny their force or validity are treated as cheap apologies for perjury. In Holinshed's day, the succession of Henry VIII's two daughters by virtue of parliamentary acts had, in effect, changed perceptions in England about the feasibility of female rule. Holinshed's inflexible view of the oaths sworn to Maud also seems to reflect his contemporaries' uneasiness about disputed successions in case they reopened the civil wars of the previous century. He takes for granted a right to succession according to the arbitrary whims of the ruler. This satisfied many men in his own age. Holinshed admitted that, in the beginning, Stephen's reign was 'nothing bitter or heavy to his subjects but full of gentleness, lenitie, courtesie and mildness', but this he reckoned to be what happens under princes who 'attain their estates more through favour and support of others than by any good right or title which they may pretend of themselves'. Allowing subjects to bargain with rulers opens the way to dissent and turmoil. This depressing conclusion is deepened by the chronicler's guarded recognition of princely arrogance: 'We may also consider the inordinate outrages of princes and their fanatic fierceness who esteem not the loss of their subjects' lives, the effusion of innocent blood, the [?de-]population of countries, the ruinating of ample regions ... an so their will may be satisfied, their desire served.' Holinshed, despite recognising princely failings, thought it better to leave them to dispose of the crown as they chose; election has no attractions for him.

Despite these sixteenth-century foretastes of the way the past might have

meaning for the present, history only developed its full potential for incul-
cating lessons in political sagacity from the political conflicts of the
seventeenth century. Earlier, a wave of antiquarian interest in the past almost
submerged any fresh attempt to reach conclusions about the correct answers
to political problems from past events. The position in the early seventeenth
century may be illustrated from the work of John Speed, whose *History of
Great Britaine* was published in 1611,[3] and of Samuel Daniel, who concluded
the original version of his English history with the reign of Stephen in 1612.[4]

Speed's idea that 'so powerful is ambition where the object is a diadem
and so weak are all assurances built on the wavering multitude that King
Henry [I]'s providence was soon defeated' clearly owes much to Holinshed.
Other parts of his narrative have a different emphasis, one which remained
influential till the eighteenth century. Apart from the way the bishops were
drawn into the acts of perjury, the secular nobility traitorously avowed that
'it was baseness for so many and so great peers to be subject to a woman',
a view that after Elizabeth I's reign was bound to seem unreasonable . The
importance of the nobles is also stressed at the end of the reign when they
brought Henry of Anjou and Stephen to agreement;

> the nobility on both parts there present were nearely linked in alliances and blood
> and how these stood affected was very doubtful yet that brethren were there
> assembled the one against the other whereof must needs follow an unnatural war
> between them and of dangerous consequence even to him that conquested.

Although Speed disapproved of Stephen's perjury, he was rather more
positive than Holinshed about his merits:

> [His] person and presence drew ever the affections of the beholders being in all
> parts complete with nature, endowments of personnage, passing comely of dis-
> position, loving, cheerful and affable to the meanest, always very liberal ... and
> in martial prowess gave place to none of that time, wherein though his whole
> reign was continually spent yet (by reason of king Henries great treasure left)
> never burthened he the commonwealth with any exactions ... neither is he taxed
> with any other observable crime save only his perjury against the empress dowager
> and her son.

Speed made more of a case on behalf of Matilda than previous writers,
though he remained rather indecisive. Discussing her resistance to the
petitioners of 1141 at the pinnacle of her success in England, Speed refers to
the common allegation that she rejected them 'out of pride, say some, but
it may seeme rather of policy, holding it safest to passe affaires of importance
not upon intreaty but by due advice and to govern the subject with a severe
austereness rather than a indulgent lenitie.' However, he clearly recognised
that, in the summer of 1141, she was still in too precarious a situation to

practise statecraft: 'this too regular strictness which might have done well in a settled government in this her yet green and unsecured estate proved not so behoveful'.

Within months Matilda was reduced to making her legendary escape from Winchester to Gloucester in a coffin, and Speed took the opportunity to generalise on the fate of princes:

> To such extremities were these two princes [Matilda and Stephen, still then in prison] at the selfsame time subject that while they turmoiled for spacious king-doms brought themselves to the very extream wants of air and elbow room but with such dalliance doth Fortune [we see] oftentimes follow her game that she maketh even monarchs the balls of her play and tosseth them lastly into the hazard whence hardly they escape with safety of life.

Speed is both more acute and more lively in his account of the reign than Holinshed. There is less of divine intervention and his comments on the papal support for Stephen in 1135 ironic rather than partisan: it 'may be conceived that his holiness either out of hatred of the empress whose [first] husband Henry [V] was no friend to the papacy or for some other holy ends had no small hand in advancing Stephen's perjured and disloyal intrusion'. It would have seemed in seventeenth-century England quite unremarkable for a pope to condone perjury. The basic incongruity of the idea never crossed Speed's mind. His references to King David of Scotland and his refusal to do homage to Stephen in 1136 probably owe something to the new interest after 1603 in the connections between the two kingdoms and go someway to fulfilling his own agenda in rewriting English history from a British point of view.

Samuel Daniel's history, published in quarto format, made it more con-venient for general reading and may have accordingly enjoyed a broader readership. Nevertheless, he was not a mere popularist, taking advantage of the recent publication of the principal chronicles of the reign to construct an account of events that is in outline quite familiar. He made little of the fact that the oaths sworn under Henry I to accept his daughter as his heir were set aside, 'upon what reasons of councell wee must gather out of the circumstances of the courses held in that time'. Stephen, being 'popular for his affability, goodly personage and activeness and therefore acceptable to the nobility', owed his 'election' chiefly to the clergy, who perceived that his lack of any 'title' would 'make his obligation the more to them and so they might stand better [secured of their liberties] than under such a one as might presume of an hereditary succession.' Daniel then moved on to discuss how Stephen prepared to deal with the inevitable challenges he would face as ruler. First, he granted 'licence to all that would build castles upon their oune lands thereby to fortifie the realme and break the force of any overrunning invasion that should master the field which in settled times might be of good effect'. Daniel pointed out, however, that 'in a season of distraction and part-taking' this was very dangerous. Stephen's quarrel with the bishops in 1139 is held to have had even greater consequences, though, according to Daniel, the bishops did not dare proceed too far and the king 'held what he had gotten'. When it came to open civil war from 1141, his account remains strangely muted: 'holding the State broken between them and no means made to interpose any barre to keepe them asunder. Their borders lay everywhere and then the ingagements of their partakers who (looke all to be savers or to recover their stakes when they were lost which makes them never give over) entertayn the contention.' Nevertheless, 'the best part was they were rather troubles than warres and cost more labour than blood. Everyone fought with Bucklers and seldom came to the sharpe in the field which would have soon ended the business.' Daniel's final assessment of Stephen confirms the impression that he was far from being hostile:

> A man so continually in motion as wee cannot take his dimension but only in passing and that but on one side which was warre: on the other wee never saw but a glaunce of him which yet for the most part was such as shewed him to be a very worthy prince for the government. He kept his word with the State concerning the relievment of tributes and never had one subsidy that we find. But what is more remarkable having his sword continually out and so many defections and rebelliuons against him, he never put any great man to death. Besides it is noted that notwithstanding all these miseries of warr, there were more abbeys built in his reigne than in an hundred years before, which shows that though the times were bad, they were not impious.

Daniel judged the king according to the standards of his own day and, though he recognised many of the problems that still preoccupy historians of the reign, he was clearly not prepared to condemn Stephen out of hand.

Though ideological disputes about monarchy under Charles I and the Commonwealth had repercussions for medieval history, after the Restoration fresh efforts were made to achieve a more empirical understanding of the period. A different approach to the reign of Stephen can be detected in the work of Robert Brady, a physician, who was for many years custodian of State Papers in the Tower of London. His *Complete History of England*, published in 1685, is as scholarly in its approach to historical writing as the seventeenth century attained, with marginal references and conscientious reliance on attested evidence rather than anecdote or fancy.[5] Yet Brady had his own political agenda. He aimed to defend the prerogatives of the crown and questioned the tendency of previous historical writers to seek justification for parliamentary pretensions in the historical record. Significantly, he noted already that Stephen's reign offered him nothing to his main purpose: 'during all of this king's reign in most of the historians we read of nothing almost but fire and sword, blood and slaughter, rapine, plunder and captivity'. Still, Brady dutifully aimed to illustrate the situation by citing a precise example rather than indulge in generalities. He did so admirably by using the continuation of the chronicle of Florence of Worcester to describe the attack on the city by the men of Gloucester and the use made of Worcester's precious relics to help repulse it. The city was defended by its earl, Waleran, count of Meulan, who returned from his counter-attack boasting 'that he neither in Normandy nor England had burnt more places and houses at one time', which gave Brady the occasion to refer to 'the way in Normandy' which

> from thence [was] brought hither: if any earl or great man found himself aggrieved by another injured or highly affronted, they frequently got together all their men at arms or knights that held of them, their other tenants and poor dependents and as much assistance from other friends and confederates as they could and burnt one another's castles and houses, destroyed their lands and small territories and carried away the inhabitants prisoners ... These were private hostilities and revenges between man and man; but if there was a title in the case and siding one for one pretender, another for another, they invaded one another after this manner with more asseverance and confidence under the notion of a public war and asserting the right of that side, they struck in withall and were almost constantly encouraged rather than checked by pretenders.

Though Brady drew on experience of recent English history for his ideas of the likely effects of a 'public war', he found confirmation for them in his sources: 'The Norman histories abound with these stories; see Ordericus Vitalis in the history of Rufus, Henry I and then king Stephen, especially wherein these inhumane ravages were as frequent and more barbarous than in England for many years.' Brady concludes by citing Camden's *Britannia*: 'In this king's reign there were in England so many tyrants as there were lords of castles, everyone pretending to coyn money and to exercise the right of majesty.'[6] As yet, this state of affairs was not called feudalism, but the notion of feudal unruliness was already latent in Brady's account and he could hardly have made it more obvious that it was introduced into England from 'abroad'.

The English history by the exiled Huguenot, Paul de Rapin-Thoyras, written in French, was originally published abroad for the benefit of foreigners interested in the history of the newly powerful United Kingdom. Nevertheless, it was rapidly translated into English and achieved a great reputation until it was superseded by Hume's *History* in the next generation.[7]

Rapin's international experience gave him advantages in seeing English history in a more detached manner, free of the prejudices of party affiliation which had prevailed amongst English seventeenth-century historians. Rapin's concern was the development of the modern conception of the 'state', and he was extremely critical of groups that defended interests of their own. In the case of Stephen, he still held the clergy mainly responsible for his election as king, but he also portrayed the nobility in a more sinister light: 'then as well skilled, as now, in the art of evading the most solemn oaths by distinctions and mental reservations'. Rapin saw Stephen as being forced to buy the support of the nobles by promising them 'more privileges … than they had enjoyed in the reigns of the Norman kings', yet they became discontented because they were 'not being rewarded in the manner they expected'. Rapin declined to go into the tedious details of the civil war, echoing Brady, because

> like the rest of that kind [it] furnishes more instances of treachery and cruelty than of glorious actions … Whilst it lasted the whole kingdom was divided, every city, county and person siding with the king or the empress according as they were swayed by passion or interest. The lords nearest in neighbourhood and blood fell upon one another in a cruel manner, burning the houses and pillaging the vassals of each other so that a terrific confusion was quickly spread over the whole kingdom. In the fatal anarchy, the barons acting as sovereigns grievously oppressed the people and were so presumptuous as to coin their own money.

Here, at last, appears the term 'anarchy', together with the notion that every part of the kingdom was racked by division on account of the disputed succession. These ideas became part of the familiar assessment of the reign found in both serious and popular histories. From this time on, the emphasis was firmly placed on the fate of government in Stephen's hands. Rapin's exceptional familiarity with the differences between the states of France, England, Holland and Prussia made him sensitive to the importance of political structures for the variable wellbeing of the people.

Rapin's personal experience of England and Ireland in the service of William III may also help to explain the attention he gives to the damage done by foreigners, and the sufferings of the 'people' at their hands, in Stephen's time. Stephen himself is not roundly condemned as ultimately responsible for these evils. The main objection to him is the difficulty of justifying 'all his proceedings in acquiring the crown and particularly the breach of his oath. Rapin reports that on account of this 'many are of the opinion he ought for all that to be deemed a usurper' and 'his breaking his word on certain occasions is moreover a stain on his memory'. Yet Rapin's verdict is not so damning. 'If the prince's character be considered in general only, he may be said to be worthy to live in better times and his good qualities to outweigh his defects ... the commendations due to his valour, clemency and generosity cannot be denied him.' Rapin correctly perceived that though 'there are historians that made it their business to blacken his reputation ... most of them wrote in the reign of Henry II or his sons'. Even the contemporary testimony of William of Malmesbury had to be treated with caution, since he is 'known to be the earl of Gloucester's creature'. In spite of what he wrote about the oaths to Matilda, Rapin admitted to some doubts about her rights to the succession.

> After all it is not easy to determine whether the Crown justly belonged to Mathilda or Stephen's election entitled him to take possession. What may be said with more certainty is that after the Conquest the Saxon laws were no longer observed and it does not appear that the Normans had yet any settled rules concerning the succession to the Crown.

However prescient in some respects, Rapin's Protestant sympathies explain his confidence that the troubles of the reign 'furnished the clergy with a favourable opportunity to exalt the mitre above the crown. The court of Rome improved also these junctures to introduce into England new laws which the English doubtless would have opposed at any other time.'

To enhance the attractions of the second English edition of Rapin's history (1732), it was provided with plates, giving imaginary royal portraits of medieval kings. The artist responsible, George Vertue, was official engraver to the Society of Antiquaries for nearly forty years (1717–56) and himself deeply interested in history, particularly that of the middle ages.[8] Before the history of each reign, a full 'portrait' plate incorporated some allusion to one of its leading events. The plate for Rufus, for example, shows a hunt in the New Forest as an allusion to his death in a hunting accident. In the portrait of Stephen, a bust of the king is derived from the models provided by two of Stephen's coins, also illustrated. Beneath the bust, a cherub holds in his left hand a small medallion with an image of the Empress Matilda and in his right hand a family tree showing the descendants of William the Conqueror. In this way, something of the character of the reign is expressed by the image itself. The desire to provide visual aids indicates a concern to make the history more vivid and, at the same time, take into account rather more than a mere narrative of events. The pictures help to render historical characters more accessible, particularly as there was as yet no attempt to distance them from readers by dressing them in period costumes. But a start had been made and, by the end of the century, publishers took great pains to secure the services of the greatest painters of the age for the purpose of illustrating historical works.

The most elaborate attempts to provide illustration for books of history were made for later editions of Hume's *History of England*, after it became the authoritative account in the late eighteenth century.[9] When his history first began to appear, Hume had immediately been criticised for his independence of mind in challenging the traditional adulation of the heroes of the constitution and his 'willingness to shed a tear' for those whose causes had been unsuccessful. Something of the freshness of his approach may also be detected in his medieval volume, published in 1762, where he expressed the view that Henry I, despite the precautions he had taken to secure the succession for his daughter, might have been instructed by 'the irregular manner in which he himself had acquired the crown' that 'neither his Norman nor English subjects were as yet capable of adhering to a strict rule of government'. Nevertheless, Stephen is credited with 'criminal ambition' for obtaining the crown; 'from this religious ceremony ... without any shadow either of hereditary title or consent of the nobility or people he was allowed to proceed to the exercise of sovereign'. (Hume's interpretation of the coronation ceremony betrays a typically eighteenth-century disdain for ritual and ignorance of its significance in the twelfth century.) In return for their 'submission', the barons are supposed to have 'exacted terms destructive of public peace as well as of royal authority – particularly permission to raise fortresses in the security of which they could tyrannise the local population.

Hume assumed that, though he had 'vigour and abilities', as a rational man Stephen was 'necessitated to tolerate in others the same violence to which he himself had been beholden for his sovereignty', and the consequence was that the 'aristocratical power ... usually so oppressive in the feudal governments, had now risen to its utmost height'. As had become usual, Hume proposed to spare his readers a relation of all the military events transmitted by contemporary and authentic historians, as they 'could afford neither instruction nor entertainment to the reader' and left it that 'All England was immediately filled with those fortresses ... unbounded rapine was exercised upon the people'. Even so, Hume attempted to moderate some excesses of popular history. Though there were civil wars and intestine disorders, he rejected the idea of 'anarchy'. Had Stephen succeeded by a just title, his qualities could 'have promoted the happiness and prosperity of his subjects', in Hume's view a laudable ambition for a king. Even for Hume, the matter of his having no 'right' to the crown was sufficient to prejudice the course of his government. But Stephen's own competence went unquestioned.

For a century or more after its publication, Hume's *History* remained unchallenged; it could still be considered authoritative as late as 1878, when it was updated for the last time. As far as Stephen was concerned, no revision of serious opinion was attempted before the end of the nineteenth century, but a certain view of the reign intended for a less sophisticated readership than Hume had written for had nevertheless become prevalent by the mid nineteenth century. This kind of history reflected the impact of Romanticism in early nineteenth-century England and attempted to meet the objections voiced by Catherine Morland: 'real solemn history I cannot be interested in ... [it] tells me nothing that does not either vex me or weary me. The quarrels of popes and kings, with wars or pestilences in every page; the men all so good for nothing.' To meet this objection, historians began to rely on their own imagination in an effort to appreciate the impact of past events. Shakespeare's history plays provided a literary model for this, and the acting of Edmund Kean was the immediate inspiration for John Keats in late 1819 when he began a tragedy based on the life of King Stephen. The play began with Stephen's heroic stand at the battle of Lincoln:

> Not the eagle more
> Loves to beat up against a tyrannous blast,
> Than I to meet the torrent of my foes.

Fighting alone against all odds, Stephen impressed even his enemies as a 'mighty soldier'

> he is no man
> But a fierce demon, anointed safe from wounds
> And misbaptized with a Christian name ...

Had Keats completed his play, Stephen might himself have come to be remembered as a particularly English kind of hero, the tragic failure, noble but doomed. Instead, an alternative Romantic way of treating Strephen's reign through its impact on the general population came to prevail. Traces of this new treatment can be already detected in John Lingard's *History of England* which had appeared earlier that same year, 1819.[10]

> Never did England, since the invasion of the Danes, present such a scene of misery as under the government of this unfortunate monarch. The two competitors alike dependent on the caprice of their adherents, were compelled to connive at excesses which it would have been dangerous to punish: and the foreign mercenaries ... frequently indemnified themselves for want of pay by the indiscriminate plunder of friend and foe. The desire for revenge also mixed itself with the thirst of power ... the christian knight gloried in barbarities which would not have disgraced the pagan forefather.

As a Roman Catholic, Lingard did not identify with the established tradition of approval for authoritarian monarchy and needed a different focus for his history. To highlight the sufferings brought on the common people by disagreement about government was intended as a way of making remote historical events seem more real to modern readers. The tendency of such interpretations to move away from what may actually be knowable about the past and settle for stimulation of the imaginations of the present has its dangers. The imagination needs to be reined in by some appreciation of what is compatible with contemporary testimony. Unfortunately, much teaching of history now appears to encourage children to think that they can conjure the experiences of the past from the unaided imagination. In the nineteenth century, imaginative reconstruction of the horrors of civil war reached its most popular expression with Charles Dickens's *A Child's History of England* (1852).[11] 'Nothing worse is known of him than his usurpation of the crown', but this was more than enough: 'the people of England suffered more in these dread nineteen years than at any former period'. Dickens accepted the literal truth of the famous passage in the Peterborough Chronicle:

> every Noble had his strong Castle where he reigned the cruel king of all the neighbouring people ... perpetrated whatever cruelties he chose ... castles were filled with devils ... the peasants were put into dungeons for their gold and silver ... tortured ... murdered in countless fiendish ways ... In England there was no corn, no meat, no cheese, no butter, there were no tilled lands, no harvests.

In place of Hume's aristocratic excesses, Dickens roundly puts the blame on the 'Feudal System which made the peasants the born vassals and mere slaves of the Barons'. This kind of language can still be heard. Dickens shifted the emphasis from the unconstitutional origin of the reign to the social evils for the general population, a matter on which he regarded himself as more of an authority.

Only slightly more sober was a little book, *The Childhood of the English Nation*, published by the accomplished Mrs Ella Armitage in 1877:

> the unhappy reign of Stephen ... this hideous reign, a time in which our England was as though she were not, her laws all sunk, her people a prey to robbers. Stephen was not a bad man; he had a great deal of generous feeling and his manners were very popular, but he was utterly unfit to cope with the strong monster, feudalism; he was far too easy and allowed the barons to have whatever they asked for. As soon as the late king's treasures which Stephen scattered with a too liberal hand were spent, the barons began to falter in their troth and Matilda found supporters to her claim to the throne ... None of the nobles of England (except Robert of Gloucester) cared very greatly about either Stephen or Matilda; what they wished for was to make themselves independent of any rule at all. It was seen then what feudalism meant, when there was no State, no strong hand above the noble to hold the turbulent to right.[12]

Not surprising she concluded by saying that 'It would be a waste of time to follow all the turnings of the warfare between Stephen and Matilda' and hurried on to deal with the reign of Henry II, 'one of the most important in the history of England'.

Kate Norgate published a full account of the reign in her book *England under the Angevin Kings* in 1887,[13] the last important work on the subject to be written within the familiar conventions of historical narrative. Her merit was to put the reign into a context of feudal rivalries as they dominated the history of twelfth-century France and therefore to break away from the limitations of seeing the reign in purely English terms. Miss Norgate strove to breathe fresh life into the topic by studying Stephen as a member of his great family of Blois, trying to identify, as it were, the salient features of that family's political ambitions and its personal characteristics. In her view Stephen was flawed because of his 'lack of steadfastness'. Lest this be attributed to some personal conflict between ambition and good nature, Miss Norgate explained that Stephen carried 'the old curse of his race' in inheriting alone of his brothers 'the peculiar mental and moral constitution which the house of Blois derived from Odo II', a paternal ancestor who had died early in the eleventh century. By emphasising the dynastic clashes between the families of the counts of Blois and Anjou, she unconsciously made use of contemporary interest in the 'survival of the fittest'. One of the advantages of her approach was to encourage the view that greater issues were at stake in the period than earlier writers had appreciated when they had deplored the tiresome and sterile sequence of petty disputes. In this way, Miss Norgate translated into typically nineteenth-century terms something of the medieval view of Stephen's ordeal as larger than life. The last in a long line, her book has not been without its influence on later writers, but its potential in this respect was not fully realised because within a few years its whole approach was quite suddenly rendered obsolete by the development of a new kind of academic history.

Since antiquity, historians had found stories from the past useful as a way to provide as Hume put it 'entertainment or instruction'. Only after the French Revolution did a new approach to the past begin to emerge. The whole of human history came to be thought of as following a particular course, like a river, the ultimate destiny of which could be discovered by scrupulous charting of all its ramifications. This made it necessary to redis-cover parts of the past that had been forgotten or overlooked. It had particularly beneficial implications for medieval history, which was at last released from preoccupation with its purely religious aspects. Instead, at-tention focused on the obscure centuries of the middle ages in which all the most venerable European institutions had first taken inchoate shape. In nineteenth-century Britain, the main thrust of historical enquiry into the middle ages was to explore the origins of parliament. Historians concluded that these could be traced back to the popular assemblies brought with them by Germanic settlers of the migration period. On these solid foundations had been imposed a strong form of royal rule at the time of the Norman Conquest. Recurrent conflicts between kings and people had eventually been resolved through the device of parliaments. In this long-term history, the period of Norman rule was commended as the time when it had served the common good for kings to establish their firm authority. Without strong kingship, the kingdom would not have been able to act as a unit, and parliaments, when they became necessary, could not have been assembled. Historians of the post-conquest period have been consistently pro-monarchist, occasionally deploring excesses of violence but insistent that kings served the country well by preserving its integrity from the forces of feudal decentralisation, providing sound money and enforcing justice. In this context, Stephen seemed unworthy of his royal office: he alone contributed nothing to the development of institutions.

As Mrs Armitage's book shows, such views of Stephen were commonplace well before academic investigation of his reign was launched. The general outlook of the new historical practitioners was shaped by their predecessors; fresh studies only served to fill out and reinforce existing prejudice. The tone of the new scholarship was set by William Stubbs, founder figure of the Oxford School of Modern History, who pronounced the reign to be one of the most important for English history,

> as exemplifying the working of causes and principles which had no other oppor-tunity of exhibiting their real tendencies ... a period of unprecedented general misery ... a most potent lesson for later times and foreign countries.[14]

Stubbs was, however, aware that men learn hard lessons from difficult times

> the terrible discipline of anarchy ... during which ... opportunity was given for every sort of development and combination ... opening the eyes of men in general to the sources of their strength and the causes of their weakness.

Less attention has been given subsequently to the ways men's eyes were opened than to how their lives were blighted, thanks particularly to the work of Stubbs's pupil, J. H. Round. His account of Stephen's reign, *Geoffrey de Mandeville: A Study of the Anarchy*, published in 1892, was still so influential a hundred years later that it inspired a commemorative book of studies which rightly saluted Round as the founder of modern Stephen scholarship.[15] In his book, Round had reckoned to display, from Geoffrey's example, the evils of feudal anarchy as they burst out when England was no longer governed by a strong man. Round was in fact happy to acquit

Stephen of the more serious charges levelled against him: 'had he enjoyed better fortune, we should have heard less of his incapacity'. He correctly pointed out in Stephen's defence both the ambivalent legacy of Henry I and the difficulty created by a rival claim to the throne. He too thought, however, that Stephen had compounded his difficulties by negotiating terms for his recognition as ruler. Overall, his defence of Stephen has carried less weight with later writers than his description of Mandeville's success. Round created an impression of aggressive feudalism in England that has dominated twentieth-century study. He believed that feudalism in its worst guise, though rampant on the Continent, had only appeared in England when the crown was weak. In his view feudal barons were no more than strong men eager to assert their local strength and get the burden of the crown off their backs. He did not consider why, if feudalism was rampant on the Continent, it did not likewise plunge France into perpetual disorder. Feudal France was the cradle of multifarious religious reform movements, of the revival of learning, of vernacular literature and 'Gothic' architecture. Only in England, apparently, did rampant feudalism create disaster.

The novelty of Round's scholarship lay less with his assessment of the situation than with his method of proving it from formal documents, normally recording legal transactions. He demonstrated how it was possible, working from one document at a time, to elucidate the text with a wealth of reference, particularly on matters relating to family connections. His brilliant expositions of what information could be squeezed out of this evidence created a style of historical analysis that persists to the present. For all his acumen, Round never wrote an extended work of history; all his work appeared in the form of essays, often short. Even his *Geoffrey de Mandeville* was composed in this way. The narrow aims of his scholarship and indeed of his political sympathies seriously inhibited his capacity for historical thought.[16] He could not take a broad view of historical problems. This would have obliged him to stretch the range of his natural sympathies and deal with topics that were not congenial. It would also have required him to expound his own standpoint at some length. This he was reluctant to do. One of his most striking characteristics was his sharp eye for the mistakes of others and his quite merciless exposure of other scholars' failings. Even his apparently courteous acknowledgement of the learning of editors, or the profundity of Stubbs himself, invariably precedes some notice of what they had got wrong or misunderstood. His controversial style of scholarship rather than his subject matter produced a new kind of historical writing. One of his chief reasons for defending Stephen at all was not due to any real insight into the circumstances of his accession, but his mischievous determination to contradict previous writers.

Never himself a formal teacher of history, Round acquired a formidable reputation in the academic world where his mode of scholarship found a comfortable perch. His focus on the formal charter as a source of information about the twelfth century encouraged scholars throughout the twentieth century to publish an enormous number of them and work out their implications. The kind of academic history which has emerged from all this has had a particularly profound impact on the study of Stephen, since the reign raises many questions susceptible to this kind of scholarly enquiry. Academic historians also changed the manner of writing about the reign. They publish their findings in periodicals with limited circulation and intended for a very narrow public of fellow experts. When they publish in book form, their studies are still weighed down with an elaborate apparatus of footnotes, not only to justify the statements of the text by reference to the original sources of information, but also in reference to alternative interpretations offered by others. Footnotes provide such refined examples of academic debate that many scholars treat them as the most valuable parts of books. Since the Second World War, the amount of space allotted to footnotes in academic books has steadily grown, to accommodate these controversial asides. Though disconcerting to the uninitiated, or the impatient, this manner of discourse has become second nature in academic history.

In the scholarly skirmishing of the last hundred years, many modifications in Round's interpretation of the reign have come to be accepted, but medievalists have in general held the work of Round in great awe and been unwilling to challenge his authority, as though even after death he might rise up and denounce them. There ought to have been much more soul-searching about the limitations of his approach. Round's personal interests in peerage and genealogy explain why he confined his attention to relations between the king and the barons. More surprisingly, this has continued to dominate discussion of the reign by historians with different social priorities.

The first tentative steps towards a modification of Round's approach were taken by Frank Stenton in his *The First Century of English Feudalism*, published just after Round's death.[17] Though Stenton agreed that 'they deserve the hard measure which historians always give them, many features ... often regarded as illustrations of baronial independence were really the baronial response to the conditions of civil war ... the barons ... have found few apologists, but the facts give no support to the view that a state of general war was agreeable to the baronage as a whole'. If they took advantage of the king's difficulties, it was in part to provide what security they could in districts subject to their power. In addition, Stenton argued that although 'it is customary to regard the barons as moved to rebellion or to frequent changes of faith by desire for independence of the crown ... the concessions which individual barons obtained were highly concrete ... in many cases ... recovering rights or possessions which once belonged to ancestors'. These claims 'illustrate feudal conservatism rather than feudal aggression'. Stenton was the first historian to credit the barons with a sense of public duty and the capacity to confront their own problems in political and not purely military, not to say thuggish, terms.

Subsequent historians are still engaged in seeking to fathom the motives and interactions of the great barons. Progress with these studies in the second half of the twentieth century owes most to the publication of the royal and princely documents of the reign by Harry Cronne and Ralph Davis in 1968,[18] – though there have been many other collections of baronial charters before and since to help fill out the picture. Making all this material available has not been without its disadvantages. Not only have charters been accorded a privileged status as formal and unbiased evidence. By encouraging historians to focus on what charters can be profitably used for, attention has accordingly been diverted from some of the weightier problems of the reign raising most controversy, for which documents must necessarily be wanting. If such controversies seem to be incapable of resolution, there will be a tendency to avoid them altogether as vain occasions for dispute. Since the reign of Stephen is unavoidably controversial, not venturing beyond the evidence of documents to confront the difficulties of contemporaries appears like reluctance to deal with the real challenges.

Even for such a remote period, to plead inadequate information as an excuse is insufficient. For Stephen's reign, historical sources of several kinds are comparatively abundant. England was exceptionally fortunate in the number of excellent writers of chronicles in this period. Interest in the intellectual activities of the English in the twelfth century has also prompted a revival of scholarship devoted to historical writing itself. In recent years new editions of all the principal chroniclers of the reign have drawn attention to their value, not merely as purveyors of facts but as expressions of contemporary opinion. This is an aspect of the past to which the late twentieth century, for reasons of its own, began to pay great attention. Without opinion polls as a guide to the public response to past events, we may consult chroniclers for this purpose. The slurs formerly levelled against credulous, monastic writers have been brushed aside. Instead, the stress has been put on their connections with the great world and their sensitivity to the cultural and intellectual achievements of the age. Academic historians without much experience of public affairs have found that they more readily sympathise with mere observers, like the writers of the period, than with the kings, the barons or the senior clergy.

Even if the 'sources' are indispensable, their reliability needs to be tested. They may have been ill-informed, biased or blinkered by local conditions. This also applies to formal records; they do not necessarily tell the whole story; they were specifically designed to settle old scores, not provide disinterested evidence for the past. Sources need to be 'interpreted'. In the elucidation of their meaning, their potential ambiguities may be enhanced rather than resolved. The newly discovered difficulties of interpreting texts can become so many excuses for treating historical debates as mere differences of opinion between schools of exegesis. Interest in the past is in danger of being swamped by fascination with the slanging matches between practitioners, a foible encouraged by the present fashion for shifting attention from the text to the gloss. It can seem as though looking for the truth about the past is so much effort frittered away.

Indispensable though the documentation must be, it is necessary to remember those aspects of ordinary life for which no written evidence can ever be adduced. For earlier periods of history, like Stephen's reign, this includes many matters where writing would now be expected. In the twelfth century even legal agreements were still only exceptionally committed to writing. The foundations of numerous Cistercian abbeys at this time have also left only the barest trace in the record, so the implications of such an expansion do have to be worked out from what is known about the general history of the order. They cannot be disregarded simply because the direct evidence is wanting. How powerfully the religious life continued to call throughout this period in England, just as it did in anarchy free France, indicates something significant about the state of the kingdom. Even less is known about the ways the English participated (to some effect) in the expeditions to the Holy Land, known as the Second Crusade of 1147–48. How contemporary political and military events bore on the conventional practices of religion is a matter not easily grasped in modern conditions. For the more mundane activities of everyday life, now considered so fascinating, the evidence available can only prompt unanswerable questions. This cannot excuse ignoring them altogether. For example, during this reign numerous royal grants were issued authorising weekly markets in various towns. In one case, Stephen was besieging Wycombe when the bishop of Lichfield obtained his permission to hold markets in Staffordshire, an area anyway often thought beyond Stephen's regular reach.[19] Can we argue from such evidence that turbulence in one part of the kingdom had not apparently diminished the effectiveness of extending the royal peace to those who attended markets elsewhere? To what extent were the familiar routines of daily life interrupted at all? If these royal charters had been totally ineffectual, would they have been obtained or preserved?

A comparable problem concerns schooling. Henry of Anjou himself is recorded to have studied as a boy with Master Matthew of Bristol. He was not alone in getting an education in these years. According to a controversialist of the 1130s, there were as many professional schoolmasters in England (not only in 'urbibus et castellis verum etiam in villulis'), as there were royal tax-collectors, a clear insinuation that they were expected to be ubiquitous. England was no intellectual backwater in the twelfth century. There was a high level of commitment to learning, even to scientific innovation and study of formal Roman law. According to Torigni, Master Vacarius was in this reign brought over from Italy to teach law at Oxford in 1149. What this means has been much discussed. For Torigni, clearly, it was not incongruous to suggest that some important new development in English learning had occurred in a year marked by renewed political agitation in the north of England. At Oxford, conditions made it possible to attract a distinguished foreign jurist. Whatever the disturbances of the reign amounted to, they cannot have suspended the activities of all schools.[20] This in turn becomes evidence about the degree of civil disorder we are entitled to expect.

As usual, the fate of the country population, the majority, remains the most obscure of all. At Ramsey abbey Abbot Walter is known to have granted some of his rustics their freedom.[21] What lies behind this? Did the disturbed conditions give serfs opportunities to improve their lot ? It is usually supposed that they suffered rather than benefited from the troubles. Disruption also offered favourable opportunities for rustics to abscond to towns, or perhaps engage in military activities, if only as forced labour. Some may have simply sought or been offered greater security on other estates. The monks of Jumièges, who complained early in the reign of Henry II that many of their *nativos* had fled from their English estates since 1135, had hopes of recovering them, most likely from neighbouring estates.[22] The monks' grievances do little to enlighten us about the reasons for the departure of the estate workers; their ultimate fates can only be speculated upon. Modern experience offers many different possible explanations for how and why people move in disturbed times. Some better themselves by it; others suffer. Did the men of Hertfordshire who withheld rents and customary dues from the abbey of St Albans take advantage of the 'troubles' to evade their obligations, or did they have quite independent grievances?[23] The extent to which ordinary life was disrupted would have had implications for the mobility of the population. Chroniclers report that roads became dangerous because of the cunning of men who preyed on travellers and abducted likely victims to extort ransoms. Such conditions cannot have prevailed all the time or everywhere. Writing in the 1140s, the author of the *Gesta* reported that the hot springs at Bath were much visited not only by

the sick in search of relief and cures but by the healthy for recreation.[24]
Nothing is said to imply that these salubrious pleasures had been disconti-
nued on account of unsettled conditions. Visiting the hot springs may seem
to us like an improbable occurrence at such times, but our notions of general
conditions should not be based exclusively on the partial information of
querulous monks.

The kind of evidence available is simply inadequate to allow us to draw
a complete picture, however much we feel inclined to fill out the details of
disaster for ourselves. To their surprise, archaeologists have discovered at
Winchester that the devastation denounced in the chronicles did not leave
deep scars in the ground. Within seven years of the ransacking of Winchester
in 1141, the bishop's survey of the city also shows effectively no sign at all
of the destruction reported by chroniclers.[25] If this is true of one of the
main theatres of war, how much more must this have been the case with
many other parts of the country? We know from the present time how
ordinary people are capable of carrying on their lives and surviving the most
terrible effects of modern wars. Perhaps the disputes about the crown we
think so important did not have such dreadful repercussions everywhere.
There is a risk of drawing too deeply on the well of Romantic imagination
to depict the horrors of civil war and suppose that what happens to be
known for one place must have been a common experience. It is also
important not to allow recent events to colour our impressions of what
happens when governments 'break down'. In earlier times, governments had
not become so integral to the lives of all their subjects as modern living
requires. A sense of proportion has to be retained and a tight rein kept on
what is read into the twelfth-century evidence.

3

English Kingship in 1135

University study of English history from its inception in the late nineteenth century made the development of constitutional government the core of its programme. The earliest great formulation of English liberties, Magna Carta, which sought to restrain the unbridled prerogatives of the king in financial and judicial matters, became the first of the great thirteenth-century statutes venerated by common lawyers. The procedural peculiarities of common law were confidently traced to the legal innovations of Henry II, whom Stubbs appropriately designated the 'original hero of the constitution'. As medieval historical studies grew, interest shifted from confrontations between kings and barons to the ways kings had actually governed the kingdom, as revealed in the abundant records of royal administration. By the second half of the twentieth century, historical interest in the medieval constitution had in effect been replaced by one in the management of royal affairs. Intensive study of Domesday Book demonstrated how the Norman kings exploited their conquest, and Henry I's role in shaping English royal government in the next generation at last began to receive adequate recognition. Naturally enough, historians came to assume that by the time of Henry's death in 1135 the promising start made in the royal administration of justice and finance was capable of future development and elaboration. All that was needed for this was a ruler capable of continuing Henry I's good work. Their disappointment with Stephen for not being able to sustain the impetus for better government is palpable.

Whether anyone living in 1135 thought in such terms is another matter. What in retrospect seems an admirable achievement for more effective government was at the time more likely to have been regarded simply as a means of making the king richer at his subjects' expense. Apart from leading members of Henry I's administration, with their own reasons for wanting to remain in office, no one else had obviously gained much or could, at the time, have had any inkling of the future to come under Henry II and of the duty incumbent on Henry I's successor to keep his administrative apparatus in good working order as a basis for later improvements. In particular, those most directly affected by his administration had good reason to take an informed view of what Henry I had 'achieved'. Whereas some great men had bought judicial favours from the king, others had just as clearly suffered in consequence. Those who failed to appreciate the advant- ages of royal interference in the legal process may now be considered somewhat imperceptive observers of longer-term developments, but their blindness inexorably affected their judgments. If Henry I's 'admirable' new system was not as carefully looked after in the following two decades as most historians think it deserved, one of the reasons could have been that its merits had not in fact won it unqualified acceptance. At the very least, if it faltered, it cannot have already made itself indispensable or created a cadre well-entrenched enough to survive neglect. To what extent the Hen- rician system did break down is anyway arguable, but the conviction that Stephen did not appreciate his uncle's administrative innovations has shaped interpretations of the reign for over a hundred years.[1]

Henry I's ability to surmount the many troubles of his reign attracted to his service men able to make dazzling careers by deploying their talents for his benefit. Ordericus Vitalis, using a biblical phrase 'men raised from the dust', noted that royal favour exalted those born without great expectations.[2] Because such an idea appeals to twentieth-century aspirations, this phrase is widely understood to mean that Henry I promoted merit over noble birth. Regrettably, this interpretation misses the significance the phrase had in the twelfth century. We do not know how low down the social scale Henry sought his minions, but attributing low birth to his servants probably only voiced a conventional prejudice that Henry passed over those with more obvious claims on his patronage. The really low born would have had neither the qualifications for office nor the opportunities to draw themselves to the king's attention. Henry made use of adroit ministers (the word minister originally meant a mere servant) devoted to his interests because they had no distracting commitments to others than themselves and their families. If necessary, they could therefore easily be dismissed without causing pol- itical ructions. Their usefulness to the king hardly commended them to the king's subjects, who resented and feared the promotion of persons without 'connections', because they were justifiably suspected of having no scruples. Henry's motives for preferring ministers entirely committed to his service did not proceed from disinterested concern for finding the best men for state-building but from his determination to exploit the resources of king- ship for his exclusive benefit. Henry's legacy lay not with his administrative apparatus but with the consequences of his patronage. Judgment of the king's wisdom ultimately depends on how the character of this enigmatic ruler is read.

Unfortunately for historians, since contemporaries did not openly debate about the most desirable forms of government for their own times, it is not a straightforward matter to explain what kind of king or government the English were looking for in 1135. Since there are differences of opinion about what might best suit our own times, it is sensible to assume that men were not all of one mind then. Though it is difficult to describe what the differences might have been in 1135, several writers of history in Henry I's England do at least indicate that Henry I's style of rule did not entirely meet contemporary requirements. Some of them were circumspect, even reserved, with their comments. This itself has been held to indicate the fear the king inspired, as though chroniclers already dreaded the descent of royal thought police, a fantasy inspired by very modern developments. Admittedly, Henry I's savagery is not in doubt: Orderic Vitalis provides two famous instances in Normandy. The king allowed two of his own grandchildren to be blinded in vengeance on their rebellious father, and ordered the execution of a critical versifier whose lampoons on the king had got under his skin.[3] Henry I punished those who publicly defied or derided him; but there are no grounds for suspecting him of paranoia in trying to suppress what monks thought or wrote about him in the cloister. Clerical writers were no doubt timorous creatures anyway, not disposed to be disrespectful of kings, whether or not they anticipated royal wrath for any incautious criticism.

In England, the clergy had for centuries looked to kings for protection and patronage. Henry I had provided them with security and it was not difficult for them to find things in him to praise. One of the English historians, William of Malmesbury, was encouraged in his work by Henry I's first queen, Matilda, and later by Henry's bastard son, Robert, earl of Gloucester. What he wrote about the king had to be acceptable to such patrons. In these circumstances, that he wrote favourably of Henry I is only to be expected. Even so, close reading reveals Malmesbury's own reservations. In his *History of the English Kings*, William's fifth and last book concerns the first twenty years of the reign of Henry I.[4] Much of this part of the history has little to do with England at all but with European affairs in general. Most of the royal action described in it concerns Normandy and relations with the kings of France. In his preface to this section, the author attempts to deflect any possible criticism that the book narrates 'so few of his deeds', for 'fame no doubt will trumpet the rest and lasting memory transmit them to posterity'. The excuses he gives are curious and awkward. First, he offers conventional self-deprecation: to do justice to Henry's deeds 'requires an abler hand than ours'. Then he pleads further deficiencies. 'To unfold in detail all his profound counsels, all his royal achievements' is matter 'too deep for me and requires greater leisure than I possess'. Moreover, as a monk, 'far from the secrets of the court', Malmesbury could only 'touch on a few events' and withheld 'his assent from doubtful relators, being ignorant of his greater achievements'. This enigmatic remark seems to imply that he was unwilling to trust some of the stories he had heard. He insisted, moreover, that, just as he could not know everything about what Henry had done, 'he ought not to relate all that he knew, lest he stretch the limits of his readers' patience'.

In his assessment of the king's character, Malmesbury stresses the king's wisdom, preferring to get his way where possible by counsel, that is by taking thought, rather than warfare. William's determination to make the best of Henry is famously revealed by his claim that Henry was 'completely free during his whole life from fleshly lusts', and that his exceptionally large number of bastard children was due 'to indulging in the embraces of the female sex ... from love of begetting children and not to gratify his passions'. Given this blatant whitewash, it is not difficult to understand what lies behind his descriptions of Henry's ability

> to restrain the rebellious by the terror of his name ... he was a most severe requiter of injuries, constant in enmity, giving too much indulgence to the tide of anger, depressing his enemies even to despair, exalting his friends to enviable condition, inflexible in the administration of justice, suffering nothing to go unpunished which the delinquents had committed repugnant to his dignity.

Henry's unpopularity in some quarters may be imagined. William acknowledges that an attempt on his life was made by one of the low-born servants of his bedchamber. Suger, abbot of Saint-Denis, went further. He believed Henry to be so terrified of assassination that he frequently changed his bed, increased his guards and kept a weapon at his bedside in case it was needed.[5] Since Henry was himself afraid, he ruled by trying to inspire terror in his subjects. It is not surprising that Henry needed to be constantly on the alert. England may itself have been quiet, but his was not a tranquil reign. The brunt of disorder was borne by Normandy, which Henry had seized from his brother Robert Curthose in 1106. Robert remained his prisoner, not seen or honoured in public, for most of the rest of the reign (he did not die until 1134) and Henry's own title to the duchy was never confirmed by the king of France. The king's mercilessness did not earn him universal approbation. His firm character was not even sufficient to keep his Norman barons submissive. As should have been expected, his high-handedness itself provoked unrest. The account of the first half of his reign given in the 'Hyde' chronicle concentrates on Henry's activities in Normandy, tracing the 'principal root' of all the evils of his time in Normandy *and in England* to the difficulties arising out of his treatment of his brother Robert and Henry's continuing unpopularity in Normandy.[6] Henry is presented here as ruthless and detestable. That Henry's rule in Normandy can be considered as much upset by rival claims to rule as Stephen's in England is often overlooked. Whatever his merit for modern writers, some of his subjects had reason to breathe a sigh of relief at the death of this long-lived king.

The other main historian of Henry I's reign, Henry, archdeacon of Huntingdon, who wrote at the behest of his bishop, Alexander of Lincoln, did not need to be quite so careful about what he wrote as William of Malmesbury. Though Bishop Alexander's uncle, the bishop of Salisbury, was Henry I's principal minister, the chronicler made no attempt to extol royal administration. His account is most useful for its plain narration of events. This reveals how the king was in regular conflict with different members of the nobility and how little he satisfied them as a ruler. There are also references to his imposition of taxation in England, even to his fining the clergy for their concubinage to his own profit, which sabotaged the efforts of the bishops to extirpate this clerical failing. Often the king's enemies are praised: both his brother Robert and Robert's son, William Clito, who also defied the king, receive a striking eulogy; on the other hand, the king's counsellor, Robert, count of Meulan, praised by Malmesbury, is treated by Huntingdon as foolish and defiant of the clergy.[7]

Henry I's success as a ruler was achieved against heavy odds. When Henry I died, Huntingdon indicates that some frank opinions of his life were voiced: praise for his wisdom, military victories and wealth had to contend with criticism of his greed, cruelty and debauchery. No contemporary comments on his part in shaping organs of government have been recorded, apart from disparaging remarks on the king's promotion of persons of low birth to positions of great eminence in the kingdom. His reign may have given the English general peace and prosperity, certainly by contrast to the disorders of much of the eleventh century, but the king's preoccupations in Normandy may have made him more determined to squeeze what money he could out of the kingdom through his willing subordinates. The bishop of Salisbury, widely recognised as the king's chief instrument, inspired respect, not admiration. His acquisition of several valuable churches in addition to his bishopric point to the way he feathered his own nest. Little is known about the effects of Henry I's government on the general English population, but the chronicler John of Worcester reported that the king dreamt he was threatened by all three classes of his subjects – his clergy, knights and peasants – for his ill-treatment of them. The gravity of what he reported was reinforced by drawings of what the king had seen.[8]

Impressions of contemporary political expectations may be drawn not only from their accounts of Henry I but from what such historians wrote about the more distant English past. Both Malmesbury and Huntingdon freely praised and censured earlier rulers, not merely projecting back their own ideals of what kingship should provide but offering a historical context for political understanding in their own day by writing up remote events. Calling attention to the piety of some pre-conquest rulers was not simply nostalgia for an earlier golden age; they advanced models of a kind of kingship which had been more respectful of the clergy than that of Rufus, for example, had been.

The clergy's dissatisfaction with the Henrician regime is the most easily understood because articulated in most detail. At the beginning of the reign, the impieties of Henry's predecessor, William Rufus, had prompted the new king at his accession to repudiate his brother's abuses of the church and promise to rule more in accordance with clerical expectations. In 1135 the clergy, if not equally outraged by Henry's treatment of the church, were sufficiently discontented to seek reassurances from Henry's successor. The leading spokesman for the clergy at this point was Henry, bishop of Winchester, nephew of the late king and brother of the new one; the prelate, it might be supposed, least likely to damn the memory of the one or hamper the government of the other. If the bishop of Winchester demanded changes, it may be imagined what less favoured prelates thought of Henry I.

The fullest criticisms of Henry I's treatment of the church were voiced by the author of the *Gesta Stephani*.[9] Although Henry was praised at the opening of the book as 'the father of his people, source of peace and righteousness and law, under whom England had been the mirror of religion', the author presents a king who had ridden roughshod over the church's freedom. At his hands, the church had suffered disgraceful wrongs, as, like a second Pharaoh, he ensnared the clergy in litigation, exacting gifts and services, practising simony, interfering in marital business, taking church lands during vacancies, seizing altar offerings and persecuting clergy who protested. At a council early in Stephen's reign held at London, the new king listened patiently to such complaints and graciously conceded freedom to the church, respect for canon law and clergy of whatever rank. The author believed Stephen's intentions were honest. Any later lapses were excused as the fault of advisers or the result of urgent necessity. In some measure the reforms asked for did achieve their objective.

A number of distinct strands can be identified amongst these objections, but in part they all relate to one. Henry I reigned thirty-five years, longer than any previous king of England had ever personally ruled the whole kingdom since its unification in the tenth century. Inevitably he outlived the circumstances in which he had been raised. His brother Robert had at least gone on crusade and seen something of the world; Henry had not. He had twice met popes in France, but from these encounters derived a false impression of their relative ineffectualness. He also remained unmoved by the new waves of monastic piety and ecclesiastical reform current in his day. One of his proudest achievements was the marriage made by his daughter Matilda to the German emperor, Henry V, and he remained unimpressed by papal criticisms of secular power, as revealed by its controversies with the empire. Henry I himself disposed freely of bishoprics. If his bishops were promoted on account of their royal services, they were not released on translation from their previous obligations. By 1135 Henry's style of relations with the church was distinctly old-fashioned, according to the best standards of the age. Some of the senior clergy thought change was overdue. Henry's abuses did not need to be on the same scale as Rufus's to excite comment. In the light of the different expectations of the time, they were equally unacceptable. Continental churchmen of the time not only expected greater independence in running their own affairs; they had obtained recognition of their superior rights to direct the lives of the secular nobility; by their international solidarity in monastic orders like Cluny and Cîteaux, and under papal leadership, they had more impressive strength than their predecessors and reckoned to break free of purely royal patronage. Kings might still be useful, but only as and when the clergy chose to call upon them.

Wringing concessions from Stephen may not in practice have been as detrimental to royal influence in the church as it seems, but the senior clergy attached a symbolic importance to getting royal approval of their rights to privileged treatment, and it gave them more confidence in their special role in the kingdom. The real reason for demanding concessions was not any perceived new weakness in the king himself but the greater assurance of the clerical reformers, and of the papacy in particular, since the end of the dispute with the empire in 1122. Some of the implications had already become clear in Henry I's last years. Henry had been too old to adapt easily to the new situation, but the clergy of Bishop Henry's generation were eager to get a clearer endorsement of the privileges clergy were entitled to from the new king. Stephen, son of a crusader, benefactor of the new religious order of Savigny, made no old-fashioned difficulties about this.

Since the essence of the reformed programme was to liberate churchmen from the unwelcome attentions of lay lords, the clergy inevitably tried to draw a sharp distinction between the religious and the secular life in order to make clergy more aware of their superior responsibilities. The tendency to exaggerate the evils of the secular style of life made the clergy poor observers of its virtues and disposed them rather to castigate the shortcomings of the laity than sympathise with their problems. This is unfortunate because the writings of the clergy constitute most of the evidence available about secular affairs. The clergy must, however, be considered highly unreliable witnesses. Wrapped up as they were in concerns with their own ecclesiastical rights, the clergy wrote little to any purpose about how kings should conduct themselves in secular matters. Their calling blinded them totally to what the lay majority may have expected of rulers. The aspirations of the clergy to a stricter form of religious life have been sympathetically treated by modern historians, but their very professions of idealism should not be accepted at face value. Some laymen at the time were admittedly susceptible enough to offer them patronage, but others resisted the clergy's attempts to enlarge the scope of their privileges and were accordingly denounced for their ungodliness. The clergy praised the meek and adhorred the others. This makes understanding the basic assumptions of lay life more difficult.

To get round this we may begin by trying to take stock of the general situation. At the time of Henry I's accession, the Norman conquest of England was only thirty-four years old and the continuing connection between England and Normandy uncertain. Throughout much of Rufus's reign and at the beginning of Henry's, the major preoccupation of the king and the leading barons was how relations should be managed between the kingdom and the duchy. Henry I had in the end successfully imposed a regime that united them under his rule and defeated all attempts by the king of France to dislodge him from Normandy. By the end of the reign, this arrangement was taken for granted. All parties within the realm seem to have assumed that Henry's successor would rule both together without question. The principal difference between the situation in 1135 and in 1066 was that, whereas William had conquered England from Normandy, Henry had reimposed the union from England which properly reflected the greater weight, resources and confidence of the kingdom by 1106. Henry I had thereafter been continuously preoccupied with maintaining himself in Normandy and appears to have expected his successor there to acquire England into the bargain. In 1135 it was surely impossible to believe that the English crown could have been won a second time by a successful conquest from Normandy. As it happened, when Henry died and his nephew became king, Stephen in England found that Normandy fell into his lap. The Norman lords accepted his kingship without being pressed. Normandy had lapsed into its more natural position as an English satellite. In fact, it was not quite so straightforward as it looked. Henry I had only retained his hold on Normandy by spending a great part of his time there and by constant manoeuvring of his French allies to stave off the interference of the French king and the Angevin count. Though England was the greater prize, it was valued only for what it could contribute to Henry's ambitions on the Continent. English kings took several centuries to resign themselves to exclusion from continental affairs.

After a reign of thirty-five years Henry appeared, nevertheless, to have re-established the primacy of the kingdom over the duchy. Born in England and married to a lady of the Old English royal house, Henry must have appeared in England as more of a native ruler than his immediate prede-cessors. By his day anyway, the Norman conquerors and landlords were themselves in some measure being absorbed back into 'English' society. Some of them, particularly of middling rank perhaps, had married into English families; the greatest had begun to found their own religious houses in England or become patrons there of long-established religious institu-tions. They had begun to take an interest in the pre-conquest English past. Confident of their position in England, some had begun to advance beyond the marches into Wales and Scotland, which had itself become a protectorate of the English kings under the brothers of Henry I's queen, Matilda. Any lingering uncertainties in 1100 about the future of the changes effected by the Norman Conquest had evaporated by 1135. Some historians do still debate how 'Norman' the 'English' nobility remained, but such discussions are unreal and turn on how the words are defined. The England of 1135 was quite different from that of 1066 and there was no expectation, let alone hope, of turning the clock back. Henry I's first queen, Matilda, might appear to 'represent' the Old English line and bequeath her 'legitimacy' to her children, but she herself had no roots in the pre-conquest kingdom. There were no Godwinsson pretenders lurking for an occasion to overturn the Norman settlement. The most eloquent of the Anglophile elements were found in the monasteries and they took the view that the Norman rulers, whatever their failings, should and could be vigorous defenders of the ecclesiastical order; anyway, success in battle had shown that God endorsed their rulership. A new order had come into being and there was no hankering after a remote glorious past. Ecclesiastical advocates of change looked to the future for more progress in getting their own way; their interest in the past was not nostalgic.

The Anglo-Norman baronage is unlikely to have perceived any need on its part to take instruction about the merits and duties of kingship from the clergy. Of any conscious attempts to articulate their own expectations, however, there is no evidence. Yet it has to be remembered that, in 1066, most Normans were neither informed about kingship nor interested in it. Initially, it was the Conqueror who had gained most from his coronation, not his barons. Perhaps within twenty years, the barons had been reconciled to the idea of royal government in return for confirmation of their hereditary rights to the properties awarded them in England; but, as events after the death of the Conqueror showed, they were not passive subjects of monarchy. They certainly considered themselves entitled to some say about whom they would accept as their king and did not all automatically accept that Rufus's coronation by the church in England had conferred on him absolute right to their loyalty. The monarchy was not therefore entirely within the gift of the English clergy, nor its nature determined by the Old English ecclesiastical legacy. Moreover, though the English hierarchy might be able to achieve its own purposes by claiming the prerogatives of the Old English church, the real power in the kingdom rested not with the clergy but with the great secular lords, whose outlook was not shaped in anyway by Old English traditions.

In 1087 it may seem as though they still behaved 'like Normans'; for them, the relevant precedents of secular government derived from Norman practice. The succession to the duchy had since 911 passed from father to son, for the most part without having to make any concessions to younger brothers; William the Conqueror may himself have in many ways ruled more like a king than a duke in Normandy even before 1066, but he still consulted his great lords about his enterprises and required their support. He did not command like a king and after his success in England he did not expect his Normans on their own to acclaim him as king. He was king of the English, only duke of the Normans. Some of the many kinds of Frenchmen who had joined his forces may even have wondered how the nominal vassal of the king of France could himself become a king in another kingdom: the situation was unprecedented. When William I died in 1087, Norman custom required him to allow his eldest son Robert to succeed him, at least in Normandy, despite the long estrangement between father and son. The Conqueror's proposal to arrange for his second son, William, to succeed him in England was controversial and, accordingly, challenged. Many preferred, for whatever reason, to acknowledge his brother Robert and considered themselves justified in fighting on Robert's behalf. After Rufus's death Robert also seemed to some barons more entitled to the English throne than the youngest brother, Henry. Henry had promptly been consecrated king, but this did not deter Robert's supporters. Did they prefer Robert on formal grounds, because he was duke of Normandy, or the eldest son? Were their reasons more personal: that they found Robert more congenial? Did they calculate that Robert would be more easy going and give them less trouble? They did not all necessarily have the same motive for preferring Robert and their particular motives are not of much import- ance. What matters is that they were not prepared to be excluded by the clergy from the business of king-making. The king was pre-eminently their lord, military commander and arbiter of their disputes. He had to be someone capable of discharging the secular duties of kingship.

Kingship was in early twelfth-century Europe an institution still in process of development. Since the Carolingian revival of the 'Roman' empire in the eighth century, educated discussion of rulership had focused on the nature of imperial rule, the only form of secular government seriously considered by earlier Latin learning. Mere kings had *de facto* authority of a very limited kind, within narrow geographical limits, though their titles made them kings of peoples, not of territories. There was no theoretical understanding of the rights of kingship, apart from what the clergy could concoct from their reading of the Old Testament. In practice, royal powers depended on the traditions of the peoples they ruled, whose ancient laws and customs they swore to uphold. Henry I did precisely this when he promised at his coronation to keep the 'laws of Edward the Confessor', not an agreed text but a convenient way of referring in this instance to the long-established ways of the English kingdom before the Norman takeover. Most medieval kings were found on the peripheries of Christendom: in Spain, in the British Isles and in Scandinavia. Aspirant political societies might seek papal approval for recognition of new kingships, as happened in Hungary and Poland. Early in the twelfth century, new kings were recognised in Jerusalem, Sicily and Portugal. These new kingdoms did not draw upon any established traditions of respect for royalty, and though the ambitions of the new rulers for a distinctive title played an important part in creating them, this would not have been sufficient to give them lasting authority without backing from the great men in their kingdoms. Without the support of his most powerful subjects, no king could make a kingdom out of papal approval alone.

To help put Henry's kingship in its contemporary secular context, it is worth reflecting on the image of kingship depicted in the 1130s by Geoffrey of Monmouth's *History of the Kings of Britain*, a work which rapidly acquired an enviable reputation as a true history.[10] What is now regarded as fiction became almost immediately an inspiration, not merely for more works of pure romance but for standards of courtly behaviour. The last great British hero before the arrival of the Saxons and the beginnings of English history was Arthur, who himself became a model of kingship in later times. According to Geoffrey, Arthur was a great conqueror who subjected all neighbouring kingdoms to his authority and who successfully defied and defeated the Roman state itself. He was a warrior, prepared to settle quarrels by personal combat and totally fearless, generous, even lavish to his knights and conducting his public affairs in great state and dignity. There is almost nothing whatever about him to suggest that he gave time or thought to the management of his landed estate or to the doing of justice. At the most, he settled occasional disputes between his greatest vassals. His regular actions were military and ceremonial. Even if Geoffrey were thought to have written mere fiction and to have had no influence on his readers, his presentation of kingship at this time bears no resemblance to the picture of twelfth-century kingship painted by modern scholarship.[11] Arthur may have been fortunate to win all his battles, but the important thing was to fight and to lead men by exemplary and undaunted valour. The secular nobility expected to find something admirable about their king which would inspire respect. The simmering support in Normandy for Duke Robert, the former crusader, and for his valiant son William against Henry I, may be explained in this way. For all Henry's merits, he may not have inspired comparable reverence. Malmesbury himself calls attention to Henry's unusual preference for settling disputes by diplomacy.[12] The importance of creating a 'chivalrous' impression in the twelfth century may be gauged from the terms in which such an ecclesiastical historian as John of Hexham could describe Stephen's resolution at Lincoln in 1141:

> Like a lion, the king stood in the line of battle, the bravest of the brave, fearing the attack of no one. He cut down all who came to challenge him until his sword was shattered in his hand; a man of Lincoln city then handed him a Danish axe. It is not easy to describe with how much courage he threatened his adversaries; at length he perceived that almost all his comrades were scattered and that he would remain alone, yet still no one ventured to lay hands on him to take him captive. When Earl Ranulf showed his wish to attack him, he struck him on the head with the axe, bringing him to his knees on the ground, and so taught the earl not to attempt more than lay within his powers.[13]

Geoffrey's Arthur figured largely in the imagination of the twelfth century, particularly in the dominions of the English king. This is shown by the use made of Geoffrey's Latin history in Wace's French vernacular and poetic version of it, the *Geste des Bretons*, or the *Brut* and in Layamon's English *Brut*.[14] Layamon's dates are in dispute but his eagerness to adapt Wace for English taste suggests a date in the twelfth century rather than later. Wace's book was completed in 1155 and written therefore either in Stephen's reign or immediately after it, well before Henry II's own reign could have completely altered the historical context. It was dedicated to Henry II's wife, Eleanor of Aquitaine, and Wace anticipated some interest in the subject matter at court and a public for it amongst French speakers in England, as well as on the Continent. Wace had been educated at Caen and Paris. Though his knowledge of Geoffrey's Latin history could have been acquired as easily in France as in England, his decision to provide a vernacular version may have given him the initial stimulus to visit scenes depicted in it; he is believed to have travelled in England in Stephen's time. Despite the closeness of his adaptation, Wace had no scruples about injecting Geoffrey's characters with the spirit of romance appropriate to poetry. Wace in particular provided exciting extra detail about Arthur's battles, the embarkation of troops, the welcome extended to his armies on return from campaigns, the élan of military life. He apparently knew other stories about Arthur than those given by Geoffrey and used them to fill out his portrait of *li bons rois*, making him in the process less barbaric and more like the ideal hero of chivalry. The point here is not to argue that Wace set up a model type of king, against whom Stephen must seem like a disastrous failure, but to insist that, for those who enjoyed Wace's story, it was the military life and the bravery of soldiers that mattered. In this respect, Stephen did meet contemporary requirements. He may not have been as successful a hero as Arthur, but he fitted comfortably into a society where Arthur would naturally be regarded as a paragon.

Layamon's translation of Wace for the benefit of English speakers shows in a general way that the spirit of the French romance were not assumed by him to be the preserve of a French-speaking elite group or totally without attraction for the English majority in the kingdom. Layamon nevertheless infused his account with a different spirit. The courtly polish of Wace wore off in the hands of this Worcestershire country priest. Layamon thought well enough of Wace's material to embellish it to twice its original length, not by adding fresh episodes but by providing more detail, drawing skilfully upon what seems to be his appreciation of the native English literary tradition for his inventions. Layamon's characters are, however, unlike Wace's, not conceived in chivalrous terms, though they are still military: fearless, self-reliant, but also impulsive, violent and cruel. Appropriately, Arthur himself is not a Romantic hero, but the greatest conquering king of all time, receiving tribute and hostages from all his royal neighbours in proof of his greatness. Arthur also commands his men rather than listens to their advice; his firmness created conditions within his kingdom that brought peace and prosperity to his people. Layamon's Arthur may even be interpreted as an implicit English rejection of an ineffective king like Stephen. His is a harsh world. Arthur asserts himself against other headstrong men. Layamon may therefore reveal indicate what features of kingship were valued in England.

Early in Stephen's reign, Geffrei Gaimar provided a history of the English in French verse for a Lincolnshire lady, Constance Fitz Gilbert.[15] According to the epilogue, the work began with the story of Jason and the Golden Fleece, but the mere six and a half thousand lines of his verse now extant begin with the last years of Roman Britain and carry the story of the peoples of England forward no further than the death of Rufus in 1100. All the earlier British part was probably derived from Geoffrey of Monmouth and would have become redundant for a French-speaking audience once Wace's superior poem became known. All that has survived of Gaimar's history relates to the later period not dealt with by Geoffrey of Monmouth, what we think of as Anglo-Saxon England. Adding little to our historical knowledge from other sources, it is of interest for showing both that French speakers in England wanted to learn about the old English past and that Gaimar was able to make use of the English vernacular chronicle for this purpose. Gaimar blithely interprets the past in terms of his own times, which justifies use of him as a guide to the sentiments of lay landowners in the mid-twelfth century.

His work has, for this reason, attracted some attention in recent years. It is remarkably untouched by the familiar preoccupations of the clergy; references to piety are perfunctory and conventional. His focus is on martial exploits and chivalrous behaviour. The action of events shows Gaimar to be aware of the many early kingdoms of England, and he remains alert to what is happening over a wide geographical area with a strong Danish element to his body of information, perhaps understandably for a Lincolnshire text. Yet Gaimar identifies strongly with the English when the successful eleventh-century Danes are presented as behaving with intolerable arrogance towards the native population. There is, significantly, no comparable comment on Norman behaviour after 1066. The notion of a Norman Conquest of England is absent. Unlike the Danes, the Normans have been absorbed into the narrative as though they had already become as English as Gaimar and his patrons. Apart from paying attention to battles and weaponry, the text takes a view of the barons which must reflect current perceptions. They are noted several times as giving their advice, or rather that rulers acted after taking their advice. Their contingents are usually defined in terms of the counties that dukes or counts commanded. They muster their friends, men and dependants for war. In campaigns, other groups that field forces include 'barons' of towns like York, as well as sergeants and burgesses. The great men of the kingdom may on occasion resolve an end to conflict and they are certainly not presented as fomenters of discord or naturally factious. Even if this puts a favourable gloss on the behaviour of secular lords, it is not without importance for telling us how they saw themselves. In his final lines Gaimar offered to extend his work to cover the reign of Henry I, if a generous patron came forward. This would enable him to do justice to 'li reis meillur ki unkes fust ne james seit e crestien fust e beneit' (he was the best king there ever was, a Christian and blessed) but he offered to do this by describing his 'festes', his 'noblesces des largetz et des richesses e del barnage k'il mena des larges dons k'il dona' (his great assemblies, his generosity, his riches, the barons he led and the great gifts he made) as well as the love affairs and jesting contests that entertained such high society. For Gaimar's circle of educated and comfortable gentry, Henry I could apparently be considered a chivalrous king. Again, there is no sign at all here of the Henry I extolled in modern political histories.

If the great secular lords wished to retain some say in their choice of ruler, they were not necessarily opposed over this by the senior clergy. The new kings of the age deliberately invited recognition from the popes and sought consecration from the chief bishops of their kingdoms. The eagerness of prelates to obtain exclusive rights for officiating at coronation ceremonies became a further element in the business of choosing and legitimising kings. In none of these monarchies could the royal office be regarded as a piece of inheritable property; it could only pass with assent and not by some incontrovertible law. Admittedly, the French monarchy appears to be an exception to this, passing by pure inheritance, first in the family of Clovis, then of Charlemagne and finally of the Capetian dukes of the Franks. Henry of Huntingdon himself describes the French royal succession as one from father to son in each of these three dynasties. Whatever Huntingdon may have thought, the succession to the French throne was not secured by inheritance but in practice by the coronation of the king's heir to a joint kingship in his father's lifetime. Even in Henry I's reign, for example, King Louis VI of France first had his heir Philip crowned at Reims in 1129. When Philip was accidentally killed in a riding accident, the king promptly had Philip's brother Louis consecrated, again at Reims, by none less than the visiting pope, Innocent II. Innocent on this visit to France was also received by Henry I at Rouen, when his daughter Matilda was there, but there is no hint that Henry discussed his dispositions for the succession with the pope, still less sought papal confirmation for them.

Although the French example found no echoes in England in Henry's time, in 1152 the English king did attempt to guarantee the succession of his elder son by this means. As it happened, this came to nothing, but a comparable move was successfully made in 1170. Instead of simply making foresighted provision for the future, it proved a total disaster. In England, the young king, egged on by his father-in-law, the king of France, promptly demanded to be treated by his father as a real ruler. This provoked open civil war and the experiment was never repeated. Yet in France the ceremony still served a political purpose in 1179, when the young Philip II was crowned in his father's lifetime so that in 1180 on his father's death he succeeded without further ado. What helped in France did not necessarily achieve the same success elsewhere. Though it was tried in Sicily three times, in 1151,

1191 and 1194, in the hope of prolonging regimes that were openly challenged, the ceremony proved insufficient on its own to save the dynasty.

By the twelfth century, the French kingship may have become a possible model for other Christian rulers, but it was not so easy for kings in the interests of their family to graft French practice into their kingdoms, because not all the king's subjects were disposed to approve it. A line of hereditary kings proved acceptable in France because the Capetian rulers themselves aspired to little more in the eleventh century than the preservation of their former authority as dukes of the Franks, under the royal title. Even the landed estate of the monarchy comprised what the Capetians had brought to it as dukes: by the time of their acceptance as kings in 987, the resources of the former imperial dynasty of Carolingian monarchs had been dissipated. This means that nowhere can the office of kingship itself be yet considered a piece of inheritable property. To be effective it needed to obtain recognition and support. Consecration in church visibly established a new king's credentials – and some realistic demonstration of the willingness of great men to acknowlege him would be required to get him into church. A few clergy could not stage a ceremony to pre-empt the outcome. The procedure of election was not formalised but the principles involved are clear and were adequate for the age.

The English monarchy had been originally established in the tenth century, but it faced similar problems to other newer monarchies of the twelfth century. The claims of the Wessex house of Cerdic to rule the whole English kingdom had been set aside three times in the eleventh century: by the Danish Canute, the English Harold Godwinsson and the Norman William. Since 1066, moreover, the 'natural' heir had been twice passed over; there were no certain 'rules' to preclude a disputed succession. William the Conqueror had left the question of the succession to the kingdom open until his death-bed, though Robert's rights to succeed him in Normandy had been confirmed much earlier. Even the Norman kings' subjects may have seen that any possible advantages in trying to bind the future might be countered by awkward and embarrassing consequences, at least as undesirable as uncertainty. The clergy benefited by an arrangement that at least accorded them the last word, namely the chance to confer the crown on a candidate too strong to be rejected, rather than merely confirm a feeble one designated in advance by royal whim. It may be imagined that the baronage would be still less attracted by any system that deprived them of the slightest influence over the outcome and left the nomination of the king's heir to the king's own fiat. Even if the king was himself popular, his free choice might not be. In modern terms the issue might be expressed as one about whether the kingship was a public office, conferred after some political discussion, or a piece of private property, inherited by the rules of customary law. In as much as even the recognition of descent of landed property in England was still in principle understood to be conditional on the acceptability of the heir to the lord of the fief, it would be understandable if the succession to the kingship was seen to be conditional on the acceptability of the heir to the people. The ritual of the coronation ceremony prescribed popular acclamation, as it still does.

In the middle part of his reign, Henry I probably felt that his own rule in England was sufficiently well established for William, his son by Queen Matilda, to be sure of a peaceful succession. Had William outlived his father, this might have been the case. William had, however, no 'rights' in Normandy and, according to the Anglo-Saxon Chronicle for 1115, Henry I, while in Normandy, obliged the Normans themselves to do homage and swear fealty to William to smoothe his way, a blatant attempt to override the claims of Henry's nephew, William Clito, son to Duke Robert. Henry's troubled relationships in these years with the Norman barons and the king of France, and his consequent anxiety to make alliances with other northern French princes, are described in detail in the 'Hyde' chronicle. Yet, surprisingly, this chronicle never mentions the swearing ceremony. Only when Henry's victory at Brémule over King Louis VI of France in 1119 persuaded Louis to recognise Henry's son William as duke of Normandy did some prospect of lasting peace open up. Even so the Hyde chronicle refers to William only as 'rex Norman-Anglorum, ut putabatur futurus' (assumed to be future king of the Norman-English), not that he had been formally recognised. In Henry I's calculations it was in Normandy and against the claims of his nephew that he had to work for his own son's succession. Nevertheless, apparently following the Norman ceremony of 1115, Henry I, according to the Worcester chronicle, required an assembly of great men and barons in England the following April 1116 to do homage to William and swear fealty to him.[16] Henry may therefore be considered to have taken calculated steps to get William accepted as his heir in both England and Normandy. To cement his standing in France, William was married to the count of Anjou's daughter.

Even so, it seems probable that, had Henry I died before 1120, some barons, whatever they might have sworn, would have certainly regarded his brother Robert, or Robert's son William, as having claims on the succession at least as good as Henry's own son. Though Robert, as Henry's prisoner till his death in 1134, remained a cipher, William Clito, who had slipped out of Henry's clutches, counted on real support from the king of France and some in Normandy until his death in 1128. Henry, who had himself no right by inheritance to the crown or the duchy, could hardly assert an incontrovertible right to dispose of it himself by rules of inheritance. He used his power to try and foist his own children on the kingdom and his subjects may have succumbed to his pressure, but they could fairly claim to have been put under intolerable stress and, according to later sources, did so in justification of their alleged perjury. Morally, they felt themselves free to repudiate their oaths when the time came.

After Henry's wife Matilda died in 1118, the king, by then well over fifty, began to negotiate a second marriage. The death of his only son William at sea in December 1120 made Henry I even more desperate for a male heir. Within a month he had taken the teenage Adeliza of Louvain as his second wife. In the meantime, however, some of Henry's barons naturally saw the claims of his nephew William Clito as correspondingly enhanced, certainly in Normandy itself. Clito himself also became more active, recovering favour with Louis VI, with his relations in Flanders, with some Norman barons and with the count of Anjou, who, no longer committed by his daughter Matilda's marriage to the cause of Henry's son, agreed to the marriage of another of his daughters, Sybil, to Clito. Henry I negotiated with the pope to get this marriage annulled on the grounds of consanguinity, by no means abashed that his own son's marriage had been equally unlawful. Papal support for Henry I may have broken the marriage arrangement but did nothing to diminish Clito's ambition or his network of friends.

Then, in 1125, Henry I's daughter Matilda lost her husband, the Emperor Henry V, and returned to her father. By that time, Henry may have already given up hope of begetting further offspring and Queen Adeliza was seeking spiritual consolation for her barrenness.[17] According to several writers, the king obliged his leading subjects in England in December 1126 or January 1127 to recognise his daughter Matilda as his heir. No steps were taken to secure recognition of her rights in Normandy, or by the king of France, probably because Henry accepted its impossibility.[18] Henry's purpose has usually been taken for granted – to guarantee in the longer term the succession of at least his own daughter, in default of a son in both England and Normandy – without adequate consideration of the immediate circumstances in which Matilda was brought forward. In 1126 Henry and his great men would have recognised that, in the event of the king's death, his most direct legitimate male heir was his nephew, William Clito, his detested enemy. At the very time Matilda was brought to England, Clito married the queen of France's half-sister, Jeanne of Maurienne, and within another two months was formally invested by Louis VI as count of Flanders. Clito's new position would have made it comparatively easy for him to launch a campaign against England for the assertion of his rights. Henry's need of effective allies in France was obvious and he must have taken the extraordinary step of making a public show of Matilda's status as his heir in 1126–27 to enhance her attractions for any future husband.

Henry did not adopt the forms of recognition chosen for her brother William in 1115, 1116 and 1119. Those were inconceivable. Instead, Henry settled for an arrangement that looks like a compromise. The archbishop of Canterbury (then also Roman legate) and other bishops and secular princes merely promised on oath to defend the kingdom of England for her after Henry's death, if the queen had not by then borne him a son. No text of the oath survives. The great men are not recorded to have done homage or sworn fealty. The Peterborough Chronicle, but not the Worcester Chronicle, mentions Normandy alongside England as part of her inheritance; but in England it may have been assumed that both would simply go together. Henry's very insistence on promises to uphold Matilda's claims as his heir after his death betrayed his recognition that, without them, her position would be precarious. Had Matilda's rights as sole surviving legitimate child been incontrovertible, if only in England, promises would have been quite unnecessary. Contrariwise, had her rights been as uncontestable as her late brother's, homage would have been performed. Further means were obviously needed to strengthen her claims. A second marriage for her was certainly anticipated; without it, the line of Henry I could not be perpetuated. On her subsequent marriage, moreover, appropriate recognition of her husband's standing might have been anticipated, since in contemporary terms it would have been her husband's duty to assert her rights. To succeed Henry in England, his daughter ought to have been kept in the kingdom, her potential subjects won over to her cause, and her husband introduced to his people and prepared for his role.

Even if he disregarded the fact that, after her return from Germany, and for whatever reason, Matilda did not inspire devotion or respect in England, Henry I cannot seriously have expected his daughter would succeed him without opposition. Since she could not do battle on her own account, a husband for her had to be found. In 1127 Matilda was sent to Normandy and negotiations for her marriage to Geoffrey of Anjou were initiated. Only Robert, earl of Gloucester, and Brian Fitz Count among the great men of England are known to have been consulted about this, suggesting that Henry I sensed the strong hostility of both his French and English subjects to the proposal. The choice of the fifteen-year-old Geoffrey, knighted by Henry I himself in 1128, made sense only for protecting Normandy in the short term from Angevin aggression and in offering Henry I the hopes of keeping a young son-in-law under his own thumb. In England it is unlikely to have been regarded with much confidence or as a satisfactory solution to the problem of the succession. In Geoffrey, however, it will have planted an understandable ambition to obtain some if not all of his wife's 'inheritance'. Any chances of reaching England would depend on his reception in Normandy. Can Henry I have supposed his Norman barons, always head-strong and independent, would eventually accept Geoffrey willingly as their duke? In 1128 the young Geoffrey's abilities as a soldier had not been tested and Henry can have had no confidence that he would prove equal to the task of asserting his wife's rights. (When the time came, Geoffrey of Anjou took eight years to achieve the conquest of Normandy.)

There were soon more immediate problems with the marriage. Within a year, Matilda had deserted Geoffrey and returned to Normandy. They were only reconciled in 1131, after the barons at Northampton in a great assembly advised that she be sent back to Geoffrey as he had requested.[19] William of Malmesbury claimed that on this occasion more oaths were sworn to her, but this time gives no specific detail and is silent about Geoffrey's rights, a matter of crucial importance.[20] Henry I may by this time have become disillusioned about the Angevin prospects. Can the birth of his first grand-son, the future Henry II, in March 1133 have made the old king more sanguine about the chances of his Angevin kin being accepted in Normandy? Until the birth of a second son, Geoffrey, at Rouen in 1134, the young Henry must have been regarded by his father first and foremost as his own heir in Anjou. Anxiety about the future may have kept Henry I continuously in the duchy from August 1133. According to Huntingdon, he was there much affected by his grandchildren, but this is probably mere surmise. That Henry I had taken no direct action to secure recognition of the succession for the Angevins is clear from the reticence of the Norman chronicler, Orderic, who referred to the young Henry of Anjou as one on whom great hopes were placed by some.[21] In Henry's last year, he is reported to have been incensed because his daughter was stirring up her husband against her father and provoking hostilities in Normandy. If true, Matilda may have become impatient with her father's own unhelpful attitude. Embittered relations did nothing to improve the chances for the success of a highly hazardous policy.

Matilda's marriage in France without getting prior approval in England indicates that his kingdom was not Henry's prime consideration: he put the problems of his continental lands first. In 1128, admittedly, it may have seemed probable that any contest for the succession would be fought in France with Clito, and that England would then fall naturally to the victor in the duchy. But, at the very least, had Henry's calculations run along such lines, Geoffrey should have been brought to Normandy, if not England, and acknowledged there as Matilda's husband and, therefore, future ruler. With-out this, Henry's subjects in England, least of all the senior clergy, who had no stakes in Normandy at all, cannot have been expected to welcome the king's Angevin son-in-law as king. Once Matilda became countess of Anjou, Geoffrey as her husband and legal representative must have looked for some guarantees of the succession. This Henry sedulously avoided. Geoffrey may have felt cheated. Even after the reconciliation of 1131, Henry failed to hand over castles in Normandy as a token of his intentions. Nor did he negotiate Louis VI's endorsement of any proposals for an Angevin succession in Normandy. Louis was not likely to have welcomed such an approach, but, unless something was done to prevent him, he could be expected to challenge it. Naturally puzzled by Henry's behaviour, Geoffrey had grounds for thinking he had been duped. Henry's treatment of Geoffrey may have successfully kept his son-in-law in suspense during his own lifetime, but just as obviously bequeathed a dangerous situation to any successor.

Henry's cavalier attitude to Matilda's position after 1128 has proved difficult to understand. If his main purpose had been to neutralise Anjou in the interests of Normandy, Clito's death in Flanders, leaving no heir, within weeks of the marriage, may have put an end to Henry's immediate worries. Thereafter, Henry may have had the quite different objective of using Matilda's marriage to keep Geoffrey's ambitions in France at bay in his own lifetime. The policy was somewhat cynical. If it satisfied Henry's own requirements, it showed total disregard of the eventual outcome. In England, Geoffrey continued to remain an unknown quantity. His attraction for Henry I lay only in what he could do for the duchy, not the kingdom. Geoffrey himself could not have nursed any hopes of an uncontested occupation of the duchy, and he may have early on discounted the likelihood of ever becoming king of England. Anyway, before he had consolidated his hold on Normandy, Geoffrey had no chance of even making a bid for the English throne.

Henry seems to have been indifferent to the implications for England of his decision to marry his daughter to Geoffrey of Anjou. If he expected that the kingdom would meekly accept what he thought best for Normandy, this was short-sighted of him. Since, in both 1087 and 1100, new kings had first established themselves in the kingdom itself and Normandy had been added afterwards, the English had some grounds for doubting Henry's own priorities. By almost immediately bundling Matilda into a continental marriage, Henry demonstrated his blindness to the political realities of the new relationship between the kingdom and the duchy, though he was himself mainly responsible for it. The Angevin marriage could alone have been sufficient to create serious misgivings about oaths sworn to her as an unmarried widow, and in England those concerned about the succession may well have discounted the oaths they had been forced to take. The king's own interest in the crown was not the only one of importance and anxiety about the future would have been understandable. Even if Matilda's husband had been accepted without question, there could be no guarantee he would prove equal to the task of ruling England from his Angevin base.

Until 1120, Henry I clearly concentrated on reuniting under his own government all the lands ruled by his father in 1087 in expectation of handing them on to his son. Although he had had many illegitimate sons before his marriage, none of them had attained prominence by 1120. After William Aetheling was drowned, however, Henry I made Robert, the eldest of them, earl of Gloucester and married him to the Fitz Hamon heiress of Glamorgan. This looks like a bid to establish Robert in a prominent position to help his father in the kingdom. The return of Henry's widowed daughter from Germany in 1126, far from diminishing Gloucester's standing, added to his prominence. Matilda, then still an unmarried widow, may have been given into the protection of her half-brother. Custody of his dispossessed uncle Robert of Normandy was deliberately transferred to Gloucester's charge at her request. Robert of Gloucester's distinction remained exceptional. Henry I, who had several other bastard sons, did nothing to exalt their status. Robert was, however, not without other rivals in the king's favour, notably his Blois nephews, the sons of his youngest sister, Adela. Adela was the only one of the Conqueror's daughters to have a large family and after her husband's death on crusade in 1102, she looked to her brother Henry I as a source of patronage for her younger sons. Henry probably did not need to be cajoled. The Blois boys were not unworthy of his patronage. After 1120, Henry probably saw in them the sole reliable male representatives of his father's line. They were closer to him in kinship than his son-in-law, Geoffrey of Anjou. Count Theobald, Henry's regular ally in France, had lands in England. The youngest son, Henry, was appointed abbot of Glastonbury, one of the most valuable monasteries in the kingdom in 1126. Most favoured and over a longer period was Stephen, count of Mortain since 1113, who married the heiress of Boulogne, Matilda, the late Queen Matilda's niece, probably in 1125; Stephen was therefore most richly set up in England, Normandy and France. Gloucester and Stephen have been regarded either as balancing one another, or cancelling one another out. In accordance with his general behaviour, Henry I may have offered no hostages to fortune; on the other hand, Henry may simply have become as fond of one as of the other.

For Stephen's subsequent succession, it proved significant that, the year after the Angevin marriage and the death of William Clito, Henry I promoted his youngest nephew, Abbot Henry, to the see of Winchester, the ancient capital of Wessex where the king kept his treasure in England. This move surely enhanced the political weight in England of Henry's brother Stephen as against Robert of Gloucester. Henry I cannot seriously have doubted that the two brothers would act in concert on his own death. The promotion of such a great man as Henry to Winchester also reaffirmed Henry I's alignment with the Cluniac order. Shortly after this, another Cluniac, Hugh of Amiens, was transferred from the abbacy of Henry's own foundation at Reading to the archbishopric of Rouen. As archbishop, Hugh was to demonstrate his strongest support for Stephen and hostility to the succession of the Angevins in Normandy for as long as he could. Neither of these episcopal appointments in Henry I's last years can in any way have strengthened Matilda's chances. The wily old king may have been deceived, of course, if his unscrupulous nephews had professed hypocritical commitment to uphold Matilda's 'rights', but this is unlikely. Henry I was not easily duped.

Henry I may have foreseen only too well what might happen. All his reign he had manoeuvred to secure his own objectives. Matilda's second marriage, which ushered her out of England, served its immediate diplomatic purpose in neutralising Geoffrey as an enemy in Normandy. Henry lavished no affection on her; he used her marriages for his own purposes. He was certainly a hard man in politics and it is naive to take for granted any sentimental commitment to his daughter's succession. What little he could do to guarantee the succession of his Angevin descendants he deliberately abstained from doing. He had no means of forcing his English subjects to abide after his death by proposals which would commit the kingdom to the authority of a Loire valley count, but he could certainly have done more to make Geoffrey look like a convincing successor. Did Henry contemplate the prospect of Stephen's succession with equanimity? He had befriended all the sons of his youngest widowed sister Adela and almost certainly preferred the company of his nephews, who were often with him, to that of his daughter, whom he hardly knew. Henry had learnt only too well from personal experience how kingdoms were won and battles fought. We cannot of course know either what Henry thought or would have preferred. We can, however, stop ascribing thoughts and intentions to him that seem plausible to us. He lived in times with different assumptions. If he did manage to deceive himself, his subjects had no reason to do likewise.

4

Stephen's Accession

If it cannot be taken for granted that by 1135 the succession to Henry I had been incontrovertibly arranged in advance, Stephen's abrupt installation as king should not be treated as blatant usurpation. All his immediate predecessors had laid claim to the throne without unimpeachable rights. Acceptance of those claims owed less to the justifications offered than the success of the new kings in seeing off their rivals. On his deathbed, William the Conqueror, universally accepted as conqueror of the kingdom and duke for over fifty years, had despatched Rufus to Lanfranc in England recommending him as king and had conceded the rights of his son Robert to Normandy as previously declared. Henry I's death-bed instructions were not so certain and his authority to dispose of the crown and duchy not so indisputable as William's. Henry's barons in Normandy were in no obvious hurry to replace him. Their priority was to arrange for his body to be brought back to Reading for burial in the great abbey he had endowed; some delay in achieving this was unavoidable, but delay was unaccountably extended by transporting Henry I's body across the whole of Normandy, first to Rouen, then to Caen, instead of shipping it straight over from upper Normandy. For whatever reason, a month elapsed between Henry's death and burial. Huntingdon makes much of the inevitable consequences of this dilatoriness as the king's corpse putrefied. At first there may have been some intention of deferring the choice of a new king until after the burial in England, followed by coronation presumably in London, or in the monastery at Westminster built by Edward the Confessor. A new king of England could hardly have been raised outside England itself.

Nevertheless, more than two weeks after Henry's death, some lords in Normandy, for reasons not made clear, thought better of further procrastination and began to look for a new ruler for the duchy. Geoffrey of Anjou's invasion of Normandy in December may have made them realise that finding a successor to the late king was more urgent than they had first supposed. They had begun to canvass the choice of Theobald, count of Blois, when they received word that his younger brother Stephen had already been consecrated king in England. This was sufficient to resolve their doubts; no alternative candidate from Normandy itself was proposed; the great lords in Normandy accepted the decision taken in England, despite their own absence, with little further ado. Robert of Gloucester, who had most misgivings, joined Stephen in England within four months, perhaps after sounding out opinion on the chances of resistance and concluding that there was in effect no alternative to Stephen. The prompt adherence to Stephen indicates that there was no general inclination on the part of the baronage to take this expected opportunity either to challenge royal authority in general or Stephen's assumption of it in particular. Nothing in our sources indicates that the claims of either Matilda or Geoffrey to be accepted as ruler in Henry I's place were advanced in Normandy, though before Christmas Geoffrey himself sent Matilda, who was again pregnant, into the duchy to assert her rights; he followed her shortly after. Some border castles in south-west Normandy were surrendered to them, but Theobald of Blois then negotiated a truce, and the Angevins had clearly lost their chance to establish their credentials.

Several chroniclers report that the death of Henry I immediately precipitated disorder in England, though according to the *Gesta*, the new king was able to restore a sense of security within a matter of weeks, if not days.[1] This makes it seem as though the extent of disruption had been exaggerated, but news of the old king's death probably did arouse considerable anxiety and unleash violence in some places. To re-establish enforcement of the king's peace, suspended by Henry I's death, the most urgent requirement was to find a new king as quickly as possible. In the meantime, some men seized what seemed like a golden opportunity to settle old scores with impunity.[2] In the north, King David promptly invaded to reassert his claims over areas he believed to be subject to Scottish kings and unjustly appropriated by Rufus and Henry I. Prior Richard of Hexham's account of the disturbances David caused at the beginning of the reign hints, however, that violence was not confined to border disputes.[3] In face of all his difficulties, the new king did not allow himself to be deterred or embittered and the Hexham chronicler never suggests that these troubles arose because his enemies fancied him to be easily bullied.

Whereas David's intervention in the north may have been the specific source of strife there, when the Worcester chronicler makes a similar observation about the widespread break down of order in 1135–36 he names no names.[4] From how far away the Worcester chronicler gathered his information is unclear, though the comment that the situation was worst in Wales suggests that he was thinking in terms of the west country rather than of the kingdom as a whole. According to this account, unnamed men were taking the law into their own hands. In particular, the *optimates* used their power to oppress the weak because they were fearful for the future, seeking to cover themselves against all eventualities and no longer living in dread of the 'royal terror'. The death of the old king also provided a long-awaited opportunity for those wronged by him to seize their chance. These men, the so-called 'Disinherited', did not believe in waiting in hopes of kindlier treatment from a new king. They naturally preferred to help themselves and leave negotiation for royal endorsement till later. Contemporary notions of right depended more upon family connections or sense of obligation to patrons than respect for an abstract concept of the public weal.

Chroniclers and others were understandably prepared to welcome any king able and ready to restore the royal peace without delay. Henry I's death in Normandy had left England rather ill-prepared to meet the emergency, since many of the great men were abroad. Faced with a prospect of continuing uncertainty, the government apparatus, such as it was, required a new ruler with adequate qualifications to take charge as soon as possible. Nevertheless some assessment of the likelihood of success must have played an important part in winning acceptance. To Stephen's credit, he wasted no time in pressing his suit, appeared to have most of the personal qualities required for kingship, and, as a grandson of the Conqueror, an unexceptional claim to be considered for the royal office.

Against Stephen we cannot be absolutely certain that any formal protest was made in England on account of Matilda's rights. As countess of Anjou, she was barely known. She could not possibly be expected to arrive promptly and take over the responsibilities of rulership as the situation required. Her very access to England was dependent on a peaceful Angevin occupation of Normandy itself, which must have seemed totally improbable, given the hostility of most Norman lords.[5] Even to voice the formal possibility that Matilda's eldest son Henry might be acknowledged as his grandfather's heir would have raised a host of unnecessary complications. Not yet three years old, the succession of the young Henry would have involved a long minority, a situation that had no precedent other than that of Aethelred II, of unhappy memory, who had succeeded in 978. The most likely regent would have been either a woman, Matilda herself, or her Angevin husband, neither of whom can have seemed desirable, even to those who did not know them personally. Those who argued that Henry I had commanded such a succession had no reason to think that this course offered the kingdom's subjects a practical solution to the immediate problem of finding an effective ruler immediately. Why should the late king's whims prevail over all other considerations? In December 1135 a king was required who could exercise all the authority of the kingship at once. The prompt appearance of Stephen as a candidate seemed providential. How could Matilda have seemed likely to make a better ruler than the late king's favourite nephew, known and respected in the kingdom? From first to last, Matilda had nothing to back up her claims except the promises made in 1126, and the sole grounds for challenging Stephen proved to be the charge that as a perjurer he was unfit to govern.

Outside some (not all) clerical circles, the matter of the 'oaths' previously sworn to her did not obviously enjoy the credit usually accorded it. This does not mean that men were indifferent to the seriousness of oath-breaking. They had, however, developed a strong sense of when it was appropriate. That Henry I even had the right to demand such oaths was doubtful; that what he proposed would provide successful government of the kingdom was extremely improbable. In matters of such importance, oaths could not be regarded as sacrosanct. All the same, most writers since, following Matilda's own lead, have maintained that this issue determined the outcome and beset the whole course of Stephen's reign. There is, however, no incontrovertible evidence that in 1135 much attention was paid to it. In the first edition of his chronicle, completed about 1130, Huntingdon, for whatever reason, made no allusion to the oaths which Henry had forced his barons to swear in 1126. A more serious lapse appears to be his failure, even in the first continuation written after 1138, to call attention to Matilda's status in 1131 as Henry 's heir, when he recorded Henry's discussions with his barons at Northampton about her future. Had the matter of the oaths been publicly raised in 1135 as an objection to Stephen's coronation, Huntingdon's indifference to them early in the reign would be quite inexplicable.

Most of the sources that deal with what happened at Stephen's succession were written well after the Matildine arguments had entered the public domain. They therefore attempted to deal with these objections as though they had been raised from the very first, namely in December 1135. However, the earliest certain evidence for the voicing of these objections points to the year 1139, when Matilda's case was argued at Rome at the second Lateran council.[6] Even so, only a somewhat partial account of this argument, insufficient to resolve all the points at issue, has survived. What is clear is that, in this ecclesiastical forum, Matilda raised the moral question without success. This decision probably does not reflect mere ecclesiastical prejudice against a woman as such, though in modern times such an explanation has been proposed. Such an argument does nothing to help bolster Matilda's own position. She had herself chosen to drag the church onto the judgment seat by pressing her rights on moral grounds. Moreover, since, on an allegedly moral issue, Rome judged her case to be insufficient, or unproven, there is at least a prima facie conclusion that the matter of oaths was never quite so clear-cut as she made out. Her very insistence on their importance sidesteps two major difficulties. First, if the oaths were so important to her claim, she must have accepted that her rights as Henry's sole surviving legitimate child were themselves insufficient to make her ruler of England; secondly, on her marriage, the vindication of her rights had by customary law become her husband's responsibility. In practical terms, she was seeking to have Stephen replaced by Geoffrey, an option for which there was no English support whatever. Naturally Matilda preferred to insist on her own 'right', as though marriage had made no difference.

After 1139 some discussion about the validity of the proposals of 1126 obviously continued, proving that the papacy's rejection of her case, if it carried some weight, did not allay all doubts, and these she continually fostered. They were considered sufficiently disturbing to inspire a number of different explanations as to why the oaths might have been set aside. As it happens, though William of Malmesbury does not record that the matter of the oaths was raised as an objection against Stephen's coronation, he gives one possible reason why they were not considered of any significance. In his *Historia Novella* (a historical work intended for Robert of Gloucester), he slyly reported Roger, bishop of Salisbury, as claiming to be himself absolved from what he had sworn, on the grounds that Henry I, contrary to his word, had married Matilda to Geoffrey without prior consultation.[7] Roger's excuse would have served others as well, though not Robert of Gloucester himself who had been one of the few privy to the marriage plans. In effect Malmesbury's admission of this technical difficulty in Gloucester's own case bears out Roger of Salisbury's story, though only at the cost of making it more difficult for him to explain Gloucester's own muddled behaviour.

Malmesbury recognised the inconsistencies of Robert's position between 1136 and 1138, and argued that Robert was so conscience-stricken by his recognition of Stephen's kingship in 1136 that he consulted the papacy itself about how to resolve his dilemma. Malmesbury even asserts that the pope sent a letter strengthening Robert's resolve to return to Matilda and promises to insert this letter in due course into his narrative. He never did, presumably because Robert never actually produced it. Malmesbury may have been tricked into thinking such papal authority had been obtained, which would at least excuse his remarks. If the pope ever considered easing Gloucester's own conscience in this way, in every other respect Innocent II never deviated from his recognition of Stephen as rightful king. He treated the oaths of 1126 as irrelevant. Malmesbury's concern to show the purity of Gloucester's motives for joining the Angevins appears to accept the morality of clearing his own conscience by creating civil war. If Gloucester's motives were not so conscience-stricken, his hypocrisy is even more odious.

Whether the oaths were used by Matilda's friends as an excuse or not, the importance which had come to be attached to them by sensitive clergy may be illustrated from the *Gesta* itself. Here even one of Stephen's most devoted supporters sought ways to exculpate him of perjury. Writing not before 1142, and knowing little if anything of the situation in 1126, he claimed that the archbishop of Canterbury did raise this objection before crowning Stephen in 1135. His objections were overcome on the grounds that Henry had compelled rather than directed his great men to swear. Moreover, knowing that such forced oaths would not be kept anyway, Henry had on his death-bed released the barons from their obligations.[8] This very unspecific story, perhaps then still relatively new, was amplified later on, citing Hugh Bigod, the king's steward, as swearing that he had been present and heard Henry's recantation. This was alluded to by Huntingdon in the speech put into Gloucester's mouth at Lincoln in 1141 (written before 1146). According to John of Salisbury writing in 1164, Bigod's oath was used at Rome in 1139 as one of the objections to Matilda's advocates.[9] After the archbishop's death within a year of Stephen's coronation, some writers chose to see in this God's punishment of the prelate's own perjury. The Bigod story may have been elaborated in connection with attempts to blacken or vindicate the archbishop's memory, and may also have some bearing on Bigod's contemporary reputation, since his loyalty to Stephen was never consistent and the empress's party could not regard him as very reliable. If Bigod was widely distrusted, the story acquires an extra piquancy. It does not have much to commend it as truth, whether Bigod was with Henry on his death-bed at Lions la Forêt or not. The story is both improbable and unnecessary.

In Normandy, Henry I would have needed to make a much more public repudiation of Geoffrey's rights than a muttered death-bed wish, had such a move been considered necessary at all. The situation at the bed-side may well have been confused; Henry's last words could have been easily garbled or misheard. However, the archbishop of Rouen, Hugh of Amiens, who was certainly present at the time, wrote promptly to the pope about it, making no comment on the succession. He was himself a consistent supporter of Stephen as lawful king as long as he was a free agent, that is until Geoffrey of Anjou occupied Rouen in 1144.[10] The archbishop cannot therefore have regarded Stephen as in some way disqualified for the kingship by his oath, or have supposed that any last minute injunctions of Henry I had any significance. Hugh's credentials as a loyal churchmen of Henry I are unimpeachable. In 1126 Hugh, as abbot of Reading, received a precious relic brought from Germany for his abbey by the widowed empress and was in an unrivalled position to know the full story about the promises and their implications. If all the principal prelates and barons had taken the oath, Hugh, as abbot of the king's own foundation, can hardly have evaded taking the oath himself. Historians may harbour all sorts of doubts about the integrity of various English prelates, but Hugh is beyond reproach. (As a 'foreigner', of course, he usually gets little attention from English historians.)

Whatever some clerical writers thought after 1139, in 1135 the matter of the succession to Henry I appears to have been treated by the principal parties as an entirely open question. Richard of Hexham reported indeed that in January 1136 David of Scotland had made the men of Durham swear to uphold Matilda's rights and give hostages, but that this was mere subterfuge to cover his real purpose became clear when he agreed terms with Stephen only weeks later early in February without a fight.[11] Nothing more was heard in the north of Matilda's partisans. Though as king himself David declined to do homage to Stephen, he had no objection to his son Henry doing so as earl of Huntingdon, or to his fighting actively on Stephen's behalf. For both David and Henry, accepting Stephen's kingship meant repudiating any obligations David had himself sworn to Matilda. Admittedly, later in the reign, David joined Matilda in England and subsequently received and knighted her son Henry; he is accordingly regarded as a consistent supporter of her cause. Nevertheless, at the crucial point, after Henry's death, he did not consider his oath of 1126 as morally binding; he treated it merely as a bargaining counter in his own calculations.

Curiously, the moral basis of Matilda's stance, and the only one with any impact on the outcome, may not certainly have come to the fore until after Matilda had failed to convince the papacy of its force. This appears to be because the only way she found to discredit Stephen as a ruler was by alleging his moral lapse. Subsequent historians have tirelessly repeated Malmesbury's own claim that Stephen's only fault was being compromised by his oath. Medieval writers, puzzled by his misfortunes, found it plausible that he should be punished directly by God for his perjury. John of Salisbury made it the basis of his vitriolic attack on Stephen. Later writers, however, who do not accept that God punished Stephen's perjury, find it rather difficult to show in practical terms how his perjury damaged him. At best, like Hume, they rationalise, claiming that his own bad example showed his subjects how to go back on their word to him. For the most part, the imputation of perjury to Stephen is left as a smear and its usefulness in this regard may not be discounted. A charge of perjury can still be invoked to discredit politicians not obviously vulnerable by other means. It should not be regarded then (or now) as a decisive argument. Henry I had notably failed to keep the oaths he had sworn in his own coronation charter without this being held against him as an unatonable sin. Most medieval chroniclers consistently described Stephen as most pious and refrained from abusing him as a perjured tyrant. The evidence that his perjury compromised his ability to rule is tenuous in the extreme.

Since Stephen was crowned king about three weeks after Henry I's death, there was little time either for discussion about who should be king, or indeed for the more unfortunate consequences of a hiatus in government to become manifest. On the other hand, had Stephen seized the crown with the aid of a small group of cronies to the utter outrage of rivals, his action would surely have provoked immediate opposition, just as Henry I's comparable action in 1100 had precipitated his brother's invasion of 1101. The evidence suggests rather that, even if some of the great lords were taken aback, they immediately rallied round as though glad the matter had been resolved in such a satisfactory manner. At the very least, a goodly number of interests were engaged with the new ruler and expected the kingdom to be ruled accordingly. Of the anarchic tendencies of the Anglo-Norman baronage there was no sign, apart from the vague reports of the Worcester writer about the reactions of the *optimates*, probably with the peculiar situation of the Welsh march in mind.

Whether by chance or not, Stephen had not been in Normandy at the time of Henry I's death and would have surely found it difficult to make a dash for England had he been there. He learned of his uncle's death in his county of Boulogne. From there it was easy to slip across the Channel and take a risk in bidding for the crown. According to a Canterbury writer of the late twelfth century, Stephen was rebuffed on his arrival at Dover, but Stephen's unacceptability there has been convincingly explained as a consequence of the castle being held on behalf of Robert of Gloucester.[12] The fullest account of his coronation campaign, given in the *Gesta*, stresses the exceptional role assumed by the city of London in conferring the crown. This may reveal an aspect of the practical realities of kingship insufficiently reflected in normal expectations of the constitutional forms; by the time he wrote, the author may also have been influenced by his awareness of the importance of London's partiality for Stephen, as shown in the crisis of 1141. Though the reasons for it are not specified, that London was itself strongly in Stephen's favour is not in doubt. The only known text of Stephen's coronation charter, in which he confirmed all the good laws and customs of Henry I and of King Edward the Confessor, is preserved in a London source.[13] It is possible that Stephen was well known in the city. His natural son, Gervase, after he became abbot of Westminster, provided a house for his mother in Chelsea, which raises the possibility that London had been the venue for his parents' liaison. Certainly as count of Boulogne since his marriage in 1126, and a great landowner in Essex as lord of the Honour of

Eye, Stephen must have been familiar with many of the leading citizens. The comments of chroniclers on his affability with men of all ranks may refer specifically to his good relations with townsmen. Unfortunately, the *Gesta*'s picture of king-making by the London citizenry is not corroborated elsewhere. As it stands, the initiative of the Londoners cannot be an adequate explanation for his success.

The speed with which Stephen concluded the affair suggests he may have had a contingency plan worked out beforehand with his youngest brother, Henry of Winchester, who at this point began to assert a major influence on public affairs. The prominence enjoyed by the Blois brothers in England under Henry I is understandable. As sons of Countess Adela, William the Conqueror's last surviving child (possibly 'born in the purple', after William had become a king), they had been Henry I's favoured nephews.[14] As the only surviving legitimate grandsons of the Conqueror himself, they were persons of some consequence. Their elder brother, Theobald, was by any measure one of the great men of France and his children extended the high reputation of the family as rulers of Champagne in the next generation. Rather than planning a sordid little *coup d'état*, Stephen and Henry may have discussed taking sensible steps to defend their grandfather's legacy when their uncle died. Henry of Winchester, appointed there by Henry I in 1129, was inevitably in a strong position to influence the changeover when it came, because the king's treasure was deposited in Winchester under his very nose. The *Gesta* itself notes the importance of Henry's negotiations with the royal treasurer for the release of the late king's hoard of money. Henry may also have foreseen a role for himself in any coronation ceremony. The archbishop of Canterbury, William of Corbeil, was already old and ill in 1135; had he died sooner, or even been incapacitated, another bishop would have officiated at the coronation. In the absence of Archbishop Anselm at the time of Henry I's coronation in 1100, the bishop of London had acted, but the London bishopric was itself vacant in 1135 and Henry himself had taken charge of diocesan administration there. Henry's eminence in the English church could have been challenged only by Thurstan of York, distinguished, but old and remote from southern affairs. Henry was a commanding figure who enjoyed public life and managed business with exceptional flair.

An alternative 'party' of bishops has been discerned in Roger of Salisbury and his two nephews, Alexander of Lincoln and Nigel of Ely. Roger had been Henry I's chief minister and had known how to take advantage of the king's confidence in him to make his own fortune and that of his family. The king's subjects recognised his power and treated him with appropriate deference. His role in the development of branches of royal administration has won him many modern admirers. He is now widely regarded as the effective head of royal administration, a concept not certainly then in vogue.[15] Whatever his abilities, he and his family are unlikely to have been popular. Roger's obscure origins in Normandy may have inspired some scorn – and his subsequent eminence, envy. Roger was a powerful figure in England but, after his royal patron's death, his main hope must have been to retain his influence and wealth, rather than initiate new policies of his own: he was a powerful servant of kings, not himself a maker of policy. Stephen was prepared to retain his talents in his own service. In consideration of such assurances Roger would have raised no difficulties about Stephen's kingship, had any occurred to him. He had no alternative candidate to propose and no political credit outside his own family to put at any rival's feet.

Quite apart from any sympathy Henry of Winchester felt for Stephen's ambitions, he is presented as expecting his brother's succession to be a God-given opportunity not merely to rectify relations between the ruler and the church but to inaugurate a programme of reform which would release churchmen from the old-fashioned strictures of Henry I's regime. Stephen's promises at his coronation to satisfy the church's demands were elaborated within months by the publication at Oxford of a charter of liberties for the church in April 1136. Though more detailed, this charter actually drew on the precedent of Henry I who had likewise issued a charter in 1100 promising to abolish the evil customs of the previous reign and to restore the good old practices of hallowed memory. Granting the charter is not therefore a sign of Stephen capitulating to the demands of those who had chosen him as their pliable creature. Like all new governments, Stephen offered a new deal and asked for confidence in his sincerity. As always, not all the promises were kept, but some defaulting on ideals is only to be expected. At the very least, like others, Stephen found that it is not actually so easy to govern as planned. Nor do governments necessarily find all their proposals so attractive when the time comes to implement them. Despite the carping of some chroniclers, Stephen was no more dishonest than others in a similar position. This does not detract from the importance of the charter, for it clearly shows, like that of 1100, what those surrounding the new king at least hoped to achieve. Stephen did not buy allegiance with the charter. The charter proclaimed a programme.

The absence in Normandy of most of the great lords had made it impossible for Stephen to have set about buying their support for his 'unlawful' regime by offering rewards and favours to his barons, as is often alleged. Some historians claim that he not only made concessions to obtain support, but did so on such terms of equality with his barons as to admit their right to break with him if he defaulted on the deals. This interpretation seems to be based on the assumption that Stephen was very simple-minded and is then used to argue that his rule was necessarily compromised from the first by being conditional on his own good behaviour.[16] This seems like a wilful misrepresentation. In a sense all kings accepted that they were bound to show consideration for their vassals' rights. Stephen conceded no more than this. For the rest, the new reign and the death of the old king were surely considered proper occasions for rejoicing and promising a different style of kingship, more fitting for the modern age. Stephen was not desperately buying support but cheerfully giving a display of what a younger and more confident king should be. Spending lavishly would not have been judged a profligate dispersal of Henry I's accumulated treasures but a happy augury of the king's generosity. Some chroniclers sniffed disdainfully that Stephen squandered Henry I's treasure and modern writers use such remarks to justify their criticisms of the king's profligacy. In fact, chroniclers knew nothing of the virtues of political economy. What they objected to was that laymen not clergy had been the main beneficiaries of royal bounty. In their view the money should have been given to the church, so that Henry's soul might be properly prayed for. Medieval appraisals need to be understood for what they were; they are not easily appropriated for modern polemic.

About his relations with very few of the great men of the kingdom are we informed in any detail. The case of David of Scotland is the best known. David's invasion of northern England had obliged Stephen to go north at the very outset of the reign. David's ambition was to reverse those advances which William II and Henry I had made into northern territory, at a time when David's elder brothers were too dependent on English support to defend the interests of their own kingdom in the region. The rights of the English kings were at best contentious and, in the twelfth century, it was not only the boundaries of the two kingdoms which were still not agreed. The pretensions of the archbishops of York also extended across the whole of Scotland, since the bishops of Glasgow, St Andrews and of the Orkneys were all claimed as suffragans of the York province. (Scotland had no metropolitan bishop till the fifteenth century, and the special relationship which made the pope the direct superior of the Scottish bishops was not negotiated till 1189.) David would have seen Henry I's creation of a new bishopric at Carlisle in 1133 as a bid to consolidate the very recently imposed English control over Cumbria.[17] David's own government in Scotland since 1124 was shaped by his determination to restore some independence of action after years of English protection, and his plans involved recovery of lands not only in Cumbria but in northern-eastern England, which he believed to be properly subject to the kings of Scotland.

David was the real architect of the medieval Scottish kingdom and he owed much to his earlier experiences in England as earl of Huntingdon since 1114. The extensive lands of the earldom and its political importance since the eleventh century gave him unprecedented opportunities to play a prominent part in English affairs for more than a decade before he himself became king in Scotland. David naturally wasted no time on hearing of Henry I's death in asserting himself and would have behaved no differently with any other successor to Henry. Stephen's concession to David, granting him Carlisle and Cumbria, have on the other hand been judged weak. Henry II, after all, easily recovered these properties from David's heir, Malcolm IV. Henry had, however, confirmed David's possession of them only a few years previously and would not have found it so easy to snatch them from David himself. The original concession to David had been made by Stephen in order to acquire the loyalty of David's heir, who did homage for his father's former earldom. This appeared to restore good relations between the two kings on a potentially enduring basis. Stephen may not have regarded his concessions to David as shameful surrender of national territory, as it is bound to seem now, but a sensible restoration of good relations with his wife's uncle by withdrawal from exposed positions only recently acquired by Henry I. Whether this should be considered an example of Stephen's casual bargaining for recognition or not is at least an open question, but if he did, he might have been well satisfied with the outcome: David had distanced himself from the Angevin cause and shown what he really wanted.

The adherence of Robert of Gloucester to Stephen as king in 1136 is both better documented and yet more mysterious thanks to William of Malmesbury, writing probably after the later total breach between king and earl in 1138, and obviously in some unease about Robert's erratic course.[18] First, he alleges that by recognising Stephen's position as king, early in 1136, Robert had seen no alternative way to look after the young Henry's interests. Secondly, Malmesbury tries to make out that Robert's recognition of Stephen in 1136 was provisional, doing homage and reserving fealty only as long as Stephen kept faith with him. Most historians take Malmesbury's comments at face value and find themselves accordingly obliged to criticise Stephen, both for his weak acceptance of Robert's conditional homage and then for his treacherous reactions to Robert's conditional loyalty. Stephen's position cannot be fairly judged one way or the other, but Malmesbury's evidence is so obviously *parti pris* as to be suspect.

Had Robert stipulated openly that his fealty was only provisional, Stephen like everyone else would have been warned what to expect. In a sense all fidelity in such a society was reciprocal and provisional, for vassals could not be expected to be loyal to lords who betrayed them or vice-versa. This means that mutual respect was required on both sides. To call attention to it deliberately would have occasioned comment. Malmesbury may in fact be trying to make a more explicit excuse, relying perhaps on Gloucester's confidential admission to his chronicler of his mental reservations when joining Stephen. This makes Robert's original decision to recognise Stephen at all seem hopelessly irresolute later on. The simplest explanation is that Robert saw Stephen's position in England to be sufficiently secure to leave him no option. The Welsh unrest in Gwent on hearing of Henry I's death had probably made it sensible for Gloucester to return to England from Normandy promptly, if his own Welsh lands were to be protected. At Cardiff castle his men were in the front line. Nor will Gloucester have been confident in 1136 that Bristol, his greatest English stronghold, would be able to resist a siege if he provoked the king. Only after the failure of Stephen to capture Bristol in 1138 did Robert realise the potential of his stronghold in the west country. In 1136, however, this was no moment to dither.

In 1136 Robert may have been prepared to go further than this and endorse Stephen's kingship wholeheartedly. The breach in 1138 could have been induced by fresh grievances. To all intents and purposes, Robert appeared for two years to have become one of Stephen's supporters and encouraged the king to think of him as such. If he had mental reservations from the beginning, then he was certainly guilty himself of tricking Stephen into a false sense of security. Malmesbury's story that Robert only turned against Stephen when the king planned to ambush him in Normandy would only look persuasive if Robert himself had been unequivocally loyal. This story itself seems contrived, since Stephen had been at least six months back in England before Gloucester published his renunciation of fealty. Malmesbury's shifty attempts to exonerate Robert from all blame make it more likely that Robert and Stephen had been been wary of one another throughout. That they were perceived by their contemporaries as natural political rivals is suggested by a later fictional elaboration of the story of the oath-swearing in 1126 from Gloucester abbey, which alleges that the oaths were renewed in 1128 and that Robert and Stephen then vied for the honour of swearing first.[19] The story at least gives an instance of the likely way the promotion of the king's son and his favourite nephew, in comparable measure and in the same period after the loss of the king's son William at sea, inevitably provoked emulation. Robert as a bastard accepted that he had no hopes of the crown itself. This itself would have been sufficient to make him resent Stephen's success. Perhaps before the event he had ruled it out as improbable; but, once done, Robert did not immediately see what he could do to challenge Stephen's new position.

An aspect of their relationship concerning the affairs of south Wales deserves more attention than it often receives.[20] In Henry I's last years, Welsh unrest was already simmering and, immediately his death was known there, Welsh princes aimed to overturn the settlement imposed in Henry's time. Unlike the position in Scotland, there was no single Welsh leader capable of leading a united force directly into England itself, no coherent strategy for achieving their objectives and no possibility of attracting border barons into an alternative lordship, as King David aspired to do in the north. Welsh actions took the form of local assaults on the several different lordships set up to parcel out responsibility for the region. The response was equally piecemeal. The marcher lords had considerable experience of the situation and knew how to take advantage for themselves of the divisions amongst the Welsh. Nevertheless, within eighteen months, two of the most important agents of English royal supervision in Wales, Richard Fitz Gilbert of Clare and Payn Fitz John, had both been killed in separate incidents. To all intents and purposes the impressive reinforcement of royal power achieved there in the previous reign was rocked to its foundations.

Stephen's negligence in not launching a campaign to reverse Welsh successes has been contrasted with Henry I's vigour, but Henry 's reputation in fact rests on shallow foundations. He had made only two personal interventions in Wales, in the spring of 1114 and again in 1121, both against the king of Powys in north Wales. At the time this was an unavoidable direct responsibiity of the king, since the lordship of the earls of Chester was in the king's hands and the two post-conquest earldoms of Hereford and Shrewsbury were in abeyance. In north Wales the situation was stabilised not by creating new English lordships but by Henry's recognition of a client Welsh king. In south Wales, where the violence occurred in Stephen's early years, the advance of Norman lordships had proceeded without much direct royal intervention since the reign of Rufus. The only indication that Henry I had taken any special interest in supporting his barons there was the confiscation of the Montgomery lands and the settlement of Flemings in Pembrokeshire under royal supervision. He also set up a royal castle at Carmarthen. Whereas the situation in north Wales could be manipulated by the use of a client Welsh prince, this option was not available in the south. Moreover, access to the royal installations in the west lay across the lordships of various Norman barons, cunningly insinuated alongside Welsh princes. These barons had hitherto managed their own affairs with the minimum of royal help and may not have welcomed greater royal involvement in their affairs. The stability of these south Welsh honours was such that they became desirable prizes in themselves. The most conspicuous, the honour of Glamorgan, built up by Robert Fitz Hamon, passed with the heiress Mabel to Robert of Gloucester. Likewise, the other great heiresses of the region, Sybil of Lacy and Sybil of Neufmarché, were married respectively to Payn Fitz John and Miles of Gloucester. More blatant interference is shown by the transfer of the honour of Abergavenny from the heiress to Brian Fitz Count, another of the king's most trusted men.

Although most of south Wales was not a direct royal responsibility, Stephen nevertheless dispatched various forces in the early months of the reign to put down the troubles. They did not achieve their purpose and the main royal stronghold at Carmarthen was lost to the Welsh. Both the king and the other parties involved are said to have postponed further concerted action in the (correct) expectation that the Welsh would soon revert to their normal practices and turn on one another. Stephen did not turn his back on the problem. At the end of 1137, he was still sufficiently involved in the affairs of the Welsh march to be invited to ratify the marriage settlement between Miles's son Roger and Payn Fitz John's daughter Cecily.[21] After Gloucester renounced his allegiance in May 1138, however, Stephen's ability to add royal weight to efforts for reversing Welsh successes was hampered because Gloucester's lands lay across his routes of access. Nevertheless, the same year, for the purpose of trying to salvage royal assets in the far west, Stephen made the slain Richard Fitz Gilbert's younger brother Gilbert earl of Pembroke. At the end of 1139 Stephen's authority was still respected enough for Maurice, the new bishop of Bangor, to do him homage and Uchtred, the new bishop of Llandaff. probably did the same, since they were both consecrated at the same time by Archbishop Theobald.[22]

To make Stephen's alleged neglect of Wales a major factor in alienating baronial sympathy in the region is not at all convincing. The motives for any later disaffection must be sought elsewhere. Once Gloucester had come back to Bristol, he used his influence to try and combine the forces of many, though not all, of the greater south Welsh lords but not for the purpose of dealing with Welsh resurgence. On the contrary, Gloucester and his allies established relations with the Welsh in order to hire seasoned troops for use in their English campaigns. In this way the marcher lords themselves showed less interest in securing royal assistance for the recovery of their old authority than in advancing a quite different cause. Naturally, as later under Henry III, the Welsh took advantage of English internal disputes to recover lost ground. If Stephen distanced himself from his Welsh obligations, this was a trifling factor when compared with the reactions of the marcher lords. Whatever their reason for rejecting Stephen's authority, it had nothing to do with the wish to provide for a more effective defence of their Welsh lands.

Were it not for their intimation of worse to come, all these various challenges to Stephen at the start of the reign might be regarded as rather run of the mill problems. Any ruler would have been confronted similarly on his accession to test his resolution and the degree of his support. Nor can it be argued that in the process Stephen acquired a reputation for appeasing his opponents rather than defeating them. The *Gesta* indeed reports on one of these episodes at some length as an early example of Stephen's valour and devotion to duty. If Stephen's authority seems at first most contested in the west and south west, it was because the author of the text shows most knowledge about events in that region. The localised defiance of Baldwin of Exeter was encouraged, according to the *Gesta*, by some unnamed royal supporters eager to disconcert the king.[23] These dark hints of conspiracy cannot be followed up and may reflect only the gossip current in the early 1140s about the shaky support for the new king. More significant is the report that Baldwin abused his authority in Exeter itself, arrogating to himself rights that infringed the king's. This provoked the citizens of the city to call on the king to intervene. There is no pretence that Baldwin was concerned to raise a standard for Matilda. His interest was more direct, not ideological. Stephen's campaign against Baldwin involved a siege of Exeter castle which lasted many weeks and reduced the castle garrison to extremities when the wells ran dry in the summer. There were differences of opinion in Stephen's camp about how to bring the business to a rapid conclusion and, subsequently, some dissatisfaction with the generous terms on which the defeated garrison was allowed to surrender. In spite of the comments made then and since, this campaign was successful. Only after he was driven from the country (to take temporary refuge in Anjou) did Baldwin openly become identified with Matilda's rights, but even this is not sufficient to show that he had initially rebelled on her account. He soon left Anjou for Normandy, where he cooperated with other friends and relations in pursuit of his ambitions there. His interests appear tangential to the issue of the succession. If there is any truth in the idea that his rebellion was prompted by his loyalty to the empress, its chief historical significance is that it had evidently failed to inspire any more general rising on her behalf. She can have drawn scarce comfort from such a situation. Baldwin's rebellion was snuffed out; it sparked no conflagration.

On the whole, Stephen dealt energetically and effectively with the problems of his early years and the proof of his effectiveness was that to embarrass him Matilda had by the autumn 1139 no better plan than to come to England in person to stir up trouble. An additional reason why Matilda came to England was her husband's lack of progress with the conquest of Normandy. In a sense her initiative was vindicated, because Matilda did, briefly, achieve dominance in England, but her victory in England still did not settle the fate of Normandy. Though Geoffrey may have been able to take advantage of Stephen's impotence in 1141, his conquest was still far from complete when Stephen recovered his throne at the end of the year. Some historians nevertheless claim that Stephen made a major error in not taking better care of his position in Normandy in his early years. Typically, such critics fail to propose an alternative viable strategy. By 1135, as is shown by the reaction of the Norman leaders in the duchy to the news of Stephen's coronation in England, the kingdom of England was perceived to be the principal prize. Henry I had proceeded to conquer Normandy from England and Stephen correctly understood the importance of getting recognition in England first. That Normandy then became his without effort was a bonus he had not sought.

Had Stephen presented himself in Normandy immediately after Henry I's death as a candidate for the succession, he probably would not have obtained general recognition since, there, his brother Theobald was regarded as a more suitable candidate. Stephen's coronation, an English not a Norman ceremony, trumped any rivals. Stephen certainly did not intend to fight for Normandy if this entailed losing England. In 1136 the first problem was presented not by Normandy but by the north of England. Only after David had been bought over could Stephen prepare his first visit as king to Normandy. Orderic thought he was then distracted by a rumour that Roger of Salisbury had died, making it impolitic to leave England at such an awkward moment. The Norman campaign was accordingly deferred a whole year. Orderic deplored the fact that Normandy all that time still found itself without a firm master, being inclined to the view that the Normans were a very restless violent people in need of strong rulers.[24] Yet Stephen's absence did not make the Normans in general any more willing to accept Matilda and Geoffrey.

As in England, many men in Normandy had taken advantage of Henry I's death to reopen private feuds; the succession to the duchy was not for all of them the most urgent concern. There were some lords who favoured Geoffrey, though Orderic does not name them. Their motives may have had more to do with their own grievances than with Matilda's rights. Given the lack of urgency, Theobald of Blois, on his brother Stephen's behalf, negotiated a truce with Geoffrey to last until May 1136, which suspended immediate hostilities. By the time the truce expired, however, Geoffrey had been handed the southern strongholds of Domfront, Argentan and Exmes by Henry I's vicomte of Exmes, Guigan Algason, described by Orderic as 'low-born' to explain not only his treacherous behaviour but his inability to influence men of greater consequence to do likewise. When Geoffrey duly invaded Normandy in the summer of 1136, he was accompanied by William, count of Ponthieu, who wanted to reassert the claims of his family in Séez.

Three border castles, Ambrières, Gorran and Mortemer, formerly belonging to Juhel de Mayenne, were also obtained and restored to Juhel in return for his promises to help Geoffrey. These exploits were similar to those occurring elsewhere in which local interests prevailed. Angevin attempts to extend their hold in the region involved such violence that the outraged Normans drove the Angevins out of the duchy.

When Stephen failed to arrive in Normandy, as expected, an attack was led against Exmes by Stephen's supporters, but they were defeated by William of Ponthieu. In September 1136 Geoffrey himself led a great army of confederates from Anjou and its neighbours into Normandy and made a raid on Lisieux, which was put to the torch before Waleran, count of Meulan, could recover it. The Angevin raid lasted about a fortnight and Orderic describes in great excitement the atrocities committed and the Angevins' shameful retreat at the hands of the Normans, even though the Norman efforts were not coordinated by a leader. More serious disorder in Normandy seems, however, to have been caused by the feud of the twin brothers, Waleran of Meulan and Robert of Leicester, against Roger of Tosny. When Henry of Winchester went to Normandy, during the winter of 1136, the sufferings of the province were brought to his attention. He made efforts to improve the situation by imposing ecclesiastical sanctions. Orderic himself believed that Stephen's own presence was needed to contain the troubles, not merely from the foreign, Angevin, enemy but from the Normans themselves. Whatever problems awaited Stephen when he arrived in Normandy, fighting for recognition of his title was not one of them.

The precise sequence of Stephen's Norman adventures in 1137 is not certain.[25] One of his first engagements was to suppress the revolt of Rabel, the chamberlain of Normandy, at Lillebonne. Next, Stephen came to terms with his brother Theobald, who, as his elder, is said to have 'expected' some financial compensation for the derogation of his 'rights' to the English crown. From his great store of money, the king offered Theobald two thousand marks a year. Then in May Stephen clinched his hold on Normandy as Henry I had in 1119, not by himself doing homage but by obtaining for his ten-year-old son Eustace recognition as duke of Normandy from King Louis VI of France. Shortly after this, Stephen's brother Theobald, then high in Louis's favour, escorted the king's young son, Louis, to Bordeaux for his marriage to Eleanor, the heiress of Aquitaine. By the time of his return the old king, Louis VI, had died. The new king, Louis VII, remained on friendly terms with the Blois family and the understanding with France was subsequently strengthened by the marriage of Eustace to Louis VII's sister, Constance, celebrated in 1140.

While Stephen was still in Normandy in 1137, Geoffrey of Anjou had led a large army of knights into southern Normandy. Stephen promptly planned a campaign from Lisieux to attack Geoffrey at Argentan, but according to Orderic, Stephen's magnates opposed such a direct confrontation. These differences of opinion may have inflamed another dispute at Livarot, eleven miles away, between the two parts of Stephen's forces: his 'Flemings', possibly recruited from his county of Boulogne; and the Normans. This effectively put paid to any ambitious campaign against Geoffrey. Stephen agreed instead to a truce for two (or three) years and is said to have also offered Geoffrey two thousand marks a year to keep the peace. Though admittedly it was desirable to dislodge Geoffrey from the castles he had obtained, it was hardly perceived as urgent, and Geoffrey's unwanted presence, if anything, exacerbated Norman dislike of the Angevins. Stephen certainly did not fear any wholesale desertion from his side. Peace, after a fashion, had in any case been restored to Normandy. Stephen remained long enough to settle some local disturbances, at Grossoeuvre (Evrecin) and Guitry (Vexin). His men dealt with St-Pois (Avranchin) and Bretons near Mont St-Michel. At the end of the year, Stephen was obliged by events in England to recross the Channel and never himself returned to Normandy. To maintain his presence in England was more important. Just why he is thought to have been mistaken about this, is never made clear.

About six months after Stephen's departure, in the following spring of 1138, Robert of Gloucester, who had remained in Normandy, formally renounced his homage to Stephen and threw in his lot with Geoffrey. Gloucester's motives have been much discussed in the light of Malmesbury's far from impartial evidence. The only 'reasonable' explanation we are likely to advance for his change of position lies with calculation of self-interest, though Matilda may have also played on any fraternal regard he may have had for her. Whether Stephen could really have prevented Gloucester's defection must be doubtful. They were rivals of long standing. For Stephen to have put more trust in Gloucester and turn against his other friends on Gloucester's account would have been a serious political error. This has not deterred some writers from deploring Stephen's excessive confidence in such barons as the Beaumont brothers.[26] Gloucester may have been brooding over his standing in Stephen's kingdom, realising that he was no longer the king's son, but now only the late king's son, and thinking himself demeaned to be no longer Stephen's rival but his vassal. Since Gloucester's decision was made in Normandy, and did not bring him back to make an immediate challenge in England, the most likely explanation lies with Geoffrey's own desperate attempts to attract at least one powerful lord in Normandy to his wife's cause. Gloucester will have been sensible of the greater value of his friendship to Geoffrey than to Stephen. Even after Gloucester's defection, however, Geoffrey still made little progress in his campaigns of 1138 to acquire the duchy: Gloucester's defection had not encouraged other prominent Normans to follow his lead. Gloucester must have had mainly personal reasons for defiance; he was not even able to assume the leadership of a sizeable pro-Angevin faction in the duchy: there was none.

The best contemporary evidence for Stephen's government in Normandy comes from Orderic Vitalis, the English monk of Saint-Evroul in southern Normandy where the Angevins were particularly unpopular. Orderic's final pages record the capture of Stephen at Lincoln but show that Normandy was, at that point, still well beyond Geoffrey's grasp. If Stephen could afford to 'neglect' Normandy, it was because of his confidence that the Normans preferred their traditional link with England and resented the Angevin intrusion. Norman clergy continued to come to England to receive confirmation of their offices or to get royal concessions. At the end of 1138 the English took an archbishop of Canterbury from the abbey of Bec; as late as 1143, Robert of Gloucester's son, the bishop of Bayeux, was succeeded by Philip of Harcourt, Stephen's chancellor, a disappointed candidate for the see of Salisbury vacated by Roger in 1139. Hugh of Rouen remained loyal to Stephen until January 1144.[27] The reasons for Geoffrey's eventual conquest of Normandy after 1141 do not lie with any mistake Stephen made at the beginning of the reign, but in the way the situation developed after Stephen's imprisonment.

Over all, compared with the beginning of Henry I's reign, Stephen made a very creditable start and, though there were still problems, nothing less could have been expected. Stephen gave every sign of knowing what he had to do and of behaving sensibly and effectively. His government was not compromised because his enemies called him a usurper; his rule was not on that account doomed. Henry of Huntingdon indeed presents his Norman campaign as a victory against Geoffrey, who had been induced to propose the truce. On Stephen's return there seemed to be no more immediate problem to deal with than the disaffection of Miles of Beauchamp, constable of Bedford castle, who objected to Stephen's proposal to marry Miles's niece, the Beauchamp heiress, to Hugh of Beaumont and make him earl of Bedford.[28] Behind this, however, simmered the problem of King David's dissatisfaction with the settlement agreed with Stephen in February 1136.

Stephen's recognition of Henry as earl of Huntingdon had not deterred the king from also accepting the claims of Henry's elder step-brother, Simon, as earl. This had possibly involved some diminution to the estates of the earldom of Huntingdon itself. But David was also ambitious to recover other territories in northern England that he regarded as properly subject to the kings of Scotland. Taking advantage of Stephen's absence in Normandy,

David repudiated the peace treaty of the previous year and summoned his army after Easter in 1137, in order to set about the pillage of Northumbria. Stephen nevertheless managed to get his earls and barons to muster an impressive force at Newcastle upon Tyne to resist any invasion of England and David was obliged to accept a truce for six months. When this expired at the beginning of Advent, and David refused to renew it, Stephen had no option but to leave Normandy and deal with the implications.

Several writers believed that David had been worked upon by the empress's party to challenge Stephen's kingship outright.[29] As in 1136, if David was happy to use Matilda of Anjou's claims to justify his further invasions of northern England in 1137 and 1138, he did so for reasons of his own and not to pluck chestnuts out of the fire for the Angevins. Whatever cover David may have used, his invasions do not need to be explained by reference either to the empress or even to any perception on his part that Stephen's position had become shaky enough to invite further intervention. As king, David could hardly resist the temptation to go on playing the active role in English affairs he had enjoyed as an English earl, but as king he had his own agenda. He was himself a direct descendant of the Old English royal house and his 'legitimist' credentials were not forgotten in the north. His marriage to the heiress of the eleventh-century English earl, Waltheof of Northumbria, enhanced his claims to respectful attention. His behaviour cannot be regarded as immoral, irresponsible or selfish. His motives are clear and comprehensible. They are typical of the way political arrangements operate at any time. His efforts to strengthen his standing in the north of England necessarily kept the region agitated. Far from welcoming David as the champion of Henry I's unjustly disinherited daughter, all the northern chroniclers deplored the barbarism of the Scots' invading force. Their hostility to the Scots strengthened their commitment to Stephen.

When David duly invaded England early in 1138, Stephen, with his customary vigour, promptly went north to chase David back into Scotland. When Stephen returned south, however, David himself advanced again into the kingdom. Stephen was not anxious a second time about events in the north, thinking it sufficient to send one of his followers to help Archbishop Thurstan of York and other Yorkshire barons coordinate a force to oppose the Scots. The battle of the Standard became one of the great set-piece battles of the period.[30] The Scots were not only soundly defeated, but local grandees had shown their capacity to cooperate in the defence of their homeland. It was a local triumph. A few Yorkshire leaders had wavered originally, because David, as a king in the north, had strong powers of attraction for them.[31] Nevertheless, in the end, most Yorkshiremen rallied to resist David and thereby showed their wish to remain part of the English kingdom, even without Stephen's personal presence. The way the battle was commemorated by the chroniclers reflects something of the way it was perceived as a 'national' victory. The implications of this for pointing to Stephen's personal acceptability in the kingdom should not be missed. There was no hankering after independence from the kingdom in Yorkshire and no sense that Stephen was perceived to be so 'weak' as to create an opportunity for seceding into regional autonomy, or opting for the empress's Scottish champion. In the north, counting on the king's support against Scotland made loyalty to the king a local requirement.

Meanwhile, in the south, Stephen had not been idle. In May 1138 Robert of Gloucester had repudiated his allegiance. The coincidence of these events raises the suspicion that there was some concerted plan. It is, however, equally possible that Gloucester simply took advantage of David's second invasion to cover his own treachery, for David's actions were themselves contingent on the course of events in England and could not have been neatly timed to coincide with conspiracy abroad. Gloucester instructed his men at Bristol to cause as much havoc in the kingdom as they could, so Stephen promptly set about besieging the castle, to impede such depredations. The siege was, however, abandoned when his barons pointed out that it was in fact impregnable. Not discouraged, Stephen took some other castles of Gloucester's adherents and even proceeded in June to Hereford, where he effectively drove out the rebellious Geoffrey Talbot. In August he also advanced against Shrewsbury, obliging William Fitz Alan to flee. Since the castle garrison refused offers of peace, Stephen took the place by assault and had nearly a hundred men hanged for their insolence, showing that he could on occasion be merciless. Meanwhile, Gloucester's men in Kent, who had also defied the king, failed to carry the day. The queen herself obtained naval forces from her county of Boulogne to force the surrender of Dover, and Gilbert of Clare captured Gloucester's castle at Leeds in December 1138. All these separate and isolated outbreaks of disaffection inspired by Gloucester's defiance were stamped out before the end of the year. Gloucester had nothing to show Geoffrey for his pains. His men's rebellion had not inspired the English baronage in general to rise in support for the Angevins. Were it not for the failure to capture Bristol, Stephen could have considered 1138 a good year for his reign.

The victory over the Scots in August 1138 was not followed up with a form of peace until March 1139. David's persistence and strength made him a formidable enemy in the north and negotiations had to settle for what was possible. The papal legate who had arrived in England during the summer of 1138 travelled into Scotland to prepare the way. No historical source suggests that David raised the rights of the empress with the legate:

they were not relevant to his main concerns. The chronicler Richard of Hexham believed that the terms eventually agreed at Durham owed much to the intercessions of David's other niece Matilda, the wife of King Stephen, whose activities on the king's behalf have been consistently underestimated.[32] The chronicler also believed that her personal relations with her uncle and her cousin Henry played their part in securing peace. Unlike Matilda of Anjou, who had been sent as a child to Germany, Matilda of Boulogne had probably spent a lot of time in England both before and after marriage and had certainly had more occasion than her cousin to know her mother's family. If David allowed sentiment to influence his conduct at all, he is more likely to have been moved by his feelings for Stephen's queen than for Stephen's rival. The only attraction of Matilda of Anjou to David was the chance that, if she had become ruler of England, she would have made concessions to him over the Scottish border. If David could obtain in practice from Stephen, already in power, what Matilda, given the chance, might grant in the future, he had no good reason to dither.

After the battle of the Standard, the peace of Durham reaffirmed David's recognition of Stephen *de facto* and acceptance of the fact that Matilda of Anjou was unlikely to replace him in the immediate future. David also wanted the earldom of Northumberland for his son Henry, on the strength of Henry's mother's rights as Waltheof of Northumbria's heiress. Stephen was initially loth to grant this, but in the end gave way, taking Henry's homage for the earldom to demonstrate that, though the earl was a Scot, the earldom was as much part of the kingdom of England as Huntingdon was.[33] As a further guarantee for a lasting settlement in the north, Henry of Northumberland was married to the sister of Earl Warenne, to reinforce his family ties in the kingdom. Stephen's goodwill to Henry is indicated by the story that Henry was personally rescued by the king in an incident which took place shortly afterward when Stephen attacked the rebellious garrison at Ludlow.[34] Henry's willingness to fight for Stephen against the rebels openly declared his loyalty and his acknowledgment of Stephen's real authority. Stephen certainly believed in trying to cultivate good relations to ensure success in his rule, something no doubt which helped to make him popular. Rulers who want to be liked are regarded by some historians as pathetic.

The completeness of the victory at the Standard makes the terms of peace with David look surprisingly generous. Such a view reflects the belief that the victors have the moral right as well as the power to impose their own terms on the defeated. The Yorkshire barons having won the battle were still concerned to remain on good terms with King David and reach an agreement that would give enough satisfaction on both sides to rule out further hostilities. The English royal presence in the north had been established barely fifty years before when Rufus had founded a castle at Newcastle upon Tyne; Northumberland had not been surveyed by the king's commissioners in 1086; nor for that matter had the lands of St Cuthbert between Tees and Tyne, the later county Durham. A way had been found to satisfy David without surrendering royal rights. The battle of the Standard had saved Yorkshire from David's ambitions. By the summer of 1139, Stephen could look back on nearly three and a half years of a strenuous, but not unsuccessful, reign. His fortunes were about to change.

5

Trouble

The early years of Stephen's reign were not notably more turbulent than those of his immediate predecessors since 1066; their survival had initially looked no more secure than his. Huntingdon remarked on how precariously the reign of Henry I had begun and how contemptible he appeared until after his victory at Tinchebrai: not until his seventh year did his regime begin to look safe. Warfare marked the first twenty-five years of his long reign. In this context Stephen's reign was not anomalous. Stephen's intrusion is often considered sufficient explanation of his later misfortunes. Yet the troubled years immediately following William I's conquest or Henry I's confrontations with his crusader brother Robert are not thought to have fatally compromised the prospects for the rest of their reigns. Indeed, whereas Henry I faced persistent opposition for the first six years of his reign, Stephen's beginnings in contrast seem almost uncontentious. If the explanation for his later difficulties does not lie with the origins of his kingship, alternative ways of accounting for what happened must be sought. Here there must be differences of opinion about what has to be 'explained' before their 'real' causes can be sought.

That Stephen had defects as a ruler is not in doubt; all rulers, however accomplished, have their shortcomings. On their own these are rarely adequate to bring about ruin. Notoriously, some wicked rulers even manage to survive, not necessarily to most of their subjects' disadvantage. To be brought down rulers need enemies able to exploit weaknesses and prompt to seize opportunities for their own advancement. Since Stephen persevered in his kingship despite everything until his death, even Stephen was never decisively defeated. The purpose of historical discussion is frustrated if it is supposed that the outcome was predetermined. To argue, for example, that his perjury had blighted all chances of a successful reign, whatever his other merits, implies that Stephen could have done nothing after his coronation to salvage something from his criminal ambition, whatever his other merits. Or, if the root cause of Stephen's weakness was a trait inherited from his father, Count Stephen, defamed for infamously deserting the first crusading expedition, his fate was decided at birth.[1] Since much less is known about the father than the son, it also turns the evidence upside down. If contemporaries remembered his father with such contempt, how is it that his distinguished brothers, Theobald and Henry, did not incur comparable odium, and how did they bring themselves to acquiesce in Stephen's promotion to the throne? Kate Norgate's account of the great family feuds between Blois and Anjou was hardly any more convincing as an explanation of what we know to have happened in England itself. 'Explanations' of what happened in England by reference to events long past in remote places slip into determinist mode. By emphasising the long-term factors, they minimise the immediate circumstances for which alone the king had any responsibility.

Modern authorities are not the only ones to have probed for the 'deeper causes'. Medieval authors when otherwise baffled detected the hand of God in what occurred for good or bad. Though they were on occasion bewildered by God's decisions, they never discounted human sin as the most likely reason for God sending down unexpected punishments. If the sin was not glaringly obvious, it must at least have been latent and no less deserving of retribution. If the slightest incident carried a dire presentiment, notable events could not be attributed to mere chance. Those who think about human history have pored over the dramas of Stephen's reign, convinced that they must be a rich source of lessons to be learnt.

At what point in the reign did contemporaries themselves begin to suspect there might be something particularly unfortunate about the new king? Some idea of this may be derived from the way Henry of Huntingdon successively updated in Stephen's reign the narrative of English history he had originally compiled under Henry I.[2] In his first addition, his references to the character of Henry I show that, early in 1136, the old king still had some stern critics as well as admirers. Such views were only modified as the new king's faults began to make men less critical of the old. But how soon did Henry I's reputation recover? Revising again in 1141, when Stephen's reign appeared to be over, Huntingdon summed up Stephen's first two years as successful, his third still tolerable, and only the last two disastrous, suggesting that things had turned against him in 1139 and 1140. In Huntingdon's view, writing as he was for his bishop, Alexander of Lincoln, the critical moment came in June 1139 at Oxford when the king had arrested Alexander, along with his uncle Roger of Salisbury. Huntingdon regarded this as an act of terrorism perpetrated against God's chosen ministers which was properly punished without further ado.

Subsequent writers, for rather different reasons, also condemned the arrest of the bishops as an example of Stephen's foolishness because it destroyed the effectiveness of the whole royal administration, a view authoritatively advanced by Stubbs in the 1870s.[3] Salisbury's part in Henry I's administration is not in doubt, but a 'system' of 'government' that collapses with the fall of one minister is an odd concept. Defenders of such a view were no more able to show in detail how the arrest caused the administration to crumble than Huntingdon could trace the connection between the arrest of the bishops and divine vengeance. In the one case it was sufficient that Huntingdon believed Stephen to have offended God by touching the bishops; in the other it is taken for granted that kings needed administrators and that in this case the aged bishop of Salisbury was indispensable for the management of the kingdom. What would have happened had Roger still been 'in office' when he died in December? Stephen cannot be expected to have had his government run for him by Salisbury for ever. The notion of Salisbury's 'system' is a modern chimera. Henry I and Salisbury had acquired immense wealth for them both, through the workings of the exchequer, but this is hardly the same as conferring an obvious benefit on the kingdom in general.

Huntingdon did not himself record any collapse of administration on Salisbury's arrest. He attributed Stephen's disasters to divine punishment for his maltreatment not of a royal minister but of a bishop, and not because he was either particularly holy, or indispensable, but simply because he was a minister of the church. Modern writers do not believe that the arrest of the bishops automatically triggered a divine punishment for the king. They reject Huntingdon's explanation for what followed, while still accepting, for reasons of their own, that the episode was the turning point of the reign. The arrest of the bishops has impressed both medieval and modern writers, though for different reasons. Neither way does this incident lead directly to what happened later. By this act Stephen cannot even be shown to have lost the confidence generally placed in him by the clergy, and so provoked their distrust.[4] Within eighteen months of his arrest, the bishop of Lincoln, Huntingdon's patron, was calling Stephen back to intervene in the affairs of his city. However much chroniclers threw up their hands in conventional horror, the leading clergy did not unite in defiance of the king to defend clerical privilege. In the summer of 1139, there were serious problems involved and taking up postures of outrage was quite out of order.

Assumptions about the clergy's reactions are in part no more than surmise. The position of the English church and bishops, like that of the western church as a whole in the period of the Anacletan Schism (1130–38), demands scrutiny. Jumping to facile conclusions has done nothing to help with understanding the difficulties, which had a direct bearing on Stephen's own affairs. At the beginning of his reign, Stephen offered a chance of a renewal in the English church to be effected through an alliance with his brother, Henry of Winchester. They acted in concert with Pope Innocent II who, though supported by the north European churches, had been obliged to take up residence in Pisa and leave his rival Anacletus II in Rome. The recognition by Stephen and Innocent of one another's rightful succession was a basic plank of policy on both sides. When Innocent was eventually able to return to Rome after Anacletus's death, the pope did not renege on his ally. By 1138 the main problem for the English church had become finding a successor to William of Corbeil, archbishop of Canterbury, who had died in December 1136. Henry of Winchester certainly aspired to the archbishopric. Embassies went to and from Rome for the purpose of securing the necessary papal permission for his translation from one see to another. Some writers impatiently suppose that Stephen himself could have insisted on the translation, though these are often the same critics who denounce Stephen for promising freedom for the church and then disregarding his promises.

Over the translation, Stephen was powerless. Since the Norman Conquest there had been only one instance of a bishop being translated from his first diocese to Canterbury. The case of Ralph of Séez, who had been moved by royal fiat in 1114 from Rochester to Canterbury, had provoked papal wrath. More than twenty years later, such royal high-handedness was inconceivable. Innocent II could certainly have authorised such a move for Henry of Blois, but translation was still unusual and not, as now, regarded as a routine matter of promotion. Innocent II did not have any grudge against Henry of Winchester. On the contrary, he appointed Henry as resident papal legate in England, over the head of two archbishops. This unprecedented sign of favour for an English bishop has a contemporary parallel in France, where the reliable bishop of Chartres had served as papal legate in the ecclesiastical provinces of Aquitaine throughout the 1130s.[5] If Henry was disappointed not to get Canterbury, his consolation prize as legate was magnificent. Only in England could he appear to have been snubbed and speculation as to any 'reason' for it is otiose.

During the months between the death of William of Corbeil and the choice of his successor, various objections to Henry's promotion must have been raised. Any intrigue mounted by possible secular enemies of the king and his brother is unlikely to have had any success. The view that the king himself secretly lobbied at the curia to defeat his youngest brother's ambitions, thus creating a rift between them, ultimately with dangerous consequences, is not even plausible. More to the point may have been objections raised by the monks of Canterbury, whose formal responsibility it was to choose an archbishop. Henry, unlike William of Corbeil, was at least himself a monk and potentially attractive to them on that account, but he was also a notorious pluralist: not only bishop of Winchester but abbot of Glastonbury, and head of other churches as well. At Canterbury, the monks could have persuaded themselves that Henry would be too much like Stigand, a political prelate of notorious memory and not sufficiently amenable for their purposes. What they wanted was a monk who would work exclusively for the glory of the house of Canterbury.

The appointment at Canterbury was certainly one of the outstanding difficulties of the kingdom, but not the most urgent, which the pope entrusted for settlement to Alberic, himself a former Cluniac monk, once abbot of Vézelay and but lately consecrated bishop of Ostia, sent as legate to England and Scotland in 1138. Only after his return from Scotland at the end of his mission was a new archbishop of Canterbury chosen, presumably by general agreement. Alberic had been long enough in Britain to sound out opinion, even to consult the bishops of the province as to their expectations. Finally, in December, the choice fell on Theobald of Bec. Like all his predecessors since the Conquest, William of Corbeil alone excepted, he was a Norman abbot. Bec was also the Norman house with the closest ties to Canterbury. He was therefore highly acceptable to the monks. Theobald, who had only recently become an abbot himself, was both a relatively unknown and an apparently undistinguished monk, with no important family connections or ecclesiastical allies. However welcome at Canterbury, he was not likely to be any match for, let alone rival to, Henry of Winchester. Much has been made of Gervase of Canterbury's late comment that Henry was indignant because the formal election took place while he was conducting an ordination service at St Paul's, but it is impossible to believe that Henry was confronted by a petty *fait accompli* and that his acquiescence had not been secured in advance.[6] The nature of Henry's relations with Rome and the unobtrusive, generally helpful character of Alberic's legation imply good coordination between the parties, not cheap and cunning ruses. The choice of Theobald itself indicates the considerable thought given to the matter. Tact had prevailed.

Early in 1139 Theobald left for Rome, with those English bishops summoned to the Lateran council Innocent II had called to deal with the aftermath of the Anacletan Schism. Before the council met early in April, Henry may have already received his appointment as papal legate in England. There is no evidence for his own presence in Rome at this time, though it is hard to believe that the legatine commission would have been conferred *in absentia*. Both Theobald and Henry could have expected a warm welcome from the pope they had consistently supported. Why should either have taken grievances against the king to poison the pope's mind against him? The scope of Henry's legateship is not clear. As legate, Henry did not supersede the archbishops, but must have been expected to act as the pope's particular representative. In this period, perhaps with his encouragement, English churchmen first began to make regular use of the right to take ecclesiastical disputes on appeal to Rome. From Innocent II's point of view,

Henry's reputation for good management of the valuable properties of his benefices may have recommended him as a safe pair of hands for channelling money to the curia. A letter from Henry, as legate, to the prior of Worcester deploring tardy payment of Peter's Pence survives as proof of his zeal.[7] As junior archbishop to Thurstan of York, Theobald could not have himself expected to receive such a commission in 1139, and he was no doubt reconciled to the deference already accorded to Henry as the king's brother. Henry had certainly been consoled by the pope for any disappointment he had felt over Canterbury, and he may have appreciated the distinction of the title sufficiently to care less for what accretion of real power it might bring.

The second Lateran council gave Matilda her first known opportunity to voice her complaints about Stephen's kingship in the presence of an English contingent totally opposed to her.[8] It was left to the bishop of Angers, acting on a special brief from Count Geoffrey, to raise the matter of Matilda's rights to the throne. This did receive some attention, though not perhaps very much. The pope had himself met both Henry I and Matilda at Rouen in 1131. Cardinal Peter Ruffus had been present at the Northampton council where, Malmesbury asserted, Matilda's rights had been reaffirmed. Innocent II cannot therefore have been personally uninformed about the question. If he was not convinced by the Angevin arguments, it is hardly surprising that others took the same view. The pope was not prepared to query Stephen's position or encourage the countess. Can the Angevins have seriously expected the pope to give a ruling against the king of the English for which there was no English support whatever? Had he done so, can they have imagined Stephen going quietly? The indifference of some ecclesiastical writers to political realities may be measured by their preoccupation with the validity of oaths taken years before. If the moral issue did matter so much to contemporaries, it was seriously damaging to Matilda that the highest possible court of appeal rejected her case out of hand. Correspondingly encouraged, the English delegation would have returned home reassured that Stephen's moral character had not been damned.

Oddly enough, the fullest account of the debate, given in a letter written in 1144 to Brian Fitz Count by Gilbert Foliot, shows that it focused not on the oaths at all but on whether Matilda was, as claimed, Henry's legitimate heir. This may seem like a devious way to deflect the argument, but it is only another indication of what ecclesiastics thought important. For them, the matter of the oaths was subsidiary to the question of whether Matilda's mother had been a professed nun before her marriage to Henry I. Foliot, who had been present at the council with his then abbot, Peter of Cluny, had by 1144 become abbot of Gloucester and needed to tread carefully with one of Matilda's most convinced supporters. Foliot argued that since the marriage had been blessed by Archbishop Anselm, it could not have been improper. Nevertheless, at the time of the council, he had not himself been persuaded about Matilda's rights. About the same time, on the Continent, Herimann of Tournai, another admirer of Anselm, commented on the same issue, reporting, however, that Anselm had himself prophesied calamity for the English kingdom from such an unholy marriage.[9] The drowning of the Aetheling had been an unprecedented disaster. Alongside Matilda's childless first marriage, it was interpreted as sure proof of God's displeasure. What may seem now like a despicable attempt to besmirch Matilda's reputation seemed no more blameworthy, or frivolous, than the charge of perjury. Foliot's allusions to the way the lawfulness of the marriage might all the same be defended betray his own uneasiness about it. In 1139 he had had no scruples about recognising Stephen as king when accepting appointment as abbot of Gloucester. Writing to Brian in 1144, he found Brian's intemperate defiance of papal and ecclesiastical opinion extremely troubling. Foliot's reservations do not seem to have been adequately appreciated. Though professing sympathy for Brian's own moral predicament, Foliot was far from endorsing Brian Fitz Count's political position. Whatever his intemperate abuse of Stephen, when necessary Foliot made no difficulties about recognising a royal authority confirmed by the pope. The feelings of moral outrage indulged on both sides in fact made little practical difference.

By the early summer of 1139, Stephen's future may well have seemed reasonably safe. With the treaty negotiated by his wife with her uncle David of Scotland, the most troublesome of his problems looked resolved. The settlement of the Canterbury issue had actually cemented the bond with the papacy which had declared itself firmly opposed to Matilda's pretensions. Had Matilda by the early summer of 1139 come to accept that Stephen was firmly ensconced, resigning herself to the loss of her inheritance would have been perfectly understandable. Matilda, deserted by those she may have expected most from, clearly had no one but herself to rely on. Perhaps exasperated by the failures of Gloucester's men the previous year, Matilda decided to interfere in person, either on her own account or on behalf of her sons. Whether what she now set out to do was planned with her husband, or in spite of him, is not known. Geoffrey consistently showed no interest in Matilda's ambitions for herself in England; but Geoffrey appreciated that, by stirring up trouble for Stephen in England, Matilda at least distracted Stephen from defending his rights in Normandy. In the early summer of 1139 Stephen may have seemed to both Geoffrey and Matilda as poised for a successful reign. She herself may have become impatient with her husband's slow progress in Normandy, or, scornful of his efforts, wished to show how much better she could do for herself in England. Stephen's apparent triumph could alone have been enough to goad Matilda into taking desperate measures. If she did not anticipate immediate success for herself, she resolved at least to take the smile off the king's face.

She had probably begun to take soundings in England as soon as her embassy returned empty-handed from Rome. When the king summoned his great men to a council at Oxford in June, the political situation was already tense. The most likely explanation for this has to do with the expectation that Robert of Gloucester was planning his return to England in order to be seen as more active on behalf of the Angevin cause. His 'invasion' probably did not take place until September, but rumours of his impending arrival may have been circulating long before. He is likely to have sent out feelers for potential support for his reception in England, and Stephen may have become justifiably uneasy about the loyalty of some of his barons. The *Gesta* states as plain fact that Roger, bishop of Salisbury, had been approached and had secretly agreed to support Matilda if she arrived with Gloucester. Whether or not Salisbury had compromised himself to such an extent, it is scarcely credible that overtures would not have been made to him. Gloucester's forces crossing to England from Normandy would be anxious to link up with their base at Bristol, and would be obliged to enter and traverse the diocese of Salisbury to do so. The neutrality, if not support, of the bishop would be essential. He was not only a commanding figure in his own right, he also had four fine castles, at Old Sarum, Sherborne, Devizes and Malmesbury, in his diocese, all possible hurdles to be surmounted on the approaches to Bristol.

Their importance in military affairs was soon manifest. The Gloucester chronicle explicitly mentions Stephen's anxieties about the castle at Devizes and his summons for Roger to come to court and surrender it to the king.[10] Its value may be appreciated from Robert Fitz Hubert's reported boast that from Devizes he could gain possession of the whole region between Winchester and London. Whether Bishop Roger had actually conspired with the Angevins or not, it was serious enough that he was suspected of doing so. The idea is not absurd. Possibly put out by the influence now exercised over the king by Henry of Winchester, Roger no longer enjoyed his old supremacy as the king's surrogate, however useful to Stephen he remained. Matilda could have tempted Roger by offering to restore his former pre-eminence as chief adviser in England. On setting out for the June assembly, Roger spoke openly to William of Malmesbury about his uneasiness: he had premonitions of impending disaster.[11] This may reflect his own guilty conscience; at the very least, it shows he was aware of the suspicions against him. Some chroniclers, duly echoed by later writers, speak pitifully of Stephen's bullying tactics, or alternatively of his guile, in getting the poor bishops into his toils. This approach fails to stress how tense the situation appeared and how provocative the recalcitrance of the bishops was bound to look. Roger of Salisbury was no harmless Anselm, but a man with nearly forty years of seasoned politics behind him. Clerical writers with a clerical agenda chose to see Stephen's treatment of him as an outrageous insult to God's minister. Historians can afford to be less dewy-eyed.

As a result of a scuffle between the bishop's men and those of some secular nobles in Oxford, in which a knight was killed and others wounded, the bishop was summoned to explain himself and required to surrender his castles to the king. When he refused, he was 'arrested', along with one of his two episcopal nephews.[12] The other nephew, the bishop of Ely, escaped and by his subsequent defiance more than confirmed the worst suspicions of Stephen's supporters. To obtain surrender of the castles, the king is said to have starved the bishops into submission. How many meals they missed is not stated; their real sufferings may have been comparatively minor. Neither bishop was known for austerity and for their supporters physical ill-treatment counted for less than the insult to their high ecclesiastical rank. Once the king obtained possession of their castles, the bishops recovered their liberty. Was all this contrived beforehand? Malmesbury describes the key incident as an ill-mannerly brawl. Orderic Vitalis, possibly to excuse the king, presents him as urged to take action by youthful hot-heads hostile to the bishops, so modern accounts duly take for granted a conspiracy to bring about the downfall of the formerly great minister and his family for personal reasons of spite. Responsibility for this is widely attributed to such a 'younger' noble as Waleran of Meulan, already thirty-five years of age and no tyro in politics. The testimony of Malmesbury excludes the possibility that Roger walked unsuspecting into a trap, but the evidence does not even support the sinister interpretations usually proposed.

The inevitable rivalries at court and a highly volatile situation easily explain how harsh, even casual words could lead to a spontaneous fight; once blood was shed, this led to accusations of treachery. That murder occurred in the king's court made the matter even more serious. When Roger refused to give up his castles, suspicion became certainty and demanded urgent counter-mesures. If Roger was not being truculent or disloyal, why should he refuse to surrender his castles? Roger was never known as a stickler for ecclesiastical privilege and his long years of political service must have inured him to the arbitrary ways of kings. His obduracy in this instance prejudiced any fair hearing at the time and his apologists since have failed to suggest any adequate justification for it. Whether or not Roger had seriously con-sidered making his castles available for Gloucester's purposes, his castles gave him some political clout of his own which he was clearly reluctant to forfeit. After the quarrel at Oxford, his presumption in resisting their surrender was indefensible on political grounds. He lost his credibility as a loyal minister and his resistance confirmed suspicion of his treachery.

Matters did not, however, rest there. Malmesbury claims that at this point Henry of Winchester made public his appointment early in March as papal legate and summoned an ecclesiastical council to decide whether the arrest of the bishops had been an infringement of ecclesiastical privilege. The legatine commission had turned out to be a useful weapon in his armoury. Malmesbury's reference to it was, however, somewhat disingenuous. By early June, if not sooner, Nigel of Ely himself must already have known of Henry's legatine commission, since the earliest surviving papal letter to the new legate commanded him in late April to back up Nigel's efforts to recover the lost properties of his see.[13] Nor is Stephen likely to have been ignorant of his younger brother's commission. Malmesbury is a subtle writer and his text deserves to be read with close attention. His very detailed information about the legatine council must be read in its political context. While those at court, including the bishops, will have perfectly understood the nature of the political problem, many of the lower clergy may have been entirely taken up with the apparent assault on the rights of churchmen to exemption from secular judgment.

How widespread any criticism of the king was on this account is impossible to determine. Huntingdon, writing for one of the arrested bishops, Alexander of Lincoln, not surprisingly made much of this episode, but the manifest embarrassment about the arrest of the bishops shown in the *Gesta*, a text totally sympathetic to the king, points to more general fears that the king had indeed incurred divine retribution by his brutal action. Significantly, the author of the *Gesta* was bothered by the arrest of the bishops, even though he had no doubts whatever about the bishops' intended treachery. For him, the bishops, however compromised, ought not to have been treated like laymen. The clergy in the bishops' own service would have raised the matter of clerical privilege, if only as practised men of affairs ready to try every possible angle of legal resource. These accusations would need to be rebutted or appeased, even if they had not seriously threatened the king's practical command of affairs.

Henry of Winchester himself is commonly assumed to have needed no prompting from others to launch an enquiry into his royal brother's precipitous error of judgment. He is seen as an eager defender of ecclesiastical liberty, newly empowered as legate by a reforming pope and naturally feeling the same sense of shock as other clergy. What is more, Henry has been suspected of looking out for a chance to bring Stephen to heel after suffering a rebuff over his own ambitions for Canterbury. This is not supported by any contemporary testimony and rests upon mere assumptions about the vindictive behaviour to be expected of his frustrated ambition. Malmesbury's report shows, however, that Henry's intentions could have been more complicated. Though the council is alleged to have been called to punish some clerical outrage, in the end it did nothing to vindicate the arrested bishops. Malmesbury himself reports in detail the spirited defence made for the king's action by a layman, Aubrey de Vere, the king's chamberlain. Henry, though legate, then chose to defer taking any decision himself until the arrival of his fellow Cluniac, Hugh of Amiens, archbishop of Rouen, who had already expressed his support for the king's position. Hugh was then allowed the last word: 'show from the canons that bishops may hold castles and their legitimate property will be restored to them'.[14] The final episode of the council, in Malmesbury's account, saw Henry and the archbishop throwing themselves before Stephen and asking him for a gesture of accommodation.

Stephen was not therefore condemned. Brief references to some token penance remain quite unspecific. From this evidence it is unwarranted to conclude that Stephen had been humiliated; rather, by going through the motions, the council had in effect exonerated him. Confronted by the clerical protests, Henry had used his legatine authority to investigate the issue and, after a thorough examination, had deferred to the opinion of his fellow Cluniac, a respected figure from outside the kingdom, whose opinion was not contradicted. Nor did this verdict betray the papal trust placed in him to defend the clergy against the secular power. Had Innocent II ever thought of bridling Stephen's desire to meddle in church matters, he would surely never have chosen the king's own brother as the papacy's most trustworthy instrument. On the other hand, had the pope's own legate, Alberic, on his return from his long spell in England reported unfavourably about Henry's reliability or suspected any wish on Henry's part to pay Stephen out for excluding him from Canterbury, the pope would hardly have opened the way for trouble by appointing Henry as papal legate. To make Henry legate can only have been intended to endorse the close working relationship of the brothers, in operation since Stephen's accession. Henry's council was designed to satisfy clerical opinion. Clergy were expected to feel reassured by the formal enquiry and accept that any loss of dignity Stephen had suffered was sufficient punishment, never mind that in fact Stephen's action had been condoned and Salisbury had not recovered his castles. On Salisbury's death, a few months later, Stephen, quite unabashed, confiscated the late bishop's enormous fortune, made only too obviously from diverting into his own hands the profits of his long royal service. Contemporaries were not deceived about the value of Roger's commitments to the public good.

The disgrace of Salisbury might have given Matilda further occasion to pause before doing anything hasty, but, undeterred, she decided to come to England anyway. Any uneasiness about Stephen's position after the arrest of the bishops can hardly have been substantial enough to have improved her chances and in point of fact seems to have played no part in her calculations. The opportunity was provided by an invitation from her young stepmother, Adeliza of Louvain, who had recently remarried, to stay at Arundel castle. Since Adeliza's new husband, William d'Albini, proved a consistent supporter of Stephen, Adelaide's invitation cannot be regarded as sinister. However regrettable with hindsight, it might have been intended as a way to try and reconcile the cousins. Adeliza is more likely to have badly misjudged the situation than to have positively intended to precipitate harm. Matilda of Anjou's acceptance may seem like the greater miscalculation. She must have felt the time had come for her to do something herself. With three healthy sons, she no longer needed to think of further pregnancies and she had their futures to think of. Maybe, tempted by the opportunity to cross over with Gloucester, when he at last chose to visit his lands in England, she offered to accompany him, attracted by the prospect of the adventure. By the midsummer of 1139, had she drawn some comfort from the recent success of her late husband's nephew, Conrad of Hohenstaufen, whose claims by inheritance on the German kingship had at last been endorsed by his election to succeed Lothar in 1138?[15] For ten years the Hohenstaufen party had contested the validity of Lothar's election with the assistance of the German bishops in 1125; in the end, the 'cause' of hereditary kingship had been vindicated and defiance of a king backed by the church shown to be not such a lost cause after all. Matilda might have derived further comfort from recent events in south Italy.[16] In April her envoys at Rome would have heard the pope excommunicate Roger of Sicily for usurping the title of king; they may have then felt some sympathy for this other victim of Innocent II's intransigence. Before Matilda came to England in the late summer of 1139, had she heard that Roger by force of battle had obliged the pope to give up his hostility and accept him as king of Sicily? The pope was not after all invincible and might be made to change his mind. What had she to lose? History has on the whole vindicated her. Most writers have accepted that she had inviolable rights to the royal succession.

Even before Matilda's arrival, Baldwin de Redvers had returned to England and taken possession of the port of Wareham and of Corfe castle.[17] Stephen had probably already begun to besiege Redvers at Corfe when news of the landing at Arundel was received, although one chronicler was sufficiently confused by events to think that the king was conducting a siege at

Marlborough. Reports about the rapid succession of events that summer may well have bewildered contemporaries. Taken together, reports of dis-affection have been interpreted to show how dissatisfaction with the king was coming out into the open and was now prepared for confrontation. Yet their disparate character also proves that there can have been no concerted plan of action to topple Stephen himself. If Matilda had already planned open defiance of Stephen, she was very circumspect on her arrival probably at the end of September 1139 (some chroniclers date this some weeks sooner).[18] She was escorted to Arundel by Gloucester and 140 knights, but the occasion to raise the standard on her behalf in England was not then taken. Rather than openly defy Stephen in the south, Gloucester himself unceremoniously left Matilda at Arundel and slipped away with a mere dozen knights to his stronghold at Bristol.

Many aspects about the visit of these two remain mysterious. Contem-poraries were as puzzled as we are, not merely by their motives, but, more practically, as to what to do about them. Gloucester had renounced his own fealty to Stephen and might be treated as an avowed enemy, but he did not go so far as to deny Stephen's kingship altogether or openly call for Matilda's acceptance as ruler in his place. His return to England suggests that, since his presence in Normandy as Geoffrey's ally had failed to achieve any significant improvement in Angevin fortunes, he came over to dem-onstrate the value of his support in England. What, however, did he aim to do? He did not find the kingdom already slipping out of Stephen's weak grasp and eager to embrace either an alternative ruler or an opportunity to throw over the traces altogether. His surreptitious departure for Bristol proclaims the character of his protest. He was simply defiant, refusing himself to submit to the king and intending to remain his own master, by securing such domination of the western regions as lay within his reach. Bristol became in effect the capital of Gloucester's 'principality' where, after Stephen's failure to capture the castle the year before, Gloucester might be considered invincible.

With regard to Matilda, a woman non-combatant, daughter of the late king and Stephen's kinswoman twice over, it was a different matter: courtesy was not to be denied. Since Matilda had not come in open defiance of the king, she could not be treated as a certain enemy. Stephen took such action as he could and immediately advanced on Arundel where neither Adeliza nor her husband made any attempt to keep Matilda under their protection. Had they ever encouraged Matilda to think that her visit had political implications, they displayed no willingness to compromise their own rela-tions with the king on her account. Once the king was reassured about this and had Matilda in his charge, there was, however, no question of trying to keep her in prison. The situation was awkward and it was not clear what course of action to take.

Could she have been deported to Normandy? The problem was resolved by Bishop Henry, Matilda's cousin, who arranged for her to be escorted to Bristol, where she could be left with Gloucester and where their joint intrigues, whatever they turned out to be, could at least be concentrated in one place. This turned out to have been a mistaken calculation. Writing probably in 1141, the chronicler Orderic already deplored Stephen's naivety or stupidity in disregarding the likely consequences for himself and the kingdom. After the event it was easier to see that it had been a mistake, but at the time it no doubt made the botched kind of sense often resorted to in perplexing circumstances. At least, it saddled Gloucester with responsibility for Matilda, which he was probably reluctant to shoulder since he had originally left her at Arundel. If, by accepting her step-mother's invitation in the first instance, Matilda had dreamt of being able to use Arundel as a base to rally support in the south, her brusque departure under escort from Sussex at least nipped such plans in the bud. Disappointed in the south, Matilda perforce made the most of her opportunities in a region where Gloucester already commanded some support and sympathy, but also where keeping contact with the Continent was more difficult to maintain.

The awkwardness of their relations is further apparent from the fact that, within weeks, Matilda had surprisingly left Bristol, to find a more compliant host in Miles, castellan of Gloucester. Miles had hitherto been one of Stephen's reliable henchmen and the king is not known to have done him any injury which might excuse his treachery. The rational explanation for Miles's adherence to the empress was probably his recognition of his relative weakness in any confrontation with Robert of Gloucester. Unlike most barons, Miles had all his landed assets concentrated in one part of the country, namely in the west where, if Robert attacked him, Stephen's assistance would not certainly have been sufficient to save him.[19] Rather than fight doggedly on Stephen's behalf, Miles would on this showing have preferred to make himself Gloucester's willing adjutant in the west. While still in Normandy, Gloucester could have already put Miles under pressure to join him, and Miles may have acted as go-between with Salisbury, held to be a close political ally. Cornered into conspiracy, Miles duly took up the cause with conviction, perhaps to give himself moral justification for disloyalty. He became the most active of those who fought for Matilda, ravaging both Gloucestershire and Herefordshire and even venturing as far east as Wallingford, to assist Brian Fitz Count.

Brian's landed interests were more widely dispersed around the country than Miles's.[20] The estates of the Honour of Wallingford, which he held by right of marriage, stretched from the Chilterns across the Thames into Berkshire and Wiltshire. He may have been powerful enough to act in accordance with his sentiments and finer feelings rather than according to calculation of self-interest. His castle at Wallingford, which defied Stephen for over thirteen years, played a major role in helping to keep central southern England uneasy. Brian is known to have acted several times in the past together with Robert of Gloucester, so they may have been political allies of long standing. Like Robert, he is singled out for his part in the negotiations over the Angevin marriage. He was, however, not really part of the established English baronage and brought no other friends into the Matildine camp.

The ensuing disturbances took Stephen himself into the west country, close on Matilda's heels. The king had attacked Wallingford castle, raised counter-works to keep it under siege and recaptured the castle at Malmesbury all before the end of October. An attack on Humphrey de Bohun's castle at Trowbridge was abandoned. Stephen then arrived at Worcester shortly after it had been sacked by the men of Gloucester. Hearing that Geoffrey Talbot, once again rebellious, and Miles were pressing royal forces in Hereford, Stephen attempted to relieve his men there, but was forced to withdraw. A truce during Advent was then agreed, though returning south Stephen led his knights in an attack near Bristol and raided into Somerset where William de Mohun successfully defied him in Dunster castle. Here, Stephen left Henry de Tracy of Barnstaple to keep Mohun in check.[21] By December Stephen had returned to Salisbury on the death of Bishop Roger.

Probably in the new year, Robert of Gloucester and Miles recovered some of the castles they had lost. According to Orderic, they then unleashed a mighty force of wild Welshmen to cause devastation in England. It was to be a troubled year. Reginald, one of Henry I's bastards, who had assumed authority in Cornwall after his marriage to the daughter of William Fitz Richard, the chief baron there, was driven out by Stephen, who appointed in his place Earl Alan of Richmond, probably because one of his forbears, Count Brien, had enjoyed authority in Cornwall under the Conqueror. Stephen successfully beat off Robert of Gloucester's efforts to challenge this settlement, but once Stephen himself had willy-nilly been obliged to withdraw from Cornwall, Gloucester was geographically better placed to reimpose Reginald. The defeat of the king's efforts in Cornwall proved the most lasting reverse of the year. Malmesbury states that Robert of Gloucester himself installed Reginald as 'earl'. Some historians have cavilled at the idea that Gloucester could have 'created' an earl because it offends their ideas of constitutional niceties, but the countess of Anjou had no better 'right' to make earls than Gloucester himself. From a practical point of view, 'Earl'

Reginald managed Cornwall without obvious opposition from then until the end of the reign, so the Matildine party did not have to worry about being attacked from the rear.

Closer to the scene of most unrest, some time in the early summer of 1140, Stephen's party regained possession of the castle at Devizes, which had been seized by one of Gloucester's hired Flemish mercenaries on his own account. In August Stephen's forces also defeated an attack Gloucester made on Bath, only six miles from Bristol itself. The appointments of a new bishop of Salisbury and of abbots at Malmesbury and Sherborne, the monasteries Roger of Salisbury had appropriated, proceeded this year under royal authority, as indeed did the election of a new abbot of St-Evroult in Normandy where Stephen's permission was duly obtained. Both William of Malmesbury and the author of the *Gesta* describe the state of the kingdom as extremely disturbed in 1140, but even in the west country, where most of the trouble seems to have been concentrated, Stephen was neither inactive himself nor lacking in support. The 'Gloucester' chronicle writes bitterly about the way Matilda had Stephen's supporters treated and the horrible tortures inflicted by her adherents on those who denied her pretensions.[22] Her arrogance in disposing of public affairs, as though by right, gave offence. The chronicle never hints that her cause was popular.

Matilda's presence must in the nature of things have encouraged a sense of unease. The *Gesta* at this stage in the king's history has a long chapter bewailing the miseries that now descended on England, implying that strife was widespread throughout the kingdom. Though such passages often recur in several chronicle accounts of the reign, they are rarely illustrated by examples that support the generalisation.[23] Instead of providing useful information about the raids launched by Gloucester and Miles, both William of Malmesbury and the author of the *Gesta* give closest attention to the more localised activities of the Flemish professional military captain, Robert Fitz Hubert. The scope of his belligerence, however cruel, appears to have been both short-lived and restricted. Fitz Hubert, no lover of monks, captured Malmesbury castle and incurred the inveterate hostility of the monastic interest, though his occupation of the castle in October lasted no more than two weeks. About six months later, Fitz Hubert got possession of the castle at Devizes, an even more valuable acquisition. Confident of his fresh importance, he offered John the Marshal, castellan of Marlborough, his alliance. He was quickly outwitted. The Marshal seized him and tried to get possession of Devizes for himself, but Fitz Hubert's men would not surrender, even though their captain was hanged before their eyes.[24] In revenge, the garrison eventually surrendered the castle to Stephen's son-in-law, Earl Hervey. These events show that in 1140 Stephen's cause was far from lost in Wiltshire itself. Nor do they seem to add up to such a dire state of affairs as to justify the belief of the *Gesta* that only in this way could God punish the English people as a whole for their sins: luxury, drunkenness, gluttony, indeed every vice. Stephen, though watchful and active, could not turn away the anger of the Lord. He was not held to be directly to blame.

Other parts of the kingdom were also troubled. In 1140 the Isle of Ely became, briefly, the scene of disaffection under Bishop Nigel, until he was forced to flee and take refuge with the main opposition in Gloucester. Only from that point may Nigel's opposition be considered part of the empress's campaign. Even then, he was only an opportunistic supporter and not a consistent adherent of her cause. After the failure of the Bath expedition in August 1140, Gloucester was lured the next month by Ralph Paynel into an adventurist attack on Nottingham reported by the Gloucester chronicler. This raid appears to show that Matilda had picked up some support in the midlands, since some knights of the earl of Warwick had joined in. This may indicate that the earl himself had already declared for her. Nottingham was not held by one of Matilda's adherents for very long and its capture had no obvious impact on Stephen's recognition in the region.[25] If the Matildine party had any policy at all, it amounted to little more than the creation of havoc where it could. Matilda attempted to get persons of consequence to renounce their previous submission to the king and accept her lordship and call her 'lady' – *domina*. She is not reported to have claimed any rights as queen, probably recognising that to assume that title she would need previous public and religious acclamation in London. At best she may have hoped to settle for a *de facto* recognition in the kingdom until Stephen's death or other disaster provided an opportunity to do more. Her arrival in England had certainly failed on its own to prompt any spontaneous uprisings on her behalf.

Her mere determination to show herself may, even now, seem almost heroic, were it not for her total indifference to the disruption she caused by trying to encourage men of influence to rally to her cause. Without the justification she offered them, they would possibly not have engaged in persistent opposition to the king. Of course Stephen would, like his predecessors, have expected discontent and military confrontations with his barons from time to time, but Matilda's appeal could have offerred those who opposed the king, for whatever reason, 'political' justification. Out of this situation, a 'cause' may have emerged, just as under Henry I a sense of loyalty to his brother Robert and Robert's son William had flared up on different occasions almost throughout the reign. In Stephen's time, however, from this point on until within months of Stephen's death, Matilda, and later her son Henry, did not so much take advantage of any latent antipathy to Stephen as deliberately seek to stoke the fires of disaffection. Despite their efforts, they really achieved very little for themselves, whatever unrest their activities provoked in the kingdom.

It is far from safe to assume that whenever trouble developed between the king and his great men, his opponents thereupon declared themselves Matildine sympathisers, though such a change of allegiance is usually taken for granted. As we can tell from modern times, governments may for a variety of reasons provoke any number of opponents who notoriously prove unable to forget their own differences to coordinate their activities in opposition. Governments, both strong and weak, survive essentially on the innate inability of their enemies to unite on an alternative programme. The slender support demonstrated for Matilda even in her most triumphant moments should prove sufficient indication of this. Stephen is often presented as dealing with risings on her behalf all over the kingdom throughout the reign. Had he had to confront such a united cause, he could never have won through. Matilda in fact made little headway in 1140: if Stephen was unpopular in various quarters and the kingdom in disorder, it was not because of any mounting support for her cause. Their grievances neither made his enemies willing instruments of Matilda's campaign nor persuaded them to regard her as a likely source of remedies.

More difficult to account for is what looks like reluctance on the part of Stephen's own supporters to assist the king in taking more decisive action against Gloucester. In part, the tested impregnability of Bristol and his own circumspect acts of aggression may have spared them from having to face the need for a proper show-down. Perhaps they took the view that Gloucester, as the late king's son, might be allowed to get away with personal defiance of the king. They may well have expected that, as a great baron, he was anyway entitled to manage his own lands and vassals without too much interference, though by later standards such a supine attitude teeters on complicity with rebellion. On the other hand, the baronial reaction shows there was no general willingness to join Gloucester, or display open indifference to Stephen personally. The barons do not appear to have been eager to take a leaf out of Gloucester's book on their own account. The barons may simply not have known how to deal with this unprecedented situation for the best. Since Stephen could still carry the fight into the west country itself, Gloucester's pretensions did not go unchallenged even there, but his great power, resources and standing made it almost impossible to think of attempting to destroy him altogether. In this situation, the disarray of Stephen's barons may seem at least slightly less inexcusable. The main difficulty we have with interpreting their behaviour is our own innate lack of sympathy with the dilemmas of great barons. They did not behave in

ways we think correct, and so, without further ado, we think they must
have been in the wrong.

The principal source of information about English events over the sixteen
months between September 1139 and the beginning of February 1141 is the
Historia novella of William of Malmesbury. His narrative is both sweeping
and unspecific, probably set down in the summer of 1141 when Gloucester
wanted a record made of the extraordinary things that had happened *magno
miraculo dei*. Gloucester's patronage and the way things looked then probably have something to do with Malmesbury's account of both Stephen and
his brother, Henry of Winchester. Malmesbury accepts that the year 1140
was extremely turbulent, but presents Gloucester himself as having acted
with restraint, nobly protecting both the clergy and church property. Though
Malmesbury inadvertently admitted that Gloucester had initiated hostilities,
he is not blamed, but rather commended, for observing his solemn oath to
defend Matilda's interests. Malmesbury admits that the party built up on
Matilda's account, which geographically clustered around Robert of Gloucester at Bristol and Miles at Gloucester, had relied not merely on sympathy
for her cause but also on force of arms to consolidate its hold. Confirmation
of this is found in the Worcester chronicle, which leaves no doubt about
how aggression from the men of Gloucester disturbed the region of Worcester. The town population had taken refuge in the cathedral in search of
protection, seriously disrupting the round of monastic worship. The king
and the local earl (Waleran, count of Meulan) did their best to repulse the
attacks. The sentiment of the Worcester community remained strongly
royalist, if only because of its innate hostility to the men of Gloucester.[26]

Malmesbury's reticence on the degree of backing Matilda received in 1140
indicates her limited appeal. All the same, the legate, Henry of Winchester,
was sufficiently impressed by the capacity of Matilda's supporters to cause
trouble (not least because his own lordships, particularly Glastonbury, were
seriously exposed) that he tried to negotiate a settlement. Without any
preliminary truces, discussions dragged on for several months, with the
legate even going to France to talk things over with other clergy (probably
Archbishop Hugh of Rouen), with his older brother Theobald and with
King Louis VII. Malmesbury describes Matilda as ready to fall in with any
plans for peace, while Stephen resisted all talk of settlement. Malmesbury
naturally omits to call attention to the fact that any negotiations at all could
only be to Stephen's detriment and appear to concede Matilda's alleged
rights. No details of a potential form of accommodation are given, though
negotiations in France show that Normandy as well as England must have
been considered. Perhaps Geoffrey hoped to secure the cession of Normandy,
or at least part of it, in return for peace in England. Any serious willingness

to bargain at all would have implied that Matilda's rights to the crown itself cannot have been insisted on and that her party must have been prepared to accept less. Since she seems to have never contemplated any such renunciation, Henry's diplomacy had little chance of success, but Henry could not give up. He was aware of his special responsibilities, as legate, to find a way out of the difficulty and was desperate to achieve something. This did not make him a willing instrument of Angevin schemes to trim his brother's lordship. Stephen had to defend the integrity of his kingship; the legate, like many clergy, simply put peace before any other principle. Matilda's party, which was making little headway on its own, and may have incurred some odium for its behaviour, had every motive for pressing the legate to negotiate something quickly on its behalf. When Malmesbury's narrative breaks off at the end of 1140, with negotiations still in the air, the chronicler no doubt expected to be able to show in the sequel how the matter had been resolved in a far more satisfactory manner when the war-mongering king had duly received his divine punishment at the battle of Lincoln and been replaced as ruler by Matilda. In fact Malmesbury did not resume his narration until the year 1142, by which time events had taken another quite unexpected turn.

The most dramatic and unexpected event of the reign was Stephen's capture at Lincoln on 2 February 1141. English kings have rarely been captured in battle. This extraordinary situation left contemporaries totally unprepared. The issue has two distinct aspects: how it came about, and how it might be followed up. For the first, it has to be noted that Stephen was at Lincoln not to confront Matilda and her party, but at the request of the citizens of Lincoln and the bishop in their opposition to the earl of Chester. Though his cousin Nigel of Ely continued to defy Stephen, Alexander of Lincoln, who had actually been arrested in 1139, bore the king no grudge. The king's assistance was needed because Earl Ranulf was trying to enforce what he regarded as his rights on Lincoln castle. By a cunning move Stephen was able to blockade the castle with Ranulf's wife and half-brother, William de Roumara, inside but Chester himself escaped and sought aid from the earl of Gloucester, his wife's father. His dispute with the king over Lincoln had originally nothing whatever to do with Matilda. Whatever mistakes Stephen may then have made, or not, in handling this dispute, he clearly did not think of it as connected in any way with her cause. Likewise, Chester himself had appeared hitherto totally uninterested in Gloucester's commitment to Matilda. Gloucester, either on his daughter's account, or in the hope of being able to broaden his campaign against Stephen, marched hurriedly to Lincoln, for some reason deliberately leaving his troops in the dark about their ultimate destination.

The battle provided chroniclers with every incentive to write at length about an outstanding military encounter. Stephen fought with great courage and resource to the end. Many of his supporters fled to fight another day, but Stephen would not flee. Finally, he surrendered, trustingly, to his cousin and enemy, Gloucester. With this victory, Chester was promptly able to assert his position in Lincoln and many of the civic militia loyal to the king were slaughtered without compunction. At one swoop, both the local and the national problems appeared to have been resolved. This should not be allowed to obscure the fact that the local dispute had been only most indirectly connected with the king's right to rule. Not only had Chester shown no interest in Matilda's claims; Stephen's involvement in Lincoln's affairs at this time indicates how little he had allowed Matilda to monopolise his attention. This may be used to argue that Stephen was somewhat obtuse, but this is to take the Matildine case at its own estimation. Stephen may have been correct in thinking that Chester's threat to royal interests in the east of the kingdom was potentially more dangerous than Gloucester's isolated defiance in the west. Dramatic though the victory had been, it had come about incidentally and not as the result of a battle fought to vindicate Matilda's rights, let alone in the expectation of getting posssion of the king's own person.

Victory proved embarrassing. Stephen had been disarmed and Matilda could never have imagined such a favourable outcome. Yet it speedily became apparent how difficult it was to exploit. Gloucester himself was surely disconcerted by the extent of his success, for in his most sanguine moments he can only have hoped to recover possession of Lincoln castle for his son-in-law and force the king into a humiliating retreat. Death in battle over such a trivial grievance would have been foolhardy and running away from defeat, however inglorious, a more likely outcome than capture. Malmesbury's references to compromise and negotiations in previous months show that Gloucester had not been expecting to dethrone Stephen, only to encroach on his power. Whereas Gloucester might have been prepared to skirmish indefinitely to achieve some concessions, he was certainly not expecting to have to discharge the responsibilities of the whole kingdom, nor could he have been confident of his ability to command obedience in Matilda's name from the other great men of the kingdom. As Gloucester's prisoner, Stephen had become more, not less, of a problem than before. His courage in fighting to the last confirmed his reputation for bravery. William of Malmesbury insisted that Robert of Gloucester treated Stephen with the deference due to an anointed king and not with the ignominy appropriate for a usurper. Nor did Stephen allow himself to be humiliated by captivity. By later standards, it may seem extraordinary that means were not found to murder him and so get him out of the way, as happened to four English kings in the fourteenth and fifteenth centuries. In the twelfth century, the murder of a king would have hopelessly compromised the position of his successor. Even to keep him in captivity was considered infamous; when Matilda began treating Stephen, her royal cousin, inconsiderately, this seriously detracted from her own reputation, not his.

The period of Stephen's imprisonment and eclipse was comparatively short, but as drama it has no parallel in English history. Unfortunately, little consideration seems to have been given to the difficulties it opened up for all the parties, mainly because of a persistent tendency to see in it a straight issue of conflicting claims to the throne, as in the Wars of the Roses. During the next four months, Matilda's party tried to draw the maximum advantage from its possession of the king. Matilda herself appears to have expected simply to take up the reins of government without more ado. This proved more difficult than she had supposed. Matilda may have exacerbated her own problems. She insisted on her right to exercise power in person, disregarded advice and behaved arrogantly. All this was considered unbecoming in a great lady. Such an attitude must have been galling for Robert of Gloucester, however well he kept countenance. Matilda's disregard of her husband did not either draw Geoffrey into her plans or make him seem any more attractive to potential English subjects. The problem Matilda presented to the English baronage seems strangely unappreciated. For seventy years the barons had expected their ruler to be an active military commander. Matilda was no captain for soldiers. It is unreasonable to condemn the barons for their prejudice. The royal office required the king to be active in the field. Matilda as ruler would have had to allow Gloucester, or her husband, to assume military command. Unwilling to take a back seat, she hopelessly compromised her own chances.

Though, according to Malmesbury, Gloucester had repudiated his allegiance in 1138 because Stephen had unlawfully claimed the throne, Gloucester initially treated his captive with respect. Whatever his own views about the validity of his oath to Matilda, Gloucester could hardly deny that many others had sworn no oath to her and had lawfully recognised Stephen as king. Stephen had been approved by the pope; his royal standing was undeniable. Malmesbury, by the time he came to write about the year 1141, had also become concerned to present the two prisoners, exchanged for one another in November, as comparable in quality. Gloucester is said to have argued that, since Stephen was a king, it was manifestly unfair for Matilda to release him in return for a mere earl like Gloucester. If Malmesbury's purpose was to show that when the exchange occured all the same, Gloucester's quasi-royal standing was openly acknowledged, he had only done so by showing how Gloucester himself respected Stephen's dignity. From first to last, Malmesbury aimed to give Gloucester credit for honouring the king, as it befitted his own honour. Matilda did not behave with comparable decorum and Malmesbury lets it be understood that Gloucester was not impressed by her behaviour.

Brought to prison in Bristol, Stephen was soon confined in leg-irons to hamper his freedom of movement and treated with less deference, allegedly on the grounds that, by straying from his guards, he aimed to escape altogether. As a captive, Stephen ceased to be an active protagonist in the rest of the drama. In his place stood his brother, Henry, and further off his own wife Matilda of Boulogne, who more effectively than her cousin, Matilda of Anjou, proved capable of raising troops and bringing them to bear on events. Neither of these relations have received their due from historians, who have concentrated at this point on Matilda of Anjou at her apogee. Taking advantage of Stephen's detention, Matilda asked the legate to receive her immediately in the church and kingdom as Henry I's daughter, whom all England and Normandy had sworn allegiance to. It took a month for negotiations during Lent to achieve even a mere meeting with the legate in Winchester. On Sunday 3 March 1141, she and the leading members of her party promised to allow the legate control in all major royal business, especially over church appointments, provided he accepted her in holy church as 'domina' and remained loyal to her. The following day she was escorted into the cathedral attended by several bishops and abbots. The archbishop of Canterbury did not put in an appearance until several days later and put off swearing fealty until he had obtained Stephen's permission to do so. Malmesbury implies that Stephen gave his consent and that Theobald and others then fell in with the legate's plans, but he refrains from saying that fealty was sworn. Fobbed off with this preliminary ceremony, Matilda was again made to wait another month, passing Easter without pomp in Oxford. Her slow progress towards the crown may be contrasted with Stephen's breathless campaign in December 1135.

Only after the festival did the legate open an ecclesiastical council at Winchester, attended by Malmesbury himself whose account is therefore that of an eyewitness, though one highly partial to Matilda's cause. The legate began by explaining the reason for summoning the council: to discuss the peace of the kingdom which had suffered a great shipwreck. He gave an account of how Stephen had become king but how the great hopes placed in him had been disappointed. Now God had allowed him to fall into the hands of powerful men, it was necessary to save the kingdom from collapse by finding a new ruler. The legate declared that, in a meeting held the previous day, the chief clergy had already proposed to elect Matilda of Anjou as *domina* in England and Normandy. In effect, he asked the council to confirm the prelates' choice as though the clergy had sole rights in the matter. All this appears to show that the whole business of the council had been prearranged to install Matilda as ruler. If 'fixing' seems the only possible explanation, the outcome makes Henry look rather more subtle. When a little murmur of support from the council was duly forthcoming, the legate, far from wrapping up the proceedings, announced that he had sent a special summons to the Londoners, 'who on account of the greatness of their city hold the leading place in the kingdom'. Since they had not yet arrived, he proposed to adjourn further deliberations until the next day; and indeed the council was made to wait yet another day after that.

When the Londoners duly spoke their mind, however, it was not to concur with the deliberations of the legate's council but to demand the restoration of Stephen. Malmesbury himself, far from suppressing information so prejudicial to the Angevin cause, reports that Stephen's queen had also sent a clerk to appeal for her husband's release. In Malmesbury's account, the legate is admittedly described as horrified by what had happened, sticking to his guns and getting the council to agree to the excommunication of the many who still adhered to the king, insisting that the Londoners bear back the council's resolutions to the city. It is, however, difficult to believe that Henry can have been quite as disingenuous as Malmesbury pretends. Henry had himself deliberately delayed proceedings to allow the Londoners, though laymen, to appear in his ecclesiastical council. He cannot have been ignorant either of the popularity of his brother or of the determination of his sister-in-law. Despite the ecclesiastical censures, and the clerical 'election' of a new ruler, the crucial problem was, as it turned out, to obtain the consent of the Londoners to Matilda's nomination, without which she could not realise her objectives. The legate's concern about the Londoners was justified. Malmesbury himself reveals that, for all the legate's pressure, the Londoners still made no concessions for nearly twelve more weeks. Nor had Henry attempted to use his legatine power to pre-empt opposition by formally investing Matilda in his own cathedral. Possibly Matilda herself insisted upon being received in London. If so, the legatine reception was perceived to be inadequate on its own, a mere prelude.

The precise course of events through April, May and most of June is not known.[27] For such a short period, only charters provide much help. There are about three dozen of these, most not precisely datable. The hazards of survival make conclusions based on such a sample very shaky. Such as they are, they show that she did not venture north of Oxford, though she reckoned on obedience of her instructions as far away as Shropshire. She made one grant of land in Rutland, and authorised a market in Warwick. She anticipated that payments would be made at the exchequer audit at Michaelmas. That she was recognised as potential ruler throughout the kingdom is a mere assumption. If Matilda's party, under Gloucester's guidance, took on some of the responsibilities of government, it did so without securing any formal recognition. It appears indeed to have marked time, waiting for the ritual confirmation of her title to be enacted in London itself.

The Londoners put up considerable resistance. Probably in connection with this, Stephen's chamberlain, Aubrey de Vere, was murdered in May 1141. His death may have opened the way for the pro-Matilda party in the city to get its way; but, less than a week after Matilda's arrival in London, she was driven out again. These few days were, no doubt, too eventful and confused ever to have been fully grasped, let alone recorded, but some relevant factors may be identified. When she arrived, the small number of great men she could muster in her entourage would have shown the Londoners the predominantly west country nature of her following; this itself may have provoked contempt or hostility.

In his later letter to Henry of Winchester, Brian Fitz Count provides the names of all those who witnessed the legate's call on the barons to help Matilda obtain her due. These names may plausibly be regarded as evidence for the constituents of her party at its height, as it must have been therefore at London in June 1141. Durham and York being both vacant, it included all the English bishops. Adelard of Carlisle had come south with King David. Of the thirty-seven secular barons, Brian names as earls only three (Robert of Gloucester, Ranulf of Chester and Bigod of Norfolk), though four others, three already 'promoted' by Stephen (Mandeville; Chester's half-brother, William of Roumara; and Gilbert Fitz Gilbert, brother-in-law of the murdered Vere) with Roger of Warwick appeared without the title on his list; five other barons on Brian's list were shortly afterwards made earls by Matilda. Of the rest, fourteen of the thirty-seven witnessed Matilda's documents of these months. Apart from Roger de Valognes (Hertfordshire), Miles de Beauchamp (Bedfordshire) and the two William Peverells of Dover and Nottingham, however, all of those identified came from the west country.[28] Matilda's position in London was no doubt compromised by the rivalries between the different parties in the city which had led to the murder of Aubrey de Vere, father-in-law of Geoffrey de Mandeville, castellan of the Tower of London. Matilda obviously needed to be sure of Mandeville's support, but instead of also trying to placate the Londoners by promising to restore the customs which her father had revoked, she alienated all goodwill towards her. The Londoners were not a negligible force in their own right and Matilda's partisan attitude cost her dear. In London, moreover, she rejected pleas to release Stephen even on very hard conditions and refused to assign the county of Boulogne, his mother's inheritance, to Eustace, Stephen's son. Without having accomplished her purpose, she was obliged to leave the city precipitately, though (according to Malmesbury) with military discipline.

Driven from London, Matilda found her plan of campaign in ruins and retired to Oxford. For want of other evidence, the charters she issued there can be used to show how she attempted to rethink her strategy. Here she perceived that she needed some more big names on her side: Gloucester on his own was insufficient. She was therefore obliged to create new earls to boost her entourage. Miles of Gloucester became earl of Hereford and she offered to make the count of Guisnes, Aubrey de Vere (son of the murdered chamberlain), earl of some English shire, not knowing quite which. She seems to have anticipated that her uncle King David might object to Vere in Cambridge and lamely suggested that the earl of Gloucester, and Vere's brothers-in-law, the earls of Essex and Pembroke, would advise Aubrey which one of four other possible counties he might choose for his title. The most revealing indication of her disarray is the unprecedented invocation of her absent husband's authority, possibly at the instance of Vere himself, which offers us a glimpse of the baronage's own recognition of Geoffrey's importance, however much Matilda liked to pretend otherwise. Vere may have been looking for greater security than Matilda could offer after her disarray in London.

The most commented on of Matilda's moves at Oxford, however, related to Vere's brother-in-law, Geoffrey de Mandeville, whom Stephen himself had appointed earl of Essex and whose services it was imperative for Matilda to retain if she was to nurse hopes of returning to London. Round and others have made much of the two charters Matilda issued for Mandeville within weeks of one another in the summer of 1141.[29] Since Mandeville had abandoned Matilda by September, Matilda's concessions can never have become effective. They are interesting only as evidence of what she was prepared to offer in order to tempt Mandeville to remain on her side. Their value to him would have been negligible once it became clear that she had no power to command obedience in the areas where Mandeville might appreciate royal concessions: London, Middlesex, Essex and Hertfordshire.

By the end of July she had settled on a new plan: to attack not London but Winchester, to deal with the legate. He had chosen the moment of Matilda's flight from London to throw off his mask of compliance and join his sister-in-law's campaign of resistance. Like Mandeville, he has been blamed for being unprincipled, without much consideration for his situation or responsibility. On the basis of Malmesbury's tendentious report of his speech to the Winchester council, his conduct from that point has been deplored as time-serving. Though it is not impossible that Henry wavered in his natural support for his brother, his behaviour in his dealings with Matilda deserves at least to be viewed in context. Instead of suspecting that he had harboured grievances against the king since 1138, and had rejoiced in his downfall, it would be more natural to believe that Henry, like everyone else, was completely taken aback by Stephen's capture. Moreover, he had the unenviable responsibility of having to find a way out of the mess, both as Stephen's brother and as papal legate. As legate, Henry could not escape playing a leading role, so he can hardly have delayed consulting Rome, which had flatly rejected Matilda's claims less than two years before. If he was to act in the pope's name, Henry needed advice and perhaps papal instructions.

We do not know in what terms Henry broached the matter to the curia, but at the very least he had to string Matilda along for two months or so until his speediest messengers could return from Rome. Even assuming that Henry had despatched letters to Rome early in February, he could not have been confident of receiving any reply by the time of his council at Winchester. Later in the year, Malmesbury heard that the pope had rebuked the legate for evading the task of getting his brother released and had strongly urged on him the importance of doing so by any means, ecclesiastical or secular. No such letter now survives and when it might have been issued is uncertain, but Rome's attitude to the question is not in doubt. Awkward though Henry's position in England might be, he probably viewed the matter in a similar way. Until some kind of papal letter arrived, however, Henry would need to tread carefully. He made no attempt to pre-empt Rome's intervention, for example by securing attendance from great secular lords at his legatine council at Winchester in April. Its clerical composition, under the papal legate, raised the possibility that its decisions would be provisional until the pope had confirmed them. Some response from Rome could have arrived before Matilda reached London; possibly, Henry only received papal instructions while he was there. This would help to explain a lot about his subsequent conduct. As things turned out, Henry did not have to play the Roman card, but from the summer he was no doubt strengthened in his new resolve by expecting Roman endorsement for continuing the struggle against Matilda.

If so, through the spring, Henry would have played for time, making proposals for the future but hoping he would not have to take any irreversible step. Some formal deposition of Stephen might have been thought unavoidable. Malmesbury could quote the legate's words about the decision taken by God in battle, but this meant only that Henry acknowledged a matter of fact; Stephen was in prison, but he was still perceived to be king.

The archbishop of Canterbury actually sought Stephen's permission to repudiate his oath to him, in effect acknowledging his royal power even in prison. Though no others are known to have done the same, it seems unlikely that Theobald was the only baron with some misgivings about what to do. Some public pronouncement was needed. Could a consecrated king be lawfully set aside simply because a rebellious baron had taken him prisoner?

Had the pope been prepared to pronounce formal deposition, the way forward for Matilda would have been clear. When, on the contrary, he emphatically demanded Stephen's restoration, he probably expressed a widely held view of Stephen's status. The pope did not anticipate that the way to a settlement would come by an exchange of prisoners. This outcome was in some ways unfortunate because it left the Angevin party undefeated and unrepentant. In Innocent II's view Stephen should have been released without conditions simply because he was king. If Malmesbury is correct in stressing Gloucester's concern for moral principles and papal endorsement, Gloucester would have been disappointed by the papal refusal to ratify Stephen's deposition and obliged to accept that depriving Stephen of his kingship de facto was insufficient. Stephen, moreover, remained popular, whereas Matilda quickly showed by her haughtiness that she had no natural aptitude for government. She would get nowhere if she could not command the wills of the great men of the kingdom. Stephen also retained the loyalty of an effective body of troops which his spirited wife, Queen Matilda, was able to muster. The fiasco of Matilda's abortive visit to London put fresh heart in the opposition to her and it must have seemed only a matter of time before Stephen would be restored. If Henry finally received his instructions from Rome about securing Stephen's release in late June, he will have decided that further temporising with the Angevins was inopportune. If necessary, he was now prepared to fight.

Malmesbury is such a detailed and convincing witness that enough allowance has not been made for his basic commitment to Gloucester and the difficulty he experienced in writing anything to Gloucester's disadvantage. Moreover, though Malmesbury may have been well-informed about Gloucester's side of the question, he knew less about the legate. By the time he wrote, the legate had become a scapegoat for all that had gone wrong with the Matildine campaign and Malmesbury no doubt relished the opportunity to put Henry in a bad light. Malmesbury's account of Henry's speech may be read as a cruel paraphrase of what he had, in an awkward situation, actually said, but slanted to imply more than he intended. The words may represent the best case Henry could advance at the time for going along with Matilda, but Malmesbury still manages to show, by the cunning way Henry made it possible for the Londoners to drag things out even longer, that Henry had not fully committed himself to repudiating his brother, still less to hoisting Matilda onto his brother's throne. Malmesbury even gives in detail the words of the queen's clerk's speech. Henry's reaction, feigned or otherwise, was clearly embarrassing for him by the time Malmesbury wrote. Malmesbury had not needed to be so explicit on this issue, and he is remarkably reticent where more detail would have made Matilda's case. Malmesbury, though writing for his patron, may himself have been unwilling to overlook some of the more difficult aspects of Gloucester's arguments, preferring to point the way towards certain knowledge of events rather than indulge in mere propaganda. Arguably, Henry did his best to retrieve the situation for Stephen, even at the risk of incurring censure of himself for his deviousness. A great burden had been suddenly thrust upon him and, if he wavered at all about how to proceed, it is hardly surprising. In the event, he managed to emerge and to see his brother restored to office without forfeiting papal trust. We vainly hope to understand more about this fascinating situation. Even without the necessary testimony, we can and should recognise the constraints within which Henry operated, rather than accept uncritically what Malmesbury tried to make out about him.

6

Turmoil?

The best opportunity for negotiating a complete settlement of the dispute over the crown in the autumn of 1141, while both leaders were in captivity, foundered for two reasons. The royal party was desperate to secure Stephen's release in return for Gloucester's; Gloucester appreciated their position and took advantage of it to refuse negotiations on other issues. According to Malmesbury, he was prepared for long confinement in Boulogne rather than agree to make peace. The impasse was only broken because Matilda herself became frantic for Gloucester's release, since without him her own party could do nothing. On her account Gloucester nobly consented to be exchanged for Stephen, but conceded no more. This was not sufficient to restore the *status quo ante*. Stephen recovered his throne, but the limitations of his rule had been exposed. Worse, Gloucester's release without conditions provided the king's enemies with an unyielding leader acknowledged to be of equal consequence in military terms to the king himself. Before 1141, a trial of strength between the king and a rebellious faction had been only an ominous possibility; the events of 1141 had brought open confrontation and left the opposition defiant. Admittedly, Stephen's restoration had in effect conceded the legitimacy of his rule. Gloucester must have understood this, but would not accept its implications. Thoroughly committed to opposition and raised by his recent experiences to quasi-regal standing, Gloucester did not contemplate ditching Matilda and submitting to Stephen. Unable from his own resources alone to carry the war again deep into Stephen's territory, he remained disaffected and withdrawn. Even had Gloucester for his part been prepared to compromise, Stephen's kingly instincts would have prevented him from signing away any part of his authority. He must have expected that in due course defiant vassals could be induced to conform. The uncertainties of this situation continued; both sides were naturally reluctant to give up hopes of improving their respective bargaining positions.

To call the outcome a civil war conveys an erroneous impression of a kingdom riven by two equal parties committed to persistent conflict. Stephen was in fact recognised throughout the greater part of the kingdom as the one and only king.[1] His misfortunes in 1141 were not perceived as having compromised his status. He remained active in dealing with enemies but his title to rule was presented as in itself uncontentious. All eastern England acknowledged him, including the major centres of population, London, Norwich, Lincoln and York. The region of disloyalty began in the south, on the border between the dioceses of Winchester and Salisbury. While the main Angevin strength was concentrated at Bristol and Gloucester, there were outliers at Wallingford, Marlborough and Devizes. Far out at Hereford, the bishop sternly denounced the disorders created by Matilda's earl. At Worcester too, there was a similar disagreement between the bishop, the town and the castle, which gave Stephen different opportunities to interfere. Further north, the earl of Chester normally showed no disposition to put his considerable strength at Matilda's disposal, nor indeed any need to pose as her supporter in order to cover any truculence. If the other midland earls did not apparently do much to help the king, nor did they make any attempt to impede his government, for example by blocking his movements when he made forays to the north. They are not known to have given him any trouble. Stephen's kingship extended far into the north. At Durham, notably, the king of Scots' nominee for the bishopric was ejected in 1144. Stephen was far from being confined within a small part of the realm. His ability and willingness to move about in it may be contrasted with Henry I, in whose reign, nearly twice as long, the king was less widely seen by his subjects.[2]

In modern terms Stephen might seem entitled to an exclusive claim on men's allegiance and saddled with the duty to insist on help in suppressing rebellion. Desultory warfare was resumed in the new year of 1142, until Lent imposed a lull in hostilities, but Stephen's campaigning appears to have been hampered by something as commonplace as illness, possibly related to the aftermath of his ordeal. Matilda's party could take little advantage of this. What realistic options were open to her? Her bid to get universal confirmation of her position in 1141 had fallen flat. Can she have seriously anticipated having better luck another time round? Her reverses in London and Winchester had exposed her shortcomings: she was in no position to offer an alternative government, still less the re-establishment of peace, except by renouncing her pretensions. Rather than that, she determined to make Stephen's rule as difficult as lay within her power. No wonder she was branded as a trouble-maker.[3] By early March 1142, her party already accepted that its own resources were inadequate for this purpose and appealed to Matilda's husband for help, as was his duty. Significantly, Matilda declined to go to Normandy and beg in person; likewise, Geoffrey prevaricated on the grounds that he knew none of her English envoys and asked for Gloucester to come and discuss the situation with him. Gloucester, who may have felt humiliated by the need to invite Geoffrey, left for Normandy in June. The dependence of her English supporters on Angevin assistance demonstrates how slight they perceived domestic support for the legitimist cause to be. In Gloucester's absence, Matilda ventured as far east as Oxford. Stephen pursued her there and, after capturing the town, besieged her in the castle throughout the autumn months. No support could be mustered in England to effect her rescue, not even from nearby Wallingford. Meanwhile, Geoffrey, deferring discussion of the situation in England, made use of Gloucester to help advance his own methodical conquest of Normandy. When it came to the point, Geoffrey flatly refused to accompany Gloucester back to England, though some additional troops were sent. Geoffrey's nine-year-old son Henry also came, a gesture giving notice that Matilda's struggle would continue into another generation. To persist in rebellion so long, her party would need rather better succour than this. Even to get back into the kingdom Gloucester had first to recapture the port of Wareham, his point of entry, from Stephen's forces. Stephen did not himself abandon his siege of Oxford castle. Nevertheless Matilda cheated his hopes of taking her captive at the end of the year, when, now desperate to escape, she fled from the castle at night across the snow. To her enemies, as well as her friends, it seemed to show that God was even-handed with his blessings.

The drama had nevertheless already exposed the fragility of her position in England by the winter of 1142–43. If she continued the struggle, it was not because she had any immediate prospect of once more turning the tables on Stephen. Keeping Stephen tied down in England at least helped Geoffrey complete his conquest of Normandy without any danger of Stephen's re-appearance on the Continent. Angevin calculations cannot be faulted and it is obtuse to think that Stephen should have risked all in England by launching another Norman campaign himself. Geoffrey did not find the going easy even after Stephen's capture in 1141[4] and it is easy to see why he declined to extend his own operations into England at his wife's behest. He took another three years to gain complete possession of the duchy, proof enough that the Normans remained hostile to Geoffrey's rule. Indeed, when the news about the battle of Lincoln was known in Normandy, the Normans' initial reaction, according to Orderic, had not been to capitulate to Geoffrey, but to invite Theobald of Blois, Stephen's older brother, to take the duchy. Theobald, who already had vast domains to manage, declined the further honour, but took advantage of the occasion to offer Geoffrey a deal: Normandy in return for Stephen's release and the city of Tours for himself, conditions which Geoffrey declined. By trying to negotiate, Theobald did not simply use the occasion in his own interest; he showed some concern for his brother and he wanted Geoffrey to surrender something for being offered Normandy on a plate. Theobald's conditions show that Geoffrey still could not expect an easy time in Normandy and that opposition to him was not considered hopeless.

Theobald's own unwillingness to assume responsibility there himself nevertheless deprived the Normans of a leader capable of organising resistance to Geoffrey. Even before Orderic gave up writing his history, Geoffrey had achieved a major success with the occupation of Lisieux, surrendered by its weary bishop, John, who died weeks later, on 21 May 1141. Some Norman leaders made separate submissions to the Angevins. Rotrou, count of Mortagne, had already broken with Stephen over the king's refusal to release Rotrou's nephew from prison at Breteuil. In the spring of 1141, Rotrou managed to achieve his purpose when Robert of Leicester, lord of Breteuil, negotiated a truce with the Angevins, accepting that he was too vulnerable in the Risle valley to continue hostilities. Even so, the Beaumonts did not yet concede victory to Geoffrey. Robert's twin brother, Waleran, count of Meulan in the Vexin, continued to support Stephen's cause in England at least as late as July; only after his return to Normandy later in the year 1141 did Waleran reconsider the position. Waleran appears to have agreed a division of labour with his twin. Because his stake in the Vexin kept Waleran in France, he came to terms with Geoffrey for his Norman lands, while Robert returned to England to supervise the twins' interests there. This arrangement was a practical means to salvage what they could and may have been taken with reluctance; their half-brother, Earl Warenne, continued the fight for Stephen in Normandy for a further two years. Geoffrey's position did gradually improve. The lords of the Roumois between the Seine and the Risle acknowledged Geoffrey; the surrender of Falaise in the same year secured his lines of communication between southern and Upper Normandy.

This was the situation when Gloucester returned to Normandy in 1142, asking for Geoffrey's help. Instead, Geoffrey took advantage of Gloucester's presence to get reinforcements for his campaign in Lower Normandy against the county of Mortain, Stephen's own honour. After they had captured the four main castles of the Avranchin (Mortain, Tinchebrai, Cérences and Teilleul), the Côtentin too gave up resistance, though Cherbourg sustained a long siege until the following year. In 1143 the mopping up was still not complete. Verneuil on the Avre and Vaudreuil on the Seine only fell at this stage, and the great men of the Pays de Caux, including Walter Giffard, also resisted until this point. Launching the triumphant final campaign early in 1144, Geoffrey was at last admitted to the city of Rouen itself on 20 January. Even then the men of Earl Warenne defied Geoffrey from the castle until their supplies ran out. Geoffrey now assumed the title of duke of Normandy and obtained recognition of this from the king of France in return for surrendering the border fortress of Gisors.[5] This reduced the pockets of resistance to Drincourt under Earl Warenne and Arques under William, called *monachus Flandrensis*. Another marcher lord, Hugh de Gournai, submitted to prevent the devastation of his honour. William Flandrensis was accidentally killed in 1145 and Arques then surrendered. The long resistance put up against Geoffrey in Normandy proves that well into the 1140s his cause was far from popular; he had to fight every inch of the way. All the time Geoffrey was kept fighting for Normandy, English barons with Norman lands had no reason to think of throwing in their lot with Geoffrey's wife to forestall losing their lands across the Channel.

Whatever the merits of his claim on Normandy as his wife's husband, Geoffrey became duke by right of conquest. Matilda was not received in Normandy as Henry I's heir. This provides a clear demonstration of what contemporaries expected of an heiress's husband and goes a long way to explain what would have been expected in England too. Since it had taken Geoffrey eight years from Henry I's death to achieve his conquest of Normandy, it is not surprising that he gave his wife's cause in England itself so little help. He may well have considered her English expedition of 1139 as no more than a useful diversion, with the added bonus of getting her out of the duchy. After his occupation of Rouen, Geoffrey could perhaps have contemplated an invasion of England; but, for whatever reason, nothing was tried. Geoffrey's main interest was keeping Normandy out of unfriendly hands; after a mere six years, he found the earliest possible occasion to hand over the duchy to his son Henry before he became seventeen in 1150. Possibly he thought Henry might be content with this and allow Anjou to pass to a younger brother. Geoffrey consistently showed little interest in his wife's claims on England, sensibly dubious about his chances of conquering a kingdom where even his wife commanded so little loyalty. Geoffrey had adequately discharged his obligations to his son by securing his inheritance in Normandy. In the long term, Henry's control of the duchy after 1150 gave him some leverage on barons in England, promising to restore any lands forfeited in return for their support. As far as Geoffrey himself was concerned, the acquisition of Normandy was itself a sufficient bonus. What it offered as future bargaining power was irrelevant.

By remaining in England until 1147, Matilda stolidly insisted that her rights were not negotiable. In the one instance known of her 'terms' *c.* 1147, she refused to renounce her pre-eminence (*primatum*).[6] There was actually no room for compromise here. A display of patriotic self-denial in the interest of peace should not be expected. She stuck to her last. She had no status except as Henry I's 'heir'. She had never been formally recognised as queen and was never in a position to constitute an alternative royal government in waiting. Rejecting her title 'countess', which gave her no standing whatever in England, she may have intended to show not merely that she was not her husband's decoy in England, but that she intended to keep him at arm's length. Her preference for the style 'empress' (though in fact she had herself never been crowned empress by the pope) asserted a superior sort of title which may have been considered, by her supporters if not herself, as an appropriately humorous sobriquet, playing upon aspects of her character, while offering her ostensible flattery. Is it possible that as 'empress' she thought of acting like the German empress regents, Adelaide, Theophanou or Agnes of Poitiers, her first husband's grandmother? Those great ladies had enjoyed prominence in their own right. Her campaign was, like theirs, maintained in the long-term interest of a son to rule the kingdom. In 1141, however, she made every show of wishing to rule in person. This may have been as disconcerting for Robert of Gloucester himself as for her husband. While her maternal concern and personal involvement are understandable, it is dubious to what extent this proprietary attitude inspired loyalty in others. They could have been unwilling to accept her direction, preferring to wait and see what would happen when Henry of Anjou came into his own. At best, her presence may have helped to rally her dispirited supporters, or to give their defiance of the king a spurious legitimacy, but there is no hard evidence as to the true sentiments she inspired. Rather than live under the protection of the earls of Gloucester or Hereford, as she had done before 1141, she apparently maintained an independent 'court' at Devizes, the bishop of Salisbury's castle, which had fallen into Angevin hands after the battle of Lincoln.

About seventy of Matilda's English charters survive as the main proof for her activity. Many of them cannot be dated very precisely; most certainly belong to the years 1141–42.[7] Some may have been issued at any time in the next five years she remained in England. Disposing of royal lands and granting royal privileges, she issued documents for those who rallied to her or whose lands lay in the zones of her influence. A mere handful, belonging to the years after her return to Normandy in 1147, prove that her name might then still be usefully invoked in western English shires and on the Welsh borders.[8] The sympathies of the west of England for the Angevin cause were sufficiently widespread even by 1149, when Henry of Anjou returned to England, to enable him to travel across England from one friend to another as far as Carlisle. Gilbert Foliot went so far as to describe Henry in 1153 as lord of much of the English kingdom, but this was an occasion for flattery.[9] However staunch the west remained, strong bases there were far too peripheral to be used for mounting campaigns to dislodge the king from his more commanding position in the kingdom as a whole.

'Matildine' territory did not form a homogeneous bloc. Angevin government amounted to no more than what the leading lords could impose in their own regions. Apart from Gloucester (and on occasion Chester), Roger of Warwick was the only earl of Henry I's reign who is named as ever going over to Matilda.[10] Possibly the Warwick interest in the lordship of Gower made him susceptible to pressure from the other marcher lords of South Wales, Miles and Brian Fitz Count, who had become Gloucester's allies. Warwick was described by the *Gesta* as a man without military reputation and played no significant part in bolstering Matilda's support. How long he stayed loyal to her is not known. In 1153 his commitment to the king was unshaken by the return to England of Henry of Anjou. The feeble support Warwick was able to offer meant that Matilda could not count on any substantial cadre of support beyond the range of Gloucester's military might. Matilda herself may not have inspired sufficient respect to muster the forces of local government, but those who dominated the shires within Gloucester's orbit probably appropriated the traditional powers of sheriffs or earls and perhaps received authority to do so from her.[11] The revenues and resources of the crown in western shires could have been commandeered by the men on the spot, but they were not pooled for the purpose of relaunching a major offensive against Stephen.

Whether Matilda's men enjoyed untramelled authority in their zones or remained fully engaged on a local basis in holding on to their own positions is impossible to specify. Some of them obviously had problems. In the case of William de Mohun, styled earl of Somerset, she clearly failed to find an effective lieutenant; after founding Bruton abbey in 1142, he is no more heard of and his earldom was never claimed by his heirs. He was singled out early on by Brian Fitz Count for his disloyalty to her, but what lies behind this accusation is not known. In Somerset, Henry de Tracy, whom Stephen had authorised to deal with Mohun, may have gained ascendancy across Exmoor. Equally ineffectual as Matildine earl was Aubrey de Vere, generally styled earl of Oxford, though he had no lands there. After Stephen's recovery of the city in 1142, Aubrey can have had no role at all as earl and by 1144 had made his own peace with the king.[12] In these instances, Matilda's attempts to promote barons to strengthen her grasp in the regions simply came to nothing. In the far south west, in Devon and Cornwall, however, her earls enjoyed more success. In Cornwall, the royal party had been eliminated before 1141. For the rest of the reign, Earl Reginald effectively blocked any efforts by Stephen's surviving friends to maintain his rights. Though Reginald is assumed to have been consistently sympathetic to

Matilda, he is not recorded as having fielded any military force on her behalf. This would be understandable if his responsibilities in Cornwall kept him busy there; if so, his rule as earl must have been more troubled than it looks. He certainly fell foul of the bishop of Exeter. His only known intervention in political affairs further afield was as a negotiator.

The position in Devon was not substantially better. Matilda had recognised Baldwin de Redvers, the rebel of 1136, as earl of Exeter by the summer of 1141. He was not accepted as earl by Stephen until after the settlement of 1153 and is accordingly counted among the empress's party. Yet there is no record of his ever appearing in Matilda's company after 1141 or participating in any military campaign on her behalf. He could have profited from the general situation elsewhere to become his own master in Devonshire. Belligerence of a sort continued intermittently between hostile parties in north Devon and Somerset because Henry de Tracy and others fought on in Stephen's name, but their quarrels may have arisen out of their local differences.[13] The fate of the kingdom would obviously not be settled in Devon anyway and to describe what happened in partisan terms could misrepresent its real character.

The part of the kingdom most consistently troubled seems to have been Wiltshire, where royal rights were considerable and coveted.[14] Hervey, Stephen's nominee as earl, was expelled after the battle of Lincoln, but the king's party in the shire recovered some ground after his own release from prison. Malmesbury castle was already in royal hands in 1144 and remained so until 1153; even when its royal castellan, Walter de Pinkney, was taken prisoner, his men refused to surrender it to the Angevins. Malmesbury had probably been retaken for the king at the same time as Sherborne castle, which Matilda extorted from the castellan, William Martel, the king's steward, after he was captured at Wilton in 1143. Stephen's assault on Wilton had been an attempt to salvage something from the military campaign that had failed to take Wareham back from Gloucester. At Wilton, the king had himself nearly become a prisoner again and escaped only with ignominy. Gloucester's second victory did little for the Matildine cause and damaged his own reputation. The chroniclers disapproved of his savage treatment of the nunnery there and thought it was properly punished by God when a number of Gloucester's adherents (one of his sons and Miles of Hereford amongst them) died within the year. Although Gloucester had defeated the king's Wiltshire campaign, the Angevins were still in no position to dominate Wiltshire outright. An Angevin 'earl', Patrick of Salisbury, is not named until 1148 and how exactly he achieved prominence is not known.

In Herefordshire on the Welsh border, which had been plagued by recurrent warfare since the beginning of the reign, the appointment of Miles of Gloucester as 'earl' did not bring peace. It may have been more of a licence to impose himself where he could. Miles had accepted Matilda with enthusiasm as early as October 1139 and campaigned against both Worcester and Hereford the same year. He had also provided for all Matilda's wants. She still did not nominate him as earl of Hereford until after her expulsion from London.[15] For two and a half years he continued to give her strong support until he was killed in a hunting accident in December 1143, but he did not enjoy unchallenged control of his shire and the bishop did not approve of the earl's military activities.[16] Miles was succeeded by his son Roger, an active west country baron with an agenda of his own, through his additional responsibilities as husband of Cecilia, daughter of Payn Fitz John, heiress of the Lacys. Roger never matched his father's personal devotion to the empress and features in the *Gesta* as a slippery politician playing for his own ends.[17]

For shires without earls, information is even more sparse. In Dorset, the monks of Cerne became an object of concern to senior clergy when they expelled a new abbot, a former prior of Gloucester. Abbot Gilbert of Gloucester conducted a long drawn out campaign on behalf of the new abbot, from which the monks can be seen to have defied all authorities invoked against them, including both the pope and the earl of Gloucester.[18] Gloucester could have held Wareham and other castles along the routes north, but still been powerless elsewhere in Dorset. The volatile situation of Wiltshire may have had a limited parallel in Berkshire, since the Abingdon chronicler complained that what one lord confirmed, was rejected by another, suggesting shifting lordship. Even an 'ally' might prove untrustworthy. The abbot bribed the constable of Wallingford to use his forces to protect the monastery's property and was outraged when he raided one of its estates. In 1147 the abbot sought papal support for getting ecclesiastical sanctions against several named individuals, including William Martel, Stephen's steward, and John Marshal, his enemy. If these attacks were coordinated, it indicates that political enemies might join forces to assail monastic property. More probably it shows that monks in buffer zones were as likely to suffer from one side as another. Berkshire never had an 'earl' and the sheriff made the most of his opportunities. The abbot of Abingdon regularly paid him an annual sweetener of one hundred shillings in return for lenient treatment of the monastery's men and property in the shire and hundred courts. This indicates that the sheriff remained an influential figure in the shire, where campaigning in and around Wallingford might have been expected to disrupt traditional administration. Reading abbey, with properties in Herefordshire and Gloucestershire, was also awkwardly placed and obliged to take note of Angevin authority. This must have nominally extended as far east as Blewbury since the empress granted it to Reading abbey after 1142, probably because her hold on it herself had become precarious.[19]

The attitude of the clergy though circumspect was not always servile. Though the bishop of Exeter was obliged to recognise Baldwin de Redvers as effective earl, he nevertheless dated some of his own documents of this period as issued in the reign of King Stephen.[20] Prelates who had perforce to recognise those with effective authority in their regions are often described as though they too had become committed supporters of Matilda. This is surely an error. Abbot Gilbert of Gloucester had no choice but acknowledge the earl of Gloucester's practical power. It was no more than polite to refer to Matilda as *domina*; what else could she be called? This did not commit the abbot to stop recognising Stephen as king. Since his abbey owed no military service to the crown, he had no obligation to provide troops; after 1141 he witnessed only one of Matilda's charters and his presence at her court did not as such brand him as a supporter.[21] His abbey also had properties in other parts of the kingdom and the abbot maintained close relations with fellow prelates committed to the king. Foliot wrote abusively of Stephen to Brian Fitz Count, but his lament that 'tot reges patimur quot municipes angustamur' (we are harrassed by as many 'kings' as there are townships) reflects no strong approval of the consequences for the west country of the Matildine cause. Gilbert was well aware of papal support for Stephen and was unwilling to find himself out of step. If he did genuinely hope that Celestine II would pronounce in Matilda's favour, he will have been disappointed by subsequent papal behaviour.

By 1144 the hard core of Matilda's active party had been reduced to Robert of Gloucester and Brian Fitz Count. Despite their loyalty to her cause, they could in fact do little to turn back the tide against her. Exceptionally, Brian Fitz Count took to her defence not merely by holding Wallingford against the king but by disputing about her rights with the clergy in writing. His letter to the legate, Henry of Winchester, shows that he was quite unimpressed by Henry's standing, arguments or integrity. Though Brian is thought to have joined Matilda as soon as she returned to England in 1139, in his letter he justifies his support for her on the grounds that Henry had recommended this course of conduct in 1141; Brian saw no reason to change his allegiance again in 1142 just because the legate had done so. His answer to the legate is a piece of splendid invective rather than an honest exposition of his reasons for joining Matilda in the first place. Not satisfied with mere contradiction, Brian also wrote a propaganda tract, perhaps intended to persuade fellow barons. This little work has been lost and is known only from comments in a letter of Gilbert Foliot to its author.[22] Brian accepted without question Henry I's rights to dispose of the kingdom as his property to Matilda as his natural heir. He argued that her rights were unimpeachable, and so in effect independent of any oaths.

Brian had, nonetheless, recognised Stephen as king for nearly four years and had not appreciated Matilda's better rights until she herself came to plead her cause in England. His change of heart may have been influenced by the fact that, as a bastard son of a Breton count, he owed his own eminence in England to Henry I's patronage and in particular to Henry's decision to marry him to the heiress of the honour of Wallingford. Brian shared the assumption of all great lords that honours were inheritable and appears to have convinced himself that the kingdom was no more than a great honour. Since he had no sons to inherit his honour, he could even afford to be reckless about the future and please himself about what he did. After 1139, if not before, Brian was prepared to defend his new commitment to Matilda at much personal cost. Resistance at Wallingford remained a thorn in Stephen's flesh till 1153, but, as Matilda's plight at Oxford proved, its offensive range was limited. Hemmed in by people loyal to the king, it was physically rather isolated from the main body of Matilda's support, and efforts to succour it from the west stretched Matildine resources to the limit. Probably to reduce his own responsibilities, Brian surrendered to Miles of Gloucester his rights to the honour of Abergavenny, which eliminated any question of conflicting baronial rights in south-east Wales.

The distressing state of the kingdom prompted the author of the *Gesta* to compose another lachrymose passage about the period 1143–45, but the information he gives fails to establish just how the general situation had deteriorated. It seems to have been inspired by the wickedness of individual castellans, like John the Marshal at Marlborough, and various mercenary captains in the immediate vicinity. The chronicler soon affirms with equal conviction that the king achieved a remarkable triumph at Faringdon in 1145. This tendency to hyperbole makes it impossible to take his comments literally.[23] Still, there can be no doubt that Stephen had severely frustrated Robert of Gloucester's effort to link his part of the country with Brian's by constructing a castle at Faringdon. The 1145 campaign proved to be Gloucester's last important military initiative. Further plans for challenging the king petered out on his death in 1147. Gloucester can hardly be judged to have done his utmost to secure an Angevin succession in England. In fact, he may have consciously limited himself to defining a zone within which he could operate independently. Whatever the explanation, Gloucester was no ordinary baron and his example set no precedent. Nor was he able to take advantage of his extensive possessions all over the kingdom to persuade any of the great barons outside the west country, not even Chester his own son in law, to join him on a regular basis. Gloucester probably lost control over most of his extensive properties outside his home territory, though even this is not certain.[24]

By the time of Gloucester's death, Stephen's position had already begun to look much more secure, even if by then he was still committed to military campaigns against the earl of Chester. When the fourteen-year-old Henry of Anjou brought a body of mercenaries to England in 1147, his campaign collapsed so disastrously at Cricklade that the young man was hurried back to Normandy by the king himself. After the death of Gloucester, his heir William, not surprisingly, is said to have recognised Stephen as king; his younger brother, Philip, had become Stephen's vassal in his father's lifetime.[25] Even the one bishop Matilda had appointed, at London in 1141, became reconciled to the king at the pope's request, on the understanding that even if he could not swear allegiance (presumably pleading an earlier oath) he would swear to abstain from any harm to the king and the kingdom.[26] The same year, Stephen knighted his elder son, Eustace, and advanced him to comital rank. By this the chronicler presumably had Eustace's recognition as count of Boulogne in mind.[27] In 1147, probably before the death of Robert of Gloucester, but after the aborted campaign of her son Henry, Matilda quietly slipped out of the country and never returned.[28] Her party did not seek another open confrontation; if it played for the longer term, it gave the impression of being at its last gasp. Stephen had reason to be confident the worst was over and that he could soon apply himself again to his continental interests.

The degree of respect accorded to the empress during the six years succeeding the battle of Lincoln needs to be assessed realistically. The only men of consequence steadily at her service were her half-brothers, the earls of Gloucester and Cornwall, Earl Miles and Brian Fitz Count. She had gained no lasting adherents by her successes in 1141 and over the years, particularly after the deaths of Miles in 1143 and of Robert of Gloucester in October 1147, her strength ebbed away. Geoffrey's successful occupation of Normandy in 1144 did nothing to make her seem a more attractive prospect in England. The willingness of a few disaffected Angevin supporters in the west to defy Stephen's authority may be attributed to their sense of duty to uphold her rights, had they not all earlier in the reign accepted Stephen's kingship. The west country, however disaffected or rebellious, could never on its own create problems for the king all over the kingdom; it did not become an effective haven for Stephen's other sundry enemies; nor from their castles at Bristol or Devizes did Gloucester or Matilda plot with sympathisers elsewhere for Stephen's overthrow.

Historians have, nonetheless, been quick to conclude that, whatever difficulties Stephen faced, they may ultimately be traced back to the matter of Matilda's rights. On this account, King David has himself been considered Matilda's strongest supporter, Gloucester apart, though it is difficult to see how David's efforts to strengthen his standing in the north of England could have given Matilda any satisfaction. Had Matilda been accepted as Henry I's heir in 1135, David would certainly not have desisted from attempting to reclaim what he regarded as lost Scottish land. His interventions in the north at the very least threatened to keep the region agitated and obliged Stephen accordingly to make several visits to the northern limits of royal power in the course of the reign. Stephen's ability to keep his hold on Yorkshire is all the more noteworthy, since, without his persistence, David might well have effected a permanent shift in the Scottish frontier much further south. There is no reason to think that any of the northern lords who wavered in their support for Stephen had Matilda's interests in mind. They felt susceptible to pressure from David because of his own powers of attraction.

Applying the principle that all political problems in this reign involved confrontation between two parties for the succession has meant identifying every baron who ever fell out with the king as a committed supporter of Matilda's cause, as though it were impossible for barons to have quarrel-ledwith the king over personal grievances or any other issue. This is clearly mistaken. To understand the nature of the unrest under Stephen, it does not help to put all his different problems together and regard them as aspects of Matilda's challenge to his kingship. At best, the 'legitimist' claims created sufficient uncertainty to provide cover for others to pursue their own objectives and prevent Stephen from dealing with only one problem at a time.

To what extent did barons make use of the legitimist distraction for their own purposes? The insignificance of the dispute about the crown itself seems obvious enough from consideration of the several occasions when the king was in conflict with the earl of Chester. What took Stephen to Lincoln in 1140 originally had nothing to do with Matilda. Already by September 1141, Chester was so little committed to her that he tried to rejoin the royal forces. Yet his attitude to the king remained unpredictable. In 1146, apparently confident of Stephen's good will, he sought royal help over his difficulties with the Welsh. Stephen's advisers persuaded the king that he was being led into a trap. The earl was seized and obliged to answer for his unfulfilled commitments to the king and had to surrender Lincoln in return for his release. Behind this episode, there clearly lay previous inconclusive efforts to secure Chester's loyalty. Once more free, he resumed his active hostility to the king; and, though our sources do not give much detail, the king remained committed to serious warfare against him, with mixed success. The king's quarrels with Ranulf of Chester gave him grounds for demanding the surrender of castles belonging to Ranulf's nephew, Gilbert, earl of Hertford, who had stood as a guarantor of Ranulf's loyalty. This in turn provoked protests from Gilbert's other uncle, Gilbert, earl of Pembroke, who claimed the forfeited castles as family property. Stephen immediately took action to obtain his castles too. Both Gilberts were fairly soon reconciled with the king. These quarrels had not been occasioned by Matilda's rights and the disturbance they caused did not materially advance her interests. John of Hexham admittedly believed that, to revenge himself against Stephen, Chester eventually encouraged Henry of Anjou to return to England and challenge the king, but this attempt to manipulate Henry for his own purposes hardly makes Chester much of an Angevin supporter. In 1149 and later, when he is alleged to have 'gone over' to Henry of Anjou, he never actually fought on Henry's behalf.[29] Similarly, though Hugh Bigod was credited with helping Stephen to justify his seizure of the crown and actually fought for the king at Lincoln, he also defied the king on and off throughout the reign, for reasons which remain obscure.[30] What is certain is that these grievances and hostilities were not concerted by the earls together and formed no part of any plan to make Matilda ruler in Stephen's place.

Nor did all the conflicts of the reign arise from the ambitions of the greatest men. The *Gesta* explicitly attributes the rebellion of Turgis of Avranches to fear that he was about to be deprived of the custody of Walden castle.[31] Similarly, the trouble caused by Walter de Pinkney, the former royal castellan of Malmesbury, was the result of taking personal vengeful action when, after enduring a spell in Robert of Gloucester's dungeons, he seized his chance at Christchurch in Hampshire to occupy the castle.[32] Neither incident had anything to do with support for the Angevin claim to the throne; they were spontaneous and autonomous. In the case of Turgis, the king was able to deal promptly and effectively with his treachery; at Christchurch, Pinkney, operating as a freelance in a zone subject to Baldwin de Redvers, was eventually killed by the townsmen themselves.

Because confrontations between armies were unusual, the ability of castles to hold out defiantly, at least for a time, became the major source of unrest. This should not be interpreted as evidence for 'feudal' indiscipline. The assumption that lords were entitled to untramelled enjoyment of their castles was shared by clergy who felt under no obligation to surrender them on demand to the king. The importance of ecclesiastical castles is proved by the prominence of both Malmesbury and Devizes in the record. Ecclesiastical defence of rights to castles indicates that the problems castles presented cannot be laid at the door of feckless barons. In other respects, too, clergy pursued their own own affairs with comparable self-confidence, utterly careless of the consequences. The prolonged dispute about the succession to Archbishop Thurstan of York, for example, proceeded quite independently of Matilda's claims to the throne. Stephen became committed to an unending task of defending the rights of the crown and did so with great energy. Throughout the reign, he persevered particularly with siege warfare, a matter to which he gave much attention and expertise, as the *Gesta* admiringly recorded.

Just how unruly the kingdom as a whole became on account of these various operations is now impossible to assess, though few medieval subjects have been more closely studied in modern times. The arguments continue because the evidence is not and cannot be comprehensive. This is not actually surprising on general grounds: there is no shortage of disagreement about the extent of the damage caused by many twentieth-century conflicts. What should be expected in these circumstances is not total agreement but the exercise of some sense of proportion. According to the *Gesta*, parts of the country where ordinary life had at first continued undisturbed were also eventually plagued by plausible rogues from Bristol, who abducted victims and demanded ransoms. Does this text authorise us to believe that the whole kingdom was affected? Or was the author still thinking in terms of a very limited range of brutality? The men of Bath, only six miles away, had been able to check an attack from Bristol in 1140 and the castle of Malmesbury, twenty miles off, was held for the king: the men of Bristol cannot have been as free to lay the country waste as a literal reading of the text would suggest.[33]

Contemporaries were most struck by what they described as the simple contrast between the peaceful, affluent times of Henry I and the disturbances under his successor, which reduced the country to misery. A foreigner, Herimann of Tournai, commented to this effect in the 1140s when the outcome was still uncertain.[34] This state of affairs was unusual for England, but how widely the whole kingdom was affected remains unclear. The source most frequently quoted in support of the worst outcome is a passage inserted into the last seven pages of the vernacular chronicle of Peterborough.[35] After Stephen's death, a single scribe copied out an account of the years 1132–54, compiled from three distinct elements: a narrative about a new abbot, Martin, a disorderly set of annals and the famous long lament of about seven hundred words on the horrors perpetrated in the terrible nineteen years of Stephen. This passage begins after recording the death of Henry I, Stephen's consecration, his visit to Normandy and the arrest of the bishops. 'When the traitors saw that Stephen was a good-humoured, kindly and easy-going man ... they committed all manner of horrible crimes.' 'They' are nowhere named. 'Every great man built him castles' and the atrocities then described are perpetrated from these strongholds. Again, no places are specified. At the close of this general passage, the scribe gives an account of Martin's abbacy. 'During all these evil days, Abbot Martin governed ... under great difficulties.' All the more remarkable in these circumstances that Martin provided everything necessary for the monks, visitors and beggars, extended the church, adorned and roofed it, went to Rome, recovered lost properties, admitted many monks, put up new domestic buildings for them and changed the site of the town. Under Henry II, another account of Abbot Martin was written up in Latin, again without specific details about the problems he confronted.[36] Stephen himself, 'mild and humble', made at least two visits to the abbey, adjudicated in their favour, gave the monks gifts and privileges, and venerated their miracle-working relics. Stephen had hardly abandoned his responsibilities to the monks.

Whatever the passage might claim about the general state of the kingdom, Peterborough itself cannot have suffered as severely from the terrible state of affairs said to prevail elsewhere. This alone makes it impossible to accept the allegations of the famous passage as they stand. Only after the eulogy of Abbot Martin does the chronicle report 'something of the events of King Stephen's time', offering a confused set of annals where the dispute about the crown is at last introduced. The earlier passage had attributed the blame for the devilry described to the simple contrast between Henry I, 'a good man, held in great awe ... who made peace for man and beast' and Stephen, 'good-humoured, kindly and easy-going who inflicted no punishments'. Misery was caused not by military confrontations but from the 'great men's' castles. This charge was repeated by other chroniclers. In this case, however, no particular castle is singled out and since, in fact, the Peterborough region was not itself densely studded with castles, the generalisation must have drawn on information about the situation much further afield. Some of the tortures described in the passage are vouched for at Durham, where the supporters of Cumin are accused of comparable barbarism. If the Peterborough writer did draw upon reports of this kind, however, his failure to provide any proper names diminishes its own value for historical purposes. Surprisingly, it makes no allusion to the damage inflicted on the neighbouring monasteries of Ely and Ramsey, which would have added credibility to its account. Ely was only twenty-five miles across the fens.[37] How reliable can its information have been about events even further away?

In contrast to the muddled testimony of the Peterborough chronicle, the two main historians of Stephen's middle years offer information that is precise and ordered. Huntingdon saw fit to update his chronicle at several points in the reign. After Stephen's capture at Lincoln in 1141, Huntingdon brought his narrative forward only to the battle of the Standard in 1138, so that it was not until after Stephen's crown-wearing at Lincoln in 1146 that he completed the narration of Stephen's first decade. A mere two years later, he offered an updated version to the new bishop of Lincoln, Robert de Chesney, his former colleague as archdeacon of Leicester. This makes it easy to perceive how local history impinged on Huntingdon's view of events. The chronicle is systematically organised by Stephen's regnal years and Matilda is not mentioned after her escapade of 1142.

The *Gesta* is a fuller but in some ways more baffling text to use for an understanding of the reign. As history, unlike Huntingdon, it did not enjoy any popularity in its own day; only two manuscripts of it are known, both from France and its author is anonymous. Most monastic writers leave clues as to the house of their monastic profession; secular clergy had patrons or benefices. This author cannot be located, even in a very general manner, though, given the little he knows about London or the east, his affiliations seem to lie rather in the south and west. He provides an account of the whole reign divided into two books, the first devoted to the king's first six years and the somewhat shorter second book dealing with the rest. His history concludes with the accession of Henry of Anjou in 1154, so the author knew the eventual outcome of the reign. At what point was the work written? Was it all composed after 1154? Was part of it composed during the reign and only completed later? Can any change in its attitude be detected at any point in a seemingly continuous narrative? For the first part, Stephen is presented as a king never downcast, constantly grappling bravely and un-tiringly with the vicissitudes of fortune. Does the more summary second part indicate that the author had lost interest in royal heroism and hurried over the last years? Stephen's capture of the castle recently built by Robert of Gloucester at Faringdon in 1145 is described in great detail as the crown of his good fortune, followed by some spectacular improvements in respect for his authority, among others by the earl of Chester. About this time, the papal call for the Second Crusade inspired the 'vigorous youth of the whole of England' to leave for the Holy Land. Unfortunately, this did not cause the civil strife to abate and the new evil doers were more zealous and less experienced. Stephen's successes had not therefore brought the troubles to an end.

At this point in the narrative, the author reintroduces Henry of Anjou, whose arrival in England in 1147 with a body of troops initially stirred considerable alarm. Henry is here described for the first time as the 'just heir' of the kingdom. On this account a change in the author's political sympathies has been proposed. This phrase apart, however, the author hardly falters in his sense of commitment to Stephen. When Henry's expedition fizzled out, he was in such need of money to get back to Normandy that he appealed to Stephen himself for help. The *Gesta* records that Stephen was blamed for acting childishly in giving money to his enemy, but expresses his personal approval of Stephen's kindliness, considering it both more profound and more prudent, because by treating enemies well they are made weaker and more disposed to repentance. From this it can hardly be argued that by this time the author has joined the party of the 'just heir'. Nor is it plausible to suggest that by 1147 Stephen's cause seemed desperate, or that his historian had begun to falter in his admiration of the king. Since his text concludes immediately after Henry of Anjou is accepted as king on Stephen's death, it makes better sense to regard the last fourteen chapters of the second book as being written in the last few months of the reign, by which time Henry was everywhere accepted as the 'just heir'.

The author had begun the second book of the *Gesta* with the sensible expectation that Stephen's release in 1141 would speedily restore peace and order; he shows, in fact, how Matilda's continuing defiance disappointed any such hopes. The narrative is, however, devoted to recounting a succession of episodes in which several named military chiefs seize castles and then devastate the surrounding countryside. Great emphasis is put on the damage inflicted on clergy, church property and other defenceless people, followed by accounts of the way the wicked were punished by God for their lawlessness. These episodes include sweeping generalisations about the outrages committed by the earl of Chester in the north, and the erratic behaviour of Hugh Bigod in Norfolk, but the chronicler's precise information mainly concerns Wiltshire, Somerset and Gloucestershire. His belief that the key to the fate of the kingdom lay with Sherborne castle indicates the limits of his strategic sense. Even in that small region, Stephen could count on supporters, but the nature of the *Gesta*'s stories does not offer any coherent explanation of alignments of forces or even suggest that disorder resulted from consistent opposition between two political 'parties'. The role of Robert of Gloucester is emphasised in the *Gesta*, but his efforts fail to coordinate the activities of even local dissidents; the narrative accordingly focuses on individual wicked men, many of secondary and only local importance, who seize their chances to take castles, supplies and prisoners, indulging private grievances, and indeed sadistic and lustful passions on occasion.

The author longs for peace and order, but displays a taste for macabre stories. His accounts of devastation, precisely tied to the perpetrators of wickedness, nevertheless aim to conjure up an impression of frightful horror, that somehow falls flat. The wicked leaders rarely come to violent ends. There are many threats to hang captains unless castles are surrendered by their men, but most of these opt for life. Several survive brutal imprisonment and are allowed to go into exile.[38] The tameness of the outcome hardly provides convincing evidence of embittered conflict. The chronicler's exaggerations of violence may misrepresent its real character. That the text needs to be read with some care is clear when the author takes the somewhat unexpected line of blaming some bishops for taking to warlike activity and wearing armour (though not to fighting in person). This could indicate not so much a collapse of episcopal integrity as the response of well-born clergy to the challenge of providing adequate defence of their own people. Since the author does not belong in any recognisable context, it is difficult to regard him as a spokesman for any particular interest. Rather like a modern journalist, he collected stray stories and wrote them up in heightened prose, apparently having little rapport with the native inhabitants; writing, as the manuscripts imply, for a readership abroad, perhaps in or around Boulogne. Journalists still report contemporary atrocities in similar style to stir up pity and outrage in their readers. While such stories cannot be discounted, the tone of indignation makes it more difficult to assess their evidential worth.

For illustrating the situation in the north, the chronicle completed by John of Hexham within a few years of Stephen's death at least proves how loyal to Stephen's kingship the most remote part of the kingdom remained. The close proximity of Scottish power no doubt enhanced the north's determination to insist on its English allegiance. King David succeeded in attracting very few great northern lords into his own camp as a better or more acceptable ruler, and any efforts he might have made to advance Matilda's cause by violence had negative consequences for her acceptability elsewhere. John of Hexham has a glowing account of Stephen's courage at the battle of Lincoln that leaves no doubt about his admiration. Throughout his account, Stephen's kingship is taken for granted and the king's enemies get short shrift. Inevitably, the main interest of the chronicle lies in its accounts of the disorder experienced at both Durham and York over the election of new prelates. At Durham, the chronicler is notably hostile in his account of the intrusion of William Cumin, backed by the Scots. At York, he offers an indulgent view of Archbishop William Fitz Herbert and leaves a strong impression that he thought the opposition to William was unfair. This chronicler also shows that William's rival, Henry Murdac, even after his reconciliation with Stephen, still did not obtain support in York itself, and that by that stage, Stephen's son Eustace had a firm grasp on the city. John of Hexham reports of the allegedly pro-Matildine pope, Celestine II, that he was the *alumpnus* of the Angevins, a contemptuous expression that surely betrays his unwavering loyalty to the king.[39] After 1144, at any rate, continuing disturbances in the north had little to do with Matildine intrigue or royal incompetence. The very persistence of violent clashes between the supporters of the rival archbishops at York indicates how little the clergy cowered in terror from the rampages of secular barons. The clergy who

deplored secular violence were unconstrained by secular conflicts and free
to indulge their own vendettas and partisan disputes without shame, pleading high principles, of course, in justification.

   Not without relevance for twelfth-century attitudes to the disturbances of
the reign are several stories collected as evidence of marvels wrought by
several different northern saints for their devotees: Cuthbert, Oswin, king
and martyr, venerated at Tynemouth, Germanus of Selby and John of
Beverley. Apart from setting these stories in the context of disorder under
Stephen, none of them pays much attention to the general state of misery.
At Scarborough, the scene is simply set ('Earl Ranulf broke in one morning
with an armed force and laid it waste') to explain how a young fisherman,
probably from Tynemouth, had been gathered up with others and carried
off to Malton castle where he had been kept and ill-treated until his family
paid for his ransom. He had escaped, thanks to his prayers to St Oswin.
Chester's Scarborough raid is known only because of this miracle on behalf
of the poor fisherman. Likewise, the clerical son of a citizen of Lincoln
escaped from the clutches of Robert de Stuteville at Cottingham because of
his prayers to John of Beverley. At Selby, St Germanus rescued four unnamed
individuals suffering from the oppressions of soldiers. The appalling state
of dearth in this reign becomes the background necessary to explain why
St Cuthbert had to work a miracle for the survival of his devotees on the
Durham estate of Hatherne in Leicestershire. To what now seems the most
important aspect of their stories, the evidence for violence caused by private
war, the clerical authors were basically indifferent.[40] Is this because conditions were not in fact so terrible but were only made to seem so, to enhance
the quality of the miracle performed? Can the hagiographers have really
been so blind to appalling suffering that the only matter of interest to them
was the intercession of the saints on behalf of a few helpless innocents? Such
stories offer no help with understanding the military actions alluded to. We
can draw no conclusions from what is known about victims innocently
caught up in the troubles. References to prisoners escaping when ransoms
for them were withheld cannot be expected to explain whether ransom
agreements were extorted or freely entered into as reparations for damage
caused. It may be natural to suspect the worst, but without knowing more
about the circumstances we must reserve judgment. Untoward occurrences
are still reported regularly, even from police stations; but, despite the hasty
comments of journalists, such incidents do not justify general distrust of
public officials. Miracle stories provide no surer evidence for the general
state of the country in these years.

   The importance all twelfth-century writers attached to what happened in
their own localities did not make them indifferent to the affairs of the

kingdom as a whole, but their local perspective at least prevented them from concentrating their attention on the dispute about succession to the crown. They continued to take the unity of the kingdom for granted, but the information they received about events further afield cannot have been very objective and the use they made of what they heard bears little resemblance to modern practice. Chroniclers were neither trained as journalists to get to the bottom of atrocity stories, nor as historians to analyse causes and understand motives. Their inclination on occasions to burst metaphorically into tears about the current state of affairs needs to be understood in their own terms, and not interpreted as the kind of conclusion required by the rhetorical conventions of modern historical writing. The belief that life was highly disturbed everywhere throughout Stephen's reign relies on the assumption that some notable cases of local violence were replicated all over the kingdom. Only if this were true would it justify the opinion that the king's peace had totally broken down. Instances of violence and private war certainly occurred, for no civil society exists without crime, but such instances as are known hardly add up to the kind of conclusion historians have felt the passage in the Peterborough chronicle authorises.

To offset the impressions created by chroniclers, modern historians rely for more specific information on formal documents. This material is not so useful as might be expected. It may not be generally appreciated how few official records were kept at all in the twelfth century. Modern scholarship has of course been responsible for assembling collections of privileges and mandates issued by rulers from what has been preserved over the centuries, mainly from the archives of religious houses. Twelfth-century royal administrations kept no copies of any such documents, and the fact that kings could rule without recognising any need of an official archive indicates how differently England was then governed. Most men in Stephen's time had very little to do with royal government at all. Yet, without exception, modern historians of Stephen are disposed to contrast the state of disorder under him with what is believed to have been the effective way affairs were managed in the reign of Henry I.

The modern reputation of Henry I's royal administration rests almost entirely upon interpretation of the single surviving pipe roll of the exchequer which audited his financial interests in land and jurisdiction for the year ending Michaelmas 1130.[41] While the interest of this document cannot be doubted, its real character must not be forgotten, not so much a record of government as one showing how the king's agents accounted to him for their management of his lands all over the kingdom. According to the evidence of Domesday Book, the king's stake in the kingdom amounted to less than a fifth of its assets; responsibility for the rest was shared out very unevenly amongst a couple of hundred barons, about fifteen bishops and up to a hundred religious institutions, many with extensive powers of jurisdiction over the lands they held. The king in addition had legal rights of a more abstract kind, also generally supervised in his name by others. Many of his great men, likewise, had similar, if lesser, jurisdictions, but no one of them had resources remotely approaching his. The evidence for royal administration in this 1130 pipe roll indicates what could be done to extract financial advantage from royal rights of lordship. The king is seen to have been prepared to sell judicial favours at a price in matters of particular importance to his feudal vassals, and to have sent royal justices out into the localities to check on the punishment of serious crime (royal pleas). Even if such visitations of royal justices are now regarded as beneficial improvements, rather than as an unprincipled means of screwing extra money for the king from manipulation of the law, they had not by 1130 become an indispensable part of doing justice. The king's willingness to interfere for a price with the ordinary processes of law may not have pleased even successful and generous bidders; those rejected became resentful. A king like William the Conqueror had rewarded his barons generously for their help with his conquest; Henry I made his subjects pay dearly for what they had come to think of as their customary rights. The king's hand also lay heavy on his subjects through imposition of the geld tax, a national burden. Even so, this was collected by locals, not by paid officials of the crown, and was accounted for at the exchequer by sheriffs who themselves paid the king an agreed 'farm' annually for the right to manage the royal interests in their shire. The style of Henry I's administrators was almost certainly not what leading contemporaries appreciated most about their king.[42] Kings themselves did not devote their attention to administrative detail; nor was the effectiveness of royal rule measured by the yardstick of how efficiently specifically royal interests were looked after.

Despite its manifest shortcomings, Henry I's administration has been enthusiastically admired in modern times and Stephen's failure to keep it in effective order consequently deplored. Were it not in fact for the exceptional survival of the 1130 pipe roll, as little would have been known about Henry I's administration as about Stephen's. Comparing or contrasting them is equally difficult. How royal administration was affected by disorder in this reign is largely a matter of surmise. The Henrician system may have been allowed to continue, though at a more gentle pace; in contrast, some historians have believed that it collapsed altogether as a result of Stephen's folly in arresting Bishop Roger. It has also been suggested that it was deliberately replaced by a policy aiming to decentralise government and entrust earls, rather than sheriffs, with local responsibilities. This last idea attempts to build on the observation that most shires in the course of the reign were provided with their own nominal earl and that this must in the nature of things have diminished the former standing of the sheriff as the king's agent.[43] That in Stephen's early years anyone consciously set out to reform shrieval administration is unlikely. Circumstances simply arose for which the appointment of earls seemed the appropriate response; changes in local administration would have simply followed on from this.

The importance historians understandably attach to written evidence explains why they are disposed to interpret any reduction in the sheer quantity of administrative evidence available as conclusive proof that Stephen's affairs must have been less well managed than Henry I's. Yet this argument is not convincing. Analysis of the handwriting of Stephen's original charters has concluded that the actual number of scribes at work producing charters for the king declined during the reign. Yet in his early years the royal chancery is judged to have reached a high point of achievement and the total number of Stephen's known charters (c. 750) is not out of step with those of Henry I (c. 1500) in a reign twice the length, particularly if, in part of the kingdom, the king's authority was ignored.[44] Such figures do not provide adequate proof of serious diminution in the scale of royal activity. More damaging has been the lack of any exchequer records. The survival of the single roll of 1130 raises a problem about why the series was not renewed until the autumn of 1155; the gap between 1130 and 1155 has given rise to the suspicion that exchequer operations had been altogether suspended under Stephen.[45] The 1130 record may, however, create a misleading impression of the general orderliness of Henry I's administration. Without it, the scale of exchequer operations in the early twelfth century would never have been guessed at. The exchequer is barely mentioned in Henry I's own charters and figures as often in Stephen's, relative to the number of documents from a shorter reign.[46] The 1130 roll is regularly cited to imply a categoric contrast between Henry I's and Stephen's administrations. We do not in fact know whether these rolls were normally preserved for more than a year or so under Henry I. They may have been discarded when thought to be no longer useful. Nor do we know for sure whether the lack of rolls for any of Stephen's years is to be explained because no rolls were ever compiled, or because they were simply lost, like most of Henry I's.

For obvious reasons, the early history of the exchequer has fascinated English historians since the eighteenth century. They have tended to describe it with almost the same reverence as was lavished on it by the late twelfth-century treasurer, Richard, son of Bishop Nigel of Ely, in a treatise he composed on its operations.[47] Not surprisingly, Richard attributes to his father, himself a former treasurer, considerable administrative gifts which were devoted to the development of exchequer practice. Nigel's administrative career has, however, further significance for our understanding of royal government because he became a bishop and was written about by the monks of Ely. We are therefore in the fortunate position of seeing how his ability was rated when he left royal service.[48] For the reputation of the exchequer in the 1130s as a sound agency of account, it is not reassuring to realise that the ex-treasurer, Nigel, did not measure up as bishop to the requirements of his monks.

After the death of Bishop Hervey, Henry I made the monks of Ely wait three years before they were allowed to proceed to a new election, and then only on condition that they chose his treasurer, Nigel, nephew of Roger, bishop of Salisbury. Nigel was duly received at Ely with great pomp and immediately promised the monks to be a good guardian of the church and to recover its alienated property. He began, presumably drawing on his experience in the king's service, by appointing a former monk of Glastonbury to be manager of his bishopric. He charged his deputy with compiling a description of all the church's properties in land, rents and services so that nothing should be lost. All the church's valuable plate and gems were also listed. Ironically, this later made it easier for the monks to identify which pieces the bishop himself had been responsible for purloining or losing. For, not surprisingly, Nigel's idea of management, however much applauded in modern times, did not benefit the monastic community at all. First, the community was eased out of control of its own affairs by the bishop's agent. Then, far from keeping his promises to the monks, Nigel pursued his own ambitions, unscrupulously using his church's treasure to meet the costs. Though under Stephen he may seem to have been caught up in the downfall of his uncle, the Ely chronicler describes him as pushing ahead with his own individual programme, deliberately fortifying a strong castle at Ely against the wishes of the monks in order to defy the king. Stephen forced his way into the Isle of Ely and Nigel accordingly fled to the empress, then in 1140 at Gloucester. Nigel's efforts to recover possession of his see proved extremely expensive, both in sending envoys to Rome and in buying off the king's displeasure. For this the monastic community naturally had to pay. As far as the monks were concerned, the appointment of Henry I's most famous fixer as their bishop was anything but a blessing. The Ely chronicler did not appreciate the benefits of being managed by a former royal official. Nor did the monks' own conventional respect for Stephen's kingship falter because of the king's inability to provide immediate remedies for their grievances. No attempt was made to put these local difficulties into a context of civil war. The blame lay entirely with the bishop's misjudgment. For them, it was the bishop's responsibility in the first instance, not the king's, to look after the interests of his church. For the clergy, at least, self-government was the best gift kings could confer on them. They did not live in awe of Henry I's administrative reforms as modern historians think they should have.

The misfortunes of Nigel were firmly attributed by his community not to the evils of the age but to his own ambitions. Nor can they be used to confirm the widespread impression created by chronicles about general calamity. Other ecclesiastical records also show that the religious interests of the professional non-combatants had not suffered overall nearly as much as it might at first appear. The regularity of senior appointments in the church, the arrival of papal pronouncements, even the preaching of the crusade, suggest stable conditions in the kingdom. The extent of the English contribution to the Second Crusade, either in the Holy Land or in the expedition to Lisbon in 1147, has been played down, but contemporary writers liked to stress the strength of the English contingents. On their own showing, they imply that the disorders of the times had not sapped the flow of military piety or exhausted any English enthusiasm for blood and slaughter.

Stephen's reign was also remarkable for the generous provision being made for the order of the Temple by the grants of lands.[49] Both the king and the queen were conscious of the crusading tradition in both their families and accepted their moral obligation to subsidise the Latin presence in the Holy Land. Stephen's father had been killed while on crusade in 1102. In 1118, when Baldwin I, king of Jerusalem, had died, his oldest brother, Matilda's father, had been expected to succeed to the crusading kingdom, but his 'rights' had been preempted by Baldwin of Edessa. Nevertheless, after Eustace's death, Matilda herself became the sole surviving representative of the Boulogne family which had created the crusader kingdom. Substantial provision was made for the Templars in nearly a dozen shires, by the king and queen, by the earls of Derby and Pembroke, and by their tenants as well as by less prominent landlords. On the Angevin side only Earl Miles donated a small property in Wiltshire. Yet it seems unlikely that the Templars would have been endowed by him at all if Wiltshire was a war zone where possession was likely to be disrupted. Over sixty charters survive for Templar property in this reign; but, had the disorder been great enough to suspend the collection of regular revenues and prevent their export, such benefactions would have been mere gestures. The preservation of the documents and the growth of Templar establishments prove the opposite. England, whatever its internal troubles, remained fully in touch with the wider world and continued to play an active part in its affairs. England cannot have been plunged into a debilitating blood bath that drained it of all energy.

The expansion of the Cistercian order and its ability to interfere in English affairs provides an even more conspicuous example of ecclesiastical exuberance. In 1135 there were only six Cistercian houses in England; by 1154, there were fifty-four, including the dozen Savigniac houses, mostly established before 1135, which became part of the Cîteaux bloc in 1147. The new monasteries had been established throughout the kingdom, with a few every year, except in the crusading year of 1147, when as many as seven houses had been founded.[50] Each new foundation represented the keen recruitment of enough new monks to its own mother house, which alone had made it possible to found a 'colony' elsewhere. Buildings were required and liturgical books, if not others, provision of which surely took adequately peaceful conditions for granted. Some of the new monasteries were situated in fairly close proximity to one another, which could be interpreted as a sign of regional isolation; but others were not. Waverley, near Farnham, established daughter houses in Dorset, Oxfordshire, Gloucestershire and Warwickshire; Fountains put down colonies in Northamptonshire, Bedfordshire and Lincolnshire, as well as in Yorkshire and Northumberland; Rievaulx, in Bedfordshire, Lincolnshire, Nottinghamshire, Huntingdonshire, Suffolk and Essex. Monks not only could move about the kingdom and set up new havens of religious peace, they could count on finding patrons and benefactors at some distance from their original bases, making use of familiar secular networks of patronage, which also therefore remained undisrupted by the troubles.

Nor were the Cistercians the only religious order to flourish under Stephen. A recent calculation of the total number of new religious foundations in the reign puts the figure at 175 houses in England, and four in Wales. Apart from Newburgh at the end of the twelfth century, the chroniclers of the age made no comment on these developments. They have to be borne in mind as evidence for a state of affairs rather different from that implied by the Peterborough chronicle's lament that God and his saints slept. Whatever damage older churches had suffered from fire and pillage (for which some great lords are even known to have paid fairly trifling sums in compensation),[51] the massive transfer of assets to new popular religious movements meant that overall the total endowments of the English church were greatly extended in this reign.

Evidence of a different kind about the condition of the church during Stephen's nineteen years comes from the two hundred surviving papal bulls issued for English houses.[52] They show that steady contact was maintained with Rome over the years, not merely by the kings and the legates but by smaller religious houses as well. They eagerly took advantage of such adventitious advantages in the mid 1140s as having an Englishman, Robert

Pullen, as papal chancellor. Pullen had previously been archdeacon of
Rochester and his cousin was prior of Sherborne. Such contacts were
naturally exploited to the full.[53] During this period, Nicholas Breakspear, an
Englishman who eventually became pope, began to rise in papal service and
his origins in Hertfordshire were neither denied nor forgotten. His first great
service to the papacy was his legatine mission to Norway, where his English
past certainly stood him in good stead.[54] The resort of English clergy to
Rome in this period was stepped up to resolve the clergy's own insatiable
appetite for litigation. Rarely did they use their opportunities to demand
papal anathemas on the secular bullies described in the *Gesta*. From the
papal deeds alone, it would be impossible to conclude that the kingdom
was in a state of turmoil: a mere handful have any bearing on the troubles
at all.[55] It is as though two different worlds failed to interpenetrate. The
largest number of surviving papal documents from any one church comes
from Ely, where Bishop Nigel had begun to seek papal help for recovery of
the rights of his see even before he fell out with the king: there are twenty-one
documents, unevenly distributed across the years 1138–40, 1144 and 1149–53.
After forfeiting Stephen's support, Nigel had perforce to turn to the papacy
for help with his problems. His complaints about how his church suffered
reflect his special circumstances, not the state of the kingdom. Encroachment
on ecclesiastical endowments had not waited on the occurrence of civil
disorder. Law suits about ecclesiastical property indicate that 'usurpations'
could as easily take place in times of peace, and may not always have been
without justification, despite what the clergy claimed. The problems of
holding on to benefactions was more general.[56]

Other aspects of church life may be glimpsed in more than a thousand
documents issued by Stephen's bishops. They illustrate interests and activities of the bishops quite different from anything found in chronicles. Not
all their documents can be precisely dated within Stephen's nineteen years,
but most show bishops pursuing all their expected activities without apparent difficulty. References to disturbances, damage to church property or
exceptional conditions in time of war are minimal, perhaps fifty documents
at most, of which nearly half occur in the documents of Gilbert Foliot as
bishop of Hereford.[57] These documents also reveal that monks from Normandy and other parts of France continued to attend to their properties in
England, activities that might have seemed likely to suffer from intermittent
warfare or a partisan approach to politics. If warfare is invoked, it is to
strengthen arguments for the appropriation of churches to mitigate the
poverty of monks, as at Tutbury, or to explain the desperation of the monks
of Fécamp. Some prelates may have offered time of war as an excuse for
their unapproved alienations of their church's property, but abuses could

as easily occur at other times when abbots did their kinsmen favours, a common abuse. An impression of order, not disorder, dominates these clerical records. In times of real disorder documents would not have been issued at all. The distribution of these documents in time across the 1140s and all over the country must help establish that chaos can nowhere have prevailed for very long. Local efforts to restore equilibrium were put in hand before making appeals to the king. Nor do the documents suggest that the clergy ever felt the need to press for extreme sanctions. At the Lateran council of 1139, the pope renewed decrees on the truce of God to contain violence; it was never invoked in England where ecclesiastical councils remained content with excommunicating those who had infringed clerical rights.[58] Warfare as such had not apparently got out of hand. Hostilities were dutifully suspended in Lent and Advent. In general, as the expansion of the Cistercian order implies, personal piety may have been on the increase rather than the reverse.

A different kind of evidence often invoked as having some bearing on the alleged breakdown of authority deserves discussion here. Questions have been raised about the effectiveness of royal government on account of coins issued in the middle of the reign without direct royal approval. In his chronicle, William of Malmesbury noted under the year 1140 a fall in the value of the coined royal penny: 'sometimes hardly twelve pennies could be accepted out of ten shillings or more'. He reported, as rumour, that the king had ordered a reduction in the weight of the coin, because he could not meet the expense of paying for his soldiers.[59] Although this comment is apparently confirmed by the discovery of many light coins, too much ought not to be made of this contemporary, but partial opinion. Comparable comments appear in the Anglo-Saxon Chronicle about the state of the coinage in 1124, so that even Henry I's 'model' government had not been able to prevent monetary abuses. Generally speaking numismatists agree that Stephen's official coinage did not deteriorate in quality. The main interest of Malmesbury's remarks is that he makes no allusion to the issue of any coins other than those by the king, though there is a widespread assumption that during the anarchy unauthorised coins were struck rather freely. Malmesbury does not try to pile up the case against Stephen.

More damaging for Stephen's long-term reputation have proved to be the casual words written at the end of the twelfth century by William of Newburgh, who claimed that under Stephen there were as many kings of England as there were lords of castles, all minting coins of their own.[60] Later historians have happily repeated the charge. Newburgh probably generalised too freely from the peculiar situation in his own part of the kingdom. In the seventeenth century, Robert Brady, a strong monarchist, already depended on Newburgh for his belief that the barons had encroached on the royal prerogative of striking coins. In much more recent times, once numismatics had established that English kings had got a firm grip over the English coinage as early as the tenth century, any infringement whatever of the king's monopoly of the right to coin money (one without parallel in contemporary Europe) became in itself a sign of ineffectual government. A great number of difficulties arise about the coinage of Stephen's reign, not all of which are ever likely to be elucidated. Nevertheless, with something like a total of five thousand specimens surviving, certain aspects of the matter ought to be clear enough.[61]

At the time of his accession, the coinage in circulation had been last struck in 1125, after a considerable shake up of the monetary system due to the large number of dishonest moneyers punished in 1124. Stephen's earliest coins were no doubt struck fairly soon after his accession (perhaps making use of the large supply of silver accumulated in the royal treasury at the end of the previous reign), at the weight and purity of his uncle's coins. The main difference in the two coinages is the revival of several mints which had not issued coins in 1125. For the most part these were in the smaller towns of the south. To argue that the king was here bowing to powerful baronial pressures is impossible. The most likely reason for the return to service of these mints is that local interests were prepared to pay for the privilege, probably for their own convenience, or for the anticipated profit. The sharp fall in the number of active mints in the previous reign after 1125 had no doubt been part of the drastic drive against counterfeit moneying in 1124. The new king in 1135 may have simply been less anxious about the revival of crooked practices.

Four main types of silver penny were struck under Stephen. The largest number of surviving coins belongs to Type 1, which has numerous subdivisions and is assumed to have been struck from the very beginning of the new reign. The experts are not agreed as to how long Stephen's first issue of currency remained in circulation, so the suggestion that Stephen intended to revert to the sytem of changing the coins every few years, which Henry I had sensibly abandoned after 1125, is not provable. Ostensibly there is no reason to believe that Stephen had in mind any calculated reform of the system of minting. His official coins throughout the reign generally maintained both the standard weight and traditional silver content. The coins themselves should be sufficient reassurance that there was no major change, let alone deterioration in the king's money. Numismatists, by their art, expect to arrange the successive types of coin in a sequence, though they have to draw on historical evidence for any precise dating system. This tends to create something of a circular motion to the arguments of historians who cite coin evidence and numismatists who quote historians. Only for the end of the reign, when another royal issue of coins (Type 7) showed a similar pattern of distribution to that for the beginning, do historians and numismatists agree on recognising it as one of the consequences of the political agreement between Stephen and Henry of Anjou. Coins of this type are firmly dated to 1154 and were considered to be of good enough quality in the next reign to remain in circulation until 1158. Comparatively few specimens of these coins have been found.

While the position of the royal money at the beginning and the end of the reign is not in dispute, several problems about the coinage of the middle period remain contentious, since a remarkable diversity of solutions has been proposed. Although the arguments invoke coins in proof, the discussion always turns out to be based on assumptions about political order. The first difficulty is obviously connected with uncertainty about how long coins of Stephen's first type remained in circulation. Coins of this type have been assigned to four distinct categories based on a steady reduction of the king's title on the obverse from *Stephanus rex* to a mere *Stiefne*. This is not itself a sign of deterioration in quality control: such degeneration is a familiar feature of medieval coinages. Some time would be needed to account for this steady development, but certain scholars have curtailed this period by arguing that this coinage must have ceased at least by 1141, when the king was in captivity. This argument is not conclusive and proceeds from a false appreciation of the position in that year. Most recently it has been suggested that the coinage lasted to at least 1145, giving plenty of time for all four of the variants to circulate. If so, the king's government did not lose control of its traditional supervision of the provincial mints during the first ten years of the reign. Since Stephen's authority received an additional boost after Faringdon in 1145, the coinage is not likely to have suffered seriously thereafter.

After Type 1 was given up, however, two new official types (2 and 6) were issued, presumably in succession, for which the dating may be as narrow as 1145–54, with each of barely four or five years each. One peculiarity of the two mid-reign issues is that, although the traditional practices of sending out standard die designs to the mints was retained, there was a marked drop in the number of mints striking these coins: fourteen of the thirty-six mints of 1136 produced no coins at all. Both Types 2 and 6 were geographically confined to the south east of the kingdom. The second problem about them is why, unlike Types 1 and 7, these coins were not struck all over the kingdom. One obvious suggestion would be that during this period the king's authority was not acknowledged outside the central southern zone of Stephen's strength. To some extent, there is no dispute about this. In the west and south west, some of Matilda's supporters continued to defy Stephen's authority. Yet these zones of Matildine influence account for a comparatively small part of the area concerned. If this were the explanation, it might be thought that a breakdown of respect for Stephen would be compensated for by the issue of coins in the name of his rival, The only places which did this were Cardiff, Hereford, Gloucester and Wareham, and, during the short period of her presence there in 1141–42, Oxford.

The Matildine coins themselves, of which rather more than one hundred specimens are known, were much lighter in weight than any of Stephen's official issues. They are not thought to have been struck in great numbers or to have been widely distributed. Places like Exeter or Taunton, where Stephen had had coins struck after 1136, apparently produced no coins at all. In 1994 a hoard of coins found at Box in Wiltshire brought to light for the first time about thirty coins struck in the name of Robert of Gloucester himself at various mints, Cardiff, Cirencester, Bristol and Christchurch, along with a few in the name of his son, Earl William.[62] The significance of these coins has not yet been openly debated. Some coins have also been found in the names of former kings, William and Henry, as though those responsible were unwilling to attribute coin-striking authority to Matilda herself. A small number of 'barons' from this zone are known to have struck coins in their own names, though they bore the head of a crowned king on the obverse. At the very least, these variants prove that, in their own zone, Matilda's friends did not attempt to create an Angevin currency block. Moreover, these coins were issued on such a small scale as to make it difficult to assess their practical impact. They were all of inferior weight, quality and workmanship. In the north, where the Scots had established their dominion, most of the coins were struck in the name of David I or his son Henry, earl of Northumberland. After his occupation of Carlisle, David had easy access to the freshly exploited silver mines in Cumbria and the coins struck at Carlisle represent the beginnings in Scotland of a native coinage.[63] The same is true for those coins struck in Wales. Such curious and interesting features of the coinages of the kingdom's extremities do not, however, reveal much about the state of Stephen's government in the kingdom.

In eight of the forty-eight 1136 minting places, where Stephen's mid-reign issues were not struck, and in a few other places, coins were nevertheless produced in Stephen's name, not from official dies but through ones locally made; invariably, too, these coins were also of lower weight than the official coins. Numismatists label these local coins, which employed a great number of different designs, 'semi–independent' issues and offer a variety of explanations for them. About five hundred specimens are known, one tenth of the total. The failure to obtain official dies for these 'Stephen' issues may be explained in one of two ways: either the loss of contact between the provinces and the 'central' authority, or a wilful assertion of local authorities against the king. These sub-standard Stephen issues were minted at such places as Sudbury in East Anglia, and at Lincoln, Nottingham and Leicester in the midlands. There is nothing about the coins themselves to boost the credit of local earls and the coins themselves give no grounds for thinking that the earls had anything to do with this ostensibly 'Stephen' coinage. The assumption that they did depends on the common belief in the earls' determination to extend their own influence and wealth at the king's expense. Their motives would be not so much political as financial, from not having to pay the king for official dies and from doing a deal with the local moneyers. Why barons should be bold enough to have their own local dies made in defiance of the king, but nevertheless plaster Stephen's names across them, is not explained. These independent issues do not demonstrate any ambition whatever of the great barons of the reign to assume minting powers for themselves. None of the tiresome earls, Ranulf of Chester or Geoffrey de Mandeville for example, who have been accorded such notoriety for being obstreperous, issued coins in their own name or obviously managed to promote 'semi-independent' issues where they were powerful. Out of the thirty-five different types concerned, only five do not actually bear the name of the king.

The interpretation of these five types remains unsatisfactory. Even identifying the 'Robert' whose name has been read on one coin depends on whether the three legible letters of the minting place-name 'ere' are read as referring to Hereford or to Leicester. Only two specimens of these coins are known anyway. Of the ten types of coins with similar ornamental motives, which have been linked with York, five carry Stephen's name. Two of the others bear the name of Eustace, or of Eustace Fitz John; two a name read as Robert de Stuteville; and the last (which has Stephen's name on the reverse side) Henricus episcopus on the obverse. Nobody has offered any plausible explanation as to why these three names should appear on York coins, given that, of the great men designated, only Eustace the king's son had any special responsibility in York, unless Henry 'bishop' refers to Archbishop Murdac.[64] The suggestion that Earl William of Aumâle who was all powerful in York had authorised these curious productions fails to suggest why he should adopt such devious means to cover his 'usurpations', or why he might think it tolerable for Eustace Fitz John and Stuteville to get their names on coins but not his own. The many types of coins involved cannot conceal the fact that there are actually very few specimens extent and the number of types itself suggests that they had an extremely localised circulation. Numismatists are nevertheless scandalised at these breaches in the

1. The prophet Jeremiah points to an attack on Jerusalem. An early twelfth-century depiction of the siege of a town. Note the town wall, the equipment of the military men, the shape of the shields, and the weapons used; the mailed knight wields an axe. Bury Bible, Corpus Christi College, Cambridge, MS 2, fol. 245v. (*Corpus Christi College, Cambridge*)

2. A twelfth-century battle depicting Anglo-Saxons driving off their enemies. The artist took an open fight between disciplined forces in close formation for granted, though there was no more uniformity in the colour of their hauberks than in their horses. From the Life of St Edmund, Pierpoint Morgan Library, New York, MS 736, fol. 7v. (*Pierpoint Morgan Library*)

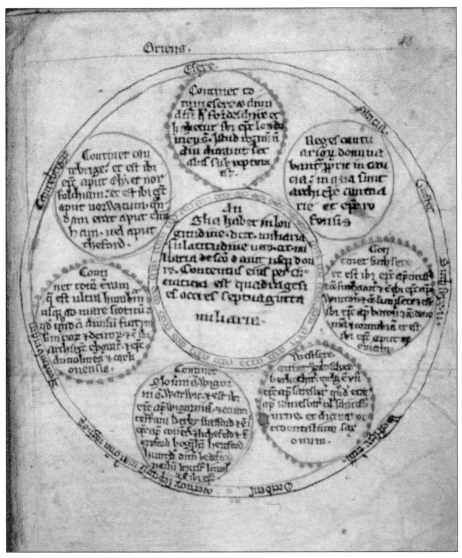

3. Schematic diagram of England, probably devised in the mid twelfth century but copied in the fourteenth century. No attempts to map England in the conventional sense were made until the mid thirteenth century. This schematic diagram, which includes a notice of the bishopric of Carlisle founded in 1133, indicates how England could be envisaged in the mid twelfth century as comprising seven separate regions. It was probably devised to accompany an early version of the Brut chronicle. British Library, MS Royal 13A XXI, fol. 40v, inserted before the texts of Wace's *Brut* and Gaimar. (*British Library*)

4. An initial from a mid twelfth-century Bible from Winchester. The initial shows a delight in providing complicated decoration to enliven the simple outline of the letter. On valuable parchment, no blank space would be left at the end of one chapter before the beginning of the next. To mark the break in the text, artists decorated the first letter of the new chapter in various original and ingenious ways. Bodleian Library, MS Auct. E infra 1, fol. 304. (*Bodleian Library*)

5. Two twelfth-century battles from Holinshed's *Chronicle*: the battle of the Standard (1138), above; the battle of Lincoln (1141), below. A variety of the set-piece pictures were used over and over again in Holinshed's text as ideographs designed to alert readers to episodes of a similar nature. Whatever the original artist had learned from observation of contemporary warfare, he made no effort to reconstruct the conditions of the twelfth century.

6. Seventeenth-century drawing of double-sided comital seals. Top: Waleran, count of Meulan (left); earl of Worcester (right). Bottom: Gilbert Fitz Gilbert, earl of Pembroke (left and right). Most baronial seals were not double-sided. For Waleran the explanation may be that he was both earl in England and count in France. Gilbert's may perhaps be explained comparably in terms of his comital status in Wales and his standing as an English baron. The representation of Gilbert on foot with a spear is apparently unique and has never been convincingly explained. From British Library, MS Lansdowne 203, fol. 16v, and Nicholas Upton, *De studio militari* (1654).

7. King Stephen by George Vertue, from the second English edition of Rapin de Thoyras, *History of England* (1736). The artist has provided visual clues to the nature of the reign: the royal arms, crown, orb and sceptre strewn on the ground; a cherub holding a medallion of the empress; and the genealogy. The demure thistle plant, in the corner, must allude to the problems with the Scots.

8. Stephen's soldiers rubbed with honey at Devizes. R. Caton Woodville's painting of Robert Fitz Hubert's treatment of captured soldiers, from Walter Hutchinson's *Story of the British Nation* (1922). Woodville had had considerable experience of supplying the *Illustrated London News* with artist's impressions of military campaigns (1877–95). Here he applied his talents to staging an episode from the medieval past. Less concerned with the past than creating an illusion of realism for modern spectators, Woodville provides a typical example of how the twentieth century has depicted the middle ages, most notably in the cinema.

royal monopoly, on however slight a scale, and regard this as a major blemish on the reputation of Stephen's government.

The matter of locally cut dies cannot satisfactorily be explained by reference to the great barons, for they even turn up in some of the places where Stephen's authority was sufficient to secure the minting of his official mid-reign coins. Here no barons can be to blame. Other lines of enquiry are possible. The short weight may reflect a shortage of the basic supply of silver. The supply of silver for the coinage generally depended on a favourable balance of trade bringing foreign coins to England, which were promptly recoined in the king's name. Ignorance of the fluctuations of trade in this period makes it impossible to track the variable annual flows of bullion, but this does not alter the facts. Stephen's possession of the county of Boulogne, and his consequent power to oversee the commerce of the Straits of Dover throughout the reign, must have been a considerable asset for his financial buoyancy, not matched by any of his subjects. Bristol's trade with Ireland cannot have been a source of comparable importance for silver, but its commercial network in mid-century may have been extensive: our ignorance must not close our minds to its possible diffusion.[65] In the east, only York may have been on occasion capable of drawing upon continental sources of money, potentially at least, slightly out of Stephen's normal range.

Minting is more closely connected with the urban centres themselves than with the earls. In Domesday Book some urban communities already paid the king the minting dues and, under Stephen, certain urban communities, most of which were on excellent terms with the king, may have taken over closer management of the town's mint and moneyers.[66] They may even have paid the king for the privilege of being allowed to strike some coins by local dies, certainly in those place where good royal coins were also issued. Whether these coin issues should be regarded as 'usurpations' of royal rights is not easily resolved. That official dies simply could not be obtained so near to London as Leicester, Lincoln or Nottingham seems unlikely; it may have been that in the late 1140s (if that is when they appear) local moneyers received some sort of permission to strike coins, provided that they were not at full weight and did not directly challenge the king's issues. Local needs may have tolerated payments in acceptable local coins. The fact that Stephen's name appears on most of these coins is surely proof that they did not aim to reject the king's authority. The appearance of similar, substandard coins in parts of England where the royal authority is not doubted should induce caution about interpreting comparable coins from remoter areas.

A small quantity of exceptional issues is left, for some of which only one or two specimens are known. Why did some of these minor barons strike coins in their own names? It is not likely that such coins were a source either of prestige or of much profit, or struck in deliberate defiance of the king, or for self-glorification. They seem more like impromptu measures to provide for requirements in the immediate locality. The moneyers were inexpert and the silver available inadequate; such coins were not likely to have been highly valued in the marketplace. These were not deliberate attempts to set up a rival monetary authority. The scandalised reactions of a few medieval chroniclers, and it must be said of most modern historians, draw from a pool of outrage very commonly frequented by writers about this extraordinary reign.

However small the number of surviving coins which have nothing to do with the king, they represent an element for which there are no parallels in the English coinage since the tenth century and indicate a notable hiccup in the monetary history of England. This does not justify extravagant assessments of what dreadful consequences flow for monetary stability from the collapse of royal authority. For Henry I's reign, when the king's power was at its height, there were also serious faults found with the coins. Problems with the English royal coinage were not therefore all due to the eclipse of the king's power. What might be different is Stephen's failure to replicate the drastic punishments Henry I had imposed in 1124, but the size of the unauthorised currency of Stephen's reign suggests a very limited circulation. The two situations are not strictly comparable. The way modern knowledge of the coinage has been acquired needs to be remembered. Most of the evidence comes from the study of hoards which were more likely to have been deposited in regions of persistent trouble. What they show is that those anxious to protect their money were trying to hang on to Stephen's coins, not to those of others. This hoard evidence is also unlikely to be very typical of the coinage circulating in those parts of England which remained most loyal and least disturbed by the troubles, areas in fact where coinage moved most readily for economic and commercial reasons. As a corrective, numismatists stress the virtue of plotting on the map the occurrence of single find specimens.[67] From this it appears that the official royal coins held an even more preponderant place in the kingdom's economy than the hoards themselves imply. That there was no shortage of money in circulation is suggested by the evidence for extortion itself. Roaming marauders expected their victims to pay ransoms in cash and even rustics and craftsmen were thought worth taking.[68] The significance of the baronial issues for the affairs of the kingdom must be considered fairly by historians, even if numismatists cannot contain their excitement about the many curious and unique features of the 'baronial' initiative.

The coinage had always been closely connected with the payment of the king's geld taxes and, at least during Henry I's reign, with the settlement of debts to the exchequer. For Stephen's reign, it has proved difficult to assess the coinage in relation to either. On the whole, the richer parts of the kingdom from which Henry I had drawn most of his revenues remained loyal to Stephen. Comparing the known values of the county farms from the only available information in the pipe rolls of Henry I and Henry II, it looks as though the most valuable counties in the zone of Matilda's adherents were Somerset and Gloucester, while the persistent hostilities over Wiltshire and to a lesser degree over Berkshire may be explained by their potential value to the victors. Apart from the loss of the pipe roll evidence from the exchequer itself (not merely for Stephen's reign but for the whole of Henry I's as well, bar one year), there is no reason to suppose that Stephen had difficulties about raising money during his reign.[69] On the contrary, he seems to have found the means to hire soldiers in large numbers almost as soon as they were needed, whereas Henry of Anjou brought mercenary soldiers over in the expectation that they would be satisfied with loot. Apart from Carlisle, in a region of active silver mining, the only mint in a major commercial town outside Stephen's zone was Bristol.

All the various kinds of evidence available about the state of England in the middle years of Stephen's reign highlight the local dimensions. This makes it very difficult to answer the questions posed in modern times about conditions overall. Any faltering in the operations of central government would nowadays seem bound to bring about a breakdown of general stability. In the twelfth century, it would only have brought the effective local authorities out into the open. Though English local government had functioned under the aegis of a united monarchy for at least two centuries, royal supervision of it had always been intermittent. It had to function normally from its own resources and was therefore capable of carrying on, even if royal attention was diverted. In such circumstances, restoring royal power may not have seemed so urgent a requirement.

In most parts of the country local government could not even have simply fallen into the hands of the local baron, because after the Norman Conquest the kingdom had not been carved up amongst baronial satraps. If some great lords took over the supervision of justice in the countryside through their private hundred courts, in most hundreds there was no one great landlord but several; the affairs of its regular court meetings could not have been run by the representative of one baronial authority.[70] Instead, the people of the district, with minimal direction from above, had to secure enough cooperation to provide for their mutual security.[71] The survival of the pre-conquest shire guaranteed a form of local governement by cooperation amongst the principal landlords. Even though the sheriff, as the king's agent, was a more commanding figure, he was not usually of established local family and could only do the king's business by securing the agreement of the landowners with long-established connections in the region. Nor was the sheriff himself a royal official in the modern sense of the term, since he leased his office year by year from the crown for profit. How this worked in detail our sources are insufficient to show.

The modern disposition to see local authorities as subject to the bullying of great lords, eager to take advantage of any faltering in royal power to enhance their own, reflects a modern prejudice not authorised by what is actually known. How effectively did even the greatest lords, like the earls of Gloucester, succeed in dominating their regions? The earl of Chester could not lord it effectively over all his own lands: they were too extensive. Every lordship and shire was riddled with local jurisdictions and exemptions, which in effect created communities feeling entitled to manage most of their own affairs with minimal interference from outside and determined to uphold their privileges.[72] The proliferation of earls with at least some executive powers may represent a conscious intention to leave responsibility for some areas to local forces. Yet it is not actually necessary to posit special conditions for Stephen's reign. Lack of information makes it equally, if not more, difficult to discern how the localities were governed in the reign of Henry I; comparison is therefore otiose. Most modern writers simply suppose that the barons habitually abused their power, taking advantage of royal embarrassments, rather than stepping into the breach for the public · good. This is doubly mistaken. Under Stephen, in the critical year of 1141, many barons had in fact had to cope without royal supervision. They did not apparently seek to prolong the 'interregnum' as more to their liking, rather than welcome Stephen's restoration. At the very least, on their own lands, where they enjoyed clearest direct responsibility for keeping the peace, they could have had no motive to tolerate disruption.

Stephen was an active king, not one content to let disorder take its course. To measure his success in dealing with his problems is not easy, but to conclude from the evidence available that in his hands the kingdom descended into mere chaos is the equivalent of concluding from newspaper reports of crime that it is not safe to walk the streets. The chronicles cannot be taken at face value. Had Stephen as late as 1147 taken advantage of Gloucester's death to carry the war back to Normandy himself, his reign might in consequence have been pronounced an eventual triumph over adversity. That he did not do so has created an impression that the inconclusive situation of the 1140s demonstrated an unacceptable breakdown of government altogether.

7

Assigning Blame

The assembled evidence for Stephen's reign projects contradictory impressions of the state of the kingdom. The repeated laments of the chronicles about violence and disorder have to be read alongside formal documents implying the familiar routines of ordinary life and signs of extraordinary vitality in religious matters. The apparent discrepancy should not come as a surprise. Everyday experience confirms that life is always lived between extremes. Modern periods of warfare and 'troubles' leave some aspects of life untouched and some even enhanced, rather than depressed, by examples of heroism or fortitude. For Stephen's reign, such familiar differences have been usually ironed out to create a simple two-dimensional view: the 'anarchy', Rapin's label for it nearly three hundred years ago. In a sense, the chroniclers' conception has here been allowed to prevail, whereas elsewhere twentieth-century scholarship has deliberately aimed to rewrite the past from more 'objective' sources. Almost alone amongst medieval kings, Stephen is still often treated as a character from a morality play, rather than a ruler with familiar kinds of problems and responsibilities.

Before examining more closely the dilemma posed for us by the contradictory evidence, it is important to confront the prejudice that disorder was simply endemic in 'feudal' times. Our own age is beset with disorder, within and without. In the twelfth century men also grappled with problems still persistent and familiar. Though we pride ourselves on having eliminated the scourge of private war, violence on a smaller scale has not been suppressed at home and in the world at large it has never before been so virulent. In the case of our recent 'troubles', it has not proved easy to agree on the reasons for them, still less resolve them. The lesser problem relating to 'spirals' in criminality remains a controversial issue in politics. There seem to be essentially three positions. Some blame the 'authorities', that is the government or the police, for not treating criminals with adequate severity; some think of crime as due to a lurking criminal element bent on private exploitation of others' assets; others blame social conditions in general for encouraging criminality or for not rescuing the susceptible from temptation or despair. No one of these explanations commands general support on its own. The belief that better laws or righteous rulers will solve all problems is fostered, amongst others, by lawyers and legislators, self-evidently confident of their own indispensability. As their influence in the state has expanded, they have defined an ever increasing number of new crimes and the incidence of criminality has accordingly gone up rather than come down. Though identification of the incorrigibly criminal remains elusive, many pundits are apparently determined to nominate whole categories of likely culprits, from capitalists to shirkers, according to taste, all willing to inflict miseries on the innocent general population. To deflect blame from individuals to social conditions is the modern equivalent of an earlier tendency to blame human sinfulness. Since it diffuses responsibility too widely, it is useless to would-be prosecutors. On that basis, as in the middle ages, only prayer can help.

The evident disagreements about the nature of current problems and how to solve them ought to make us wary of proposing categoric answers to our questions about the twelfth century. A moment's thought will alert us to the pitfalls of taking our information at face value. Events may be wrongly or only partially reported; lack of sympathy and unconscious prejudice also falsify our judgments. Even if the 'facts' are agreed, identifying those responsible is necessarily contentious. For the most part we have only the complaints of the aggrieved. Should we take their word that they were injured innocents? The complaint of the Battle abbey chronicler that in Stephen's reign justice could not be obtained has been quoted as authoritative in an influential modern work, but the chronicler's own 'proof' exposes its worthlessness. For the chronicler, Stephen's failure to restrain the original donor of an estate of three *vistas* from exacting annual monetary dues was only corrected when the abbot succeeded in getting this complaint transferred to Henry II's court. A further grievance concerned churches to be granted to the monastery after the deaths of the incumbents; on account of the longevity of the incumbents, the churches had in the meantime been assigned to other beneficiaries. This dispute rumbled on into the thirteenth century. The monks' rights were evidently not incontrovertible. These highly dubious examples of injustice done to the monks were sufficient for the chronicler. Yet the same text shows that Stephen had given royal support to Battle as a *capella regis* in its dispute with the bishop of Chichester; in a dispute between the monks and the archbishop, the king had also accepted the abbot's plea that Henry I's edict on the rights of wreck became invalid on his death because it had not been approved by the barons. Only when the king did not find in their favour did the monks slander his reputation. From such biased evidence as Battle's, it is not convincing to argue that Stephen did no justice.[1] This is not to deny that there were troubles and many genuine grievances, but understanding what the troubles were all about is not made easier when testimony is so blatantly slanted.

Just as there are still arguments about social problems, so too in the twelfth century contemporaries of Stephen explained the troubles in different ways. The closest the twelfth century came to diffusing responsibility was the *Gesta*'s conclusion that the sins of the English as a whole had become so heinous as to bring down on them the dreadful judgment of God. Nowadays it is more usual to think that men are innocent and God very callous indeed to inflict disasters upon them, but educated opinion in the twelfth century believed that men collectively had no right to take divine benevolence for granted. This view at least saved them from thinking that for every calamity there must be a particular individual at fault. This sense of collective responsibility has been lost. In the process we have forfeited the possibility of grasping a relevant aspect of all social situations. We have, particularly because of the influence of lawyers, concentrated on identifying culprits who can be arraigned, tried and judged. In effect, for Stephen's reign, this means we blame either the king or the 'wicked' barons or, if in doubt, both. In modern terms, this is therefore the equivalent of accusing either the 'government' or individual evil men responsible for what goes wrong in the world; if we cannot make up our minds, we blame the 'system' that allows the wicked to rule. If modern opinion remains divided on who is guilty, twelfth-century critics were anyway less judgmental, mainly because all men were seen to have faults of one kind or another. Nor did weaknesses exclude virtues. Those who thought the king insufficiently awesome to keep the kingdom in peace nevertheless could not bring themselves to condemn his kindliness.[2] Those who took advantage of his sunny disposition were blameworthy. Modern critics take a sterner view of royal obligations. This makes them unwilling to condone rulers like Stephen whom they judge negligent. This is to impose false expectations on the past.

Modern beliefs about political society have had even more damaging effects on the ability to understand feudal barons. They are normally treated as the culprits, whether described as aristocrats, nobles, feudatories or, most recently, mere thugs. In the twelfth century chroniclers may have accused particular barons of committing outrages, but they could not denounce barons in general. At the time they could not be regarded as obstacles to royal government, for they were the ordinary pillars of society. Not that twelfth-century witnesses thought in such sociological terms. They dealt with individuals, not with institutions. If they were reticent about baronial failings in general, it was because some barons were kinsmen of prominent prelates or patrons and deserved respect; those who violated church property or privilege incurred odium.

Whereas educated opinion took social order for granted, it had no respect for professional soldiers, men from outside the 'system'. Such prejudice still lingers. Fighting men, however much respected by their enemies, are often still accused of blood-lust by their educated contemporaries. Soldiers, unless they are patriots, cannot expect favourable notice from historians. Since it is virtuous in soldiers to get on with their tasks rather than to write about them, their opinions are not easily reconstructed. Historians have found this very difficult to allow for, particularly after they began writing about war for civilian populations rather than for noble patrons. This continues to have deleterious implications for medieval history. A peculiar form of social 'order' called feudalism has been foisted on to it in which the relationship between the king and his barons is assumed to be inherently unstable. Whenever kings have problems with their barons, these can then be confidently explained as an inevitable consequence of feudalism.

Many of the difficulties we experience in thinking about twelfth-century England are obviously created by the ways we ourselves choose to approach its problems. We cannot disown our limitations, but we can try to recognise them for what they are. The twelfth-century evidence offers valuable clues about the way contemporaries thought and these can help us understand their situation more clearly. Some writers thought that the troubles of the present stood in sharp contrast to an earlier golden age, an idea still very familiar. This was the view taken in the famous passage from the Peterborough chronicle, where, in contrast to the stern Henry I, Stephen was judged too easy-going, with the consequence that the wicked took advantage of him for their own nefarious purposes. Another familiar contrast was that between England and Normandy. According to Orderic, Ivo of Grentmesnil, the most powerful lord of Leicestershire early in the reign of Henry I, made war on and burnt the lands of his neighbours, a crime almost unknown in England. For this the king exacted a heavy penalty.[3] In Normandy, Orderic simply expected such behaviour, even under Henry I. If forty years later, such occurrences are believed to have become commonplace in England and to have gone unpunished, what was responsible? The baronage as a group had not significantly changed for the worse. If Henry I had not been consistently more successful in containing violence in Normandy, why must Stephen's difficulties in England be explained in terms of his weaker character? The fault lies with our own inveterate habit of blaming the government. At the end of the twelfth century, when William of Newburgh sought explanations for Stephen's troubles, his first idea was similarly to find fault with Stephen's 'softness', but seeing that blaming Stephen accounted inadequately for what happened, he then invoked the machinations of Satan. This way out has become closed to us, but draws attention to twelfth-century assessment of calamities. The clergy had only two alternative approaches: if human wickedness seemed insufficient on its own they fell back on the idea that, by the inscrutable will of God, the Devil was allowed to do his worst.

The outlook of the educated clergy in the twelfth century inevitably influenced the way they reported the affairs of their age and we must therefore begin the investigation into responsibility by assessing these wit- nesses. Like educated persons at all times, they were inclined to disapprove of the whole range of activities they identified as lying outside those of superior persons like themselves. In the twelfth century, those who did not dedicate their lives to God's service were necessarily engaged in unworthy activities. In the hurly-burly of the wicked world, the clergy were the peace-loving men of God, through whose vicarious prayers for forgiveness alone their unregenerate contemporaries might obtain redemption. This attitude to the laity makes the clergy highly erratic witnesses of secular activity. Their preoccupation with the sins of others also made most clergy exceptionally blind to some of their own failings. Only the most austere religious reformers never tired of pointing out that many clergy too often behaved like laymen, castigating their worldliness, sexual promiscuity, greed, quarrelsomeness and pride, and other behaviour at variance with their clerical profession. A few devout exceptions apart, it seems the clergy did not behave so differently from laymen.

Nor was it just a matter of the individual failings of certain clergy; pillars of the ecclesiastical establishment were themselves also responsible for at least some of the difficulties facing the kingdom. The crisis of June 1139, widely regarded as the first serious problem Stephen had to face, was precipitated by the determination of three bishops to deny the king pos- session of their castles. Whether or not their defiance was justified is here unimportant.[4] Their disrespect for royal authority more than matches any baronial high-handedness. Shutting his eyes to the similarities, Huntingdon was outraged by the arrest of the bishops as an affront to the clerical order, using it as the basis of his generalisation that Stephen had always been hostile to the clergy. The blanket condemnation is not a historical judgment; it is the expression of pique and prejudice.

In John of Salisbury's view Stephen's treatment of the clergy was suffi- ciently hostile to warrant criticism of his whole reign as one of unmitigated evil. Salisbury is a writer much respected by modern scholars, but his long sojourn in France had made him critical of English clerical attitudes to the king and he used historical incidents for his own polemical purposes. Writing first for Becket within five years of Stephen's death, he denounced Stephen as a tyrant.[5] With a different grievance uppermost in mind, Salisbury affirmed in 1164 that, though the English baronage had been divided in its support for Stephen, the English church had been consistently loyal, even in his view servile. On both occasions, Salisbury is found, somewhat unexpectedly, berating Stephen for his dominance of the church, and of being capable of driving the unfortunate archbishop of Canterbury into exile twice, in the hallowed tradition of Anselm, thereby setting Becket an example of long suffering even closer in time.[6] This judgment on Stephen is quite at variance with modern received opinion. Clerical writers of the period could therefore arrive at sweeping and contradictory conclusions. They did not share our concern to reach a balanced judgment. They focused attention on the particular ecclesiastical interests they most held dear, Henry of Huntingdon for the church of Lincoln, John of Salisbury for Canterbury and its devotion to the papacy. Their opinions have no value until the reasons underlying them are understood. Faults denounced in the baronage could be found in the church as well. The problems created by these failings go deeper than chroniclers allowed for. The clergy never accepted that they might themselves have any share of responsibility for the troubles of their times. Because of their complacency, the troubles of the reign are still invariably traced back to laymen alone.

Our conception of the difficulties of the kingdom in this reign can be usefully extended by considering how the clergy comported themselves in relation to the papacy. Papal bulls issued for English houses during Stephen's nineteen years may not be a very rich source of information about the damage inflicted on the churches by warfare or secular hostility, but they amply illustrate how the clergy bothered popes with their own endless quarrels. Despite their petty character – the payment or the division of tithes, grievances about boundary disputes, the exercise of episcopal jurisdiction – litigants were prepared to face the expense and anguish of several visits to the Holy See, if necessary, in order to obtain definitive judgments in their own favour. Though it could be urged in the clergy's defence that law suits at least had the merit of offering peaceful solutions, this argument is somewhat specious. Some of these disagreements were so persistent and bitter that on occasion these too flared up into violent actions against both church persons and property.[7] Conditions in England placed no restrictions on these contacts with Rome. Litigants went easily to the curia, returned with desired warrants and expected to get them implemented. Far from cringing and urging peaceful accommodation at all costs in a situation of perpetual danger, clergy confidently took up whatever challenges they met on behalf of their own churches and principles, pursuing their quarrels with relentless determination. Royal weakness did not make clergy more willing to invoke the papacy or the king less able to prevent this. Resort to Rome was typical of the changing situation in the western church as a whole.

England was not in exceptional need of papal protection and not as well placed to benefit directly from it as France.

The factious parties in England used whatever influence they had at Rome in favour of their own interests. As a result, England's affairs were subject to the vagaries created by five successive popes with different agendas during Stephen's reign. The papacy did not wilfully interfere in English affairs, as earlier generations believed, but, dragged into local issues by the English parties themselves, its responses were obviously affected by its own situation as much as by English requirements. The drawbacks of this did not cause litigants to regret their membership of the international ecclesiastical community. Until the death of Innocent II in September 1143, Stephen himself found the pope a reliable ally, but with the expiry of Henry of Winchester's legatine authority, relations with Rome became less predictable. Under Innocent's short-lived successor, Celestine II, they become opaque.

Gilbert Foliot in a letter of 1144 tried to soothe Brian Fitz Count by hinting that Celestine was well disposed towards the empress. Writing in 1164, John of Salisbury also thought of Celestine as a friend of the Angevins, though his brief comments on this are puzzling.[8] According to Salisbury, the new pope had told Theobald of Canterbury not to contemplate any innovations in the matter of the crown because any *translatio* was contrary to law. In Celestine's pontificate, however, Theobald was in no position to contemplate making any changes in the kingship and any ban on a *translatio* would have been to Stephen's advantage not Matilda's. Had Celestine offered advice in connection with Geoffrey of Anjou's effective occupation of Normandy by January 1144? Did the pope then caution Theobald against any precipitate recognition of the rupture between kingdom and duchy? Whatever Celestine intended, Salisbury asserted that his advice, or command, was confirmed by his successors, Lucius II and Eugenius III. That neither Celestine II nor his equally short-lived successor, Lucius II, renewed Henry of Winchester's legatine commission may seem like repudiation of Innocent II's favour to the Blois brothers.[9] On the other hand, neither pope offered Theobald the legatine office enjoyed by his predecessor at Canterbury, though, with the persisting uncertainties about York, Theobald might reasonably have hoped for this. Lucius II was certainly not hostile to Stephen as king and sent to England and Normandy a legate *a latere*, Ymar, bishop of Tusculum, whose mission was cut short within three months of his arrival in 1145 by the pope's death.[10] Lucius's successor, Eugenius III, lived long enough to have greater impact on events. He was not an entirely free agent but a Cistercian who spent most of his pontificate exiled from Rome and some part of it in France, where he was much more accessible to English petitioners and even more susceptible to the relentless exhortations of his mentor, Abbot Bernard of Clairvaux. Bernard's interventions in English affairs were originally prompted by the wish to help the monks of his Cistercian order, particularly those in Yorkshire, who were determined to meddle in the dispute about the succession to Thurstan, archbishop of York, and resist what they denounced as the attempt to impose a royal candidate.[11] The whole extraordinary affair was protracted over fourteen years. One of the king's cousins, William Fitz Herbert, was elected and consecrated, but encountered such opposition that he was obliged to defend his appointment at the papal curia. Rejected by Pope Eugenius, William went into dignified exile in Sicily, where he was welcomed by his kinsman, Roger II, an avowed enemy of the pope. William's disgrace left the way open for Henry Murdac, the Cistercian abbot of Fountains, to become archbishop. Murdac was consecrated by the pope himself but naturally had some difficulty in obtaining recognition from Stephen, who was able to withhold the temporalities of the see for three years. Murdac eventually came to terms with the king on somewhat uncertain conditions, but did not live long after. By a remarkable twist of fortune, William Fitz Herbert returned to the archbishopric after the deaths, at short intervals, of his rival Murdac, of Bernard and of the pope. Within months he too had died, possibly poisoned. He was widely venerated thereafter as a saint.

In the long run the business of the York election was not such an unqualified success for the 'reform' party against the king. It is better treated as another attempt by a special interest group to advance its own cause in an unsettled situation. Like other such episodes, the way things turned out depended upon a host of local variables. Bernard was on excellent terms with Stephen's brother, Theobald of Champagne, lord of the district in which Bernard's monastery of Clairvaux was situated. Bernard also enjoyed amiable relations with Peter, abbot of Cluny, in these years, so Bernard's opposition to the influence of Henry of Winchester in this matter reflected not any supposed rivalry betwen the orders of Cluny and Cîteaux but a personal attack. The failure of the lobby opposed to Fitz Herbert to convince the curia, except under the Cistercian Eugenius, indicates how insubstantial the case against him was. Though issues of principle were said to be at stake, they were not the only factors of importance. When Bernard told Stephen that the troubles of his kingdom were God's way of punishing royal interference with the appointment of a new archbishop of York, he discounted his own part in stirring up trouble in the north.[12]

This was no straight conflict of principle between right and wrong, but one complicated by many factors; we are exceptionally fortunate in this instance to be able to gauge its dimensions. For other quarrels, the evidence is more limited and partial. Clerical intransigence in purely ecclesiastical disputes underlines an aspect of the clergy's own behaviour that can be easily overlooked when reading chronicle accounts of secular violence.[13] The similarities in their behaviour ought, perhaps, to have made clerical observers more sympathetic to the objectives of laymen, but partiality for their own institutions determined their judgments. At Ramsey, for example, Geoffrey de Mandeville was remembered for pillaging the monastery. By the canons of Waltham and the Templars, Mandeville was respected as a benefactor. How can we judge the baron in objective terms from such tainted testimony?

Rather than recognise their human solidarity with laymen, learned clergy in the twelfth century were disposed to exaggerate the fundamentlal diff-erence between the two social orders. The reasons for this merit attention. The whole programme for the reform of the church was conceived as a way of eliminating laymen from any share in the running of the church. Refor-mers demanded for the clergy the privilege of settling all their affairs amongst themselves. If the church asked for secular help, it claimed the right to receive it on its own terms. The clergy here established a precedent deeply prejudicial to traditional notions of respect for royal authority. Nor did clergy who defended their 'rights' acknowledge how much their success owed to the willingness of laymen to surrender traditional powers of patron-age and yet to keep up their contributions to ecclesiastical endowments. Merely to found new monasteries required secular support, gifts of land or seigneurial tolerance of settlements, all of which made reformers dependent on well-disposed secular patrons. Recruitment to the clerical orders was secured by the self-abnegation of laymen willing to accept direction from bishops and abbots. Insistence on a professional clergy of celibates had the consequence that, as the old clerical families, even dynasties, died out, new clergy had to be recruited from secular society. New religious orders, such as the Cistercians, declined to accept boys into the cloister and demanded adult conversions. The new clergy and monks had therefore, necessarily, therefore, themselves been brought up as laymen. Their clerical vocation required them to renounce the kind of life they had led and to entrust themselves to a new kind of society, the clerical order, which had to compensate them for all they had abandoned in the way of natural affections. This was not easy and the new dedicated clergy had to make heroic efforts to distance themselves from ways of life they had been brought up to. Inevitably in the process, they tended to opt out of accepting responsibility themselves for society at large, provided only that their own persons and properties were specially protected.

Simon and Waltheof, the two sons of the early twelfth-century earl of Huntingdon, provide an illustration of the situation. They grew up together and, in spite of their different careers, remained close throughout their lives.[14] Fifty years after the death of Waltheof as abbot of Melrose, the author of his life retailed stories of the way the brothers had played games as children. From childhood, their futures were marked out as distinct by the games they played. A passing holy man prophesied what these fore-shadowed. As the elder, Simon pretended to build castles by piling up boughs from a tree, to bestride a branch as though on horseback and charge, with a wand in his hand, like a lance; the younger, Waltheof, played at being a priest singing mass and opening his arms in blessing. In the pious biography Simon was eventually persuaded by his brother to repent and endow religious houses, but the narrative shows that in life Simon had done everything he could to prevent his brother from giving himself up to religion. When Simon had presented Waltheof to King Stephen, he was angry because his brother's modest attire made him ashamed for his family's reputation: 'You can see, my lord, how my brother, your kinsman does us honour.'

Waltheof, like Ailred of Rievaulx, another Cistercian abbot, had been brought up at the Scottish royal court and turned to religion, disgusted by the smutty conversation and boisterous behaviour of his fellows there. Waltheof may have lived up to his ideals, but the author of his 'Life' regarded him as exceptional and took the opportunity in this work to deplore the way pride in birth, finery and wealth continued in his own day to corrupt not only the laity but the spiritual life of high-ranking clergy. Secular values permeated the whole social order and even the noblest clergy struggled against it. Perhaps because clergy and laity resembled one another so much in practice, clerical writers were obliged to insist on the theoretical incom-patibility between the religious life and life in the world. The less idealistic, that is the great majority of clergy, simply devoted themselves to the particular interests of their own church without concern for the wider implications. Clerical criticisms of secular values could be unkindly repre-sented as deliberate attempts to deflect attention from the clergy's own cussedness. Rather, they were desperate attempts to contrast what was with what ought to be. In practice, though the clergy behaved in many respects no better than others, they were still able at least to claim their privilege of being spared judgment in the courts of laymen. Out of respect for their clerical status, they could expect more indulgent judgment from their clerical peers. The interests of religion as such was not at stake here; it was an issue of privilege and, though laymen might find it difficult to reject the clergy's claims as what was due to God's ministers, they were not all convinced that the clerical arguments were irrefutable.

The attitude of the twelfth-century clergy to the secular life was compli-cated in another respect. Clerical reformers were not content to concentrate on improving the clergy and defending ecclesiastical institutions. Many became committed to finding ways of bringing religious experience into the lives of laymen. In practice this tended to blur the formally sharp distinction between clergy and laity. To put the religious life more within their reach, reformers made surprising concessions to characteristic lay behaviour, as when the Cistercians themselves undertook manual labour and accepted hard-working lay-brothers into their communities. Most extraordinarily, the traditional requirement that a life of religion involved total renunciation of the shedding of human blood was abandoned when fighting for Christ in the crusade was positively encouraged. In the religious military orders, it was officially sanctioned by the church. Justification for this was found by reference to the Old Testament, but the reason for the change lay elsewhere. By approving bloodshed in the name of God, the church accepted that laymen's commitment to the military life was ineradicable and decided to make use of it for the church's own ends.

The idea of the crusade for religious goals has been much criticised in modern times for its irrational blend of idealism and violence, but there are still many educated persons prepared to approve the use of the most destructive force for what they regard as idealistic 'humanitarian' purposes. The twelfth-century conception of war as praiseworthy, if launched for the right motives, still commanded wide support in the twentieth century and cannot be considered a peculiar medieval aberration. However justified the clergy might believe some wars to be, they were never prepared to condone warfare in general and strongly condemned any damage done to the church's own interests: to assail churches in times of war was by definition proof of ungodliness. The clerical attitude to secular enthusiasm for fighting may now seem like proof of their own more civilised outlook, but it must also have prejudiced their ability to understand important aspects of secular society. English church councils in Stephen's reign, for example, took no obvious steps to bring about a general cessation of hostilities (even assuming that it might have been within the clergy's powers to do so). Instead, they concentrated on proclaiming spiritual penalties against those who inflicted damage in times of war against clergy and their property.[15] This looks like a very narrow preoccupation with the clergy's own interests. The same concern for the impact of events on their own particular affairs appears in the comment of the Abingdon chronicle that the dispute between Stephen and Matilda troubled the English church for many years in various ways, as though secular society had not been affected at all.[16] In this frame of mind, it is easier to understand why many clergy took the view that, if they put up castles, bishops were entitled to hold them even in defiance of the king: bishops were privileged and not subject to secular jurisdiction; if they played at soldiers, they still claimed their right to ecclesiastical privilege. Clerical indifference to the real impact of all castles on the total military situation indicates how much their real preoccupation was with the defence of ecclesiastical interests rather than with the cause of religion or morality.

This ecclesiastical detachment from their own role in matters of legitimate concern in lay society makes their writings unsatisfactory evidence for understanding the outlook of most people in the twelfth century. It is not that they were unprincipled in using religion as a justification for their privilege, for they naturally identified their own interests with those of God and exaggerated the chasm between the godly and the unregenerate lay world. Perhaps the very ambivalence in the clergy's own background encouraged them to portray the secular world in its most depraved state if only to strengthen the resolve of those who turned away from it, contrasting religious idealism with the ways of the world they had renounced. From clerical writings it may seem impossible to grasp the real character of secular society, but what temptations the clergy strove hardest to reject probably indicate what twelfth-century laymen enjoyed most: combat and weaponry, women and families, food and drink. At the upper social levels, laymen flaunted fashionable clothing and jewellery, monumental building and lavish entertainment; they were enthusiastic sportsmen, owners of prized hawks, fine horses and hunting dogs. The clergy disapproved in principle of all these worldly pleasures.

Since the great majority of laymen obviously did not share the clergy's outlook on these matters, the clergy cannot be accepted as reliable witnesses for secular behaviour. Yet there is a tendency for historians to treat clerical writers as though they were high-minded, disinterested critics of social vice, the medieval equivalents of the nonconformist conscience, speaking up in the name of religion for the poor and the defenceless. There is no warrant for this assumption, apart from what clergy then and since like to think about their public role. For this period, it is particularly suspect, because of the growing importance of ecclesiastical institutions and their claims to special treatment. The interests of religion did not necessarily gain from the multiplication of new ecclesiastical establishments and the strengthening of clerical power was not a mere consequence of greater respect for God. The clergy did not invoke the sufferings of the poor to stimulate greater charity but to shame evil-doers. The lower orders were not the main beneficiaries of ecclesiastical largesse and were themselves denounced as immoral and brutish. The clergy did not treat the labourers on their estates any differently from the way secular lords did. Far from thinking that the clergy should be regarded as spokesmen for the inarticulate majority, it is important to recognise to what extent the lower orders of secular society had more in common with the great lords. English society was not significantly divided by degrees of wealth, whereas the clergy themselves insisted on the importance of a clear legal distinction between them and the others. This legal barrier was reinforced by clerical confidence in their own moral superiority. Because all laymen by definition declined to enter religion, they were all equally sinful. Those who think gambling immoral draw no irrelevant distinction between the humblest punters on the racecourse and the playboys of the casino. There can be no greater wedge thrust into human society than the one separating the sheep from the goats. The great social barrier raised in modern times by formal education between the educated and the rest had, in the twelfth century, no significance because the greatest men could be as illiterate as the humblest. Social rank depended on quite different criteria. Over matters of importance, such as sport and war, both great and small probably shared common values and interests.

The clergy's own evidence proves that many laymen did not share the clergy's own estimation of their importance as God's ministers, entitled to great respect. Whether this really amounted to irreligion is doubtful. The great number of new religious foundations suggests some widespread enthusiasm for religion, particularly perhaps for new-fangled styles of piety in religious orders consciously breaking with established models. Since many of these also denounced traditional religious practices, lay dissatisfaction with the clerical establishment may be considered to have been endorsed by some clerical reformers. Unhappily for historians, laymen as such were not given to sophisticated defences of their conduct. The enthusiasm of some laymen for religion may have exacerbated tension between the church and their less pious fellows. The sons of generous religious patrons, for example, not surprisingly often attempted to recover alienated properties or secure adequate compensation. The clergy were affronted. The church naturally commended only the consistently devout who humbly accepted clerical direction. It would hardly be surprising, or blameworthy, if many laymen remained hostile to clerical presumption. How can laymen have been expected to show sympathy to clergy who insisted on their entitlement to special privileges and judgment by their 'own' law, and at the same time took the high moral ground and disapproved of the way most men conducted their affairs? The clergy were not all peace-loving bystanders. They were frequently confused, compromised and irresponsible. If historians have been misled by the tendentious evidence, not all the clergy's contemporaries are likely to have been taken in by the clergy's claims to moral superiority. They could see more clearly than we can how self-serving the clergy often were. Laymen who defied sentences of excommunication and were duly denounced by the clergy for their irreverence, were not necessarily hostile to religion as such but rejecting the abuse of spiritual sanctions in worldly affairs. When laymen did not exhibit dutiful submission to the church, the clergy described this as scoffing at religion. Their testimony only proves that laymen were far from living in morbid dependence on the truths of religion in an 'age of faith'. On occasion they treated holy places with scant respect; they pillaged and burnt churches and ecclesiastical property, laid rough hands on clergy and women dedicated to the religious life and covered the clergy with abuse and ridicule.[17] Something more than mere irreligion probably lies behind behind this. Possibly, like the ill-educated of modern times, some twelfth-century laymen simply scorned those who appeared lacking in manly virtues. Simply because we only know what the clergy thought about irreligious laymen, we are not entitled to judge the latter as unprincipled bullies. Laymen may have had sound reasons for their actions. They were not ashamed of their secular state. They struggled to combat the evangelical insistence that religion alone had any lasting significance and nursed such traditional beliefs as the value of heroism and family solidarity. Efforts to make laymen give up their own ways met with little success. Not surprisingly, most were ill-disposed to renounce the world at clerical behest. Some repented and made restitution; their pious ends were duly applauded. Others did not.

The unforgiving clergy's only satisfaction was to contemplate their likely fate in the after life; threatening hell-fire in the next world as a punishment for transgressions was the clergy's main argument. Dramatic changes in lay behaviour are, however, usually attributed to the effect of marvellous occurrences recorded in miracle stories. Religious writers accordingly still attached much importance to miracles as offering the most hopeful path to redemption. The stories they told of human wickedness can be used to create a schizophrenic picture of the middle ages: on the one hand, unregenerate and barbarous; on the other, one of incredulous piety. The source of confusion lies in the literal reading of clerical texts. The medieval world had its usual share of idealistic prophets, but clerical reflections indicate that they were not confident that their world was any more safe for holiness than it has been at other times.

Clear-sighted observation of styles of life they denounced as abhorrent cannot be expected of any cleric. Even on such a standard social institution as marriage, clerical evidence is virtually worthless. Admittedly, many senior clergy still had children themselves, but it was not possible for them to acknowledge their family lives openly. Still more remote from ordinary experience were the monks who have left the most abundant evidence in writing. Their main concerns were their own religious houses. Though monastic chroniclers have to be used by modern historians for want of better evidence, they cannot be accepted as reliable observers of secular affairs. They wrote for patrons or fellow monks, not the general public; their motive was edification not practical wisdom. Monastic chroniclers in their cloistered, self-contained communities naturally felt the least sympathy for the military activities they recorded. Monastic sources become particularly suspect when monastic precincts were themselves invaded or turned into a castle, as happened at Ramsey. At Malmesbury, the castle built there by Bishop Roger was a long-standing grievance to the monks who unavailingly sought papal intervention. Trying to understand the real reasons for the laity's interest in this castle is impossible from the kind of evidence available. What clearly mattered at the time was not what the monks thought, but what the soldiers required. The fortification of a church was considered so heinous by the *Gesta* as to seem the probable explanation for the divine punishment that followed.[18] The clergy simply fail us as basic witnesses of military matters. The force of the clergy's dislike of secular castles probably reflects their fear of them as symbols of a rival, worldly ideal. At the end of the century, William of Newburgh paid them an unexpected compliment when he described monasteries as castles of God.[19] What finer tribute to the idea of the castle can be imagined?

Military activities of prime interest to leading laymen are not easily grasped from what chroniclers have to say about them. They neither looked for convincing explanations of the conflicts nor described their course with any understanding, even on the (dubious) assumption that realistic information about the sequence of violent action is ever possible. The clergy were too concerned about the damage caused to their own property and over the sins of bloodshed committed to ask why exactly fighting might occur at any particular moment. For understanding a reign, exceptionally for England, often noted chiefly for military affairs, chronicles are woefully inadequate guides. Warfare is notoriously difficult for non-combatants, let alone pacifists, to understand. Like armchair critics, clerical chroniclers without military experience were disposed to think that more resolution would, for example, easily have secured the surrender of defiant castles. Their impatience has echoed down the centuries.

Castles presented novel problems not only for chroniclers but for soldiers: some, like Bristol, Wallingford and Devizes, had been so well constructed in stone, according to the most recent technology, that experts were baffled to know how they might be captured. This confirms the good sense of Stephen's insistence on getting Devizes into his hands in 1139 when the opportunity presented itself. Nevertheless, some castles did fall, though more often by treachery than by assault. A major problem must also have been presented by the management of work-forces responsible for the prompt erection of many small, temporary *castella* used in siege operations and the levelling of other fortifications after the surrender of garrisons. Contemporary writers tell us nothing about the logistics involved. What they did notice and complain about were forced labour services from their own properties, which were, in their view, exempt. A rare glimpse of what must have been commonplace is provided by the earl of Chichester's renunciation, possibly after 1154, of demands for money or services in connection with murage (town wall building), cartage (commandeering of transport), and the digging of sand and stone and making lime for his building works from the properties of the cathedral.[20] The number of men engaged on castle-building sites in this reign appears to have been prodigious. Exacting labour services were almost certainly regarded by the builders as within their legitimate rights as lords or agents of public order. The clergy's only interest in such matters was to secure exemption for their own properties from liability for 'public' burdens. They had no sympathy for the intentions of laymen to provide for better security.

The clergy appear to have had no comprehension of the effects of prolonged siege warfare on the military ardour of knights trained for hand-to-hand combat, or on starving garrisons. Even Stephen, who devoted much time to sieges, seems to have chafed at the tedious waiting involved and to have happily seized the chance to leave one siege and set off to arrange for investing another. Typically this has been used as proof of his inability to complete the immediate task in hand. His behaviour may be explained in other ways. The sieges at least contained the devastations contemplated by his enemies and gave evidence of the king's concern for the regions affected. Sitting down before one site and allowing enemies to ravage unchallenged everywhere else was hardly a more sensible strategy. The king was never dilatory. When a long siege was required, as at major castles like Exeter in 1136 or Bristol in 1138, the need to coordinate the forces of his barons and frustration with the lack of progress increased the chances of contradictory counsel. The account of the siege of Exeter has been interpreted to show that Stephen did not get wholehearted support from his own side, without adequate consideration of the circumstances of the operation. The garrison, running short of water, did eventually capitulate, and if Redvers did have friends in the royal camp they did not save him from banishment. The chronicler obviously took a very jaundiced view of baronial support for the king, but in this case the result was not unsatisfactory.

Since the clergy normally disapproved of combat, any hint of admiration in the chronicles for the military virtues of the secular world stands out as exceptional. In the *Gesta*, the author was clearly bothered by conduct that appeared disloyal and treacherous. He despised soldiers who showed more fear than judgment; it was disgraceful to flee in battle; soldiers were dishonoured by drunkenness and debauchery; hurling insults at the enemy was a recognised practice and boosted morale. Overcoming impregnable fortifications was the only way to win fame and glory; the chronicler did not ridicule this as vain and worthless. His narrative is full of wonderfully constructed castles and of ingenious devices designed to secure their capture. There are places where the description of military encounters even conveys a sense of the excitement. At Faringdon, Stephen

> instructed his men to busy themselves with a wonderful task and not without profit, namely, surrounding themselves with a rampart and stockade, that a sudden attack of the enemy might not break in to their confusion but, ensconced in a sure refuge of their own they might both provide more securely for themselves and go to meet the enemy more safely and more boldly when occasion required. And without delay setting up engines most skilfully contrived around the castle, and posting an encircling ring of archers in very dense formation, he began to harass the besieged most grievously. On the one hand, stones or other missiles launched from the engines were falling and battering them everywhere; on the other, a most fearful hail of arrows, flying around before their eyes was causing them extreme affliction; sometimes javelins flung from a distance, or masses of any sort hurled in by hand, were tormenting them, sometimes sturdy warriors, gallantly climbing the steep and lofty rampart, met them in most bitter conflict with nothing but the palisade to keep the two sides apart.

An elegiac tone can be heard in his description of the consequences of Robert of Gloucester's capture in September 1141, when the victors took many knights prisoner and

> gained plunder of incalculable value which was scattered everywhere for the taking. You should have seen chargers finely shaped and goodly to look upon, here straying about after throwing their riders, there fainting from weariness and at their last gasp; sometimes shields and coats of mail and arms of every kind lying everywhere strewn on the ground; sometimes tempting cloaks and vessels of precious metal, with other valuables, flung in heaps, offering themselves to the finder on every side. What am I to say of the knights, nay, the greatest barons, who cast away all the emblems of their knighthood and going on foot, in sorry plight gave false names and denied that they were fugitives? Some fell into the hands of peasants and were most terribly beaten; some concealed themselves in sordid hiding places, pale and full of dread, and lurked there until they either had a chance to escape or were found at last by their enemies and dragged out in shameful and unseemly fashion.[21]

That fighting was not a sport reserved for chivalrous knights appears from another unexpected source, the account written by a chaplain from East Anglia which describes the contribution made by the Anglo-Norman contingent to the Lisbon crusade in 1147.[22] Very little here displays what might be expected of a crusading text. No effort is made conceal the mundane calculations of the fighting force. Some of them openly declared a preference for leaving the Portuguese to get on with the war against the Muslims while they pressed ahead with their own plans for lucrative piracy in the western Mediterranean. The narrative does not gloss the operation.

The main value of the account here, however, lies in the evidence it provides for the capacity of a motley collection of Englishmen from different coastal ports between East Anglia and Bristol to collaborate in launching the expedition to assist the Portuguese against the Muslims. This was done without any noble leadership. The local contingents had leaders of their own, but appointed no supremo. There is no hint in this account that there was a civil war at the time which put Londoners and Bristolians into opposite camps. The text records that the English also fought alongside a contingent from Normandy, by then subject to Geoffrey of Anjou, without even a passing reference to differences of princely allegiance. Moreover, this Anglo-Norman force also acted with forces from Flanders and the Rhineland; that there were clear differences of opinion and outlook did not lead to 'nationalist' quarrels or ructions. Even more remarkably, the English forces expected to settle all their own disputes by general discussion, and declined to delegate responsibility to an inner caucus. Within days of the whole flotilla of 164 ships assembling at Dartmouth in May 1147, they had drawn up regulations for the campaign and sworn on oath to keep the terms. When difficulties later arose, the terms of the *confederatio* were appealed to and it was specifically regarded as a matter of honour to abide by them. There were nearly five thousand Englishmen on this enterprise, a force larger than the population of many towns, yet they managed their affairs successfully by agreement and without formal organisation or social hierarchy. When they met the king of Portugal to discuss the assault on the city, they were not in awe of his status. Some wanted to refuse his terms and proceed on their way; others, more charitably, asked that any fault might be overlooked in the interest of bringing the enterprise to a successful conclusion. The only person of baronial rank identified in the party was a lord from Normandy. The others were quite capable of managing their own affairs and mustering a great force for the agreed purpose from their own resources. These may have been amongst the more adventurous Englishmen of their day, but their exceptional talents of organisation in mid-century must have been first nurtured in their own local environments. The author of the narrative cannot have been a particularly well-instructed clerk; he belonged to no great religious house. He felt close to the soldiers and discharged some military duties himself[23] As a spokesman for the English underdogs of Stephen's reign his credentials are impeccable.

The military potential of the English force in Portugal raises interesting questions about who participated actively in soldiering at home during Stephen's reign. The clerical sources do not help much here. Though the author of the account of the Lisbon crusade may have taken a sympathetic view of warfare, most clerical chroniclers remained 'house-bound' and rarely took any intelligent interest in violent clashes between laymen. Despite the modern orthodoxy that most of the troubles were due to the great barons themselves, chroniclers appear to have treated the military exploits of barons with remarkable restraint, as Malmesbury, not surprisingly does for his patron, Gloucester. This conventional respect for the well-born may have encouraged chroniclers to think of deflecting any criticism of warfare as such onto the mercenary captains from abroad.[24]

The most famous of these mercenaries, William of Ypres, was actually a bastard son of a count of Flanders, and arguably not inferior socially to his own kinsman Robert of Gloucester himself. William sensibly escaped from Lincoln when he saw defeat looming. His good sense enabled him to provide invaluable help to Stephen's party in the aftermath and in due course he enjoyed some recognition as 'earl' of Kent. Chroniclers seem to have saved their greatest hatred for soldiers of foreign birth, chiefly Bretons and Flemings, though both Bretons and Flemings had been familiar figures in England for many years. Even if we could accept the chroniclers' allegations that the chief responsibility for causing most of the damage lay with foreign mercenary captains, like Robert Fitz Hildebrand or Robert Fitz Hubert, we would still be unjustified to endorse these judgments. Not only do we not know their side of the story; they have only too obviously been cast in the role of villains. The author of the *Gesta*, who took an indulgent view of chivalrous combat, certainly had no hesitation about condemning professional soldiers for the destruction they caused in his part of the country. As temporary intruders, mercenaries never became integral members of the local societies they served. Professional shedders of blood, engaged in purely secular quarrels, could not have found any apologists amongst the clergy.

At least some effort ought to be made to appreciate their situation. Hired to do a particular job, they had obligations both to their paymasters and to the men under their command, needing supplies, support and pay in an environment where they had no formal authority to command. Necessarily capable of acting on their own initiative and holding for their employers in terrain of uncertain loyalty, they were expected to fend for themselves, seizing supplies as needed, if cut off from their friends. Chronicle summaries concentrate on the damage they caused to property, particularly of the churches, and the sufferings of the defenceless rural population; but such operations would have been regarded by the soldiers as the traditional means to replenish supplies of grain or livestock, when required.[25] The chroniclers picked out very few individuals for obloquy, and few mercenaries can seriously have considered becoming freebooters. Most were not well placed to take the risk. If they felt betrayed, justifiably or not, they held their castles as best they could. The localised character of the disorder they were accused of exploiting only occurred in zones where traditional authority had already lapsed, through no fault of theirs. For their own security they were obliged to fill the vacuum and create a zone of order in their own immediate vicinity. The local inhabitants may well have appreciated this more than the clergy did. The ability of some captains on occasion to defy their nominal employers successfully demonstrated their own military confidence, and competence. If it understandably out-raged secular authorities, as well as the clergy, it is difficult to believe that the mercenaries could have done this without some cooperation from the districts in which they operated. How otherwise could they have mustered the necessary workforces, auxiliaries and supplies? By carrying out plunde-ring raids further afield and taking the lead in defending the vicinity from revenge attacks, energetic captains could even have become popular local heroes.

Chronicler prejudice against the professional soldiers deployed in England makes it almost impossible to estimate the real importance of this intruded element. Some castellans accused of cruelty and havoc were native barons of some prominence. John Fitz Gilbert, royal constable and castellan of Marlborough, deserted the king and favoured the empress's party. This seems to make him more culpable as a 'traitor' than mere captains hired from abroad. Nor were the local forces helpless victims of sadistic castellans. Wal-ter de Pinkney, another former royal castellan (at Malmesbury), who had seized the castle at Christchurch, was confronted by those who objected to his treatment of them and struck down in church by one of the townsman with an axe (the weapon Stephen himself had wielded at Lincoln).[26] The rest set about Pinkney's men and recovered possession of the castle. The general population was not dependent on the king or others to save them from military men of might. They were combatants in their own right.

The involvement of the general population in combat and the defence of its own immediate territory, if necessary by pillage of neighbouring districts, should not be underestimated. Only occasionally does the *Gesta* reveal that mere peasants or rustics took military action, but fighting was obviously not confined to professional soldiers.[27] This should not be attributed to the lawlessness of the age. In the twelfth century disputes brought to courts of law would themselves still be concluded by personal combat in trial by battle. At Abingdon, a long dispute about pasture land on the Berkshire Downs was settled in this way without prompting the slightest unease in the chronicler.[28] Modern conceptions about the proper use of violence simply have no place. What now might seem obviously intolerable was routine. Nor should this be interpreted with a disdainful shrug as typical of 'feudal' practices. Trial by battle was not mere thuggery: it took place in formal circumstances and proceeded according to prescribed rules. Such actions prove not that society was still uncivilised, but that it was one where men were still expected to provide for their own defence and had no expectation of, even desire for, getting protection from 'authority'. Such social conditions still prevail in certain corners of the civilised world, if only on a reduced scale.

In these circumstances, skirmishes between rival groups of men or neighbouring communities would not have been regarded by the parties themselves as evidence for the breakdown of law and order. They were ways in which wrongs might be righted or avenged or defensive action pre-empted. Since local communities expected to defend themselves, rather than wait meekly for the centralised forces of law and order to rush to their rescue, they cannot always have been victims; they could both ward off enemies and take their own revenge. The burgesses of Southampton inflicted such damage on the forces of Robert of Gloucester that he contemplated retaliation. From this he was dissuaded by some of his other confederates, a seafaring band known as the Veals, who had family connections in the town which they did not want compromised.[29] Here a three-party conflict, quite independent of Gloucester's 'main' political struggle, was conducted according to careful calculation, not instinctive hooliganism. Clerical writers let slip information of this kind, but rarely give much detail. They took no interest in such aspects of conflicts that mattered to secular combatants.

The general importance of townsmen in the military conflicts of twelfth-century England can easily be overlooked. Towns had their own militias and, though most of the evidence relates to their use by Stephen, the forces of Bristol and Gloucester were put at the disposal of Matilda's partisans and at Southampton, they acted for their own purposes. *Burhs* had originally been founded in ninth-century England for military purposes as places of refuge capable of sustaining assault; the construction of castles in towns after the Conquest had by the twelfth century enhanced their military potential. The Normans are usually thought of in English history in exclusively baronial terms, so the importance they attached to towns as centres of organisation can be overlooked. Rouen had a commune before London in the twelfth century. The Jews in England came originally from Rouen and were sufficiently confident of royal protection in Stephen's reign to spread to towns outside London. With over a hundred boroughs accounted for in Domesday Book, it is estimated that one tenth of the English population at this period consisted of townsmen. Stress is commonly laid on the still rural character of much urban activity, but however inchoate their institutions these had begun to take firmer shape in the early part of the century and had received a measure of royal recognition before its end.

Urban communities were flexing their muscle throughout the twelfth century; they had particularly ample opportunities for deploying it in Stephen's time. Rivalries with other towns made them willing to obtain royal and baronial assistance where they could. At Worcester, the men of Gloucester were the enemy.[30] Winchester and London were in competition as proto-capital cities. There was no 'class conflict' between barons and townsmen as such. Many different barons had property in towns, though it was unusual for a baron to have a town entirely under his own dominion, as Leicester was under its earl.[31] Many of the principal engagements of Stephen's reign took place in towns. Lincoln, London, Winchester, Oxford, Wilton, Bristol, York and many smaller places all saw action. Sieges of strongholds rather than battles in open country were the norm. Most towns had to make arrangements to guard their walls; many had militias able to fight at some distance if required. The *Gesta* alone makes passing reference to the employment of the non-knightly soldiers of Barnstaple, Bath, Bridport, Bristol, Cambridge, Christchurch (Twynham), Lincoln, London, Sarum, Winchester and York.[32] To think of them as urban communities vulnerable to unprovoked aggression misrepresents the situation. In 1086 Wallingford was already the first town of Berkshire. Though it received no borough charter until after Stephen's death, its capacity to defend itself under Brian Fitz Count had by then been more than adequately demonstrated.

Towns were much more autonomous than is often allowed for. Many possessed mints for striking coins. For all their various activities there were already local customs, some in writing.[33] Some towns borrowed approved customs from other places. Before the end of Henry I's reign, Lincoln had been allowed to pay the king directly to manage its own affairs without interference from the king's sheriff. If Lincoln was exceptionally favoured, in practice other towns enjoyed degrees of independence. Stephen sent writs to civic authorities expecting them to have the means to discharge executive responsibilities. Burgesses collectively made gifts to churches or infringed their privileges.[34] Urban communities, a few thousand strong at most, disposed of the resources necessary to regulate the ordinary business of their lives, without need of prodding or obvious signs of dependence on royal help. By the next reign, when novel practices of criminal procedure were developed in England, the boroughs' attachment to their own 'borough customs' was sufficiently robust to enable them to resist royal innovations. To later common lawyers, these customs seemed archaic and reprehensible; but in the twelfth century, the ability of boroughs to stand outside the system of common law is proof rather of their desire and ability to run their own affairs themselves. In this, they demonstrate a very familiar trait in English history. There is no reason to think of them as victims of an incompetent royal government, but, like most of their fellow-countrymen, members of communities at least as well prepared as the clergy to look after themselves. The main difference was that they took less trouble than the clergy to record their achievements in writing.

Set in the total context of English twelfth-century life, contemporary expectations and requirements of English kingship are not as easy to assess as is often assumed. Kings still took themselves on tour round the kingdom to show themselves to the people. Though received as king, in each place the king was his people's guest and to that extent at their mercy, as Matilda discovered to her cost at London. Kings were generally aware that they had no power to tyrannise their subjects. Kingship was achieved only with the consent of the people. Even the Conqueror had owed his crown not to the death of Harold in battle but to acceptance at Berkhamsted. There was little rulers could do to boost their personal popularity by 'propaganda'; they lacked the means, apart from royal appearances in public and solemn crown-wearings, at best occasional occurrences. The emphasis on the impersonal demonstration of kingship demanded a religious setting, with the king formally vested in his robes, with the crown as a symbol of his authority. Henry I is said to have neglected such ceremonies; Stephen may have 'appeared' more often.[35] The support offerred Stephen by Londoners appears to have sprung from a more spontaneous, less purely dutiful, loyalty; the commitment of the men of Lincoln to Stephen incurred vindictive vengeance from his enemies. Such slight evidence is hardly adequate for assessment of the general popularity of Stephen's kingship.

Only the greatest men in the kingdom, seculars and ecclesiastics, had such regular dealings with kings individually and in great public assemblies as to develop more of a sense of political relationships. We can perceive their requirements and expectations from the kind of favours they sought. If the senior clergy held to a rather inflexible concept of the mutual obligations of the king to the 'church', the king's dealings with the greatest land owners of the age, his 'vassals', were less stereotyped. These relationships must have been affected by personal preferences, matters that are always difficult for outside observers to understand, but the sources do not make much of such subjective aspects. Irrespective of his personal feelings, the king was expected to behave consistently and respect his vassals, not treat them wilfully. This was itself a challenge. They were not only those most immediately engaged with his affairs but, potentially, the most vulnerable to his displeasure.

The term 'baron' has acquired overtones of meaning which carry some sense of disapproval, but it is still current enough in certain contexts, like 'barons of industry' or 'press barons' to retain something of its twelfth-century meaning. In the twelfth century, when there was still no parliament, let alone a House of Lords, the idea of the peerage was still far off. The barons were not a privileged elite of gracious aristocrats but the real men of power in the kingdom, with whom the Norman kings shared responsibilities of government. Through their lands and vassals they had their own immediate obligations; as persons of consequence, they were expected to raise families who would in turn do kings stalwart service. About two hundred baronial families holding their baronies directly of the king have been identified by historians.[36] All these great men exercised authority over congeries of estates, many of which they had assigned to 'vassals' in return for 'services' performed by men of knightly quality. If only on account of their great military potential, they commanded respect. Kings could not expect to discharge their own public obligations without receiving a substantial show of support from the majority of these men.

Since the Norman Conquest, the English baronage had become rooted in English society. The post-conquest land settlement took for granted the king's need to distribute power throughout the kingdom. Domesday Book shows already that half the kingdom's wealth was shared out unequally amongst the tenants-in-chief. The Conqueror had shown no inclination to offer equal shares all round; he rewarded his faithful supporters in a totally capricious way. Nor did he assume that they would measure out their loyalty to him in proportion to their rewards. At this level in society, inequality may have been accepted as natural rather than unfair. In a general way, it probably gave enough satisfaction to his barons to avert disaffection, though some may have been on the look out for opportunities to enlarge their landed estates on behalf of younger children. In expectation of loyal service and aware of likely common interests between the king and the baron in perpetuating the arrangements, these honours normally passed from father to son.

There was nothing novel about the Conqueror's sharing out the spoils of conquest. Such arrangements had been familiar in England throughout the period of interregnal conflicts since the original Anglo-Saxon settlement and after the Danish successes of Sweyn and Canute. The peculiar importance of the post-conquest settlement was that it was not only much more comprehensive than previous ones, it also proved lasting. The pattern of landholding was not again comparably disrupted until the dissolution of the monasteries released an extensive amount of property for the enrichment of laymen. This sixteenth-century 'revolution' permanently weakened the ecclesiastical estate of the realm and inaugurated a complete reorganisation of social power in England. Comparably, in the eleventh century, the Norman Conquest established a new social order that lasted many centuries. Earlier settlements had perhaps barely endured a generation before being called into question by a change of ruler. By Stephen's reign, however, the Domesday pattern had become an enduring feature of English society. That this called for some adjustment of relations was inevitable, though not necessarily by formal means. Greater cordiality between king and barons could do much.

Henry I had modified these arrangements only in minor ways. By exercising his powers of patronage to dispose of the marriage of heiresses, he was able to promote men in his favour rather than those who were already powerful; by dispossessing great barons who had supported his brother Robert, he provided for his own henchmen. Henry I's affairs had kept him mainly in Normandy, where many of his barons had estates, or at least relations and friends with property. They accepted the idea of the king's campaigning there without signs of grumbling that such wars were no concern of theirs. The nature of disputes leading to conflict meant that they were not necessarily always engaged on the king's side, but even so the king did not invariably confiscate the estates of the defeated. When successful, the king might pardon enemies, if only because he calculated that it was worth buying back their loyalty by proving magnanimous; forfeiture only encouraged endless plotting for the recovery of what was regarded as rightful property. Henry I was a cold calculating ruler, difficult to oblige, but he could be generous and knew what was needed to hold his dominions together. He too accepted that the barons had to be treated circumspectly.[37] Some barons in the twelfth century had only recently been raised to eminence in the kingdom but the newcomers established themselves by the same means as the others had done, through royal benevolence and great landed property. As against those who gained, there were families that faltered. Those who had lost their standing under Henry I inevitably harboured grievances and hoped for better days.

The general situation was not unstable. The tone of the baronage as a whole was set by the great majority who had inherited their responsibilities from fathers and grandfathers, established in England by William the Conqueror in return for their help in his conquest. By 1135, it is unlikely that 'Norman' barons were regarded as foreign interlopers lording it over an oppressed English nation. Though formal pronouncements were still addressed to the king's subjects, both French and English, the expression carried no social implications: it was becoming difficult to separate the two peoples. The barons' own French language and culture were being acquired well beyond their immediate households; they provided leadership for traditional English institutions in local, military and religious affairs. They had constructed a social network out of their tenurial relationships and begun tentatively to prepare themselves for a political role. Quite apart from the different political climate, the geographical extension of the kingdom had slowed down after the early Norman inroads into Wales and Scotland. On the borders of the kingdom, the problems were of a different order: how to hold on to what had been gained, not press for more.

By the time of Henry's death, after thirty years of generally quiet occupation, baronial families, even the newest, took their rights for granted. This generation did not think first of thanking the king for what they inherited from their fathers, whereas those dispossessed by Henry I nursed hopes of recovering their family's lands when he was dead. A sense of family right came naturally to both groups. In Stephen's time, the relation between the king and his barons entered a new phase. Because of his own easy accession, Stephen had neither to reward supporters nor dispossess enemies. Unlike Henry I in 1100, Stephen in 1135 had few landless supporters to provide for and no need or occasion to create a new baronage devoted to his cause. Collectively, the barons had become the substantial core of the body politic. Together, they might be well placed to curb royal whims by offering sound advice or, if provoked, by calling on their friends and dependents to defy the king. If the affairs of the kingdom were to run at all in the twelfth century, the barons had to be satisfied with the way kings conducted themselves. Barons did not, however, easily cooperate for such purposes. Their personal grievances were not necessarily of any concern to other barons. They did not pursue common 'class interests' since they were often rivals for favours or influence. Each was responsible for his own network of men and estates. In this respect, they differed from the clergy, who (despite their own rivalries) accepted at least in principle that they all belonged to a privileged order subject to papal jurisdiction and bound by canon law. The only coherence to baronial activities came from their dependent relationship as tenants-in-chief owing military service to the king.

Yet increasingly the barons began to cultivate a new sense of their own *esprit de corps*, through an informal code of conduct observed by all men of noble birth all over western Europe. Both royal and baronial assemblies provided environments for the cultivation of personal reputations for courtliness in peace and valour in hand to hand combat. To surround himself with distinguished men added to the *éclat* of the king's court. Kingship itself adapted to the new expectations, becoming more ceremonious and less dependent on the church for presenting itself impressively.

'Chivalry' was still in its early days in the mid-twelfth century, but the author of the *Gesta* already takes many of its maxims for granted.[38] A sense of what is honourable in peace and war; the way friendships were made and hostilities resolved; the importance of offering warranties of good behaviour and keeping the terms agreed; the proper treatment of prisoners; respect for envoys come to parley; observance of agreed terms for truces; appropriate behaviour by kings and princes with regard to their own vassals; the importance of taking counsel and kings behaving with dignity and not by whim. These social norms could not be written into code. Disputes were settled by discussion rather than arbitration. When matters were resolved, it was sufficient to shake hands in good faith: 'dextris datis et acceptis' to use the words of the chronicles. Some military men did not happily abide by all these new rules. Ill-treatment of prisoners, for example, suggests that cruelty or revenge could on occasion still prevail over the sense of what decency required. Such lapses occur even in modern times without undermining normal expectations. Allowance should be made for the twelfth century when some military practices had still not hardened into agreed convention.

The adoption of heraldic devices, which had begun in northern France in the early part of the century, had quickly spread to England, but was still not universal amongst the barons in Stephen's time.[39] Heraldry reflected conditions of warfare. Emblems of knighthood acquired extra significance when military shields were emblazoned with patterns indicating affinities of relationships and distinguished ancestry, but knightly shields were still personal. Fighting men did not operate as disciplined troops and wore no uniforms, unlike modern military contingents. Military engagements were opportunities for the display of personal valour. The impetus for personal heraldry came from noble families themselves, not from the king. Because the development of heraldic practices was still in its most fluid personal stage, there was no 'national' flag or symbol for 'England', no lions *passant gardant*, no St George and no red cross on a white ground.

If heraldry grew out of the practices of war, the concomitant growth in the use of seals to authenticate baronial documents was borrowed from the procedures of the royal writing office, reflecting the increased use of written instruments outside the circles of royal government, and baronial familiarity with the sophisticated possibilities of writing. They were not backwoodsmen.[40] The most common type of seal used accordingly came in the form of an equestrian figure with an inscription, derived from the reverse of the royal seal of majesty. In particular the graceful horse found on Stephen's second seal proved a popular model. The types of twelfth-century baronial seals were not fixed and responded to changing fashions in such matters as the choice of horses and preference for the short sword over the couched lance as the favoured knightly weapon.

The most conspicuous sign of noble status had by the 1130s become the stone castle, built to command admiration and to represent stable lordship.[41] Developments in castle-building from the early twelfth century almost certainly did not arise from the exigencies of war but to provide an appropriate lordly residence – offering security, not terror, to dependents. Of course, most castles were constructed in such ways as to make them defensible, but this was expected to be an occasional hazard, not a permanent problem. Built to last, they proved within a short time of their construction that they could indeed be impregnable. As such they became conspicuous features of the landscape for five centuries.

The barons themselves were not ashamed of the military features of their lives. Even making religious benefactions might be symbolised by the laying down of daggers or knives on the altars of the churches. The barons' closest relationships were those with their tenurial tenants who constituted their military strength. To these men, and to the regions where they enjoyed commanding positions, the barons had obligations. Their actions were no more self-interested than those of the leaders of modern trade unions or political parties, who would be outraged if their claims to a superior sense of responsibility for defending the interests of their supporters were dismissed as flimsy fig leaves for their own cold ambitions to obtain power and rule others. The motivation of political leaders is never easy to discern, and always easy to impugn. At least in earlier societies, where leadership was vested in a given social order, there was less opportunity for the purely ambitious to thrust themselves forward. As men of high social rank came of age, they had no option but to assume the unavoidable burdens of their status; they had indeed been groomed for this role. There was no alternative social order in waiting, able to take over if the existing one faltered. It had to work for better or worse.

Faced with unfamiliar situations, the twelfth-century barons may have hedged their bets, put off making decisions, or rashly taken sides according to what seemed best to those they consulted, more or less well-informed, in more or less tight corners. Their actions must have provoked contemporary comment as much as those of great men do in modern times; but, if they made mistakes, their social rank protected them from the consequences of any personal shortcomings. This means that their social and political situations have to be taken into account; on their own, personal failings counted for little. For the most part, Stephen's barons cannot be shown to have taken unfair advantage for themselves, either of his situation or his affability. Much of what is alleged about them is derived from current beliefs about baronial society rather than from any specific evidence.[42]

Since no baron left even a personal memoir about how he viewed Stephen's government, our understanding of the reactions of the twelfth-century baronage rests on what historians have been able to read into the information available about a mere handful of great earls. Earls cannot even be regarded as representative of the great majority: of about two hundred baronial families, only a score or so received the additional dignity of a comital title. What chronicles or documents issued in their names, mainly for the benefit of the religious houses they patronised, may reveal about them hardly enables us to construct their political identities. For most barons, we have even less information. One of the most striking features of the reign, however, is the great increase in the number of English earldoms. In 1135, there were only six earls in England; by 1141 there twenty-one.[43] This in itself requires to be explained somehow. Although historians refer to the creation of earldoms, in fact there is no explicit evidence at all about how earls were created and for what purpose. They were certainly not appointed by charters or issued with instructions about their duties. Probably they were designated in a ceremony, perhaps investiture with a belt or sword of honour, or, more simply, publicly entrusted with a military command. The dates of their 'creation' are not precisely known, since chroniclers only notice their status after it became public knowledge, never at its origin. Earls were not necessarily identified by reference to a shire. Earl Simon (de Senliz), as the only Simon of that rank, rarely had need of any further distinction. In the case of common names like Robert and William, some way of distinguishing them became important. One earl, Robert de Ferrers, was as often referred to by his family name as by either of his shires, Nottingham or Derby.

Stephen's creation of a number of earls has been regarded as a concession to so-called feudal notions of government, but since the new earls appeared as a direct response to some of the early challenges he faced, it is simpler to suppose that they were ennobled to serve a practical purpose. King David's agreement with Stephen early in 1136 about the earldom of Huntingdon, for example, had wider repercussions. David had originally acquired the earldom by his marriage to the widow of Simon de Senliz, to whom she had already given a son, also Simon, more than old enough in 1136 to get recognition of his own claims to his father's and mother's inheritances. Though Stephen admitted David's son Henry to the earldom of Huntingdon, his older half-brother Simon witnessed a royal charter already in the spring of 1136 as earl. Since he is later occasionally styled Earl Simon of Northampton, the lands of his father's earldom may have been partitioned to provide for him.

Even without this, the mere doubling of earls connected with the honour would have diminished the former distinction of the earldom as David himself had enjoyed it. Shortly afterwards, Henry, as earl of Huntingdon, also found himself further hemmed in, when Stephen designated William de Roumara, the earl of Chester's half-brother, as earl of Cambridge and Gilbert de Clare as earl of Hertford; Stephen even had plans in 1137 to make Hugh de Beaumont, earl of Bedford. This looks too deliberate an encroachment on the old honour of Huntingdon to be mistaken for anything but a ploy to undermine the unique standing of the former earls of Huntingdon in the English midlands.

David's determination to interfere in northern England seems to have provoked similar precautions. Certainly this offers the most plausible reason why Stephen chose to recognise a number of new earls there. Already, after the death of Stephen, count of Brittany and lord of Richmond, in 1136, his son Alan was recognised by Stephen as earl; after the battle of the Standard in 1138, the lord of Holderness, William, already count of Aumâle, another Yorkshire baron with a continental title, became an English 'earl', and Robert de Ferrers, lord of Tutbury, earl either of Derby or Nottingham. If these earls were expected to discharge military duties, these moves make sense in connection with uneasiness about Scottish intentions. Comparably, when Stephen made Gilbert Fitz Gilbert earl of Pembroke in 1138 it was surely intended to reinforce the military organisation of south Wales. The next year, the installation of Matilda of Anjou in the west country provoked further military action there. Almost at the same time, in 1140, Stephen is thought to have assigned comital responsibilities in Worcester to Count Waleran and in Hereford to Waleran's twin brother Robert, earl of Leicester. To Cornwall, Stephen sent as earl Alan of Brittany, earl of Richmond. These men were already of comital status; they were not being 'promoted'. In the early part of the reign these responsibilities seemed to be designed as measures for additional military security. Stephen's appointments in this sense pointed the way for Matilda to do likewise.

This impression is strengthened by reference to the earliest known document to deal with the appointment of an earl, amazingly still extant in the original. It records without date that Stephen had made Geoffrey de Mandeville earl of Essex; this was probably some time in 1140.[44] The appointment involved no special concessions of land; without further elaboration, Mandeville is stated to have acquired the familiar rights and duties of the earl's office. Though his appointment cannot be justified in terms of any explicit military threat, his previous standing as castellan of the Tower of London since 1137 underlines his military potential. All Stephen's new earls were chosen from prominent families, most well provided for already with lands, tenants and followings. They were not jumped up men on the make, though a few younger sons of great families without prospects were on occasion promoted. They were chosen as persons trusted to fulfil what was expected of all great men. This means that they enjoyed positions in which they might have to make their own decisions and even act independently. They were not temporary officials, to be easily replaced if they did not come up to expectations. Even when they were generally known by their family name, their office appears to have given them special connections with a particular shire, where they were probably expected to stiffen local military forces, with their own existing retinues.

They made little provision for additional military tenures. The royal enquiry into the provision of knights' fees in 1166 revealed that only about one twentieth of the total fees recorded had been newly endowed since 1135, that is probably in Stephen's reign.[45] Most of the new fees had added very small numbers to the existing provision. A combined extra endowment of nearly 150 knights had been added by only ten great barons, including the earls of Gloucester, Essex, Northampton, Norfolk, and Derby, with the lords of Totnes and Lacy, all in regions of some military activity. In short, the troubles of the reign had had only marginal impact on the provision for extra military tenancies. It confirms the impression that, if additional forces were required, they were hired on a temporary basis and rapidly mustered. Many mercenaries were probably not foreign at all.

Nor can any uncertainty about the reasons for the great increase in the number of earls in this reign be resolved by what is actually known about how they carried out any 'comital' duties. Most, though not all, English shires had earls of their own in Stephen's reign. This would have had implications for the role of the sheriff, as *vice-comes*, if only in military matters and for custody of royal castles: it probably also had a knock-on effect for the collection of revenues from royal estates. If income was spent locally, for example on military purposes, less money would have been paid in at the exchequer audits; the financial attractions for would-be sheriffs in offering lump sums to the king to farm the royal revenues of the shires would have declined. The evidence for some shires shows that the earls' own stewards could act as sheriffs, leaving earls effectively without official rivals. The result has been described as a new style of decentralised government.[46] Though probably not intending to cut back the powers of the crown in general, Stephen may at least have consciously devolved greater responsibility to those he had good reason to trust in regions where he did not expect to exercise direct responsibility himself. Only the assumption that barons were by nature enemies of royal authority makes Stephen's policy seem mistaken and naive.

Some great lords with lands and dependants in exposed positions between Matilda's adherents and Stephen's men may have confronted difficult situations, uncertain quite how to react for the best on occasions of local disorder; unless forced to do otherwise, they may understandably have preferred to keep their options open. Rather than denying Stephen the help he needed in his own ceaseless campaigning, they may have considered their immediate duty to stick to their posts rather than rally to the king's assistance. For us to suppose that we now understand his barons better than Stephen could have done and how they ought to have reacted seems somewhat presumptuous. Our generalisations about the baronage are based on too little hard evidence. Of the earls established by the previous reign, only Gloucester, and on occasion Chester, showed any inclination to foment discord on Matilda's behalf, create mischief for the king or enjoy private war on their own account. Earls Stephen himself had appointed had even less motive to turn against him. Some great barons showed at least a comparable disposition to use their influence to keep the peace and make agreements with one another. Nor did this happen because the king was too weak to pronounce judgments himself. Henry I may have blessed comparable settlements, but no more than Stephen can he be seen regularly engaged in arbitration between his barons.[47]

Since very few earls figure prominently in the chronicles, historians have been obliged to make what use they can of such comital charters as happen to have been preserved. The total is still very small. Moreover, charters at best illustrate what the earls had to give away, who benefited from their generosity and, in their witness lists, who were in attendance on lords at different times.[48] Names which recur probably show who was in a regular position to discuss comital business, give advice and signal to what degree support could be counted on. Charter evidence gives no help at all in getting to grips with the real passions or calculations that led to action. Intermarriage amongst the small number of baronial families created over the generations many different family relationships but family connections were not alone sufficient to create political groupings. Quarrels might be temporarily patched up by marriages that nevertheless failed in the long term to heal antagonisms. The chroniclers report that families themselves were anyway often split, with brothers fighting on opposite sides. The evidence we dispose of only goes part of the way to illustrate the social bonds that presumably counted for something. We know next to nothing about how boys were brought up, as was then the practice, in the households of great lords, where they made friendships, or enmities, for life. Such experiences leave no traces in the formal documents. Great men who met at court, out hunting or in battle presumably established personal friendships with one another based on affinity and admiration or rivalry, dislike or scorn, without this being known to our sources of information – yet no less influential for all that on their conduct in political affairs, even in shaping their own ambitions.[49]

However inadequate our information about them, we have to acknowledge that they were the persons of most consequence in the kingdom. We can at least keep in mind the social contexts in which they operated. Assessing their outlook as though the only things worth knowing about them is what kings and clergy thought of them is inadequate. Royal and clerical records firmly indicate that neither the king nor the clergy cherished any illusions about great men thinking of themselves in the first instance as owing blind obedience to either king or church. Suspicions that they were by nature violent, disloyal and irresponsible arise from nothing better than modern prejudice. The oblique remarks of chroniclers about the sympathy shown for his enemies by some barons in the king's service, thus sparing them from utter defeat, offer no clues as to the reasons for such disloyalty and name no names. Historical analysis can get nowhere on rumour alone. In the earliest instance, that of the revolt of Baldwin de Redvers, his supporters at Exeter did eventually surrender and Redvers was driven into exile. His supposed friends at court did not therefore save him. His cause did not inspire others to follow his example. Any sympathy felt for him must have been related to an unwillingness to break altogether with a person of consequence who had previously enjoyed esteem, even if he had gone too far in his disrespect for the anointed king. From this incident alone it is clear that baronial support for Stephen was not unconditional; but this is not sufficient to make their conduct treacherous. Conditional respect was normal in the twelfth century, for barons were themselves men of consequence whose feelings the king himself needed to take account of. That Stephen occasionally went too far was not a sign of political ineptitude. Such things happen to those in power every day.

In his influential book, Round presented Geoffrey de Mandeville as the archetypal baron, taking advantage of the anarchy for his own 'selfish' ends. If other barons have been suspected of acting comparably, Mandeville still remains the adventurer par excellence, with unfortunate effects on both the barons in general and on Mandeville in particular.[50] His political career was in fact remarkably brief: within four years of his initial appointment as earl he was disgraced and dead. In the twelfth century he was not picked out for particular opprobrium by the chroniclers. In his notice of Mandeville, Huntingdon concentrated on his rampage against the abbey of Ramsey, his final fling, also described at some length in the *Gesta*. Malmesbury mentioned him only in passing as one who had sworn allegiance to the empress, but who had already abandoned her cause to fight for the royalists at

Winchester in September 1141. By this reckoning, the period of Mandeville's disloyalty to Stephen was briefer than that of others who accepted Matilda's *de facto* authority after the battle of Lincoln.

The fullest account of Mandeville's career, given in the *Gesta*, portrays him as most powerful only after 1142, as Stephen's *alter ego*, implying that his reputation had in no way suffered from his behaviour in 1141, now judged highly opportunist. His high standing with the king did not spare him accusations of plotting on behalf of the Angevins and he fell from grace. Surrendering his castles in return for his liberty, he then turned to pure brigandage and was duly punished by God. The *Gesta* believed firmly in Mandeville's treachery. Henry of Huntingdon agreed that he merited punishment. Yet it is now difficult to discern how any calculation of 'self-interest' in 1143 could have induced Mandeville to abandon Stephen. His eminence in Stephen's service would have made him a prime target for Angevin offers, and Geoffrey of Anjou's increasing control of Normandy would have made it possible to tempt Mandeville with the restoration of his grandfather's lands in Normandy in return for betraying Stephen. Yet on losing the king's goodwill, he did not flee to Normandy. Mandeville's standing with Stephen may also have aroused natural envy and prompted the malice of rivals. His refusal to defend himself against charges of conspiracy might as reasonably be explained as the expression of his disdain for calumny as an admission of guilt. The chroniclers were not interested or well-informed about the political manoeuvres that matter to us. They focused on his seizure of Ramsey abbey which he used, when deprived of his castles, as a centre for his revenge, like some desperado without hope of any future. A recent ingenious defence of Mandeville's standing with Stephen in 1142–43 chose to see in him the devoted public servant, one standing in his family's tradition of service to the crown, the secular counterpart to Bishop Roger of Salisbury.[51] This picture of a baronial bureaucrat owes much to later assumptions about political statecraft and seems wide of the mark. When the time came, Bishop Roger as a clerk had meekly accepted demotion; Mandeville wreaked vengeance when he fell, acting like the secular baron he was. The mysteries of his career have been rendered insoluble by the partialities of outraged chroniclers. Round's picture of the typical baron was a very misleading construction derived from his interpretation of four charters and his fixations about feudalism. These charters were still being discussed as the main basis for assessing him about ten years ago. The special interest of Mandeville's career lies not so much with his lack of scruple, but with what it shows about the anxiety of the Angevins to secure the services of a baron with such strong military potential in and about London.

His situation may be contrasted with that of Earl Ranulf of Chester, whose loyalty was not as essential.[52] He commanded no critical salient as Mandeville had done and the extent of his existing properties made purchasing his alliance potentially costly. His estates sprawled across the midlands, making him a powerful influence in the 'provinces' but giving him uncontested control only in Cheshire on the very periphery of the kingdom. Everywhere else, he felt hemmed in by the presence of other entrenched interests. Though he had in 1129 inherited the last surviving of the great regional earldoms of the Conqueror's reign, Ranulf was not satisfied with his considerable assets. Eight years previously, Henry I had taken the opportunity to cut back Chester's pretensions, albeit modestly, when Ranulf's father had been allowed to succeed his cousin; he had also been obliged to surrender his wife's lands to the king. Ranulf may accordingly have been looking forward to Henry I's death as an occasion for reasserting his 'rights' to his mother's property and reclaiming lost parts of his earldom. He has been suspected of strongly disapproving Stephen's concession in 1136 to King David of Carlisle, which had been held by Earl Richard before 1120. His discontent with the Scots appears to be confirmed by the report of the Hexham chronicler that Ranulf had reacted angrily to Stephen's generous reception of Earl Henry in 1136.

Ranulf, despite, or even because of, the extent of his lands, felt squeezed between the resurgent Scots and the disaffected Welsh; he seemed anxious to find allies, royal, princely or comital, to secure his objectives, lacking confidence in his own resources. But he made no regular friends, probably because he was perceived as too powerful in his own right to commit himself completely to anyone as an ally. If at times he seems almost diffident about taking the initiative, this may reflect an understandable uncertainty about how to manage the great interests of his family for the best. The main chroniclers attended to him intermittently, without showing any direct knowledge of his aims or continuous awareness of his actions. Even what they do report indicates that Ranulf was at least as often engaged in settling scores with other barons, including Robert Marmion and Earl William of York, as with the king. He was not allowing himself to be side-tracked. His main responsibility was to defend his own interests which were much more frequently at risk from encroachment by fellow barons than from the king.

This does not make him a part-time actor in Stephen's reign. His extensive properties throughout north central England made him a key player in the kingdom's affairs, but there is no reason to suppose he had political ambitions to settle the issue of the kingship or to disrupt royal government. He is said to have extended his power over a third of the kingdom. Not content with this, modern belief in the overriding importance of self-interest as the barons' motive force ascribes to him ambitions to extend his powers even

further, so that he might rule from sea to sea. To interpret all his behaviour
in terms of what we think of as political objectives is probably a mistake.
Neither by himself nor with his elder half-brother, William of Roumara,
could he indulge any megalomania without taking into account the interests
of the hundreds of men on his extensive estates who regarded him as their
immediate lord. Their importance was proved when he was arrested at
Lincoln in 1146, on suspicion of trying to ensnare the king by seeking help
for his wars with the Welsh. His vassals not only rushed to negotiate for
his release, but, unabashed, repudiated the terms once he had recovered his
liberty. They at least appreciated him, not as an enemy of the king but for
their own purposes.[53]

Allied by marriage to Gloucester, Ranulf was generally inclined to accept
Stephen's kingship, except if the king directly thwarted his own plans, as at
Lincoln in 1140. Despite his responsibility for the king's capture, even before
the rout at Winchester, he was attempting to make his peace with the king's
party. Whatever his discontents, they hardly predisposed him to consistent
support of the empress. For four years, 1142–46, he could have taken
advantage of Stephen's preoccupations elsewhere to do as he pleased in the
north midlands; but, after Faringdon, he was already eager to make up his
differences with the king, who was himself nothing loth to let bygones be
bygones. His recurrent difficulties with the king have been interpreted as
an indication of his hankering after the Angevin cause. More recently his
behaviour has been thought a sign of his 'neutrality'.[54] Not even Chester
could stand aloof. He attempted to adjust to the situations he found, for
better or worse. Given his real power, he may be considered a third force,
but it is striking how little he wished to throw his weight about on the
centre stage. His main concern was to look after his existing assets. The
dreadful consequences of his one bold step, at Lincoln, may have made him
anxious not to seem responsible for worse. He aspired neither to determine
who should rule nor to become an autonomous prince himself. The differences between Earls Ranulf and Geoffrey make it plain how impossible
it is to attribute common characteristics to earls and barons in Stephen's
reign. It is certainly wrong to think of them as a group with common
interests, or individually in some way natural enemies of kingship, bound
to encroach on royal authority. The absence of substantial information about
most of them naturally prompts attempts to generalise from what is known
of a few.

Since Stubbs, there has been a prejudice that under Stephen the barons
showed their true nature because the king, exceptionally, could not, or would
not, put them firmly in their place. The implications of this idea are not
only that Stephen's barons behaved differently from how they had done

before and would later, but also that their behaviour in his time was their peculiar response to the shortcomings of his personal rule. Strong monarchy before and after properly kept barons in their place as royal subjects; under weak kings, barons raised their arrogant heads. Such a conception of relations between the king and the baronage in the twelfth century would be the equivalent in modern times of supposing that the main enemy of government must be the electorate. Only in the most bizarre manner could such a proposition be defended. If democratic governments really do live in fear of losing popular support, they strive to save themselves by doing what will please voters. Governments can only govern provided they are not obstructed by those with the means to do so. An alternative approach is to argue that governments are the mere 'instruments' of dominant social forces. Were such a proposition true, twelfth-century kings would have had no alternative but act as the barons required. Neither of these notions about the relationship between the ruler and the ruled seems appropriate.

If so much historical writing about the 'feudal' period assumes that kings and barons were constantly at loggerheads, it is only because of the erroneous belief that in 'the middle ages' the top of society was composed of ruthless, unscrupulous men disposing of private armies to achieve their own ends. English historians have reconciled themselves to the presence of feudalism, because they believe that such a system was mercifully introduced into what they choose to regard as a highly centralised Old English monarchy and had been arbitrarily imposed in one piece by William the Conqueror. In consequence, English feudalism (quite unlike that in France) could only work 'properly' under firm royal direction. In this way English feudalism can be accepted as effectively 'different' and William I admired as one of those rulers who knew their own minds. Yet William I was just as regularly engaged in confronting his vassals on both sides of the Channel as any other king of his day. Admittedly, having conquered the kingdom, William had himself enjoyed an unrivalled supremacy, but his successors did not expect to survive on his reflected glory. Once the conquest had become an accepted fact, government, in order to survive, as always needed to command the support of those who mattered. Two or three generations after Hastings, rulers had to behave in ways their subjects found acceptable. The good government of the realm required a balance of interests and reconciliation of incompatibles. What made the kingdom work at all was the ability of great men to adjust awkward conflicts of interest and secure the maximum degree of harmony.

Far from accepting that twelfth-century English society involved constant interaction between king and barons as contemporary conditions required, English historians are disposed to think of barons as a constant threat to royal government. There are several strands to their suspicions. The most serious is their concern to present the united English kingship from its inception as bent on creating a strong centralised state, and their inclination to disapprove of any so-called reactionary forces that would hinder its development. For the earlier periods of English history, historians also feel no natural sympathy for powerful, military figures, who are systematically thought of as enemies of peace and order. Like the medieval clergy, whose writings they rely on for their information, historians are inclined to be pacific, educated, even, occasionally, idealistic. Like the medieval clergy, they feel little sympathy for the secular world of the middle ages. Few historians even attempt to be 'fair' to the barons. Some barons are blamed for exercising too much influence over the king; others for recurrent disloyalty; recently, some, perhaps all, have been accused of sitting on the fence. In their defence it has been alleged that they were bewildered and became unruly if the king failed to give them the leadership they needed. Even 'innocent' barons are thus made to look pathetic. If barons are by definition expected to be 'bad', historians only differ about what faults to find in them.[55] They can be treated as pampered children, making elementary mistakes, easily avoidable by the exercise of mere common sense. Whereas the disputants of the seventeenth century are still capable of exciting a strong sense of partisanship, either as Roundheads or as Cavaliers, the conflicts of Stephen's reign have failed to achieve any comparable resonance down the centuries. There is no 'issue' of any interest. If such had really been the case, it might have been more sensible to stress how little the barons chose to fight at all. Instead, the prejudice remains that they fought all the time to no great purpose, because that is all they were good for.

However great Stephen's own shortcomings are judged to be, his barons are usually saddled with considerable responsibility for his troubles. The idea that the barons had no proper regard for legitimate authority of any kind may seem incontrovertible when Matilda's own difficulties in winning baronial respect are taken into account. Yet, if the barons had cared so little for either of the rivals, this alone would make it odd to think of the reign in terms of a civil war at all. In fact, they showed no desire to disrupt the kingdom for their own purposes when the empress arrived in England to stir up trouble for the king. Few barons were willing to take up the Angevin cause. Of the major figures, only Robert of Gloucester proved Stephen's inveterate enemy. His death in 1147 would have brought Stephen's difficulties in the west country to an end, but for the renewed interference of Henry of Anjou. There was never any widespread baronial support for Matilda, except in the spring and summer of 1141 when there seemed no alternative. The barons' attitude to Stephen was never determined by their covert sympathies for a different ruler. Only Gloucester and King David ever attempted to justify breaking with the king on such grounds, and they won few adherents. Even if their show of righteousness were accepted as genuine, it does not account for everything about their behaviour. Both Gloucester and David accorded Stephen respect as king, when it suited them. Blaming the barons for the impasse created by the Angevin party's defiance in the west country is easier than suggesting how the deadlock might have been broken.

The twelfth-century English monarchy's chief purpose was to provide an overarching organisation for the many semi-autonomous institutions of the kingdom. Before the Conquest, the clergy had been the chief advisers of kings since the conversion of England to Christianity had made the unity of the English peoples possible. By the twelfth century, the prominent role of the church had in this respect already begun to decline, mainly because their urgent work of conversion had been completed, but partly too because the church reform movement strove to release the clergy from their compromising relationships with the secular world. Instead the clergy were encouraged to think of themselves as part of the universal church, entitled to privileges that set them apart from others. Not infrequently, this led to rifts with kings, their chief English patrons. Anyway, alongside the clergy, the king needed to establish a new working relationship with the Norman baronage which was bound in duty to the king and gave the English kingdom secular champions with unprecedented unity of background. The importance of this seems to be consistently underrated because imperfectly documented. During the course of the twelfth century the outlook of the secular baronage becomes clearer, through the development of a literature in the vernacular capable of giving expression to their aspirations. In itself this literature expresses their growing confidence in their own values. Twelfth-century barons were not delinquents to be chastised by royal servants but men of good sense who expected kings to respect traditional customs. The church, which looked to Rome for rules, had only limited expectations of kings. It was on the barons that the way the kingship was exercised impinged most immediately.

To be acceptable, Stephen's kingship had to meet baronial expectations. Unfortunately, though the barons must have been the best judges of the situation, their opinions can only be inferred from what is known about the king's dealings with them. This is itself a contentious issue. In part, it must have varied from one baron to another. That Stephen lived in general suspicion of baronial disloyalty has been deduced from what appears to be his habit of having great men seized at his court on supposedly trumped charges of treachery: the bishops in 1139, Mandeville in 1143, Chester in 1146.[56] The idea that Stephen's fears obsessed him is not supported by the testimony of chroniclers, who accepted the truth of the accusations without further ado. If they had reservations, it was only because to arrest great men, however 'guilty', seemed at the time ill-mannered and blameworthy. It seems odd that if Stephen had a reputation for breaking trust, barons continued to turn up unsuspectingly at court, but this may reveal something important about how both king and barons were expected to behave. The barons relied on the king to respect them, even if they knew they were under suspicion; the king, even if threatened, was not supposed to take the most obvious precautions, but rather to treat his barons as gentlemen. The reasons are plain. Stephen might be able to detain the person of the earl, as with Chester in 1146, but could not thereby disarm his vast network of support. By the same token, disputes could rarely be settled on the battlefield.

The interactions of king and baron as of baron with baron were complicated and rested on bargaining and on making arrangements that always left some parties dissatisfied. Summary detention of great lords might on occasion achieve a specific purpose, usually the surrender of castles, but it was risky. Stephen could not go too far. He did not punish the disloyal with further savagery or lock up his victims in barbarous captivity. They were necessarily left to return to their own responsibilities. Whether such arbitrary action was worthwhile would be a gamble every time. Did Stephen's reputation suffer more from this than he gained by his dubious tactics? Stephen must have calculated the risks worth taking. In such cases he was prepared to put practical considerations before good manners. This should not be interpreted as 'weakness'. Breaches of trust might be deplorable, but even chroniclers were prepared to grant that when provoked he had no alternative course of action. Stephen took exceptional measures to defend what seemed to him his royal rights, even against his greatest vassals, and continued to do so until the end of the reign. If he was not always successful in the battles he had to fight, he never allowed anyone to think that he would take defiance lying down. Stephen was resolute in defending the rights of the crown.

In modern eyes, Stephen's treatment of his barons seems feeble because of what looks like his inability to command their obedience and expel his rival. The more his military virtues are stressed, the more baffling his failure in this respect. Some of these difficulties arise from the assumption that twelfth-century English kings normally expected to keep their barons at heel. If Stephen was unable to impose his will, this only exposes his ineptitude for kingship. To explain his failure, it appears sufficient to list his faults and ignore his merits. This whole approach is fundamentally ill-conceived. The argument is completely circular, arguing from the 'facts' to the character, and from the 'character' back to the facts.

Kingship was not an office to be filled only by applicants with ideal credentials. On Henry's death there was some need to find a new king quickly, but even if the selection process had taken longer, the perfect candidate might not have been found – or if found, not have proved ideal. In practice, the kingdom had a stark choice between Matilda and Geoffrey of Anjou or some other kinsman of the late king. Can it seriously be argued that had the Angevins, together or separately, been allowed to take the kingdom unopposed, they could have ruled more successfully? In four months of prominence in 1141, Matilda played her excellent cards so badly as to forfeit all hope of returning to the table. When she refused to recognise Eustace's incontrovertible rights to the county of Boulogne, his mother's inheritance, she offended baronial sentiments and suffered as a result. Matilda may have been accorded a formal power to refuse consent, but to deny Eustace his due was not 'right'. To deprive men of their inheritances unjustly was no fit action of kings. The reactions of the baronage do not betray their selfishness, but their conviction that rulers could not brazenly flout customary law. No rulers are perfect, but to suppose that Stephen's character in some way disqualified him as king is peevish. Faced with a choice between Stephen and Matilda, as successor to Henry I, it is impossible to believe that a mistake was made.

Stephen's problems were not due to his exceptional incompetence as a ruler or to unprecedented disloyalty in his barons. They were compounded by the ability of his rival for the crown to wage war against him in Normandy and England at once. Disputes between kings and barons were not new in Stephen's time. Whatever strength of character Henry I had displayed, it had not saved him from recurrent disputes with his barons which had duly complicated his management of affairs in Normandy, if not in England, after 1102. Moreover, he had had to spend most of his reign defending his own hold on Normandy against the king of France and in the process had become committed to an alliance with the counts of Blois and Anjou. Henry's intentions with regard to Anjou become impenetrable in his last years. He seems to have expected to neutralise the ambitions of Count Geoffrey by marriage, yet by doing so, encouraged Geoffrey to think of taking over Normandy too. How did Henry I imagine the king of France would react to that, let alone his English subjects? Angevin pressure on the duchy itself had been staved off by Henry I and, until his capture at Lincoln, by Stephen. If Stephen's enemies succeeded thereafter in pinning him down in England, it was his misfortune, not his fault. Once the Angevins had succeeded in occupying Normandy, fresh problems arose, but it is unrealistic to suppose that Stephen could have then resolved his difficulties in England by resolute warfare in Normandy. There was too much at stake in the kingdom itself. Even if it could be proved that his difficulties were exacerbated by elements of his character, they more obviously grew out of his situation, a matter on which we are quite extraordinarily well informed.

Instead of recognising the peculiarities of the situation in which all the major parties, king, clergy and barons, actually found themselves in the mid-twelfth century, many historians have preferred to settle for the idea that the main problem lay with Stephen's inadequacies as a ruler. They are surprisingly confident that they have reliable information about Stephen's character and that this key will unlock all the mysteries. In this they are doubly mistaken. The characters of some of the most written about modern rulers still excite great controversy. At any time, evidence about character must be subjective and inadequate. What we know of Stephen's character is derived not from any personal information he left about himself, but from chroniclers, none of whom claimed his personal acquaintance. Domestic chaplains apart, the only educated men who had much opportunity to deal regularly with kings were the great bishops and abbots, but though they may have spoken freely of their experiences in their clerical communities, they did not themselves act as chroniclers. At best, therefore, the authors of our histories knew of the king only at second hand. This makes it necessary to assess what they have to say in the light of the purposes for which chronicles were written and in what frame of mind the clergy set down their information. Their assertions about his motives and character are no more than their own inferences from what they knew of his actions. They had no special insight into policy, in contrast, for example, to what Suger could very understandably relate of Kings Louis VI and VII. This ought to make us sceptical about the value of chronicle glosses on the king's character or his relations with the great secular barons, the core of all rulers' problems in this period.

Malmesbury's criticisms of the king are the ones most commonly cited by modern writers and may be confidently accepted as reflections of Gloucester's views. In itself this makes him a highly partial witness. Even so, Malmesbury happily acknowledged that Stephen had genuinely royal qualities. There are no grounds for agreeing with several modern writers that Stephen was not up to the job. At the worst he proved unable to retain the loyalty of some very influential men. The reason given for this usually stresses the disinterested commitment of a comparatively small number of barons to Matilda as the legitimate ruler. Were they, exceptionally, the only men of principle? Or should they, too, like other barons, be suspected of consulting their own wish to be autonomous? If they may be judged to have respected notions of loyalty, why should this have not also been the case with Stephen's own earls, who surely had equally strong motives to keep him in power? That Stephen 'failed' to control his baronage in general cannot be shown at all.

Stephen was never indolent in office. He was active in dealing with disturbances all over the kingdom. He has, however, a reputation for scurrying from one problem to another, reinforcing an impression of his ineffectualness. If he really had been so inept, how is it that, challenged by the empress and Henry of Anjou, he was still not overthrown and replaced by his allegedly superior rivals? To suppose that wicked barons preferred a weak ruler in order to have more freedom for themselves simply shifts the explanation back to them. Had the barons been arbiters of the situation, they would have been in a good position to deny Henry of Anjou the succession. Modern attempts to portray Stephen as inadequate are not derived from contemporary assessments of his abilities at all. They are based on dubious assumptions about the way twelfth-century kings ought to behave, about the reign as a disaster without parallel, and about the possibility of explaining disaster as the consequence of his weaknesses. That Stephen did not measure up to modern expectations of kingship would have been the least of his worries. Stephen's 'failure' is largely an historical illusion. Stephen stayed the course and provided for an orderly succession. Though he may have been unsuccessful in adequately protecting the king's peace, he was not accused of being remiss in challenging those who disrupted the kingdom. He inspired both loyalty and admiration to the last. On occasion he could be wildly angry and take brutal vengeance, but he was not consistently cruel. He did not allow himself to become discouraged or his enemies to provoke his blood-lust. There was never any baronial conspiracy to dethrone him, provoked by his 'incompetence' or wickedness.[57] His capture at Lincoln was not welcomed as offering the chance of a better, 'legitimate' ruler; his release seemed an urgent necessity, not a deplorable return to incompetent management. When confronted by real dangers, Stephen was capable of effective action. His scattered and occasional enemies could expect his prompt arrival on their heels. His personal courage was never in doubt. Indeed his barons became nervous about his excessive boldness in case he was captured a second time, as very nearly happened at Wilton in 1143. He remained active and belligerent to the end, but died in his bed.[58] In one respect his happy relations with his family may be favourably contrasted with those of his much admired successor, Henry II, whose stormy marriage and headstrong sons embittered the second half of his reign. At a personal level, Stephen was as ideal a king as English feudal society could expect. To deal with the men who counted, both force and tact were necessary. The contrast with Matilda of Anjou only emphasises Stephen's vastly more accomplished performance as a courteous ruler. His affability made him popular even outside baronial circles.

Contemporaries themselves were bewildered that a ruler with so many of the right qualities nevertheless experienced such difficulties. Malmesbury, writing for Robert of Gloucester, could not offer any better explanation than his perjury in taking the crown.[59] Historians do not believe he was punished by God for this and cannot show that the charge of perjury injured his reputation in general or provoked widespread disrespect. Many writers prefer to think of the circumstances of his accession as an alternative explanation for the 'weakness' of his government. This may take several different forms. Sometimes Stephen's seizure of the crown is supposed to have set a bad example and opened the way to general violence. Some accounts claim that, to gain the crown, he squandered his resources on lavish gifts in return for promises of support and forfeited respect by buying friends. These are insubstantial accusations, mere surmise. Stephen's generosity in 1136 was probably much approved. He did not apparently lack for resources when his uncle's treasure had been spent. He was not expelled when his generosity ran out.

Some historians have been so determined to find fault with his character that they perversely misrepresented even evidence given in good faith about Stephen's virtues. Thus the *Gesta*, which insists on his care to take counsel over controversial issues has been used to argue both that he was personally unable to make up his own mind and easily duped by unscrupulous courtiers. Such interpretations do not come from a plain reading of the evidence.[60] Some chroniclers did mutter because he was judged to be excessive lenient towards his enemies, but they found it difficult to condemn his mildness. Mercy was a virtue, even in kings. If anything they blamed those who abused his good nature, rather than the king. Modern writers are less forgiving and uniformly unimpressed by Stephen's mildness. They consider it a weakness and endorse with composure the idea that violent times required violent remedies. By earlier standards, Stephen was a more than passable ruler, not wanting many of Shakespeare's 'king-becoming graces':

> Justice, verity, temperance, stableness,
> Bounty, perseverance, mercy, lowliness,
> Devotion, patience, courage, fortitude.[61]

Much of the determination to find the culprits rests on the belief that the violence reported by the chroniclers was so extensive that only criminal negligence by some one or some group can explain why it was not rapidly suppressed. Conditions cannot have ever become as bad as they have been painted. There was little persistent conflict. Hostilities appear to have been dutifully suspended in Advent and Lent. Soldiers, however bloodthirsty, also respected the conventions of the day, though the chronicles rarely acknowledge as much. The extent of the violence cannot now be measured, but it must have been both patchy and intermittent. The lamentations of chroniclers about the damage to church property and mindless destruction should not blind us to the fact that there were few major confrontations between armies. No great person was ever killed in battle; no great persons taken prisoner were executed or murdered. There is no record of any atrocity comparable to that which disgraced the dispute between Louis VII of France and Stephen's brother, Theobald of Champagne, in 1142, when the king set fire to the church at Vitry-en-Perthois and burnt 1300 people to death.[62] By later standards of civil war, Stephen's may be considered comparatively bloodless. If the rumbling discontent really were comparatively petty, this would have accentuated the uncertainty about how to end it. Each time negotiations to conclude a peace foundered on Matilda's insistence on the recognition of her primacy, an unsustainable claim if Stephen was to remain king and proof of the impossibility of settling the issue with her peacefully. The sticking point had nothing to do with baronial support for her, which was minimal by then. The problem was that she would not countenance Stephen as king at all. Can the barons have been expected to find a way out of this by themselves?

In recent years the willingness of many barons at this time to settle their own disagreements by negotiation has received attention, though apparently with reluctance to recognise its significance.[63] These reservations indicate the strong centralist assumptions of most modern historical scholarship. The ability of disputants to resolve their own quarrels by agreement, choosing perhaps clerical intermediaries but not invoking the king's own help, should be recognised as another sign of that natural orderliness shown by the English crusaders at Lisbon, who could organise a fleet and a campaign without any natural lords at all. The practice of making private agreements between great men to settle disputes can be traced back to the reign of William I, so such settlements cannot be considered untypical of 'feudal' society. They stemmed from the ability to find ways of resolving conflicts in periods when powerful states did not exist and were not missed.

Some students of the reign may accordingly feel even greater impatience that, if they were so 'responsible', the barons did not act more effectively to restore peace after 1142. Nothing could be simpler or more natural. Efforts to this end were certainly made, but invariably foundered. Why? Matilda herself, who had not lived in England since childhood, must understandably have believed it right to continue the struggle on behalf of her son's claims.

At the time it would have been impossible to force Stephen to a compromise, which left him to rule for life, on condition that after his death Henry would recover the crown because Stephen had sons of his own; he could not be expected to sign away their 'rights' to succeed him. The attitude of Matilda's husband remained entirely pragmatic; he had every reason to encourage her to keep Stephen busy in England while he completed his manifestly un-popular conquest of Normandy. Less sympathy may be felt for great lords who continued to wreak havoc in England on account of their abject subservience to Angevin interests. What their national duty required of them now seems obvious enough. By this standard they failed to fulfil their obligations.

In twelfth-century England, as in many parts of the world still, there was clearly no awareness of any such 'national' imperative. Admittedly, the author of the *Gesta* does quite frequently apostrophise England, but mainly as a passive victim of disorder and strife.[64] He has no sense of an English spirit able to inspire patriotic sons to active defence of the kingdom. Stephen himself defies his enemies and responds to the various appeals of his different townsmen, but is in no position to rally the nation or treat his Angevin enemies as foreign intruders. To expect national sentiment in this context is to misunderstand the nature of the problem. The parties remained at variance and could not agree to terms that would give national order priority over other considerations. Even when Stephen had been captured and

> some rejoiced that this might put an end to strife and war, others of deeper
> insight saw that the wrong done to the king could not be atoned for without
> very great prejudice to the kingdom.[65]

The responsibility for dealing with the situation lay indisputably with the king; there was no possibility of some new leader, like the later William Wallace in Scotland, to rally to the kingdom's rescue. The English were dependent on the leaders they had. The *Gesta* claims that some Englishmen despaired to the point of leaving to live abroad; others gathered in small communities near churches in the hope of protection; others, in famine conditions, were reduced to eating the flesh of dogs and horses, or herbs and roots; others just wasted away. But the other evidence available suggests that this can only have been true, if at all, in some very confined places. The foundation of Cistercian monasteries suggests a rather more robust and organised way out for young men eager to retreat from the world altogether.

Only in 1153, faced with a renewal of open conflict did the leaders finally insist on compromise.

> it was terrible and very dreadful to see so many thousands of armed men eager
> to join battle with drawn swords determined to the general prejudice of the

kingdom to kill their relatives and kin. Wherefore the leading men of each army, and those of deeper judgment were greatly grieved and shrank on both sides from a conflict that was not merely between fellow-countrymen but meant the desolation of the whole kingdom, thinking it wise to raze to the ground the castle that was the seedbed of war and then, making a truce between the two parties, to all join together for the establishment of peace.[66]

Why had this realisation not dawned sooner? One of the reasons was that after 1145, the eclipse of the Angevins meant that the whole kingdom did not appear to be suffering, and that at any one time only the locality where conflict temporarily raged was affected. In local affairs, where personal and private grudges were at stake, the 'national' implications were of subordinate importance. At a local level, where the issues could be more precisely identified, tensions were reduced by negotiation. Not until 1153 did it become possible to narrow down comparable differences for the kingdom as a whole and find a form of agreement. This came about when Henry of Anjou returned to press his suit. Though this in effect forced the barons to find a way out, Stephen was still left in possession. Can such a result really be interpreted as evidence for Stephen's ultimate failure? His survival in these circumstances looks more like triumph over adversity.

8

Endgame

The final phase of the reign has been scrutinised in recent years with unprecedented thoroughness: such investigations highlight the extent to which it remains obscure and controversial.[1] The rise of Henry (duke of Normandy in 1149, count of Anjou in 1151, and duke of Aquitaine in 1152) may at first glance look like a triumphant progress of power and esteem, reaching its unstoppable climax with his accession as king of England in 1154. Yet these eventful five years for Henry involved constant activity and bellicosity, matched on Stephen's part by active opposition. The eventual outcome can never have been predictable, still less glumly accepted. Although most chronicle entries were written up only after Henry's final success in England was known, they still tend to stress the difficulties he had to overcome, not his irresistible progress. Had the result been different, even more would have been heard about the strength of the continuing resistance to him. The effectiveness of Stephen's government until the last is bound to appear baffling if the reign is considered more or less a disaster from the first; if contemporaries are supposed to have drawn inescapable conclusions from its course, it is unintelligible. At least until the death of Eustace in the summer of 1153, Stephen continued to entertain expectations that his elder son would succeed him in due course as king and that the future was still to be fought for. Seen in this way, his final years do not seem like a feeble last gasp but further proof of that resourceful persistence he had shown throughout.

Since Stephen has sometimes been presented as a ruler hopelessly dependent on the backing of churchmen to whom he deferred, the way he took a strong line with them in this phase of the reign deserves attention. The first occasion occurred when Pope Eugenius III, from his exile in France, summoned a council to Reims for the spring of 1148. As he had presumably done in 1139, the king decided which bishops should obey the papal summons and stoutly refused Archbishop Theobald permission to cross the sea. His reason is not known. Theobald, however, was determined not to risk incurring disapproval at Rome by any failure to obey the summons, clearly putting this before compliance with the king's will. Theobald's attitude had nothing to do with secular politics. He judged the situation very precarious for his own church at Canterbury. When Henry of Winchester's legatine authority had lapsed in 1143, the archbishop had recovered his own metropolitan standing, such as it was. In 1145 Eugenius III had agreed to confirm Canterbury's primatial rights, as granted by Paschal II to Archbishop Anselm, but this did not provide Canterbury with the authority over York which it craved. According to the norms of papal policy, the death of Thurstan of York had anyway left formal seniority with Theobald at Canterbury and the Roman privilege was therefore a mere gesture, conceding nothing controversial.

What part Theobald played in the protracted wrangling about the succession to Thurstan at York is totally passed over in silence by the sources, but it is impossible to believe that he did not try to influence the outcome at all. In 1154 Theobald achieved one of the greatest successes ever of the Canterbury see in getting his own archdeacon into the archbishopric of York. Theobald may have been contemplating such a coup for over a decade. By 1148 the long dispute over the immediate succession to Thurstan had recently been resolved when Henry Murdac, abbot of Fountains, with the backing of Bernard of Clairvaux, was consecrated archbishop in December 1147 by Eugenius III at Trier, without the king's approval. Murdac's standing with the pope was bound to make Theobald jittery early in 1148 that York would steal a march on him, above all if he himself remained absent from the papal council and was suspected there of having put obedience to the king before his respect for the pope. He cannot have been content to see Bernard and the Cistercians interfere in the northern province. Theobald perceived that he could not allow the pope to be entirely guided by Bernard on English affairs and that his own appearance at Reims was imperative.

Stephen, like other kings, cannot have been expected to subscribe blindly to Canterbury's policy and might in principle have preferred an archbishop at York not subordinated to Canterbury's ambitions. Despite the temporary setbacks when his nephew, William Fitz Herbert, failed to secure papal confirmation of his election as archbishop (though the affair had dragged on for four years), and the irregular election of Murdac, Stephen's resources were not at an end. In return for royal acceptance of his appointment, Murdac himself, when the time came, showed willingness to plead Stephen's interests with the pope. The king did not therefore share Canterbury's assumptions about how the English church should be run in Canterbury's interests. The king and Theobald had divergent priorities with regard to York.

The depth of Theobald's own anxieties about the situation is shown by his willingness to defy the king and escape to Reims. According to John of Salisbury, this episode prefigured Becket's own comparably surreptitious departure in 1164 and echoed those of Anselm in the previous reign. Since

Salisbury provides the fullest account of what followed, some allowance must be made for the reasons why he presented Theobald in such a heroic light and portrayed Stephen as a tyrant.[2] Yet the outline of the story as he gives it must in the main be true. It shows that Stephen stood no nonsense from Theobald, promptly reacting to his unauthorised departure by sequestering his lands. Theobald's attempt to counter this by pronouncing an interdict failed to command much respect. Stephen was himself spared personal excommunication; according to Salisbury, only by virtue of Theobald's own saintly pleadings on his behalf with the pope. For whatever reason, Stephen took his time about being reconciled with Theobald. If anyone, it was the archbishop, not the king, who had been humiliated, though Salisbury of course does not admit as much.

The strength of Stephen's position in the English church was further demonstrated when the pope presumed to replace Robert, bishop of Hereford, after his death at the council. Eugenius selected an English prelate at Reims, Gilbert Foliot, abbot of Gloucester, a monastic friend and collaborator of Theobald. When the archbishop, still abroad, summoned three English bishops to come out and join him for the consecration of Foliot, however, all three refused on the grounds that the king's rights to a say in the election had been infringed. Theobald, rebuffed by his own suffragans, fell back on the expedient of finding some French bishops to help him in the ceremony. Once consecrated, however, the new bishop immediately returned to England and submitted humbly to the king in order to receive the temporalities of his see. The pope could not have been more pointedly shown the real power of Stephen in his dealings with the English episcopate and the impossibility of imposing ecclesiastical censure on a king, even one who had so blatantly interfered in what the pope considered his own business. Shortly afterwards Murdac also returned to England. Though this took longer, he too realised that his prelacy was inoperable until he secured royal recognition. Even his predecessor, Thurstan, took longer than this to resolve his differences with Henry I. By 1148 it was clearly impossible for English bishops to think they might browbeat the king into accepting their demands. Salisbury was scathing about their weakness (as he saw it): the baronage might be in two minds about the king, but the clergy were united in their submission to him.

These intrigues at Reims have also been credited with a political dimension. Foliot had, according to Salisbury, been recommended to the pope by French clergy at the council, on the understanding that Foliot would do homage to Henry of Anjou. At the time of writing, in 1164, Salisbury's interest in Foliot's behaviour in 1148 was that it prefigured his untrustworthy behaviour not only towards Becket, another archbishop betrayed by him, but to Henry II himself. What actually occurred in 1148 was of far less interest and importance to Salisbury than his beliefs in the 1160s about Foliot. Outside his pages there are no grounds for thinking that the pope or the archbishop had any reason to compound their difficulties with Stephen by adopting a candidate unacceptable to him for the see of Hereford. In 1148 Henry of Anjou had not even become duke of Normandy. In England, the empress's party, often presented as dominant in the west country where Foliot had been abbot, was by 1148 on the point of disintegration. After Earl Robert's death in October 1147, Gloucester abbey's contacts with the king may have become less awkward. Can Foliot's presence at the council have been authorised by the king?

The west country did not generally lie beyond the king's reach. Robert of Hereford himself, for example, certainly went to Reims with Stephen's blessing, chosen perhaps to inform the council about the true state of affairs in the kingdom. Salisbury's word is not adequate proof that Foliot had attended the council as an 'Angevin' representative. The most likely reasons for Foliot's episcopal promotion lie not only with Theobald's advocacy but with his own curial contacts. He had already met Eugenius III the previous year in Paris and wrote regularly to the pope about his various problems. Had Foliot 'gone over' to the Angevins at this point, it would have been regarded as a great coup for them. Salisbury's account of how Foliot returned to England and did homage for the temporalities of the Hereford see was obviously designed to insinuate that Foliot had betrayed his Angevin friends. His apparent volte-face is, however, something of an illusion created by Salisbury, who had reasons of his own to misrepresent Foliot. In the present context, this does not totally discredit Salisbury's evidence about the strength of clerical respect for Stephen, which was only incidental to Salisbury's narrative. For Salisbury this story demonstrated that in 1164 Henry II was only acting as tyrannically as Stephen had done years before. This must affect perception of how Stephen operated in general. If Stephen enjoyed such deference in the English church, it undermines the familiar argument about Henry II's recovery of powers which Henry I had formerly exercised and Stephen had lost.

The evidence for Stephen's authority at this time may be reinforced by reference to what happened the following year, in 1149, when Henry of Anjou reappeared in England and persuaded his great-uncle, David of Scotland, not only to knight him but to invade northern England again, this time in alliance with Ranulf, earl of Chester.[3] Since Stephen's recovery of the crown in 1141, David had not ventured into England beyond the limits of the diocese of Durham, and his reverse over the appointment to the bishopric there in 1144 must have discouraged futher adventures. Plans to descend on York in 1149, probably concerted with Murdac to install him there as archbishop, must be considered excessively optimistic. If David thought to take advantage for himself of Henry's arrival and renew his own bid for authority in northern England, it would have proved a political error. Had it succeeded in launching a military campaign, a Scottish attack would have provoked hostility and compromised Henry's credentials in England itself. Since the whole episode was misconceived, it might be more generous to see it as a mere gesture intended to give David's promising great-nephew some encouragement: Henry may well have been itching to make a military showing somewhere. On its own the rump of support for him in the west country could not, or would not, rally enough strength to launch an impressive challenge in the south. As it turned out, Stephen had no difficulty about raising the forces needed or in getting them north quickly enough to cause the break up of the coalition. The collapse of Henry's escapade obliged him to withdraw to Normandy, sent back by his own English sympathisers, it is said, to muster more support from the Continent if he seriously proposed to assert his claims in England. This Henrician adventure had been no more successful than others in winning him friends or prestige.

Leaving aside Wallingford, the only parts of the kingdom where Stephen's kingship was disregarded in 1150 lay in the west country. Even there Stephen undertook campaigns in both 1150 and 1151 against Worcester, where the situation was exceptionally complicated. The lordship of the city had been entrusted by Stephen in 1140 to Waleran, count of Meulan, whose French base had subsequently made composition with Geoffrey of Anjou in Normandy unavoidable. Geoffrey no doubt urged Waleran to do his best to retain his Worcester earldom; Waleran's brother in England, Robert of Leicester, therefore kept a watchful eye on it. Though not otherwise known for active hostility to the king in England, Leicester dutifully defended Worcester for reasons of family solidarity and in this way frustrated Stephen's intervention. His fraternal concern did not amount to tacit adherence to Stephen's enemies and the king no doubt understood the situation perfectly well. By modern standards, Leicester's actions leave no room for harbouring illusions about his respect for the king, but in 1150 notions of loyalty and duty were not necessarily so uncompromising. Leicester took it for granted that his brother continued to have rights in Worcester which it was his own duty to defend, even against the king. Though the notion seems odd to us, it was probably not at the time considered tantamount to treachery.[4]

Theobald had also come to terms with the king and recovered possession of his see by 1150.[5] Theobald's docility with Eugenius had duly paid off: at this point he became resident papal legate for the whole kingdom of England.

At Rome, this could be seen as a useful device which simply confirmed his *de facto* seniority over Murdac at York without pronouncing on the intrinsic rights of Canterbury over York. If archbishops of Canterbury were denied the permanent primacy they aspired to, they might at least lord it over York as papal representatives, on condition that they introduced no innovations. Rome also expected Theobald as legate to get Murdac installed in his see. Murdac would not object to the extent of Theobald's authority since it would serve his interests too. Murdac was in fact reconciled with the king and entered York as archbishop in January 1151.

How Theobald intended to exercise his new role in the English church is by no means clear. Some writers believe it gave him the confidence to change his political sympathies. He did not, however, openly oppose the king and had returned ostensibly to make his peace. One of his first acts as legate was to ordain one of his own clerks, John of Pagham, as bishop of Worcester, an action of no obvious benefit to the dissidents of the west country and in its own way an indication that Worcester, irrespective of Waleran's position there, was still fully part of the kingdom. When Theobald summoned his first legatine council to London in March 1151, Stephen and Eustace as well as the English nobility were present.[6] Murdac himself went to Italy, where he spent Easter (8 April 1151) with the pope, happy enough for an excuse to be absent from Theobald's council.[7] Theobald may have relished the occasion he found to humble Henry of Winchester, who was three times required at this council to answer objections to his authority at Rome on appeal, the details of which are not known. The surviving canons of the council dealt with illegal secular exactions, part of a more general attempt to mop up the outstanding problems left over by earlier disorder. There was, however, no sign as yet of disagreements between king and legate.

Writing after 1154, Huntingdon claimed that the following spring Stephen had himself summoned the clergy in April 1152 and required Archbishop Theobald to consecrate his son Eustace as king.[8] According to Huntingdon, Theobald refused, on the grounds that the papacy had forbidden the elevation of Eustace as king, because it seemed that Stephen himself had broken his oath to obtain the crown. Stephen, 'who had never loved the clergy', flew into a rage and tried to coerce the clergy into doing his will. In exasperation, he seized their property, and Theobald again went into exile in Flanders, where he spent less than six months. Much has been made of Huntingdon's story, but it is actually difficult to be confident as to what exactly lies behind Theobald's refusal. The two most interesting features of the story are Stephen's plan for a French-style coronation for his heir and the role of the papacy. The coronation proposal must at the time have excited a great deal of discussion among those more closely involved than

Huntingdon himself is likely to have been. Could Stephen have actually underestimated the degree of opposition to his plan? Would this amount to another sign of his political ineptitude? Huntingdon gives no hint that Stephen's ambitions were considered ludicrous, only that Theobald saw no way to foil him, other than to plead papal instructions. Stephen's mistake over the aborted coronation ceremony in 1152 may have been to try and seal the future by introducing a French novelty as the best means to his end.

The proposal to crown Eustace probably originated in France itself. Louis VII had returned from the crusade in 1150 to find Henry of Anjou installed as duke of Normandy by his father Geoffrey. Louis had initially contested Henry's position and Eustace, already established on the Continent as count of Boulogne, had joined Louis, who was after all his brother-in-law, in Normandy for the campaign. Because joint-kingship was familiar in his own kingdom, Louis could very well have suggested Eustace's coronation as an appropiate means to safeguard his future. Stephen's reconciliation with Murdac had given him the chance to deploy Murdac's good offices to sound out the papacy on the matter and it was for this reason that Murdac had gone to the curia in 1151. Murdac clearly had no reason to believe that Eugenius had become an avowed enemy of Stephen's kingship, and his willingness to speak on Stephen's behalf indicates the degree of his deference to the king . After Murdac had, nonetheless, returned empty-handed in the summer of 1151, Louis VII had anyway been coerced by military action to recognise Henry as duke in August 1151. In a few weeks the situation was changed again by the death of Geoffrey. When Henry set about asserting himself in Anjou, the alliance between Louis and Eustace was promptly renewed. By the spring of 1152, Henry had mastered his difficulties there and had returned to Normandy to prepare his descent on England. These were the circumstances in which Stephen put pressure on Theobald in April to crown his son, still apparently unaware that the papacy had tied Theobald's hands. Did Theobald simply plead papal instructions to evade Stephen's orders? Given the situation in the spring of 1152, Theobald's unwillingness to comply with the king's demands certainly makes him seem potentially disloyal, but can his motives have been strictly political?

Because Huntingdon does not mention it, the report in monastic annals that, in April 1152, the earls and barons swore oaths of fidelity to Eustace as Stephen's heir probably at a council in London is usually overlooked.[9] If the immediate motive was to pre-empt Henry of Anjou, Stephen could point to the precedent in 1117, when oaths had been sworn to William, Henry I's heir. A few months later when David of Scotland's only son, Henry of Northumberland, died, the old king followed Stephen's recent example of preparing for the succession. David sent his young grandson, Malcolm, round the kingdom to receive oaths of loyalty as his heir.[10] In modern terms, Malcolm's title to succeed David may seem unimpeachable, but in mid-twelfth-century Scotland it was unprecedented for a son, let alone a grandson, to succeed to the throne. Malcolm was, moreover, under age when David died the following year. His 'rights' to succeed were, not surprisingly, challenged, though previous public recognition of Malcolm as David's heir in his life-time in the end proved adequate to establish Malcolm's claim. In England, it might likewise have succeeded in its purpose. Stephen's son, Eustace, was in 1152 already capable of taking his father's place. Such brief mention of him as appears in the chronicles suggests that he was a young man of energy and ability, capable at an early age of military activity and trusted by his father. No one knew when Stephen would die, but Eustace would certainly be a very acceptable successor and undoubtedly in a good position to assert his rights. In other respects, Stephen was so obviously behaving like a king that it would have been unthinkable to treat him as though the days of his dynasty were already numbered. The acceptance of Eustace as heir by the secular baronage at this time made Theobald's gesture look more like pique than politics. Whether or not Eustace had been crowned, his rights to the succession had been both asserted and accepted. Why then should Theobald have suffered further exile and ignominy rather than crown Stephen's heir? Had Theobald firmly thrown in his lot with Henry of Anjou, he would surely have joined Henry in Normandy and returned to England with him whenever that occurred, rather than gone to Flanders and come back before the end of the year.

Though Huntingdon implied that Eugenius III had forbidden the coronation on account of Stephen's broken oath, to explain Theobald's refusal, this is very difficult to credit, since Stephen's kingship had been categorically endorsed on at least three occasions by Innocent II. Huntingdon may here have been offerring only his own explanation of Theobald's alleged appeal to papal orders. The issue was more complicated than Huntingdon believed. John of Salisbury, writing in 1164, was anxious to assert papal rights to consultation in such a matter. He refers to an earlier decision of Celestine II forbidding any *traditio* of the English kingship, though no *traditio* was even being considered in Celestine's pontificate.[11] In 1164 it was not a mere matter of history. Henry II was then already eager to obtain the consecration of his own son as king, and Becket himself reminded cardinals that the proposal to crown Eustace in 1151–52 had provoked differences of opinion in the curia.[12]

If it is true that Theobald, for want of a better argument, declined to crown Eustace because the pope had forbidden it, the problem becomes one of trying to fathom the pope's reasons. Although it is often asserted that the pope had already made up his mind in favour of Henry, it is far from clear that papal backing would itself have been sufficient to guarantee Henry's kingship; and Eugenius is not likely to have risked committing papal policy to an impossible course. He probably confined himself to repeating his predecessors' advice not to make any changes in the position of the English crown. Why the papacy, which had consistently favoured Stephen in 1136, 1139 and 1141, would have switched its support to Henry of Anjou by 1152, is difficult to understand. No reasons for such a radical change of course in such a normally cautious institution have been offered. Whatever Eugenius thought about the English succession, a mere coronation would not have deterred any pope from future hostility, if deemed necessary. Only the year before, in 1151, King Roger II of Sicily, whom the papacy detested, had had his last surviving son William crowned as co-ruler without papal approval. The pope certainly did not regard William's coronation as having set up an insurmountable obstacle to his own plans for stamping out Roger's kingship on his death. Any papal advice offered in 1152 about not allowing innovations in the matter of the English coronation makes better sense as an attempt to prevent the introduction of the French practice of joint-kingship, rather than as a veiled expression of Angevin sympathies in Rome. After 1154, when Adrian IV became pope and Henry II king, it might have seemed natural if not expedient to antedate Roman enthusiasm for the new ruler, but the practical good sense of papal advice in 1151–52 was proved by what happened after 1170, when Henry II did have his heir crowned; it brought undesirable consequences that were inconceivable in France: a civil war between father and son.

Whatever else may lie behind this controversy, there seems to have been no problem about the commitment of the secular lordship to Eustace, crowned or not. The failure of the oaths of 1126 to effect the succession may just have prompted Stephen, whose title came by unction and crowning, to try and reinforce Eustace's position by whatever means he could. In the spring of 1152, there was, after all, a new urgency about making a formal declaration. However controversial this matter remained, in 1152 it had only temporary significance. Within weeks, Henry's marriage to Eleanor of Aquitaine in May 1152 not only postponed his expected return to England, it also reopened his quarrel with Louis VII. Eustace had anyway been openly recognised as Stephen's heir. Until Eustace's death in August 1153, this remained a cardinal factor in political calculations.

Henry's appearances in England in 1147 and 1149 had not made any real inroads into Stephen's position, and it is not clear what they had done to boost the morale of his friends. The *Gesta* claims that his supporters had sent him back to the Continent in 1149 so that he should find some means to augment his resources for a renewal of the English campaign. To give these hopes some substance, Geoffrey himself installed Henry as duke of Normandy in 1149/50, before Louis VII actually got back to France from the Holy Land. On his return, Louis showed such hostility that Henry was unable to think of assisting his English friends until the summer of 1151. The death of his father in September then drew him back to the Loire valley, a clear indication that he placed a higher priority on establishing his sole right to his father's inheritance against his two younger brothers than he did to rallying support in England. Only when Anjou was settled to his satisfaction did he return to Normandy. In March 1152, at Lisieux, he accordingly met his uncle, Reginald of Cornwall, who once again urged upon him the need to come to England and hearten his English friends. When in the same month, however, Louis VII at last secured a formal separation from his wife Eleanor of Aquitaine, Henry again deferred any plans for an English expedition and seized the opportunity to marry Eleanor himself at Poitiers in May. Although he then returned almost immediately to Barfleur in order to cross the Channel, Louis VII, now seriously angered by Henry, attacked the Norman frontier. Stephen, still confident of his strength at home, intervened in Louis's Norman war by despatching his son, Eustace, now his acknowledged heir, to act with King Louis VII and challenge Duke Henry's government there. As a direct result, Henry's fourth visit to England was delayed until January 1153.

Henry's three years back on the Continent had shown the overriding importance to him of consolidating his position both in Normandy and, even more so, in Anjou. The marriage to Eleanor, duchess of Aquitaine, which made good political sense in strictly Angevin terms, was nevertheless bound to complicate Henry's relations with Louis, to whom he had only recently been reconciled. Henry also appeared to have taken a risk in marrying a woman eleven years older than himself who had only previously borne daughters to Louis. The pair were not well acquainted before their marriage and calculation rather than passion is the most likely explanation for it, though political calculation at break-neck speed to exploit Angevin advantages along the Loire. To achieve dominance in the whole of western France from the Channel to the Pyrenees did not, however, have much to do with England. During his lifetime Henry demonstrated that he both intended to realise this and had some capacity to do so. Although the range of Henry's ambitions had begun to show at an early age, contemporaries may have assumed at first that he would simply overreach himself. His claims by inheritance on his mother's side to the English kingdom were certainly something of a distraction for this Angevin prince. Henry was, of course, not one to abandon any scrap of his rights, but it must have seemed a very dubious prospect that he would be able to manage his French interests as well as the English kingdom. Seen from England, moreover, a ruler with the focus of his concerns so far away from those of his great men with their Norman commitments would have seemed a very different proposition from previous kings. Though Henry might rule Normandy, the centre of his dominions was plainly much further south. Henry's immediate advantage was that, having consolidated his position in northern France by the time he returned to England, he had more concrete rewards to offer any adherents than had been the case in 1149. Had many English lords been dissatisfied with Stephen's limp government, they might have been more doubtful about the wisdom of accepting a ruler with so many other distractions. For others again, the extent of Henry's dominions might have offerred the attractive possibility of adventures in far off places under Henry's lordship.

When he arrived, in January 1153, Henry did not openly challenge Stephen's crown. Some of the documents he issued in the next few months refer to his hopes of recovering his rights or his inheritance; he also claimed to dispose of royal rights in districts subject to him.[13] He came to rally a faltering cause; the small force he brought with him was quite inadequate to overcome Stephen. At no stage during these critical months did he launch a direct attack on the king. Henry's objectives remained limited, even muted, at the most expecting to buy time and respite for his friends. Taking a lease on Devizes castle from the bishop of Salisbury, Henry anticipated that it might be three years before he could allow the bishop to repossess it.[14] Was his original plan to get his firm control over a few key castles recognised in return for a general cessation of hostilities? As with Malmesbury's disingenuous pleas that Matilda was ready for compromise in 1139 and that only Stephen insisted on conflict, any Angevin offers of compromise in 1153 proceeded from weakness, proposing to buy off Henry's intrusion into the kingdom, if in return Stephen would surrender at least some part of his claims to jurisdiction. The contest was not an uncompromising conflict about the right to rule but one designed to improve Henry's room for manoeuvre.

Huntingdon, writing after Henry's accession, chose to present England as figuratively pining for the Angevin's return. His narrative is far from demonstrating much willingness on the part of the English to fall in with Duke Henry's plans. Stephen had closed in on Wallingford and its fall was expected any day. Huntingdon does not conceal the concern of his English friends that Henry had brought so few troops with him.[15] He tries to brave it out by insisting that the glory of victory was the greater for the smaller force, but Henry's supporters may not have been so easily reassured. Such success as Henry achieved in the next few months was hardly outstanding. Those identified with the Angevin cause over the years were by the end of the year obliged to do homage to King Stephen and console themselves with the prospect that after Stephen's death, whenever it occurred, Henry would succeed him.[16] They had presumably not pressed Henry to return to them for an outcome like this.

Inevitably there are difficulties in constructing a reliable chronology for the next few months. The events of Henry's fourth English expedition cannot have been recorded in chronicle accounts month by month, let alone week by week. Huntingdon, in accordance with his previous practice, almost certainly updated his narrative after Henry of Anjou's recognition as king, accounting for events since 1149 in one broad sweep. On the other hand, in Normandy, the prior of Bec, Robert of Torigni, who became abbot of Mont St-Michel in May 1154, might have made entries in his chronicle intermittently during the years 1153 and 1154.[17] Both Bec and Mont St-Michel were monasteries with properties and many contacts in England, able to provide reliable and rapid reports. Torigni gives useful information about Henry's activities, some corroborated by Huntingdon, but there is inevitably more about what was happening in Normandy itself than about England. Intelligence reaching England about events in Normandy could not have always been reassuring as far as Henry was concerned. The shortcomings of the chronicles explain why historians have been driven to make use of charters issued during these months. Events are accordingly described in terms of an alignment of two distinct parties eager for a decisive showdown, with a few neutral clergy trotting to and fro, trying to patch together an agreement. Reconstructions of party affiliations mainly rest on interpretations of witness lists in charters. This puts excessive strain on the evidence. The fortuitous survival of charters makes them an unreliable guide to shifting political circumstances. As evidence of transactions certainly occurring at a precise time and place, they would be invaluable. Unfortunately, most of them cannot be dated very exactly and much ingenuity is employed to tie them in with the chronicle accounts. This does not make it impossible to draw crumbs of information from them, but only shaky conclusions can be erected on such friable foundations.

The eventual outcome, namely Henry's succession to the throne, could not have even been anticipated at any time before November 1153. While Stephen lived, Henry's hour had still not struck. The chronicles agree that Henry on his arrival did not rush to succour the threatened Wallingford garrison but instead attacked the royal stronghold of Malmesbury, in the west country. Henry may have discounted the pitiful stories about the imminent fall of Wallingford which had after all been expected for over three years. Possibly, when he arrived at Wareham with his small force, it seemed expedient or even necessary to make first for Malmesbury where an area of sympathisers was exposed to royal attack, either in order to achieve some small immediate success or simply to clear the lines of communication east of Bristol. As with Henry's other moves in the next few months, the chroniclers made no effort to expound strategy or excuse the unexpected by reference to untoward occurrences. Henry's unpredictable behaviour has been explained on the grounds that he preferred to attack his enemies where they least expected it, an ingenious idea, but unconvincing. Although Henry did cause Stephen to divert forces to meet him at Malmesbury, the siege of Wallingford went on. There is some disagreement about how the town and the castle of Malmesbury fell into Henry's possession, but both the *Gesta* and Huntingdon were convinced that God had shown his hand in a violent fall of rain from the west, which lashed Stephen's force in the face and prevented the two armies from crossing the river to fight it out. Stephen's undefeated but disheartened forces withdrew, and Henry was left with the moral victory and the possession of Malmesbury. How he followed up this success is in dispute. Huntingdon reported that he then advanced on Wallingford and cleverly outmanoeuvred Stephen's riposte. The problem of Wallingford, however, was not resolved by military action, but many months later, after August by negotiation, so Huntingdon's notice is probably misleading.

In the meantime, presumably to keep up the pressure, Henry became committed to a number of separate raiding parties. During these months Henry, far from being welcomed outright, was reduced to bribing key leaders to join his cause, mainly, as was natural, by offering to restore their former lands in Normandy, which were now in his gift. At Bristol, for example, he offered to make over the Norman lands of the earl of Leicester to Leicester's son.[18] This appears to have been sufficient to persuade the earl himself to negotiate with Henry rather than have his own son turn against him. The Beaumont family had been cleverly divided by Geoffrey in 1141. Robert of Leicester had in 1150 found himself in a compromising position in England, trying to protect the English interests of his brother Waleran of Meulan from the king himself. Leicester's anxiety about the interests of his family is understandable, but this did not make him Henry's abject instrument. In 1153 Henry was also desperate to obtain Leicester's support. This was sufficiently important for Henry to do him other favours. Thus Henry joined Leicester's expedition to seize the castle of Tutbury from Earl Ferrers, an interesting demonstration that Henry was being used by Leicester for his own purposes.[19] Henry was, however, unable to use Leicester for a direct attack on Stephen. Sometime or other the castle of Warwick was also surrendered to Henry by the countess, half-sister of the earl of Leicester. Her husband, who was with Stephen when the news arrived, is reported to have immediately died of shame.[20]

About the same time Henry negotiated with the earl of Chester, for the restitution of Chester's lands in Normandy. Chester too dragged Henry into his affairs. Henry's various dealings with the earls of Leicester and Chester indicate that the elaborate settlement of their mutual differences negotiated a little earlier had already become a dead letter.[21] Leicester and Chester may have both joined Henry of Anjou, but their own differences had been reopened. Nor did they become eager champions of his rights; their support proved illusory when the crunch came. A number of quite different minor skirmishes preoccupied the main contestants, not any coherent plan to settle the major question about the kingship, still less to establish peace and order as the clergy thought desirable. Duke Henry may have hoped that by these various pacts he would eventually build up a party strong enough to overthrow the king, but realistically he may have not expected to achieve more than bargaining strength. The various regional pacts were clearly a sign that the great men of the kingdom did not mind taking advantage of Henry's needs to recover ancestral lands, but this did not make them enthusiastic for a showdown which would oust Stephen in favour of Henry.

For his part, Stephen had not been able to rally his forces to evict Henry from the kingdom. Frustration with all this was used to explain how Eustace, driven into a frenzy, died of the consequences in mysterious circumstances in August.[22] In the long term this opened the way to a general settlement, but when it occurred the parties were still far apart. Nor did the royalists promptly melt away and acknowledge Henry as the inevitable victor. Shortly after Eustace's death, Duke Henry abjectly offered the canons of Bedford compensation for the injuries he had caused them, acknowledging his possible incapacity to discharge his obligations.[23] At the end of August, he ventured an attack on Stamford and a feint on Nottingham.[24] The townsmen of Stamford, still far from regarding Henry as an obvious winner, appealed to Stephen for help. Bewilderingly, Stephen was at the time engaged in fighting Hugh Bigod for Ipswich and had to refuse, rightly or wrongly estimating Ipswich a more valuable prize than Stamford and Bigod a more serious enemy than Henry. At Nottingham, the royal garrison set the town ablaze before Henry could take it, cheating his troops of anticipated booty. None of this suggests that Henry's ultimate victory was expected. If Stephen is faulted for skulking in East Anglia on a matter of secondary significance, Henry's inability to take advantage of Stephen's embarrassments to unite his forces and march on London is no less remarkable.

Huntingdon, who had no understanding of or sympathy for the baronage, explains their attitude in contradictory ways.[25] On the one hand, he claimed that they were unwilling to go to war and made peace among themselves; on the other, that they loved discord more than anything and did not want to support either Stephen or Henry outright lest the victor be free to lord it over them. Huntingdon has a genial story of how Stephen and Henry agreed to meet on the Thames and how each deplored the treachery of their followers. From such an encounter, the two leaders could have realised that a compromise might be found to give one immediate enjoyment of the crown and the other the reversion of it. If so, taking the initiative for a compromise could be attributed to them. Responsibility for devising a political settlement is more usually attributed to the barons. This is not said in the barons' favour, but rather ascribed to their unwillingness to back Stephen with sufficient enthusiasm by fighting it out to a finish.[26] Yet it is equally plausible to argue that they did not lend their ear to Henry's blandishments, but insisted on Stephen being left in possession of his throne, in which case their true purpose was to find the easiest means of persuading Henry to leave the kingdom as quickly as possible. The *Gesta*, far from thinking of the barons as lukewarm royal friends, claimed that a group of them urged Stephen to go on fighting and not to compromise.[27] The author did not report this with any sympathy for their loyalty because he himself thought that a peaceful outcome had become the most urgent desideratum. Huntingdon's assertion that barons simply enjoyed discord for its own sake carries no weight. They gave careful thought to limiting their own disputes; their ability to do so by negotiation and, perhaps, through the mediation of their own local clergy, proves that within their own orbits of influence they were well able to contain disorder and not dependent on the restoration of monarchical authority to achieve it.[28] They may have seen the dispute between king and duke as another conflict that could be settled by similar means. The whole kingdom did not have to be convulsed on account of the duke's own tiresome insistence on his 'rights'. Was he really entitled to make war on a king of England legitimately established whom most of the great men had at some stage accepted as their ruler?

Huntingdon's abuse of calculating barons has been willingly adopted by writers, with their own distaste for the 'aristocracy'. Little attention has been paid to the barons' own position. Nearly all of them had either consistently, or at least intermittently, acknowledged Stephen as king. They may indeed have appreciated his style of kingship, if it had really conceded them greater freedom of action than Henry I had allowed. There would inevitably be some reluctance to abandon him, if that is what Henry of Anjou required. If they had gained from Stephen's slack regime, as is widely assumed, they would by the same token have had little reason to throw him over in favour of a potentially less easy going ruler. In fact, Henry is unlikely to have offered himself as a would-be autocrat. In his favour it is usually supposed that his direct descent from Stephen's predecessor counted for much, but it is not certain that the baronage retained any sentimental regard for Henry I's family, still less for his style of government, if that was what Duke Henry's cause amounted to. Nor is there any sign that, after Stephen's bungling efforts, the whole country was dazzled by the prospect for the restoration of firm government held out by Henry. What was wanted rather was an end to the Angevin interference that openly encouraged defiance of the king's authority. Henry had deliberately attempted to make things worse for Stephen by offering bribes from Norman lands to enlarge the Angevin affiliation in England, as he did with the earls of Leicester and Chester and lesser figures too. By the early summer he had probably reached the limits of what could be gained by this means.

An alternative ploy to attract support may lie behind his decision at Gloucester, at Easter 1153, to adopt the title duke of Aquitaine for the first time, as though to call attention to his vast continental commitments.[29] Was this a way to boast of his enhanced powers of patronage, or was it an indication that with responsibilities on such a scale he was less likely to be much in England breathing down the necks of his friends? Finally, amongst the imponderables, must be mentioned the fact that Eleanor of Aquitaine was pregnant and that the birth of Henry's first son, William, in August offered some security for the succession in the long term. When he died that same month, Eustace left no children, though he had been married longer than Henry and was seven years his senior. Was this considered another sign in Henry's favour? Where William was born is not known. In England his name would have reminded men of the great Conqueror himself, though Eleanor's father had also been a William. At the time of his birth, William may have looked as much like a future duke of Aquitaine as a future king of England. Whatever his advantages, Henry of Anjou still seemed far from attaining his objective.

Most credit for the eventual settlement is usually accorded to the leading clergy, not so much because they fulfilled contemporary expectations by acting as mediators, but because they had deserted Stephen and gone over to Henry.[30] The clerical sources inevitably stress the peacemaking role of Theobald, who was, no doubt, expected as legate and archbishop to take the lead, much as Henry of Winchester had done in a similar position in 1141. Henry of Winchester certainly seconded Theobald's initiatives, as the site of the settlement in his city underlines. This episcopal intervention may seem to have played into Henry's hands, but from the king's point of view their success in bringing the conflict to an end, and getting Henry promptly out of the kingdom, makes them seem more astute. From the evidence available, it is unwarranted to ascribe sentiments in favour of Henry to the clergy.

Both sides agreed that it was preferable to avoid a decisive military solution and that negotiation would be the better way out. This is hardly proof of callow politics. A military victory for either side would have created more bitterness and would not necessarily have brought the dispute to an end. Stephen and Henry both had kinsmen to take up the cudgels if either was killed or captured in battle. Negotiation proves the political finesse on both sides. The more mellow political climate presumably gave mediators new hopes of making a deal. The break in the log jam may, however, have been initiated by Stephen's surviving son, Earl Warenne, who waived his own expectations of the succession in return for some assurances. Whether he did so willingly, or was persuaded to do so by others, cannot be known, but it is agreed that his meeting with Henry at Colchester in September or October in the company of Archbishop Theobald paved the way for the settlement reached at Winchester at the beginning of November.[31] The cornerstone was that Stephen agreed to adopt Henry as his heir.[32] The significance of this was that Henry's claim by right of inheritance had been rejected. His title depended on the legitimacy of Stephen's own.[33] These facts do not fit the modern theories at all.

Stephen may even have developed something like affection for his adopted heir. He is generally credited with strong human feelings; he had paid Henry to leave the kingdom in 1147 and the conflict of interests had never taken a personal turn. Henry too could be charming and, unlike his mother, was not one to prejudice his political interests by losing his self-control. In the succeeding few months, Stephen and Henry were frequently together and, on both sides, confidence and trust may have begun to take effect. The settlement had certainly not achieved an outright victory for Henry and his friends. By gracefully accepting the reversion of the crown, he deferred his satisfaction for the present, whereas for his adherents there were immediate implications, which obliged them to recognise Stephen's authority, though some of them had been denying this for years. The death in December 1153 of the ever troublesome Ranulf of Chester probably helped to remove a potential source of disruption. The death of several other earls (Simon and the two Rogers, of Warwick and Hereford) all in this period had their own impact on the transition from one reign to another.

According to Torigni, there were two other main strands to the settlement. The first was an undertaking to restore their properties to those who had held them under Henry I or their heirs. The troubles of Stephen's reign are generally held responsible for quite extensive dispossession of property and appropriation of estates without legal process or official approval. If so, promises to restore the *status quo ante* would be difficult to redeem and inevitably arouse resentment from those newly dispossessed. In practice, the settlement did not apparently create a new group of 'dispossessed'. Nor must the complications of implementing such a general promise become a useful device for explaining subsequent changes in the land law to protect 'possession' when resolution of disputes about 'right' proved insoluble. Inevitably, only a few cases of property disputes covered by this undertaking are known about in detail, but it seems excessive to think of them as possibly representing the tip of an iceberg. In the survey of military tenures ordered in 1166, of the more than 7500 fees listed, only for a tiny number of cases was *tempore guerrae* invoked to explain how fees had been created or services withheld. Had there been any widespread eviction of property-holders and introduction of alternative tenants under Stephen, on account of rival lordships, there would surely be more sign of disputes about military tenures than this, in an enquiry ordered within twelve years of Stephen's death. Even if, in the meantime, there had been a wholesale restoration of the lawful tenants, it seems very unlikely that so few cases were outstanding. A simpler explanation for this is that there had never been much reassignment of tenures; the purpose of the provision in 1153 was merely intended for reassurance in exceptional cases.

The second strand to Torigni's account of the settlement related to an agreement on dismantling castles erected since 1135. Interpretation of the significance of this is hampered by the impossibility of knowing how many castles were implicated.[34] Torigni's chronicle provides the only evidence about the numbers; most manuscripts give fanciful figures of well above one thousand; only one good manuscript records a more realistic 122. The purpose of the policy is also in doubt. In the late twelfth century William of Newburgh refers to the castles concerned as 'adulterine', that is unauthorised, and the expression has acquired mythic status in history books.[35] In the early twelfth century, however, obtaining formal royal authority to erect castles was neither common nor necessary. In 1153 the reason for sweeping away recently built castles may not have been that they were unlawful, merely that they were redundant in peacetime, or that they were potentially dangerous in the hands of those still feeling belligerent. The only hitch in carrying through this policy described at any length was given by Newburgh himself, about the castle at Drax, where a knight of the rebellious vassal, Robert de Gant, tried to ward off its destruction. There is no other reason for thinking that castellans were reluctant to comply with royal orders. After Stephen's death, Henry II is often thought to have demolished more castles and with more vigour than Stephen, but even this has been doubted.

Immediate responsibility for implementing what the king and duke had agreed was naturally assumed by Stephen as king, supposedly in conjunction with Henry; but since Henry left England before the end of March he can have played only a small part in this. He had no reason to anticipate that Stephen would be dead within six months. He may well have been expecting a long wait before he came into his own, happy enough, apparently, to leave Stephen in charge. Recently there has been some scepticism based on passages, mainly from much later writers, about the viability of the settlement. Some dissatisfaction is highly probable.[36] Compromise may often be the best way forward, but it never satisfies extremists who see noble principles sacrificed to the ambitions of time-serving mediocrities. In 1153–54, however, neither side allowed grievances to wreck the settlement. Political sense prevailed over faction. This makes it rather captious to twist the surviving charters into evidence for Henry's effective detachment from Stephen's government. About fifty documents, a dozen from Henry and three times as many from Stephen, can be confidently assigned to the ten months between the Winchester agreement and Stephen's death. Only a handful show both princes dealing with the same business, Henry, for example, confirming Stephen's grants, or vice-versa.

That Henry issued his own confirmations of Stephen's grants hardly proves that he was loth to recognise Stephen's acts as binding. Maybe his own men needed to be reassured by receiving his personal authority. More to the point, many of Stephen's charters addressed to his officials in shires up and down eastern England take for granted the continuing existence of local administration. No restoration was needed. The smaller number of documents addressed to the western shires may be a mere hazard of survival. Yet it is not unimportant to notice that the Austin canons of Bristol saw fit to get the king's confirmation of Duke Henry's grant of tolls; that the king instructed William, earl of Gloucester, to restore lands to Glastonbury and Patrick, earl of Salisbury, to destroy a castle, irrespective of any claim to papal protection for ecclesiastical property, because as king he had already appealed to Rome about this. Athelney abbey in Somerset thought it desirable to get royal authorisation for such an uncontentious matter as changing the track of the public highway across the moor so that a new water-course could be dug.[37] These are straws in the wind, and they show that respect for the king's authority promptly revived in those parts of the west country where it had been at best fitful for a dozen years of more. What had hampered royal administration was not Stephen's incompetence but the intrusion of a rival bent on undermining his authority. Once this irritant was removed, the normal respect for the king revived undimmed.

When he returned to the Continent, Henry made a visit as far south as

Périgueux, showing that he did not lurk anxiously within earshot of the Channel while Stephen coped in England. Fortune smiled on him and he did not wait long. After a troubled childhood, Henry was exceptionally lucky in his early years of maturity. Many of his enemies and relations died leaving him in a strong position. Henry of Huntingdon in his valedictory poem greeted Duke Henry as a young saviour of the kingdom. Some sense of his remarkable grasp on Fortune may have already excited a more general sense of new expectations. Yet, however propitious his eventual succession might seem, in March 1154 it could not have been thought imminent. Only the very short period that elapsed between the negotiation of the settlement and Stephen's death banished all memory of the precarious nature of what had been agreed. Had Stephen lived only a few years longer, the treaty might have been torn up, just as casually as Henry I's own attempt to settle the succession had been. Had Duke Henry been engaged in asserting himself in Anjou or Poitou rather than in Normandy when Stephen died, he might have been unable to claim his rights on Stephen's death, leaving space for another claimant, even Stephen's second son William, to seize his chance.

Once Henry II had become king, the settlement of 1153 was not repudiated so that the new king could act as he pleased. Rather than introducing any fresh element of his own, he seems to have carried on where Stephen had left off. The most admired and least doubted aspect of Henry II's major 'reforms' of 'government' in 1155 has been the overhaul of the audit procedures in the royal treasury, for which the king obtained the services of his grandfather's former treasurer, Nigel, bishop of Ely. Nigel may have brought a new vigour into its operations, but exchequer administration could not have completely collapsed under Stephen. No exchequer rolls for Stephen's reign are extant, but Henry II's first Michaelmas exchequer court met in 1155 in a regular way. What survives of the audit record shows that a few officials had clearly operated throughout the financial year, that is back into Stephen's own last weeks, even if most of the returns were submitted for only three quarters of the year. The record cannot be interpreted as proving that 'proper' accounting had only been resumed after Stephen's death. Stephen himself had given a quittance to the abbess of Caen from payments for assarts in the Essex forest from Michaelmas 1153, presumably an indication that some audit of the exchequer had taken place that year and that another was anticipated in 1154.[38] More significantly, the manner of presenting the accounts according to forms familar from the exchequer roll of 1130 can best be understood as indicating the continuing operation of the audit procedure throughout the reign. Many, though not all, payments in various parts of the kingdom were discharged after assay of the coins, so not even this highly technical aspect of the audit had fallen into desuetude.[39]

Exchequer procedures in 1155 could not have been brought to such a point from zero in less than twelve months. The appearance in the earliest pipe rolls of Henry II of such staples of later administrative form as payments in assayed money, payments for *terre date* and for assarts, all in their own way amount to proof that accounting had remained in place according to established usage throughout the reign. Some standard payments, particularly in alms to churches, were identical in 1155 to what they had been in 1130, which certainly suggests *prima facie* that they had been paid regularly in the interval.[40]

If annual audits had continued under Stephen, those parts of the kingdom where Matilda's supporters prevailed would surely not have submitted accounts of any kind to the barons of the king's exchequer. This raises the question as to whether an alternative form of audit had been established, say by the earls of Gloucester at Bristol. Some of Henry of Anjou's charters of 1153 refer to persons who had taken 'royal' properties at farm. This arrangement could have been a means of repaying loans rather than providing for an alternative to shrieval management. If such arrangements were common, potential sheriffs would have had little interest in taking over the farm of royal lands. This would have left the earls without rival officials in the shires.[41] In the first two exchequer rolls of Henry II's reign, the earls are prominent for rendering those accounts. Cornwall gave no account at all, but Earl Patrick in Wiltshire and Earl Redvers in Devon exercised the function of sheriffs elsewhere and barons like Walter of Hereford in Herefordshire and Gloucestershire or William Fitz Alan in Salop and Robert of Stafford in Staffordshire may have operated in the new reign as they had done before.[42] On balance it seems likely that the earls were left to collect and spend what revenues they could obtain within their own shires. Their ability to do so depended on the survival of local administrative routines, appointment and supervision of manorial reeves, even perhaps regular visitation of the hundred courts. To all intents and purposes, however, the machinery required for the collection of county revenues, taxes on town and country, even of geld, had functioned in the interval; it was all available for all parts of the kingdom within twelve months of Stephen's death. This hardly makes it likely that the whole apparatus had needed to be recreated from scratch in both royal and Matildine zones. The local machinery had surely continued to operate throughout the reign.[43]

Some development of exchequer procedures in this reign may also have occurred. The loss of the audit rolls for Stephen's reign is usually regarded as sufficient evidence in itself for the breakdown in his treasury organisation, but most of the rolls for Henry I's reign have also disappeared. What needs to be explained is how the exchequer roll of 1130 alone survived. From the writing of the 1130 pipe roll it appears that a clerk with chancery experience was used on that occasion. No distinctive style of script had yet evolved in an office at least twenty years old. The fact that there was still no specifically exchequer script in 1130 may indicate that accounting was still at an improvisatory stage. Perhaps, in these circumstances, Nigel had retained the roll of 1130 after he became bishop, since by 1133 it would have lost any of its usefulness for subsequent accounting. On his return to the treasury under Henry II, did he bring back his old copy of the 1130 roll and add it to the archive? Otherwise it is hard to see why this alone of Henry I's rolls should have been preserved. Kept by Nigel himself, it had not suffered whatever vicissitudes beset the others. The earliest rolls of Henry II's reign are, however, from the beginning all written in a script specifically identified with exchequer records. The most reasonable explanation for such a distinctive script is that it had evolved over the intervening twenty-five years, a development possible only in a steadily functioning office where clerks could be trained.

The financial operations recorded in the earliest Henry II rolls are on a much reduced scale from those of 1130, so that, even if the routines had been kept up in the interval, it would still be necessary to explain this serious diminution of the royal assets to be managed. Could this have been due to deliberate renunciation rather than to administrative collapse? Henry I's revenues had been grossly inflated by his willingness to sell favours of all kinds, over law suits and feudal incidents. These practices are likely to have been unpopular and could have been conscientiously repudiated by the new regime, much as Stephen had formally denounced Henry I's abuses in the church. If it seems unlikely that any government would willingly have surrendered opportunities for making money from its subjects, the explanation may lie rather with the way greater delegation of responsibilities made suitors less willing to offer bribes to the king to get their way at law. Under Stephen the collection and expenditure of revenue had obviously reduced the scope for the curial officials so prominent in the 1130 record. The rolls of Henry II's early years show that several properties in most shires had been granted away as *terre date*, possibly to repay loans by individuals. Since the sheriffs had to provide the details of the sums involved in order to clear their own accounts, such procedures had not been indiscriminate or been done on the quiet. Local military forces, for example, could have been subsidised by granting out the management of formerly shrieval monies to earls or others, dispensing with some of the oversight previously exercised in the king's direct favour. The financial consequences of this milder exploitation of royal rights do not appear to have been as serious for Stephen as might be supposed. He found no difficulties about raising large military forces when they were needed right up to the end of the reign. These forces seem to have been paid troops, emphasising his financial resources.

The royal exchequer is usually regarded as a venerable organ of government which Stephen should have done more to keep in good working order, but this modern view must not be allowed to obscure the fact, as a comparatively recent device of Henry I and Nigel of Ely's uncle to make money for themselves, it may not have enjoyed unqualified esteem. If Nigel on his return to the treasury in 1155 had had nothing more difficult to do than restore the old structures of the 1120s, it is surprising that he was not able to bump up the collection of royal revenues to its earlier levels more quickly. Whereas Henry I's officials accounted for £23,000 in 1130, it took Henry II's until 1176, more than twenty years, to account for so much; in only two other years of the reign was that sum exceeded. Henry I's success in raising money cannot therefore be regarded as due to the efficiency of his methods; it was a consequence of his abusive manipulation of his rights.

Late twelfth-century governments were not allowed to get away with this kind of thing. A recent study shows that it was not until the middle of John's reign that any king was able to get as much money from his subjects as Henry I had done in 1130.[44] John's demands were a leading factor in producing baronial resistance at the end of the reign, which itself suggests how much Henry I's abuses are likely to have provoked discontent. If Nigel's ability to achieve modest improvements in a few years probably owed something to his family's previous practices under Henry I, their excesses had been reined in by different expectations. After twenty years, it proved impossible to restore the exploitation of royal rights for fiscal profit. When, by the later 1170s, treasury receipts occasionally reached the levels of 1130, it was because Angevin ingenuity had found alternative ways of screwing revenue out of the shrieval administrators. The improvement of Henry II's finances in the 1170s can be directly linked with the innovations in judicial procedure for which Henry II's reign is most famous, but his reforming drive in English justice did not begin until ten years after his accession. Whatever its justification then, Stephen's inadequacies cannot fairly be made responsible, though they usually are. So far into a new reign, it must instead be explained in terms of the development of Henry's own style of rule.

Assessment of what Stephen had been responsible for requires us to examine the state of the kingdom he left in 1154. This is more difficult than might be supposed because the early years of Henry II are much less well chronicled than those of Stephen's reign. Historians have always enjoyed writing about exciting times more than about years of peace. The problem is compounded by the long survival of the new Angevin dynasty. As a new tradition of government and kingship became established, Stephen's reign was treated as anomalous. This perception was not an option for Stephen's contemporaries and it cannot have developed immediately on Henry II's accession. Writing in the 1160s, John of Salisbury could still denounce Stephen for his treatment of the church – if not a model for, at least a precursor of, Henry II himself. At the time, it did not seem as though Stephen had been a negligible factor. For these reasons we have difficulty in grasping what lessons contemporaries themselves may have drawn from their experiences of the years 1135–54. They cannot have considered the reign in isolation, as we naturally tend to do, accepting the modern argument that, in 1154, the situation of 1135 could be resumed without effort.

For a kingdom allegedly in need of overhaul, it is disconcerting that, for the first eight years of the new reign, the king spent only two comparatively brief spells in England; the first for a mere thirteen months and the second for only sixteen months: a combined total of twenty-nine months, just over a quarter of the whole period. Clearly Henry II had no impression that his constant personal supervision was called for to revive the lapsed powers of kingship, nor that he had to find time to achieve it. Though the lands in the north were retrieved from the adolescent Malcolm IV, Henry II did not devote himself to the reconquest of the regions of south Wales lost since 1135. The main difference from the previous reign was that there was now no party witholding respect for the king in any part of the country. The second difference was that Henry II himself could devote most of his energies to defending and extending his great possessions in France and was not obliged to fall back on England to defend his kingdom. In fact, Henry made only very fitful assertions of personal kingship throughout his reign. Stephen at least spent all but eight months of his reign in England. Only twice did Henry II spend more than two years at a stretch in his kingdom (1163–66 and 1175–77). Until 1163, Henry appears to have given little attention to English affairs.

Particularly in the matter of the coinage, to which great importance is usually attached, Henry II seems neglectful. In his reign, he gave up the preoccupation of earlier kings with frequent revision of the coinage, a device for acquiring a welcome profit from moneyers. Stephen's last issue of coins in 1154 continued to circulate until 1158, and the new issue then struck is described as of mediocre quality. There was no new issue again until 1180. After 1161, the king also gave up collecting geld as a tax, adopting instead a form of taxation based on the knights' fee and therefore in a sense dependent on the direct cooperation of the king's tenants in chief.[45] One of the consequences was that kings lost interest in close supervision of the hundreds as the basic units of fiscal assessment and made no attempt to halt the tendency for them to pass into private lordship. Even the famous reforms of legal procedure came through piecemeal operations, designed in the first instance to make existing courts work more effectively and then by providing supplementary legal processes for the kingdom's 'freeholders'. Those whose tenures were not recognised as 'free' were left to regulate their affairs according to local custom. In great measure they ceased to be of direct legal concern to the king, though at this point non-free tenure, or villeinage, had still not acquired the stigma attached to it later and which it has never subsequently lost. This process of providing legal benefits for the privileged holders of free tenures reinforced the structures prevailing in 1154. There was no recovery of lost royal rights, rather a contraction in what the king's government concentrated on. Of course, on a more restricted front, it may have achieved more.

If Henry II's early years are in spite of all this judged to have been more successful than Stephen's, and his personal direction of affairs was not responsible, credit for this must lie with others. If some of the great men who might have given trouble conveniently all died about this time, other key figures of Stephen's reign amongst the barons and churchmen and royal officials remained active. Robert of Leicester and Richard de Lucy became Henry II's justiciars; Stephen's constable, Henry of Essex, was also prominent early in Henry's reign. All must have drawn on their past experiences, not getting or needing much guidance from the young new king. Henry II may have been more successful than Stephen about getting respect for royal rights, but the effectiveness of his government owed less to his own character than to the fact that he had to contend with no rival claim to the throne, at least until the rebellion of his own son in 1173. This incident was sufficient in itself to serve as a reminder of what damage could be done by challenges to the uniqueness of royal power even after 1154. Although the 1173 crisis lasted less than eighteen months, it was serious at the time and proved to be only the first of several wars between Henry II and his sons which recurred on and off till the end of his life. In a sense, his many battles with his sons later on echoed the disputes of his family with Stephen, and these conflicts about disputed rights in the long run precipitated the dismemberment of the Plantagenet empire. In the late twelfth century, the reign of Stephen did not look very different to contemporaries from those of other twelfth-century kings.

One factor with uneven consequences for a limited section of the population concerns the death of several earls at this time, leaving heirs under age and baronies in suspension. This put many of those who had under Stephen enjoyed the influential patronage of great men at the direct mercy of the king, adding perhaps unexpectedly to his obligations in ways that turned out to be significant in the longer term. Potentially dangerous figures for long-term political stability, including Stephen's second son, Earl Warenne, Malcolm IV of Scotland and the king's own younger brothers, also died conveniently soon before they could show their mettle. Henry's relations with his barons in general came to differ from Stephen's because of factors like these, irrespective of whether he personally had been more suspicious of great barons as such or was eager to dispense with the system of comital management characteristic of Stephen's reign. Henry II had himself learned about rulership as a 'feudal' baron. Unlike Stephen, he had no experience in youth of what it meant to live under a domineering king. Henry passed his whole political life in England, as in France, with great men raised in noble society and looking for honours with responsibilities, whom Henry both mastered and led. He was no closet king, plotting to keep his barons in check, fulfilling the expectations of Machiavellian theorists of politics. Henry did not need earls as Stephen had done, to deal with the military challenges of his reign, but he was no less of a military figure, though most of his campaigning was done on the Continent. Yet the new king is usually presented as having learned from his predecessor's mistakes never to allow his barons to get out of hand. This makes it necessary to explain how such overmighty subjects could have meekly submitted to the reimposition of firm royal government. At the end of Stephen's reign, these same barons had calmly resolved their own disputes without help from the king's guiding hand and had been in a strong position to settle the fate of the kingdom too. Similarly, though Henry is still thought to have attempted to reassert royal rights over the church, most English clergy apparently saw no need to make strenuous efforts to protect their gains. Surely a policy to recover royal rights would have damaged enough interests to provoke rather more protest than the very personal challenge launched by Becket? If, during Stephen's reign, such groups had settled their own affairs, would they have willingly surrendered themselves again to the kinds of officials trusted by Henry I?

Accounts of Henry II's reign, based on the assumption that the new king had to reorganise government and reassert effective kingship after Stephen's weak exercise of it, do not depend solely on the belief that the young Angevin appreciated both the defects of his predecessor and the virtues of his grandfather. They rest on the assumption that the 'country' was desperate after Stephen's débâcle to recover effective royal rule, as though without an authoritative kingship the kingdom would once again be plunged into 'anarchy'. Even if it is allowed that the extent of disorder has been exaggerated and that eulogies of Henry I's firm hand go too far, the belief that firm kings are good for the country has become an article of faith. In the twelfth century, however, responsibility for 'government' was more widely diffused than seems to be commonly appreciated. In the basic provision for 'law and order' issues, for example, rapid action was needed on the spot; it was physically impossible to field effective forces from the centre, except in unusual circumstances. In most districts the inhabitants themselves expected to resolve law and order problems within the boundaries of their hundred or its neighbours. Such evidence as we have indicates that all local authorities, the great churches, the barons and the towns were willing and able to provide for their own security. On occasion this was insufficient and the king was called in, but in the first instance a local response was expected and some degree of autonomy unavoidable.

The position may be illustrated by reference to the towns which might seem the most in need of royal succour.[46] Yet Stephen sent writs expecting town authorities to be in a position to take appropriate legal action, and the references in royal documents to both citizens and burgesses seem to take their capacity for collective response for granted. We may know little about the articulation of urban government but can hardly pretend there was none. Stephen's relations with townsmen in the kingdom appear to have been exceptionally harmonious, particularly with London, which had probably recovered the privileges and status it had enjoyed at the beginning of the reign after the fall of Geoffrey de Mandeville in 1143. Nothing of the situation is actually known until 1155, by which time the king had reimposed the financial arrangements in operation under Henry I. This state of affairs is more likely to have arisen from Henry II's dissatisfaction with the Londoners than any action by Stephen himself. If so, the Londoners may have had some regrets about the change of ruler. Their city was kept under close royal supervision until the reign of Richard I, when the citizens' impatience to gain more control of their own affairs, shown under Stephen, was finally assuaged.

Some proof of the buoyant state of other municipalities by mid-century, however, is that, whatever constraints Henry II imposed at London, he tolerated a much greater degree of freedom in other towns by allowing responsibility for payment of their financial dues to the king to be taken out of the sheriffs' hands and assumed by locals, in some cases by the burgesses collectively. This was famously the case with loyal Wallingford, which received a borough charter in 1155.[47] It had in effect been 'self-governing' in its isolation for many years. This was surely true, too, of many other towns in Stephen's own sphere. That towns had somehow flourished despite the unrest is indicated by the way Jewish communities had spread outside London to nearly another dozen places before 1159.[48] Some of these colonies may have taken root only in the previous five years of Henry's own reign, but it seems more likely that they had developed gradually over two decades. The places to which the Jews had spread by 1159 were all in the eastern part of the kingdom where Stephen's own officers could, if necessary, protect them. Quite what the reasons for this dispersion were our sources are too slender to show. At the very least, if Jews could venture beyond the certainty of royal protection in London, it would point to sufficiently stable and tranquil conditions as well as respect for the king's will. In the only case reported in any detail, the attempts of the king's officials to protect the Jewish community at Norwich under attack in 1148 leave no doubt about the importance of royal protection if they were subjected to local intolerance.[49] Since these Jewish communities were also closely associated with financial operations, royal patronage may have been connected with the king's own financial advantage. The same is probably true of the evidence for Flemings, including the famous banker William Cade of St-Omer.[50] These men figure prominently in the management of royal finances in the early exchequer rolls of Henry II, but Stephen's own links with the Low Countries were much stronger than Henry II's, so the prominence of Cade and others probably dates from his reign.

Stephen was the first king since 1066 who apparently identified his English kingdom as the more important part of his dominions. Under pressure, he concentrated his efforts on retaining his kingdom. Yet he was never willing to give up his claims in Normandy, or make a deal for the separation of the kingdom and the duchy in order to consolidate his hold in England. Nor were his enemies on the Continent prepared to give him such an alternative. Indeed their own powers there proved to be their best lever for the assertion of their rights in England. In France, the crucial change came when the momentum of Angevin expansion became unstoppable. Henry I had attempted to protect Normandy by making alliances with Anjou to neutralise this danger, but Matilda's marriage looked like an offer to surrender Normandy without a fight. The king of France inevitably became committed to opposing Angevin ambitions and found natural allies in the family of Blois-Champagne.

The failure of Louis VII to prevent Henry II's creation of an Angevin 'empire' is often considered to be a major disaster from which the French kingdom recovered only under his son Philip II. The unhappy implications of his failure for England have not been so readily acknowledged. If Angevin success in Normandy eventually brought England too within Henry II's grasp, the long-term consequence was deep involvement in French affairs which persisted for centuries. Even after the loss of Normandy in 1204, the Channel proved no obstacle to contact between the English kingdom and the French possessions of its king. Only later did the Channel isolate England from the Continent, not as a fact of nature but through the deliberate promotion of a navy to patrol the seas. This may make it seem as though nothing could in the long run have been done by Stephen to stave off the eventual Angevin takeover, but it changes the context in which the reign is perceived. Henry I's own vulnerability in Normandy had made it impossible for him to oppose the Angevins more decisively. Whether Stephen and his heirs could have defended the kingdom in the longer term against its continental connections must seem doubtful. What is surely undeniable is that those who supported Matilda in England did not do so because they welcomed the tide of history running in favour of the Plantagenet empire.

The resilience of the English in surviving the rivalries about the kingship itself has greater importance for the long-term development of the kingdom than any reimposition of firm government after 1154. The most serious damage to the kingdom had been caused not by unruly subjects but by the rival Angevin claim to rule. On the whole, the reign suggests that there was not much sympathy at the time for the claims of the Angevin faction that for reasons of its own it was entitled to contest established authority. What the English needed was general acceptance of a king who personified the unity of the kingdom. The instability created by the Angevin counter-claim was not easy to correct. Challenges to established governments by those claiming superior 'moral' rights to authority, in whatever name they are advanced, can continue to disrupt civil society. They are still very difficult to combat. England was fortunate that such a challenge was mounted at a time when responsibility was public order was still widely enough diffused through the kingdom to prevent total paralysis if the kingship itself was challenged.

9

Envoi

History books do not simply stop at the end of the story; they aspire to reach conclusions. Reading about the past can be enjoyed for its intrinsic interest, but few historians or readers are satisfied to leave it at that. Historians who labour over their work understandably hope that some useful lessons may be learnt from it. Readers are rarely satisfied with the simple historical story because it lacks the artificial symmetry of fiction. They demand something more; they expect to be enlightened in some way about what 'really' happened in the murky past. The popular idea that 'history will judge' rests on the notion that in the end definitive judgments will be pronounced and the past seen plainly for it was, as in a panorama. Whereas we experience the present as confusing, what will count in the long term uncertain, and who might be trusted most problematic, the confidence that everything will become clear when the present has become history seems very comforting. It is, however, an illusion. Interpretation of the past remains controversial, and not only amongst professional historians, with a vested interest in keeping certain topics on the boil. Wars, even battles, are viewed differently by descendants of the combatants or parties, even centuries after they occured. Very little of the past ever becomes so crystal clear as to rule out disagreement. The most obvious lesson to be learnt about the past is that it must always have been at least as controversial as the present is. If we cannot see the past as sharing the vitality and discordance of the present, we have missed one of its essential attributes.

Considering that the England of King Stephen's day is believed to have been racked by a dispute about the succession to the crown, it is surprising that interpretation of the reign by English historians has never divided opinion in the same way as the seventeenth-century civil war or even the quarrels between King John and his barons. The determination to describe the period as an anarchy, which could be quickly forgotten about under a competent new king, suggests that it has the quality of myth rather than of history.[1] This interpretation of Stephen's reign was made possible chiefly by the succession of Henry II in 1154 and his alleged policy of restoring the good government of his grandfather. Historians began to work consistently to create an impression of catastrophe under Stephen which would both excuse and justify the Angevin reconstruction of English government. By arguing that Henry II restored his grandfather's style of government, historians defended a concept of the seamless development of English history in which only Stephen's reign had no part. His nineteen years did not count. For no other period of English history have historians ever considered it possible to turn the clock back and pretend that the lively experiences of the interval could be willingly suppressed as easily forgettable nightmares. Experiences, particularly those thought disruptive, are not so easily forgotten. A mere six years of war (1939–45) have left indelible scars and inspired aspirations and ideals still powerful after fifty years. The Restoration of Charles II could not efface the legacy of the Civil War and Commonwealth. Only of the anarchy are we supposed to believe that public euphoria at the revival of strong kingship was so strong as to eradicate from consciousness any positive impression of the previous nineteen years. Nothing was to be remembered but the direst calamity. To treat Stephen's reign as though it were a black hole in England's past defies historical common sense. The lesson historians have rammed home about Stephen is that everyone learnt that such an experience must never be allowed to happen again. The interpretation is entirely negative.

The two most recent substantial accounts of Stephen's reign may be taken to exemplify the practice of concentrating on what Stephen got wrong. R. H. C. Davis concluded his study by claiming that, after enduring Stephen's incompetence, the English had grasped the advantages of accepting 'the man who was the lawful heir ... the one with the best hereditary claim'. In case modern readers missed the point of this lesson for constitutional law, its importance was underlined. 'In the twentieth century a system which places ... emphasis upon the accident of birth may seem archaic and irrelevant', but 'in the twelfth century it was welcomed as a practical and progressive reform'; what 'made it attractive was that to an age of turmoil and strife it brought stability and peace'.[2] This gain in political wisdom made the whole dreadful business worthwhile. Unobtrusively we have here all the elements of historical moralising: an assessment of the character of the age – the twelfth century (unlike our own?) was a barbarous time of turmoil; the virtue of stability and peace, to be achieved, not by free choice of ruler, but under God-given heirs; finally, the intuition that the achievements of an earlier age can be made to seem justified in the present, if they are presented as progressive in their time. Never mind that the conclusion was quite wrong: Henry of Anjou became king not by inheritance but as Stephen's adopted heir, to whom the great men of the kingdom did homage in Stephen's lifetime. Despite all this, Ralph Davis's account of Stephen gained wide currency and ran through three editions. The shifting political outlook may now make Davis's unquestioning confidence in the undisputed virtues of hereditary monarchy look somewhat dated. Yet even if an elected head of state became the latest wheeze of constitutional modernisers, it is not likely to rehabilitate Stephen.

The determination to learn the right lesson for the present from the past may be illustrated in another way from Davis's book. When first published in 1967, it identified Stephen's major mistake as the neglect of Normandy. This reflected the current perception that it was no longer possible to pretend that Britain could manage its affairs worldwide without paying attention to its near continental neighbours. In this changed climate of intellectual opinion, historians began to reinforce the message by insisting that in the past, too, English history had been affected by events on the other side of the Channel and that the island history was not entirely self-contained. Since those days, another new approach to English affairs obliges historians to harness the past to a new bandwagon. Now they must devote more attention to the other peoples of Britain, a conviction that was advanced in scholarly circles well before it achieved political expression. In his substantial new study of the reign, David Crouch accordingly concludes that Stephen failed not only in Normandy but in Wales too.[3]

This account shows in other ways how expectations have changed in the interim. The personal side of rulers' lives must be taken into account. Crouch duly distinguishes between Stephen as a man and as a ruler and very properly finds something to praise in him as a man. He also recommends comparing Stephen's government not with those of the admirable Henry I and Henry II but instead with that of his younger contemporary, Louis VII of France. For all his good intentions, Crouch has not done much to salvage Stephen's reputation. What happened in France will not redeem Stephen's failures in England and his admirable qualities as a man seem likely to enhance his reputation for not being ruthless enough for kingship. Crouch in fact accepts the traditional view that Stephen's character was responsible for his troubles. A good judge of men, he was a poor judge of situations; he

> could dither when faced with complex problems of policy. There seem to have been intellectual limitations which inhibited Stephen from any creative ability with the raw materials of politics. His record proves that he was unable to sustain any world-view, nor could he visualise the consequences of his actions for others.[4]

Here the baleful message is that good men may not, perhaps even cannot, make good rulers. If true, this would be both important and depressing. The opportunity to examine it more closely has not been taken. If the good nature of rulers is taken advantage of to the detriment of the general good, how is it that the generality fail to rally to the ruler for the commonweal?

If the unscrupulous are the only ones able to provide effective govenment for modern society, much modern political idealism is based upon false premisses. Surely that deserves to be examined.

There seem to be two main strands to the difficulties Stephen's reign still poses for historians. In the first place, there is the determination to nail responsibility for what is generally perceived as an unacceptable degree of domestic unrest. The extent of disorder has proved impossible to measure, but the clerical evidence itself is contradictory and the fate of the kingdom in general cannot have been as dreadful as the plaintive narratives appear to make out. There were no recorded massacres or political assassinations. This is not to say that secular quarrels may not have caused hardship and led to unwonted cruelties, but evidence of comparatively local, often even trivial, oppression, however disagreeable for the individuals concerned, does not amount to the total breakdown of law and order. We do not need to peer into the depths of the feudal system to find what can have been responsible for such a major catastrophe. Describing the whole reign in terms of turbulence is perverse. If the limited character of disorder were recognised, stridency about identifying those responsible would become inappropriate. Just because we happen to share, for different reasons, the ecclesiastical preference for litigation and disapproval of combat, we need to restrain any automatic sympathy for the ecclesiastical authorities. In the twelfth century it was not simply a barbaric survival that many secular disputes could still be conventionally settled by 'battle'. Before patting ourselves on the back for our more civilised values, we need to observe our limitations. The concept of sovereignty which has authorised a state monopoly of violence has had awesome consequences beyond its frontiers. Quarrels between twentieth-century states have given rise to conflicts causing far worse bloodshed than anything known in the twelfth century. The twentieth century has no claim to the high moral ground. Earlier ways of settling conflicts were by our standards comparatively bloodless. This should give pause to those who think of the medieval past as more evil than our own.

The second difficulty lies with the unquestioned assumption that the proper way to view this reign is in terms of its contribution to the development of the kingship, a notion that may have roused legitimate interest for three hundred years but was not obviously one of much concern in Stephen's own time. If we divert our attention from what did matter to contemporaries, and introduce ideas of our own, it is not surprising if we then miss the point altogether. Most historians now insist, for example, on attributing all the king's troubles to the dispute between rival claimants to the throne. This diverts attention from other important problems and misrepresents Matilda's own significance.

Contrary to the assumption that all the king's enemies consciously acted in the interests of the empress, what was written about them at the time should be sufficient to rule this out. The presence of Matilda did not obviously encourage barons to pursue their own quarrels with the king. Nor does it follow that, if the king had difficulties with different barons for different reasons, the explanation must lie either with the alleged faults of his character or with the undignified way he discharged the duties of his office. Here again the legalistic desire to attribute personal responsibility and treat the kingdom as though it were a modern state entirely at the mercy of its government encourages historians to pursue lines of speculation inappropriate for the task in hand. Henry I had confronted his enemies in Normandy, as Stephen had his in England. This makes it impossible to hold up Henry I as conspicuously more successful than his nephew in handling his barons; Henry's barons were not notably meeker than Stephen's.

Political conflicts do not arise simply because of the greater or lesser political acumen of the principals. Daily experience confirms the difficulties men find in working together in the most pacific kinds of situation. In political life, members of the same government, bound by self-interest to keep it in office and by party affiliation to share certain agreed goals, nevertheless have disagreements, antipathies and contrary ambitions. This is not necessarily due to the faults of their leaders, though it is often convenient to pretend this is the case. In the twelfth century differences of opinion and conflicts of interest were played out according to contemporary conventions. Even the clergy, who in principle accepted papal jurisdiction as a means to appease their quarrels, did not always or immediately obey unwelcome papal decisions. There are limits to what authority can achieve in any sphere of life. Men are not naturally docile. They accept direction willingly only if they perceive it to have merits of its own. To force compliance on unwilling subjects, states require enormous resources and a monopoly of military force. In the middle ages, neither of these was available. The history of medieval England cannot be written in terms of the monarchy alone. Historians of later periods would naturally assess the effectiveness of governments in terms of their ability to meet the requirements of the governed. Only for the twelfth century, it seems, are governments to be judged according to what they did for posterity.

In the twelfth century royal government was not in a position to provide many benefits. Any regular royal interference in the general affairs of the kingdom was, without exception, an excuse for imposing financial demands. Resignation to the heavy cost of central government is arguably acceptable in the twentieth century as a price worth paying for the benefits it brings. In the twelfth century, only those with privileged access to the king's court gained any advantage from royal intervention in their affairs. For the great majority, it was a matter of finding local sources of patronage, of which there were many. Important though the concept of the king's peace was, the kingdom could not in practice rely on kings themselves to enforce it. In most localities, the inhabitants expected to resolve a lot of peacekeeping problems on their own. At most, royal authority provided for some degree of standardisation in the way it operated and penalised local authorities remiss in doing their duties. Though English kings were in an exceptionally strong position to make sure that local communities fulfilled their local public duties, they were not in any position to take over such functions with their own officials. They left a great deal to be done by those on the spot or by those who enjoyed and deserved respect as their faithful 'vassals'.

The position of the clergy was not in this respect different but it would be a mistake to accept the clergy as somehow speaking for the whole general interest. Some influential clergy, more than others, may have steadily invoked the king's direct protection, but what they too demanded was respect for their privileges. Nor was the king their sole support. They had in the previous reign already begun to draw stronger institutional support from the papacy, a thousand miles away and without any coercive powers except spiritual penalties. They were in some ways less commited to the kingdom's interests on that account. Their claims to privilege on account of their spirituality were recognised by according them social status as lords of estates, often with responsibility to provide for the legal requirements of their own tenants; they themselves added to political problems when they invoked their spiritual powers to protect their material interests. Under Stephen, all communities in the kingdom had been allowed, encouraged, or obliged, to assume, or extend, the scope of their activities. To what extent they became remiss, if the king's officials slackened scrutiny of their performances, is unknown, but there can have been no general preference for allowing local jurisdictions to lapse. In a few cases, local authorities may have discovered their greater vulnerability and become accordingly more desperate for protective lordship from the king or a great baron. Such evidence as we have, however, indicates little willingness on the part of the clergy, the barons or the towns to throw themselves desperately into dependence on greater lordships. Some, even many, hundred courts may have passed into protective private lordship, but this cannot have been accepted unwillingly as a last resort, for no effort was made to overturn such arrangements in the new reign as unwarranted or no longer necessary.

Angevin rulers presided over a system of government which endorsed privilege, in all its forms, if only for a price. The historical focus on the exercise of royal authority as a manifestation of 'state-power', is a sign of what historians have made of these developments. Their concern with the royal administrative apparatus was not shared by any contemporary writer. The king's writing office, his financial audit, even the sources of his revenues did not interest any of them, except when, as for example happened at Abingdon, the king was accused of confiscating the abbot's store of treasure for himself. The interest historians give to the study of the kingship reflects the modern English conviction that it is up to the government to do something about whatever problem there may be. On this principle, if in any way things were not right, then Stephen has inescapable responsibility. By definition, it was up to him.

Closer attention to the situation contemporaries actually had to face in 1135 puts Stephen's position in perspective. Henry I had left his successor a difficult legacy, both by ruling himself in such a way as to provoke a reaction and for encouraging his daughter to entertain impossible expectations in England. In Stephen's time, attention would have focused not on benefits to come for England from Angevin government, but on the sheer impossibility of leaving responsibility for the supreme political office, which carried mainly military duties, to a woman. Even today, it would be daring to make a woman commander-in-chief in the field. Stephen's contemporaries would have expected Matilda's husband to assume this role on her behalf if called upon, but Henry I hardly encouraged them to think that Geoffrey would or could do so. Trouble of some kind was inevitable. If this fact had been faced squarely, less would have been made of Stephen's ineptitude. Who, frankly, could have been expected to do better? Stephen made a show of coping well to start with. How acceptable was it that the Angevins then deliberately aimed to disrupt Stephen's government by advancing a 'legitimist' claim to the throne? Eighteenth-century historians in a parallel situation give Jacobites short shrift. Had the Jacobites recovered their throne, historians would presumably have condoned their aspirations to destroy the Hanoverian regime. Stephen's reputation was ruined by posterity and his blameworthy character offered to justify the unfairness.

Half-hearted attempts to exonerate the king have offered baronial self-interest as an alternative explanation, as though they were private individuals abusing the system for personal reasons. Such accusations are made in the confidence that no one will now venture to make a plausible case for a discredited social group. The harsh judgments made of barons in modern times stems from current political prejudice. In the nineteenth century the barons who opposed King John, for example, could still be admired for their resistance to royal tyranny and for obtaining the first constitutional charter, Magna Carta, from him. In the thirteenth century, the barons were the king's subjects most exposed to irresponsible royal power; they were also best placed to put constraints on it. Reacting excessively against the so-called Whig Interpretation, twentieth-century historians typically regarded the barons as privileged defenders of self-interest and pushed them off their Whig pedestal. They have accordingly treated the barons as over-mighty subjects whose powers over the humble people of England had to be checked by impartial and strong kings.

These interpretations reflect not so much a more critical attitude to the past as the populist ideology of the present. In the last hundred years, it has become commonplace to explain social ills in terms of conflict between social classes and the power of the privileged to impose themselves. Such faults were supposed to be corrected by invoking the disinterested impartiality of the state to provide equitable rule for all. Despite all the accumulated evidence that the state has not in practice proved entirely benevolent or disinterested, the state is still venerated by those who hope to gain access to its powers and exercise them for their own purposes. Legitimising the concept of the state has been done in part by historians who have traced back its venerable origins to the middle ages. For them, the barons have become not the champions of the constitution but disrupters of royal power; historians duly enlarge on the degree of disruption caused. The historians most willing to interpret their actions sympathetically have done little more than rationalise their actions as the pursuit of their own ends or as ways of 'tightening their grip' (a favourite phrase, with unpleasant connotations). The barons are still not treated with adequate consideration of their qualities or of their social standing at the time. The clergy have fared better because those who are highly literate are well placed to leave evidence in their own favour and this is duly trotted out by their intellectual heirs. The focus on government and finding the guilty inevitably distracts attention from the twelfth century considered on its own terms. The difficulties we find are largely a result of asking inappropriate questions.

To break with our modern assumptions, we might reflect on what lies behind the most enduring and eloquent evidence of the past to survive in what we think of as works of art. The monumental architecture from the first century after the Norman Conquest still visible at Durham, Lincoln, Ely, Winchester, Gloucester, Tewkesbury and elsewhere was raised in a society very different from our own. Tremendous energies and invention were not concentrated in metropolitan capitals or royal courts but dispersed throughout the kingdom. Such building continued even in Stephen's reign, such as the many new Cistercian monasteries or the king's own Cluniac foundation at Faversham, intended to rival Henry I's Reading Abbey, then also still being built.[5] The kingdom was densely studded with religious communities and patrons eager to provide buildings for their communities.

These were not modest in scale, but in the most grandiose Romanesque manner. They were not, however, mass produced from a prototype or subsidised by the state; each had its distinctive features, and demonstrated the self-sufficiency of the communities that put them up. This age of local magnificence has since had no parallel in English history. What we can still see is only part of the story, for many of the greatest religious buildings have not survived, being deliberately pillaged and ruined at the Reformation. This vandalism was then perpetrated by Henry VIII to destroy the power of the church, which alone offered a flicker of resistance to the sovereign authority of his state. For centuries, those who have since championed the powers of central government have continued to belittle the provinces and local autonomy. The ruined abbeys of England may have been regarded as picturesque, but an important aspect of what they represented as monuments of local pride has been systematically smothered by denigrating them on sectarian grounds as nurseries of superstition.

Even more disapproval has been heaped on the parallel secular monuments of the middle ages.[6] Nearly all medieval castles were deliberately dismantled as potential threats to central authority. What remained of them could, within a century of the Cromwellian destruction, still inspire a cultured shudder of Romantic horror. Collectively we still choose to regard them as instruments of oppression, designed to hold the kingdom in subjection to brutal military authorities. Current beliefs about class conflict explain why castles are automatically assumed to symbolise the arrogance of a military aristocracy. Their role as bastions of local order, stability and grandeur is ignored. One of the reasons for our blindness to their role is that we ourselves have lost that sense of what can be achieved on a local scale. Only in the Victorian north of England did civic authorities aspire to something comparable. In our own age, local governments have put up many buildings for public purposes. Their form betrays how short of confidence they are as expressions of local pride, a few grand concert halls excepted. In this respect they are in glaring contrast with the imposing achievements of earlier times. Misreading these monuments of the past as oppressive signs of class conflict is a typical example of how interpretations of the past help to bolster modern prejudices. We do not want to recognise what it meant in the post-conquest period for every part of the kingdom to be provided with an abundance of public buildings of outstanding quality. In order to understand the situation of Stephen's reign, we need to consider what kind of society it was that raised these massive buildings.

Works of art of a different kind allow us a glimpse of the more intimate sensibilities of the age. Because of their fragility, illuminated manuscripts are not as widely seen as Romanesque cathedrals.[7] Modern methods of reproduction, however, have served to make them better known and there can now be no excuse for overlooking the activities of medieval scribes and artists. Their manuscripts, comprising parchment books elaborately decorated with miniature painted drawings of superlative quality, survive in considerable numbers from twelfth-century England. Though it is not always easy to assign precise dates to their composition, many of them were certainly completed in Stephen's reign. His brother, Henry of Winchester, and Abbot Anselm of Bury St Edmunds were lavish patrons of such works; Abbot Ralph of St Albans is specifically commended for his devotion to books in this reign. The composition of chronicles, the writing of charters and the copying of library texts flourished in many places. Social conditions cannot have interrupted the supply of parchment and pigments; scribes remained active; and book-production organised by expert division of labour was not disrupted. If such activities are judged incompatible with times of turbulence, the solution is not to date them to some other reign, but to conclude that the times were not so troubled after all.

The value of invoking such artefacts does not depend, however, on what they may indicate about the continuing orderliness of the religious life in Stephen's own time. They allow us to confront an aspect of the twelfth century not otherwise easy to pin down. Some of the manuscripts are adorned with full page illustrations, usually of biblical stories. More frequently, the finest workmanship is lavished on initials clearly indicating where the text fell into its distinct divisions and serving therefore to indicate a deep respect for natural order. The letter form is decorated with leaves or animals, even of people; an astonishing variety of subjects is depicted in states of great agitation, climbing or wriggling within the letter and brilliant with colour. The combination of the letter shape with its internal life of animal and vegetable subjects may be regarded as a paradigm of an aspiration to orderly form that could not at the same time resist contorted embellishment. The sheer exuberance of invention illustrates the vitality and playfulness admitted even to the cloister. We need to take into account a twelfth-century world bursting with life and energy, not one tightly controlled, as ours has become, in the interests of modern factories and technology. We should not expect of them the kind of meek submission to authority that seems to us indispensable for the maintenance of public order.

The robust character of twelfth-century religion was further sustained by confidence in the miracle-working powers of native-born saints. Historians of the twelfth century tend as ever to pick out for emphasis the work of reformers like the Cistercians, the growth of logical studies in the schools or the development of new pieties like devotion to the Virgin Mary and the suffering Jesus. However significant for the future, these shifts in the religious outlook still had only limited impact in the twelfth century itself. The established popular practices of religion indicate that in England native saints like Cuthbert or Edmund king and martyr could still inspire more localised veneration. Such saints exemplify forms of Christianity now little appreciated but not then old-fashioned. The murder of Becket added spectacularly to their number as late as 1170. Religion as practised in the twelfth century, was as much a defence of older certainties as a harbinger of change. The aggressive defence by monasteries of their traditional independence against bishops bent on enhancing their supervisory powers is symptomatic of the mood. Not surprisingly, twelfth-century religious art is vigorous not ethereal.

The purpose of adducing artistic work of the period as evidence of Stephen's reign is not, in the manner of some twentieth-century writers, to hold up as hypocritical the human capacity to commit crimes and create beauty at the same time. It is not even necessary to date such works precisely to Stephen's reign. What they demonstrate, without risk of contradiction, is how most of Stephen's contemporaries operated in essentially local communities and institutions which provided for their needs and absorbed their energies. The problems of royal government did not matter to them all that much. Their own concerns did not then make them dependent on those of the monarchy. This is true of those we know about because they were literate enough to explain their position; most others probably had even more limited horizons.

To the aspirations and preoccupations of most people in the kingdom at this time historians usually devote little attention, even when they have confidently pronounced on the consequences of contested kingship for the happiness of the general population. This neglect of the local dimension is not a consequence of the kinds of historical evidence available, for the evidence is incorrigibly local. Rather, historians themselves have insisted on extracting from and conflating their sources in order to reconstruct the 'national' situation. This totally misrepresents twelfth-century perceptions.

The status of local government in England has sunk abysmally in the past hundred years, as the level of voting in local elections notoriously indicates. 'Government' is unlikely ever to do anything to remedy a situation for which it is mainly responsible. Local government has been systematically manipulated from the centre which has created its boundaries, dictated its powers and controlled its activities. We are brought up to think of it as a low-grade form of social organisation. Those who run local government are self-selected leaders of interest groups whose activities provide useful services; instead of emphasising their own local loyalties, they present themselves in terms of national party affiliations and expect their fortunes to reflect national rather than purely local opinions. The low profile of local politics is an unexpected consequence of enlarging the franchise, since it has diverted voters' attention from what they themselves can do locally to what their representatives might achieve nationally. Central government, confident of its mandate, disposes of local affairs as it chooses. What hope for local authorities can there be in such a situation? This proprietorial attitude of central to local government is a very recent development, but it has already deeply entered into our interpretation of the remote past. In each and every respect, our requirements run counter to those of the twelfth century. Over a hundred years ago, Victorian historians still retained their respect for local institutions. They even admired the sturdy independence of the Swiss cantons, in which they acknowledged survivals of an earlier age of popular government they thought characteristic of all Germanic peoples. Such an idea now seems preposterous. Typically, in modern England, the Swiss receive little credit for their remarkable history. In twentieth-century Britain such small-scale affairs inspire nothing but indifference, too petty for notice.

England, however, also developed as a kingdom from very small units only brought together in the wars against the Danes under the leadership of the kings of Wessex. English government grew originally from the bottom up, not from top down. The most important of its units in the twelfth century was the shire, which had successfully survived from the pre-conquest period and was therefore already of venerable antiquity. The settlement of the Normans in the countryside and towns did nothing to diminish the significance of the shire for both king and country. The value the king attached to his tenants-in-chief only served to strengthen the ability of local communities to run their own affairs with the help of powerful Norman lords and sheriffs. When kings interested themselves in matters of justice and finance, they had to send instructions or delegates to visit and negotiate in the countryside. Royal government did not in the twelfth century have any powers to run the country and made little difference to the way the country was normally administered. Even in the thirteenth-century eyres, it was only every seven years on average that the king's justices showed up. For most men, their ordinary affairs were settled in their immediate neighbourhoods. Responsibility for the suppression of any disorder was not the king's alone.

Not only were the men on the spot obliged by law to take immediate action to apprehend criminals or to go in pursuit of them, they had a vested interest in the protection of their own property. To defend the peace, they had to take action themselves; there was no local constabulary force and the king kept no standing army to be called on in emergencies. The king's function was as long stop: to redress injustice. The English knew what they had themselves to do to deal with violence in their communities. Criminal prosecutions had not yet become a royal responsibility but still depended on private accusations. Maintaining the peace depended on a suretyship system, the tithing. In order to get their districts working effectively, a higher proportion of the local community than now votes in local elections must then have been engaged in public affairs. Settlement of disputes had to be secured by neighbours and by appeal to the memories of the most long-lived. If it had not secured local cooperation, it would not have worked at all; there were then no career politicians nor professional lawyers.[8]

All small-scale agrarian societies, from ancient Greece to colonial America, were run like this. This kind of society lacks features we now think essential, yet its capacity to look after itself without interference from 'above' was unrivalled. The significance of this is barely remarked on, because it cannot be easily assimilated to modern democratic ideology. Twelfth-century England had nothing to be ashamed of; its resilience deserves more credit than it receives. In the twelfth century the king's subjects were sufficiently capable of managing in their own localities and lordships to have considered ideas about how much, or little, kingship they needed Occasionally, the king's help was sought. More often, it was the king who pressed the localities into serving his purposes. But only in the late thirteenth century did kings begin to summon local representatives to royal councils to get their approval for royal wars and vote subsidies for armies; not till the sixteenth century did sovereigns seek to cover the enormity of their decisions to changes in religious practice by obtaining parliamentary consent. The advantages of validating acts of government through representation of the people depended not on the extension of the franchise but on the existence of real communities to be represented.

Modern views of parliamentary government take no account of the historical circumstances in which parliament grew and developed, mainly because of the present tendency to leave political exposition to theorists without historical interests or understanding. Unlike their predecessors a mere generation ago, career politicians now usually have little appreciation of parliament's historic function. Many now only seek to represent the people as a step to becoming part of the government itself. The idea of communities to be represented has disappeared and been replaced by constituencies with artificially drawn boundaries. Politicians and journalists foster the idea that representation should be 'representative' of party strength, or rather of party appeal, for only a tiny minority of the electorate actually belongs to any political party at all. Yet some distant memory of what communities once were survives and surfaces in proposals to reorder modern societies.

Even now, therefore, it is not without interest to reconsider England's medieval past. Naturally many will belittle its achievements and reject its constitutional credentials on the grounds that, in all previous ages, political activity was an expression of self-interested parties. Strangely, the argument about self-interest is thought not to apply to modern reformers. We do not call into question the personal motives of those who clamour in our own day for improvements and modernisation. We are not entitled to believe that in past times self-interest was the only motive for activity in public life. Nor should some prejudice about the middle ages be allowed to excuse ignorance of the medieval part of our past. No one pretends that the even more remote achievements of Ancient Greece and Rome do not deserve an honoured place in general education for what they may teach us about such important themes as democracy, empire, law, culture or colonisation, to mention only the political.

Why has medieval history not enjoyed comparable esteem? Mainly, it seems, because in England the word 'medieval' is currently employed pejoratively for what is deemed archaic, barbarous, superseded, often with regard to features not characteristic of the middle ages at all. Anyone who takes the trouble to look seriously at the history of the middle ages finds that the popular use of the term totally misrepresents it; those educated enough to know better ought to give up using the word as a term of disparagement. Instead they use it defiantly, indifferent to the culture they pillory. English medieval historians have not, however, given up defending the cause. Though in general our countrymen choose to ignore the fact, it is not without implications in the present that England is exceptional amongst European states for a history of continuous government stretching over more than a thousand years. The expectation of stability is deep-rooted. Moreover, only on rare occasions over that period have governments been changed by force. The former reputation of the English as a distinguished political people rested in large measure on their ability to devise peaceful solutions to their domestic problems.

Because of this traditionally national focus to English history, English historians concentrated their defence of the middle ages on what they perceived the period to have contributed to the development of the English state. In the nineteenth century, the development of parliament as an institution, and the importance of Magna Carta as the bedrock of English liberties, received rapt attention from medievalists.[9] With the advent of universal suffrage respect for the early history of parliament might have been expected to grow. In fact, verbal deference to the value of parliament as an institution masks, even camouflages, a recognition that the growth of the administrative state has greater long-term significance than the extension of the franchise. In strict parallel with this present awareness, most serious study of English medieval history in the twentieth century has dutifully concentrated on demonstrating how medieval kings first created a unified kingdom in the tenth century and then gradually put together an apparatus through which the kingdom might be governed and national unity promoted. In this interpretation, even parliament itself has become not a bulwark against arbitrary royal government but another tool in government hands for the exaction of taxes and the promulgation of national statute law. Medieval historians have in this way made their own contributions to the idea of the deep roots of the modern English state. They may not have been conscious propagandists for its cause, but they have all believed in its virtues.

The academic defence of the subject in terms of what is now deemed important is understandable, but is not the only, or necessarily the best way, to approach English medieval history. We may also approach it to rediscover something of what we are otherwise in danger of forgetting altogether. The current fashion for condemning what vestiges remain of our medieval inheritance itself betrays some uneasiness that things so old surprisingly retain their allure. In Scotland and Wales, the nationalist causes quaff deeply on their medieval brews. The merits of the English medieval past deserve comparable recognition. If only in the interests of honesty, we should acknowledge what surviving examples of medieval architecture prove about medieval powers of imagination and technical accomplishment. Medieval poetry and philosophy may have no comparably visual impact, but intellectual engagement with them still stirs admiration and awe. Medieval men of learning displayed commendable industry and persistence in their efforts to grapple with some of the most difficult concepts of human thought. To help them do so, they found inspiration and enlightenment, not only in the available writings of ancient Rome and Greece but, less predictably, from the controversial scientific and philosophical studies of contemporary Islam. To provide a suitable environment for the cultivation of abstruse learning, an entirely original form of higher education was devised. The two medieval English universities played an important part in the process; but, instead of taking proper pride in these institutions, many critics take every opportunity to denounce their antiquated principles. Universities have continued to prove their value, however little their essential purposes are appreciated in most parts of modern society.

Barely acknowledged at all remains the ability of our medieval European ancestors to have created other viable social forms, most of which successfully flourished into modern times. Agricultural settlements developed across the Continent and town life revived, not so much by direction from above, as in the Roman empire, but by local economic initiatives, through the exchange of goods across the different geographical zones of Europe and the fostering of craft skills. The greater political entities of kingdoms were themselves riddled with semi–independent towns and enclaves of jurisdiction. Rationalist reformers of later times abominated this disorderly collection of authorities; 'modernisers' since have constantly ridiculed them. In the middle ages they had kept royal bureaucracies at a distance, permitting an exercise of local powers unrivalled since. There was never any question then that the faults in the system lay with others. Problems remained with those who created them, on the spot. Because the citizens of all modern societies (except, notably, of the United States) have been disarmed by the state and become therefore entirely dependent on it for their protection, communities reliant on themselves are now automatically considered barbarous and lawless. This is unfair. Where local communities had to defend themselves, they also developed all the practices of the customary law in assembling posses of men, devising forms of mutual security and securing judgment by oath-helpers and juries of neighbours.

Out of these ways of keeping the peace in their neighbourhoods, a system of interlocking communities developed. If required, these communities could find spokesmen or representatives to speak up for their constituencies and report back. This is how representative government on a broader front became possible. Though coordinated to suit the king, its origins depended on the structure at the base. For centuries this system kept the peace in England, probably at least as well as modern means provide in different times, if not better. We have no reason to congratulate ourselves on our superior achievements in public order. Things were different in earlier times, but no less effective solutions were found to the perennial problems of enabling men with different interests somehow to live together in the one community of the realm. Those solutions have left their mark on the country's customs, whether they are appreciated for what they are, or not.

How well local authorities of various kinds succeeded overall is shown by the very limited character of disruption in medieval England. In Stephen's reign, communities did not generally go to war against other neighbourhoods. As against instances of self-indulgent slaughter and rapine, there was manifest reluctance to fight other Englishmen and a widespread willingness by the leaders of factions to consult as to how further conflict might be avoided, and negotiate deals to settle quarrels. Several leading parties are known to have shown determination and ability to find a settlement by agreements amongst themselves. There was remarkably little willingness in England to upset the applecart for reasons of personal ambition. This does not mean that violence did not occur or that suffering may not have been common. Chronicle lamentations about the damage suffered by church property should not, however, be interpreted as giving objective evidence for disorder. They must be read in conjunction with other evidence. For quite general reasons, therefore, effective government in the twelfth century did not in fact have to await the end of civil war.

The capacity of locals to manage their affairs on their own did not make the monarchy itself an irrelevance in Stephen's reign, but modern ideas about authoritative rulers are mostly very wide of the mark. Considering how long monarchy as an institution has dominated the political life of the kingdom, it is astonishing at the present time how it is, without contradiction, systematically misrepresented. Those who claim to think 'rationally' about monarchy regard it as some kind of institutional dinosaur. The less well-educated seem to find no difficulty in accepting it as a focus of respect for the idea of the national community, a personification of what most people also effortlessly understand the 'flag' to symbolise.

The personal worthiness of the monarch is irrelevant to the concept of monarchy. To find fault with the person who carries the image is to commit the most elementary mistake of taking the appearance for the essence. To imprison the king is not a mere insult to his person, but a disgrace inflicted on his people. By virtue of his coronation, his designation and acceptance by God, Stephen as king embodied the notion of the English as a single people. Though his writs might still be addressed to his faithful Englishmen and Frenchmen, he was king of the English. To challenge his office was deeply disruptive of a task that was at all times difficult. The king himself was expected to act with propriety, and usually did so. When he proceeded to violent measures at his own court against disloyal subjects, his actions, however justified, seemed indecorous. To capture him in battle was an affront, not merely to his person, but to his office. It was not sufficient to annihilate his kingship, but it snubbed his people. It could not tarnish his personal lustre, and his restoration in fact confirmed that God had indeed chosen him and that men were powerless to unthrone him. Likewise, imprisonment did not later on damage Richard I's reputation, or even Charles I's. In some ways, royal suffering conferred greater dignity on kings and proved their power to rise above their degradation.

This is not to deny that in the event after the battle of Lincoln there were some who rejoiced that an unworthy ruler had been disgraced; but the enthusiasm of partisans was clearly not widely shared. There was certainly room for disagreement at the time about what qualities of kingship were most important. A very authoritarian view of rulership was expressed after Stephen's death by Henry of Huntingdon when he revised his earlier critical character-sketch of Henry I. To offset his vices, Huntingdon adduced in

Henry's s favour the great awe he inspired abroad. This change in Huntingdon's own judgment of Henry I may have come about as he reflected on the experiences of Stephen's reign. A comparable view had, however, been already expressed twenty years earlier by John of Worcester, who also thought it proper for men to live in dread of kings. Both these comments have been interpreted as an implicit criticism of Stephen, but they are typical rather of a certain approach to authority, still voiced in some quarters. Awe is hardly enough to establish durable rule. Later English kings who found their government at home became easier when they inspired awe abroad bequeathed to their heirs problems even more difficult to resolve. In the long term, it was not the quality of kings but the acceptability of their right to wield authority that mattered.

Whatever Stephen's own shortcomings, they were not perceived at the time as any justification for replacing him. Stephen's age, in some ways like our own, was looking for a more accessible kind of ruler, and had to learn to live with the implications, much as we do. Had Stephen tried to maintain the high-handed style of his predecessor, he might have found that it was no longer endurable. As it was, Stephen was respected for his own virtues, courtesy and affability. Surprisingly little unfair advantage was taken of his mildness, if indeed it is correct to argue at all that his affable character encouraged disorder. Too much of Stephen's reign has been glibly interpreted as a display of baronial egoism and royal ineffectiveness. Stephen was not always unwilling to proceed to extremes and he never became a mere cipher in English affairs. There was more beef in his kingship than detractors allow. As one who stayed a difficult course to the end, he deserves some commendation, as well as sympathy. He presented himself with dignity in public and remained active in the field to the last. His style was not like his uncle's, but he performed kingship in a way acceptable to his times. Stephen's overall supervision of the kingdom was not systematically opposed by the great men, though it was sorely disturbed by various individuals like the earls of Chester and Norfolk, for reasons of their own, and by those who dedicated themselves to championing the Angevins. Nor should the Angevin hegemony be seen as having significantly changed men's perceptions of kingship. Although the Angevins were allowed, after 1154, to turn the crown into a hereditary possession, there was a price to be paid. In return for being allowed to rule, the Plantagenet dynasty had to learn to live within the limits set by Magna Carta. Out of these arrangements developed a form of government that involved regular consultation with parliament.

As perceptions of the past are constantly changing, no final word on Stephen can be expected. The difficulties lie not with the past, but with the ways we ourselves seek confirmation of our perceptions of the present by reimagining the past to fit our own conceptions of what matters. We do this because the present is necessarily confusing; it offers us conflicting impressions of what is important: identifying its dominant elements is always difficult. There has been a tendency to resolve the dilemmas of the present by appeal to the past, which can be presented as fixed, showing what succeeds, the direction of time's current, what will survive in human memory, offering guidance as to how we might distinguish between what is substantial and what is ephemeral. If we did not have confidence that we could learn something about the durable elements of human life from the past, why bother with it at all?

The best reason is the discovery that human affairs are necessarily complicated; they can never be resolved once and for all because people are not all willing to think exactly alike. Arrangements have to be found to minimise the tensions human relationships involve. When the authority of the established government is contested by men who insist on their own rights and are prepared even to make war in defence of their principles (or interests), conflict is inevitable. If the government totally fails to defend the public interest, it will be superseded by the victorious dissidents; they will impose their own order, or fail in their turn. Stephen's government faltered, but could not in fact be replaced in his lifetime. His difficulties are not without some modern parallels. We can still see today how 'the troubles' may be due to a comparatively small number of people willing to create a state of tension and evade the pressure not merely of one government (or even two), but also of the feelings of the majority of the population; these minorities may see themselves as dedicated to noble causes deserving total commitment, yet seem to others entirely destructive of public order. We have also had to learn how difficult it can be to find, let alone impose, a 'solution', to a state of affairs almost universally deplored. Central governments, for all their resources, can still show remarkably little ability to repress 'troubles'. Modern governments naturally use all the resources at their disposal to conceal their impotence from the public, but in other respects some of their weaknesses look uncannily like some of Stephen's. In his day his government did not have the resources to invest in concealing its weaknesses; on the other hand, the public probably expected less and nursed fewer illusions.

Stephen's reign could easily be admitted into an account of English history that recognised the diversities of the kingdom and the localised character of its development. The reasons why this is not usually done go very deep. Even the contemporary obsession with denigrating heroes and rehabilitating the villains of history has done little to rescue Stephen from his critics. His most recent historians have been amongst the most hostile. Historians may differ as to what they pick out to criticise, but however weak or plain unlucky Stephen is shown to be, his unavoidable responsibility for 'the Anarchy' condemns him. Set in the context of a history focused on the development of royal government, Stephen cannot expect a reprieve. After more than eight centuries, something more positive and interesting ought to be discernible in this much maligned reign. Has the problem all along been that Stephen's benign character has itself been a reproach to his successors? Has he been consistently blamed for the disasters wished upon him by his haughty cousin? Did those who supported the idea of the Angevins' birthright to rule really have the right to try and impose this belief on an unwilling kingdom? The problems created by minorities bent on subverting lawful governments still elude solution.

Notes

Notes to Chapter 1: Scene-Setting

1. *Gesta Stephani*, ed. and trans. K. Potter, 2nd edn (OMT, 1976). R. H. C. Davis, 'The Authorship of the *Gesta Stephani*', *EHR*, 77 (1962), pp. 209–32, argued for its attribution to Robert, bishop of Bath. Though widely adopted, this theory has not convinced all scholars.
2. Gervase of Tilbury, *Otia Imperialia*, ed. G. G. Leibnitz, *Scriptores Rerum Brunswicensium* (Hanover, 1707), pp. 945–47, 'de regibus Anglorum'.
3. *Recueil des Actes d'Henri II*, ed. L. V. Delisle and E. Berger (Paris, ii, 1920), pp. 305–6, no. 682, issued by Henry II at the end of the reign, 1188, referring to *tempore regis Stephani ablatoris mei*.
4. Earlier versions of this interpretation are found in continuations of the *Chronicle* of Sigebert of Gembloux, compiled at Anchin near Douai and at Affligem between Bruges and Ghent, a monastery closely associated with the family of Adeliza of Louvain, Henry I's second queen. Auctarium Aquicinensis, Auctarium Affligense, MGHSS, vi (1844), pp. 392–98, 398–405.
5. *L'histoire de Guillaume le Maréchal*, ed. P. Meyer, SHF (1891), i, pp. 18–25 : on Stephen's reign, lines 23–738; William as hostage, lines 487–678: Stephen's heart full of *simplesse et douceur*.
6. *Feudal Manuals of English History*, ed. T. Wright (London, 1872), pp. 56, 83.
7. Matthew Paris, *Historia Anglorum*, ed. F. Madden, RS 44 (1866), i, pp. 244, 294–95, 301.
8. The most recent historical romances concerning Stephen are Jean Plaidy, *The Passionate Enemies* (London, 1976) and Sharon Kay Penman, *When Christ and His Saints Slept* (New York, 1995).

Notes to Chapter 2: Stephen's Historical Image

1. Polydore Vergil, *Historia Anglicana*, 26 books (Basel, 1534), pp. 194–207: book 12 on Stephen.
2. R. Holinshed. *The Laste Volume of the Chronicles of England, Scotlande and Irelande* (London, 1577), pp. 365–94 (in the more readily accessible edition of 1807: ii, pp. 78–111). The 1577 edition was illustrated with woodcuts (omitted from the second edition of 1587). E. Hodnett, *Marcus Gheeraerts the Elder of Bruges, London and Antwerp* (Utrecht, 1971), pp. 48–51; M. Holmes 'Some

Woodcuts in Holinshed's Chronicle', *JBAA*, 3rd series, 15 (1952), pp. 30–34, plates xxi–xxiii; S. Booth, *The Book called Holinshed's Chronicle: An Account of its Inception, Purpose, Contributors, Content, Publication, Revision and Influence on William Shakespeare* (San Francisco, 1968).

3. J. Speed, *History of Great Britaine* (London, 1611), book 9, chapter 5, pp. 445–54, a folio volume.

4. S. Daniel, *First Part of the Historie of England* (London, 1613), pp. 198–237; later edition (1896), iv, pp. 214–35.

5. R. Brady, *A Complete History of England from the Entrance of the Romans under the Conduct of Julius Caesar unto the End of the Reign of King Henry III* (London, 1685) pp. 272–97.

6. W. Camden, *Britannia* (London, 1586), quoting William of Newburgh.

7. Paul Rapin de Thoyras, *The History of England*; second edition, translated and edited by N. Tindal (London, 1732), i, pp. 201–21.

8. Vertue provided full-page portraits of Kings Egbert, Alfred, Canute and all kings from William I; separate engravings of their funerary monuments were also included. I. Bignamini, 'George Vertue, Art Historian', *Walpole Society*, 54 (1991), pp. 2–18.

9. D. Hume, *The History of England from the Invasion of Julius Caesar to the Accession of Henry VII* (2 vols, London, 1762), chapter 7, pp. 247–61.

10. J. Lingard, *A History of England from the First Invasion by the Romans to the Accession of Henry VIII* (London, 1819), ii, chapter 11, pp. 1–33.

11. C. Dickens, *A Child's History of England* (London, 1852), i, pp. 129–35, chapter 11, 'England under Matilda and Stephen'.

12. Ella S. Armitage, *The Childhood of the English Nation* (London, 1877) pp. 148–52.

13. K. Norgate, *England under the Angevin Kings* (London, 1887); p. 271 on Blois-Anjou rivalry; pp. 280–81 on Stephen's moral constitution. When Kate Norgate died in April 1935, the *Times* obituary described her as 'the most learned woman historian of what may be described as the pre-academic period'.

14. W. Stubbs, *The Constitutional History of England* (6th edn, Oxford, 1897), chapter 10, pp. 344–64.

15. J. H. Round, *Geoffrey de Mandeville: A Study of the Anarchy* (London, 1892); *The Anarchy of King Stephen's Reign*, ed. E. King (Oxford, 1994).

16. Round's first publication, *The Coming Terror* (Brighton, 1881), pp. 1–14, was a privately printed pamphlet intended to show how interference with the laws of nature for political purposes would inevitably lead to a reign of terror. 'Socialism being essentially antagonistic to society in its existing form can only be upheld by force.' Round aimed to warn all free-born Englishmen against the 'schemers who would rule them with a rod of iron ... What crimes are committed in the name [of Liberty] was the cry of a victim who had tasted the liberty of the Terror ... Shall we too offer sacrifice at the shrine of Anarchy?' In this rather oblique way he made use of a word that he was to illustrate to much greater effect ten years later. In both cases his use of the word is somewhat eccentric.

17. F. M. Stenton, *The First Century of English Feudalism* (Oxford, 1932), pp. 216, 217, 222, 244.

18. *Regesta Regum Anglo-Normannorum*, iii, ed. H. A. Cronne and R. H. C. Davis (Oxford, 1968).

19. *RRAN*, iii, nos 5, 118, 172, 293, 384–85, 456, 514, 777, 848; Matilda also authorised markets, ibid., nos 253, 597, 881–84, as did Henry of Anjou, ibid., nos 310, 710; R. Britnell, 'English Markets and Royal Administration before 1200', *Economic History Review*, 2nd series, 31 (1978) pp. 183–96. For great annual fairs during August, September and October authorised by the king, see RRAN, iii, nos 287, 476, 621 and H. W. C. Davis, 'Henry of Blois and Brian Fitz-Count', *EHR*, 25 (1910), pp. 297–303.

20. For Master Matthew, Gervase of Canterbury, *Opera Historica*, ed. W. Stubbs RS, 73, i (1879), p. 125; a *scola* at Christ Church, *Charters of the Redvers Family and Earldom of Devon, 1090–1217*, ed. R. Bearman, Devon and Cornwall Record Society, new series, 37 (1994), no 15; a *schola* in Derby given by William Barbe confirmed by Bishop Walter 1154–59, *English Episcopal Acta*, 14, *Coventry*, ed. M. J. Franklin (1998), p. 52, no 54; for the *magister scole* at Salisbury, *RRAN*, no 789; Robert of Torigni, *Chronicle*, ed. R. Howlett, *Chronicles of the Reigns of Stephen, Henry II and Richard I*, RS, 82, iv (1889), pp. 158–59 on Vacarius; 'Un débat sur le sacerdoce des moines au XIIe siècle', ed. R. Foreville and J. Leclercq, *Studia Anselmiana*, fasc. 41 (1957), pp. 8–118, 'totidem aut plures sunt in Anglia non solum in urbibus et castellis verum etiam in villulis peritissimi scolarum magistri, quot fiscorum regalium exactores', from p. 65. Reginald of Durham, *Libellus de admirandis beati Cuthberti virtutibus*, ed. J. Raine, Surtees Society, 1 (1835), relates miracles of St Cuthbert featuring school masters at Yarm and Norham, nos 17, 73; R. W. Southern, 'The Place of England in the Twelfth-century Renaissance', *Medieval Humanism and Other Studies* (Oxford, 1970), pp. 158–80.

21. *Cartularium monasterii de Rameseiensis* ed. W. H. Hart and P. A. Lyon, RS, 79, ii (1886), no. 390 'multos homines de servitio rusticorum francos fecit … unum rusticum fecit francum … '

22. R. C. van Caenegem, *Royal Writs in England from the Conquest to Glanvill*, Selden Society, 77 (1958–59), pp. 336–40, thought writs of naifty for the recovery of serfs were particularly numerous early in Henry II's reign, as though under Stephen an exceptional number had fled or been abducted. The examples he published show that well into Henry II's reign, after 'anarchy' had been contained, such writs were still being sought. Anarchy alone cannot explain whatever happened in Stephen's time. Jumièges: *Calendar of Documents Preserved in France*, ed. J. H. Round (London, 1899), no. 154; *The Beauchamp Cartulary Charters*, ed. E. Mason, PRS, new series., 43 (1980), no. 173 for recovery of *fugitivos et nativos* fled since 1135, issued before 1158.

23. *Papsturkunden in England*, ed. W. Holtzmann, iii (Göttingen, 1952), no. 69, for *homines* of Hertfordshire who stopped payments of *redditus* and *consue-tudines*. For *servi* in command of a castle, below p. 274 n. 35.

24. *GS*, c. 28.
25. Winton Domesday, ed. F. Barlow, *Winchester in the Early Middle Ages*, ed.
    M. Biddle (Oxford, 1976): 'The record of waste properties seems hardly to
    reflect the rate of the devastation that is said to have taken place ... even in
    Colobrochestret next to St Mary's there is little evidence of devastation in the
    1148 survey and none of the archaeological excavations in the city has produced
    evidence of a general burning in the twelfth century; the city's principal losses
    may well have resulted from looting by the victors rather than from the
    widespread destruction of buildings': comments by M. Biddle and D. J. Keene,
    ibid., p. 489. Natural causes, rather than warfare, were responsible for fires
    that consumed several cities in Stephen's early years. London was burned from
    London Bridge to St Clement's Danes in 1136: Matthew Paris, *Chronica Majora*,
    ed. H. R. Luard, RS 57, ii (1874), p. 163; Rochester and York were both burned
    in June 1137: Gervase of Canterbury, i, p. 100.

Notes to Chapter 3: English Kingship in 1135

1. R. W. Southern, 'The Place of Henry I in English History', *PBA*, 48 (1962),
   pp. 127–69; J. A. Green, *The Government of England under Henry I* (Cambridge,
   1986); S. L. Mooers, 'A Revaluation of Royal Justice under Henry I of England',
   AHR, 93 (1988), pp. 340–58; J. Hudson, *The Formation of English Common Law
   and Society in England from the Norman Conquest to Magna Carta* (London,
   1996), pp. 84, 115; W. L. Warren, *The Governance of Norman and Angevin England, 1066–1272* (London, 1987), p. 83, explained why the government of Henry
   I is not to be admired. Cp. Stenton, *First Century*, p. 218: 'the merits which
   attract a historian were less plain to the man of King Henry's own day'.
   M. Brett, *The English Church under Henry I* (Oxford, 1975); C. Newman, *The
   Anglo-Norman Nobility in the Reign of Henry I* (Philadelphia, 1988). For the
   survival of Henry I's style of government under Stephen, G. J. White, 'Continuity in Government', in *The Anarchy*, pp. 117–43.
2. Orderic Vitalis, *Ecclesiastical History*, ed. M. Chibnall (OMT, 1978), vi, pp. 16–17;
   cp. *GS*, c. 12.
3. OV, vi, pp. 210–13, 352–55.
4. William of Malmesbury, *Gesta regum Anglorum*, ed. R. A. B. Mynors,
   R. M. Thomson and M. Winterbottom (OMT, 1998–99), pp. 708–9, 742–45; cp.
   OV, vi, pp. 18–19.
5. Suger, *Vie de Louis VI*, ed. H. Waquet (Paris, 1929), pp. 190–91, cp. pp. 102–3.
6. *Liber monasterii de Hyda*, ed. E. Edwards, RS, 45 (1866), p. 321. This chronicle
   is now ascribed to a source close to Earl Warenne, possibly written at the
   priory of St Pancras, Lewes; J. A. Green, 'King Henry I and the Aristocracy of
   Normandy', *Actes du IIIᵉ congrès national des sociétés savantes, Poitiers, 1986*
   (Paris, 1988), i, pp. 161–73.
7. Henry of Huntingdon, *Historia Anglorum*, ed. D. Greenway (OMT, 1996),
   pp. 456–57 (Robert), 482–83 (Clito), 596–601 (Meulan).

8. John of Worcester, *Chronicle*, iii, ed. P. McGurk (OMT, 1998). Pictures with text: Corpus Christi College, Oxford, MS 157, pp. 382–83.

9. *GS*, c. 13; *RRAN*, no. 271.

10. J. Gillingham, 'The Context and Purpose of Geoffrey of Monmouth's *History of the Kings of Britain*', *ANS*, 13 (1992), pp. 99–118.

11. C. W. Hollister and J. W. Baldwin, 'The Rise of Administrative Kingship: Henry I and Philip Augustus', *AHR*, 83 (1978), pp. 867–905.

12. William of Malmesbury, *Gesta*, pp. 744–45: 'libentius bellabat consilio quam gladio'.

13. John of Hexham, *Chronicle*, in Symeon of Durham, *Chronicle*, ed. T. Arnold, RS, 75, ii (1885), p. 308; Torigni, pp. 140–41 for his own Latin verses commemorating Stephen's bravery.

14. Wace, *Le roman de Brut*, ed. I. Arnold (Paris, 1938–40) (translated by J. Weiss, Exeter, 1999); Layamon, *Brut*, ed. F. Madden (London, 1847).

15. Geffrei Gaimar, *L'estoire des Engleis*, ed. A. Bell (Oxford, 1960), pp. 205–6, lines 6477–512.

16. JW, pp. 138–39.

17. Hildebert of Le Mans, archbishop of Tours, seeking to comfort Queen Adeliza on her despair at not having conceived children. PL, 171, cc. 179–81, bk 1, ep. 14 ; cc. 189–91, bk 1, ep. 18.

18. C. W. Hollister, 'The Anglo-Norman Succession Debate of 1126', *JMH*, 1 (1975), pp. 19–41.

19. Hildebert of Le Mans' letter to Henry I's daughter Matilda *de contumelia filiae patris pectus induerit*, is one indication of the tension between them: PL, 171, cc. 291–92; HH, pp. 486–89, reports only that the barons resolved to send Matilda back to Geoffrey of Anjou, not that anything was sworn about the succession. William of Malmesbury, *Historia novella*, ed. E. King (OMT, 1998), pp. 18–21; Malmesbury would have known Henry I's charter confirming Bishop Roger's possession of Malmesbury abbey issued at the Northampton council: *RRAN*, ii, ed. C. Johnson and H. A. Cronne (Oxford, 1956), no. 1715; the long list of witnesses indicates who was present at the council.

20. HN, pp. 10–11. In his account of Stephen's coronation, Malmesbury makes no allusion to the disregard of the oaths by the king or the archbishop.

21. OV, v, p. 201: notice of Henry of Anjou's birth in 1133, 'quem multi populi dominum expectant, si Deus ... concesserit' may express what many people hoped, but more clearly showed that there had been no formal acknowledgement of his claims and hints that there was not much optimism about his prospects; cp. p. 228 a reference again to Angevin hopes, not expectations.

Notes to Chapter 4: Stephen's Accession

1. Disorder in 1135: *GS*, cc. 8–11; JW, pp. 216–19: in England and Normandy, 'plurima ... distirbatio ... in pluribus locis et maxima in Walia ... depopulatio et depredatio'; according to OV, vi, pp. 444–45, the troubles in Wales had

broken out while Henry I was still alive in Normandy but unable to return to England to deal with them.

2. A murder committed between Henry's death and Stephen's accession was pardoned because it occurred while there was no king to protect the peace *RRAN*, iii, no. 428. John of Marmoutier, 'Historia Gaufredi ducis Normannorum et comitis Andegavorum', *Chroniques d'Anjou*, ed. P. Marchegay and A. Salmon, SHF (1856), pp. 229–310; p. 278 on outbreaks of violence usual on the death of princes: 'libera ut in mortuo solent, judicia populi depromebantur'. The murder of Count Charles of Flanders in 1127 had immediately precipitated 'furta et latrocinia fraudes et periuria rapinae et incendia, pugnae et homicidia', Gautier of Thérouanne, *Vita Johannis episcopi Morinensis*, ed. O. Holder-Egger, MGHSS, xv, 2, pp. 1138–50, c. 13.

3. Richard of Hexham, *Chronicle*, CRSHR, iii (1886), pp. 144–45; JH, p. 287; HN, pp. 30–31, writes of David as *propriori iam senectute infractus*, perhaps to excuse his inactivity on Matilda's behalf.

4. JW, pp. 216–19.

5. Geoffrey sent Matilda into Normandy in December 1135: OV, vi, pp. 454–55.

6. *The Letters and Charters of Gilbert Foliot*, ed. A. Morey and C. N. L. Brooke (Cambridge, 1967), letter 26; John of Salisbury, *Historia pontificalis*, ed. M. Chibnall (OMT, 1986), pp. 84–85.

7. HN, pp. 24–27.

8. GS, cc. 4–5.

9. HH, pp. 728–31; HP, pp. 84–85.

10. HN, pp. 42–43.

11. RH, p. 145.

12. Gervase of Canterbury, i, p. 94.

13. *RRAN*, iii, no. 270 from BL, Cotton MS, Claudius D II, fol. 68, an early fourteenth-century manuscript containing legal material assembled in London.

14. K. A. LoPrete, 'The Anglo-Norman Card of Adela of Blois', *Albion*, 22 (1990), pp. 177–92; Adela died in March 1137.

15. E. J. Kealey, *Roger of Salisbury, Viceroy of England* (Los Angeles, 1972).

16. E. King, 'Dispute Settlement in Anglo-Norman England', *ANS*, 14 (1992), pp. 115–30; ibid 'King Stephen and the Anglo-Norman aristocracy' on Miles, p. 185–86; *RRAN*, nos 386–87; P. Dalton, '*In Neutro Latere*: The Armed Neutrality of Ranulf II, Earl of Chester in King Stephen's Reign', *History*, 59 (1974) pp. 180-94: *ANS*, 14 (1991), pp. 47–48; D. Crouch, 'A Norman *Conventio* and the Bonds of Lordship in the Middle Ages', *Law and Government in Medieval England and Normandy*, ed. G. Garnett and J. Hudson (Cambridge, 1994), p. 313.

17. H. Summerson, *Medieval Carlisle* (1993), pp. 38–49. Innocent II wrote to Stephen, 22 April 1136, Jaffe, no. 7765, reminding him that the beginnings made with the bishopric at Carlisle by Henry I needed to be followed through; perhaps he was anxious about Stephen's surrender of the place to King David.

18. HN, pp. 32–33; cp. King, 'Dispute Settlement', p. 125.

19. JW, pp. 176–83: this elaboration is entirely fanciful.

20. D. Crouch, *The Reign of King Stephen, 1135–54* (London, 2000), pp. 54–59, 341; idem, 'Robert Earl of Gloucester, and the Daughter of Zelophehad', *JMH*, 11 (1985), pp. 227–43. R. R. Davies, 'Henry I and Wales', *Studies in Medieval History Presented to R. H. C. Davis*, ed. H. M. R. E. Mayr-Harting and R. I. Moore (Oxford, 1985), pp. 132–47; *Brut y Tywysogyn*, ed. T. Jones (Cardiff, 1952), for evidence of internecine conflict amongst the Welsh princes during Stephen's reign.

21. *RRAN*, iii, no. 312; B. Coplestone-Crow, 'Payne Fitz John and Ludlow Castle', *Transactions of the Shropshire Archaeological and Historical Society*, 70 (1995), pp. 171–83. Carmarthen was briefly recovered by Earl Gilbert in 1146; Henry de Neuburg, who issued some coins at Swansea in his own name, must have recovered his family's honour of Gower at some point, but he is not mentioned in the Welsh chronicles.

22. JW, pp. 278–79, 284–85.

23. *GS*, c. 19: R. Bearman, 'Baldwin de Redvers: Some Aspects of a Baronial Career in the Reign of King Stephen', *ANS*, 18 (1995), pp. 19–46.

24. OV, vi, pp. 462–63; 456–57, 454–55. D. J. Power, 'What Did the Frontier of Angevin Normandy Comprise ?', *ANS*, 17 (1994), pp. 181–201.

25. R. Helmerich, 'King Stephen's Norman Itinerary' 1137, *HSJ*, 5 (1993), pp. 89–98.

26. R. B. Patterson, 'William of Malmesbury's Robert of Gloucester: A Revaluation of the *Historia Novella*', *AHR*, 70 (1965), pp. 983–97, esp. p. 991, endorsed by D. Crouch, *The Beaumont Twins* (Cambridge, 1987), pp. 41, 46.

27. CDF, 909; F. Lot, *Etudes critiques sur l'abbaye de St-Wandrille* (Paris, 1913), pp. 130–33, no. 73; HP, p. 44, for Stephen's defence of his rights in Normandy after 1144.

28. King David had assets in Northamptonshire, Huntingdonshire, Bedfordshire, Cambridgeshire and Rutland: *The Pipe Roll of 31 Henry I*, ed. J. Hunter (1833; rep. 1929), pp. 46, 49, 85, 104, 134. G. H. Fowler, 'The Shire of Bedford and the Earldom of Huntingdon', *Bedfordshire Historical Record Society*, 9 (1925) pp. 23–35, thought Bedford was part of the Huntingdon-Northampton earldom till 1138 when Stephen made Hugh de Beaumont, earl of Bedford.

29. *GS*, c. 25; OV, vi, pp. 518–19.

30. HH, pp. 712–19; RH, pp. 155–64; JH, p. 293; OV, vi, pp. 532–33.

31. Jocelin of Furness, *Vita S. Waldeni*, AASS, August, i, pp. 242–78, stressed the old English royal ancestry of David.

32. RH, pp. 176–78; JH, pp. 299–300.

33. G. W. S. Barrow, 'King David I, Earl Henry and Cumbria', *Transactions of the Cumberland and Westmorland Antiquarian and Archaeological Society*, 99 (1999), pp. 117–27, on Earl Henry as co-king with David. Barrow regards Northumberland as being effectively lifted out of the English kingdom; idem, 'The Charters of David I', *ANS*, 14 (1991), pp. 25–37, esp. 34–36; also 'The Scots and the North of England', in *The Anarchy*, ed. E. King, pp. 231–53.

34. On Stephen's relations with Earl Henry, HH, pp. 718–19; JH, p. 300; see also, P. Dalton, 'Eustace Fitz John and the Politics of Anglo-Norman England: The

Rise and Survival of a Twelfth-Century Royal Servant', *Speculum*, 71 (1996), pp. 358–83.

Notes to Chapter 5: Trouble

1. R. H. C. Davis, *King Stephen* (London, 1967; 3rd edn, 1990), pp. 3, 49, 73, 124, supposed Stephen and his contemporaries were haunted by the memory of his father's cowardice at Antioch. Without a trace of irony, Brian Fitz Count names Stephen's father amongst other loyal Crusaders when writing to Bishop Henry of Winchester: H. W. C. Davis, 'Henry of Blois', p. 301. Countess Adela had sent her husband back to the Holy Land to redeem his reputation and he had been killed by Muslims in the Ramla campaign of 1102 along with other 'viri illustrissimi clari et nobiles', *Gesta Ambaziensiun dominorum*, p. 198.
2. HH, pp. 698–701.
3. HH, pp. 718–21; *GS*, cc. 35–36; Stubbs, *Constitutional History*, pp. 353, 356; T. Callahan, 'The Arrest of the Bishops at Stephen's Court: A Reassessment' *HSJ* 7 (1995), pp. 101–16; K. Yoshitake, 'The Arrest of the Bishops in 1139 and its Consequences', *JMH*, 14 (1988), pp. 97–114.
4. JW, pp. 278–79, for the willingness of the bishops of Hereford and Chichester at the end of 1139 to impress on Maurice, newly elected bishop of Bangor, the duty of doing homage to the king.
5. W. Janssen, *Der päpstlichen Legaten in Frankreich vom Schisma Anaklets II bis zum Tode Coelestins III, 1130–1198* (Köln, 1961), pp. 18–30.
6. Gervase of Canterbury, i, p. 109. Did Gervase draw upon some vindictive belief at Christ Church that the legate who had once overshadowed the archbishop had felt humiliated by being passed over for Canterbury ?
7. Legate since beginning of March, 1139, HN, pp. 50–51. Henry as legate was impatient that Worcester had not paid its contribution to Peter's Pence, as other bishoprics had done and applied to the prior, in the absence of the archbishop and the bishop: *EEA*, Winchester, no. 138. Though it is plausible to explain the absence of the prelates by their attendance at the Lateran council, it is improbable that Henry's responsibility for Peter's Pence and the sluggish response from Worcester can all be squeezed into the spring months of 1139 as the editor proposes.
8. HP, pp. 84–85; *CDF*, no. 1385: for Innocent II meeting Henry I and Matilda at Rouen, May 1131. When father and daughter returned to England later, and met the barons at Northampton in September 1131, Cardinal Peter was present, *RRAN*, ii, no. 1715; he had returned to the curia, at Auxerre by December: Jaffe, no. 7518; R. Hüls, *Kardinäle, Klerus und Kirchen Roms, 1049–1130* (Tübingen, 1977), p. 193.
9. GF, ep. 26; Herimann of Tournai, *Liber de restauratione monasterii S. Martini Tornacensis*, ed. G. Waitz, MGHSS, xiv, pp. 276–317, at p. 282.
10. JW, pp. 244–49; HN, pp. 76–77.

11. HN, pp. 46–49.

12. OV, vi, pp. 532–33; and Crouch, *Beaumont Twins* pp. 43–45; HH, pp. 718–21; GS, c. 35 ; HN, pp. 46–49: does not suppose it was premeditated.

13. Jaffe, no. 8025, from *Liber Eliensis*, ed. E. O. Blake, Camden Society, 92 (1962), pp. 316–17.

14. HN, pp. 48–49, 56–59.

15. Conrad III: HH, pp. 556–67; JW, pp. 234–35, noted Conrad's relationship to Matilda.

16. Roger II: OV, vi, pp. 432–35; HN, p. 34; JW, pp. 232–33. Archbishop Hugh spent time in Italy in 1136 and Normans could have been well informed about Roger II's affairs; JH, p. 315, 318 on Roger II and Celestine II and on Robert of Selby, Roger II's prominent (Yorkshire) minister.

17. Corfe, GS, c. 39; Bearman, 'Baldwin', pp. 19–46; JW, pp. 270–73.

18. The two versions of JW, pp. 268–69 give different dates: in October and 1 August; Torigni, p. 215 gives August; OV, vi, pp. 534–35, gives autumn and HN. pp. 60–61, 30 September 1139. JW, pp. 268–69 (Gloucester version) thought Stephen was attacking Marlborough, but the castellan, John Fitz Gilbert was still loyal to Stephen in 1140, JW, pp. 285–91.

19. D. Walker, *Charters of the Earldom of Hereford, 1095–1201*, Camden Society (1964); D. Walker, 'Miles of Gloucester, Earl of Hereford', *TBGAS*, 77 (1958), pp. 64–84; E. King, 'King Stephen and the Anglo-Norman Aristocracy', *History*, 59 (1974), pp. 180–94, esp. 185–86. R. H. C. Davis, 'Treaty between William, Earl of Gloucester and Roger, Earl of Hereford', *A Medieval Miscellany for Doris Mary Stenton*, ed. P. M. Barnes and C. F. Slade, Pipe Roll Society, new series, 36 (1960), p. 143, suggested that Miles was alarmed by the arrest of his political ally, Bishop Roger. Had Miles, under pressure from his lord, Robert of Gloucester, been the one who had tried to suborn the bishop?

20. S. B. Keats-Rohan, 'Devolution of the Honour of Wallingford', *Oxoniensia* 54 (1989), pp. 311–18, suggests Brian became a monk, probably at Bec, and had died by 1150. For Honour of Wallingford see *The Boarstall Cartulary*, ed. H. E. Salter, Oxford Historical Society, 88 (1930), appendix 2, pp. 295–327. Brian was indirectly related to the Angevin comital house: his father's wife was Geoffrey of Anjou's aunt.

21. GS, c. 37.

22. JW, pp. 270–73.

23. GS, c. 40; HN, pp. 40–41, 70–73: 1138–40; Gervase of Canterbury, p. 95; JW, pp. 268–69; LE, p. 314: Stephen's fourth year, i.e. 1139.

24. GS, cc. 50–52; HN, pp. 76–77; John Fitz Gilbert had not certainly joined the Angevins until 1141.

25. JW, pp. 290–93; JH, pp. 311–12.

26. JW, pp. 272–75. Comment in D. Crouch, 'From Stenton to McFarlane: Models of Societies of the Twelfth and Thirteenth Centuries', *TRHS*, sixth series, 5, p. 189, and in D. Crouch 'Robert Earl of Gloucester', pp. 234–35, where this episode is interpreted as Robert of Gloucester's vengeance on Waleran of

Meulan, the lord of Worcester. John of Worcester does not mention Robert. Miles of Gloucester is anyway more likely to have been the commander of any force from Gloucester. John of Worcester writes as though the men of Worcester were simply terrified of the men of Gloucester.

27. Apart from Shropshire, in the west, presumably still linked with Hereford, Matilda's authority April-July 1141 cannot be shown to have reached further north than Rutland, though JH, p. 309, reports that King David at Durham on his way south ordered Matilda to be obeyed; *Chronicon abbatiae Rameseiensis*, ed. W. Dunn Macray, RS, 83 (1886), p. 307, no. 382, provides evidence of an agreement reached between the abbey and the bishop of Ely under her auspices. The evidence available is insufficient to substantiate the claims of *GS*, c. 60 that the greater part of the kingdom submitted to her, or of HH, pp. 738–39 that all England, except Kent, did so.

28. Davis, 'Henry of Blois', p. 302.

29. *RRAN*, iii nos 274, 275.

Notes to Chapter 6: Turmoil?

1. 'omnes fere consules et barones Angliae conversi sunt ad eum ut regem a captione eriperent': *AM*, ii (1865), p. 229, from Waverley Annals, 1141; LE, pp. 322–23 names Earls Warenne, Arundel, Essex and Pembroke. White, 'Continuity', pp. 131–333, refers to the revival of Stephen's government after 1141 but regards his 'control' over most of England to have been 'tenuous indeed'.

2. Henry I is recorded twice in north Wales, twice in Yorkshire, only once as far north as Durham, twice at or near Gloucester and once at Norwich. Stephen ranged much more widely in the kingdom even after 1141. D. Crouch, 'Earls and Bishops in Twelfth-Century Leicestershire', *NMS*, 37 (1993), pp. 9–20, implies that Robert of Leicester was preoccupied by 'local power politics'. Stephen directed the sheriff, not the earl, to respect Reading abbey's exemption from pleas, but if the date for this document is *c.* 1137, the earl would then have still been in Normandy: *Reading Abbey Cartularies*, i, ed. B. R. Kemp, Camden Society, fourth series, 31 (1986), p. 349; cp. *RRAN*, iii, no. 682.

3. 'initia dolorum hoc malum ita per totum regnum guerra detestabilis nam imperatrix cum fautoribus suis regem violenter impetebat', *AM*, iv (1869), pp. 21–22 from Osney Annals; JH, p. 302: 'emersit per eam in Anglia perturbatio valde gravis et infirmatum est firmamentum regni Stephani regis'; *GS*, c . 73; K. Schnith, '*Regni et Pacis Inquietatrix*, zur Rolle der Kaiserin Mathilde in der Anarchie, *JMH*, 2 (1976), pp. 135–57; idem, 'Zur Vorgeschichte der Anarchie' *Historisches Jahrbuch*, 95 (1975), pp. 68–87. The Continuatio Praemonstratensis also blamed her: 'Matildis ... in ipsa Anglia magnas ei molestias atque calamitates suscitat': MGHSS, vi, pp. 447–56.

4. J. Chartrou, *L'Anjou de 1109 à 1151* (Paris, 1928), chapter 3, claims that Geoffrey

had no coherent plan when he invaded Normandy in 1138 and put off a methodical conquest until after the battle of Lincoln. See also, chapter 4, note 27.

5. John of Marmoutier, p. 282; Rouen cathedral had property at Gisors and Archbishop Hugh sought the good offices of Abbot Suger of St-Denis for the recovery of his church's property from Louis VII who detained it unjustly. PL, 186, cc. 1430–31, ep. 173; Suger, *Louis VI*, pp. 102–3, 110–13.

6. *GS*, c. 95: 'comitissae fautores regni sibi primatum iure usurpantes'.

7. The only persons known to have witnessed three or more of Matilda's charters after 1142 are the two earls of Hereford, her two half-brothers, the earls of Gloucester and Cornwall, Brian Fitz Count, two Wiltshire barons (Robert de Dunstanville, Humphrey de Bohun), Walchelin Maminot, Herbert the chaplain and Bishop Bernard of St Davids.

8. Matilda issued a few documents for monastic houses in Shropshire and Staffordshire, but the extent of her authority there cannot otherwise be illustrated. *RRAN*, iii, nos 377–78, 461, 839. According to HN, pp. 6–7, Henry I had assigned the earldom of Shrewsbury to Queen Adeliza. Even so, Stephen confirmed gifts in Shrewsbury to the canons of Lilleshall early in 1145, *RRAN*, iii, no. 460. and Wenlock priory obtained a charter from Stephen in 1147: D. Cox, 'Two Unpublished Charters of King Stephen for Wenlock Priory', *Transactions of the Shropshire Archaeological and Historical Society*, 66 (1989), pp. 56–59, charter 2.

9. GF, letter 104: 'duci et regni Anglorum pro magna portione domino'.

10. Warwick: *GS*, cc. 58, 85, 119; Matilda sent him one instruction: *RRAN*, iii, no. 597; two of Stephen's documents refer to him, ibid., nos 689, 887.

11. For earls as administrators: *RRAN*, iii, nos 597, 887, 966–67; *The Cartulary of Worcester Priory*, ed. R. Darlington, PRS, new series, 38 (1968), nos 9, 47, from earls of Warwick and Hereford; Waleran claimed the geld and customs formerly due to the king in Worcester, H. W. C. Davis, 'Some Documents of the Anarchy', *Essays Presented to R. L. Poole*, ed. H. W. C. Davis (Oxford, 1927), pp. 170–71; R. B. Patterson, 'An Undated Charter of Henry Fitz Empress and Earl William of Gloucester's Comital Status', *EHR*, 87 (1972), pp. 755–57; D. Crouch, 'Duke Henry, Earl William of Gloucester and the End of the Anarchy', *EHR*, 103 (1988), pp. 69–75; E. King, 'Waleran, Count of Meulan, Earl of Worcester, 1104–66', *Tradition and Change: Essays in Honour of Marjorie Chibnall*, ed. D. Greenway, C. Holdsworth and J. Sayers (Cambridge, 1985), pp. 165–86, esp. pp. 173–74; Robert of Gloucester is reported to have kept his region in peace and order: HN, pp. 72–75; *GS*, c. 75.

12. Davis, 'Henry of Blois', p. 301; Aubrey, as *comite*, witnessed a document for Stephen in 1145, *RRAN*, iii, no. 460, but *iure uxoris* he was count of Guisnes anyway.

13. Baldwin: *RRAN*, iii, nos 275, 394; at Oxford, 1141/42, nos 634, 651. Henry de Tracy: *GS*, cc. 37, 76, 110, 115.

14. F. W. Maitland, *Domesday Book and Beyond* (Cambridge, 1897), pp. 400–1, table 1: Wiltshire was the wealthiest county for geld assessment.

15. JW, pp. 298–89, reports Miles's importance for Matilda, 'sicut ex ipsius Milonis ore audivimus'.

16. *GS*, cc. 79–80; GF, no. 2.

17. Roger's reputation is impugned in *GS*, c. 117. See also, GF, nos 77, 93–96.

18. GF, nos 51–52, 38–41, 46, 49–56, 62–64, appendix 3.

19. *Chronicon monasterii de Abingdon*, ed. J. Stevenson, RS, 2 (1858), ii, pp. 190, 200, 230; K. S. B. Keats-Rohan, 'The Making of Henry of Oxford: Englishmen in a Norman World', Oxonoiensia, 54 (1989), pp. 287–309. *RRAN*, iii, nos 703–4.

20. EEA, 11, Exeter, ed. F. Barlow, nos 49, 50; CDF, no. 729, for consecration of St Michael's Mount in Stephen's ninth year.

21. GF, letter 63 to Matilda as *domina* 1147–48, seemingly impatient with her remonstrance to him; Foliot witnessed two of her charters: *RRAN*, iii, nos 343, 111: for Glastonbury in 1141 and at Devizes in 1144, for Bohun. GF, nos 65–66 for his contacts with other English clergy outside the Angevin zone. Gloucester abbey's exchange of property with Earl Roger in 1144, *Historia et cartularium S. Petri de Glos*, ed. W. H. Hart, RS, 33 (1863), i, p. 314, was confirmed by Stephen for abbot Hamelin after 1148: *RRAN*, iii, no. 360; a charter of Stephen allegedly of 1138, was forged in 1147–48 by which time he had recovered ascendancy at Gloucester: *RRAN*, iii, no. 345.

22. Davis, 'Henry of Blois', pp. 297–303; GF, ep. 26.

23. *GS*, cc. 93–94; HH, pp. 746–47.

24. Gloucester's estates had been confiscated by Stephen when he renounced homage in 1138 (HN, pp. 42–43), but he appears to have drawn on his Kent revenues while he was imprisoned at Rochester castle (HN, pp. 116–17). Some Kentish lords, possibly holding lands of Gloucester or in his service, were at the Angevin court in Normandy in the late 1140s, driven out of England for disloyalty: R. Eales, 'Local Loyalties in Norman England: Kent in Stephen's Reign', ANS, 8 (1985), pp. 88–114, quoting *RRAN*, iii, nos 88, 432, 600, 706, 810, 836.

25. *Gesta abbatum monasterii S. Albani*, ed. H. T. Riley, RS, 28, 4 (1867), i, pp. 113, 116–18: William of Gloucester; *GS*, c. 95: Philip of Gloucester.

26. 26 June 1147, Eugenius III to Stephen to receive bishop of London *in gratia fidelitatis*; though he can't swear oath 'sufficiat ut simplici et veraci verbo promittat quod laesione tibi vel terrae tuae non inferat'. Jaffe, no. 9088; Robert appears in Stephen's charters from the latter part of 1147: *RRAN*, iii nos 402, 541–42, 555. According to EEA, 15, *London*, ed. F. Neininger (1999), no. 54, Bishop Robert officiated at the Easter celebrations in London in 1142, but no other documents show him to have been certainly in London before 1147.

27. *GS*, c. 109.

28. Matilda appears to have been present in a document issued at Rouen on 11 October 1147, *RRAN*, iii, no. 599. M. Chibnall, *The Empress Matilda: Queen Consort, Queen Mother and Lady of the English* (Oxford, 1991), argues, p. 153, for assigning this document to October 1148, but its dating clause is similar

to *RRAN*, iii, no. 735, of before Easter 1148, and shares some of the same witnesses.

29. *GS*, cc. 100–5; JH, pp. 324–25. *Charters of the Anglo-Norman Earls of Chester, c. 1071–1237*, ed. G. Barraclough, Record Society of Lancashire and Cheshire (1988), where nos 63, 64, 84, 85, 87 are cited in support of the argument that Ranulf became the head of the Angevin cause in England after Robert of Gloucester's death.

30. A. Wareham, 'The Motives and Politics of the Bigod Family, *c.* 1066–1177', *ANS*, 17 (1994), pp. 223–42; Bigod was probably recognised as earl by Matilda in 1141 at the same time as she was trying to arrange an earldom for Hugh's brother-in-law, Aubrey de Vere, and bidding for the support of his wife's brother-in-law, Geoffrey de Mandeville: not surprisingly, Bigod witnessed Matilda's two charters for those earls: *RRAN*, iii, nos 275, 634.

31. Turgis of Avranches held Walden castle in defiance of Stephen, but was so insouciant about his rebellion that he went out hunting and was captured unawares. *GS*, c. 91; Hugh Fitz Richard was also captured by the earl of Chester while he was out hunting, Stenton, *First Century*, p. 243.

32. *GS*, cc. 92, 111: Walter de Pinkney; *Charters of the Redvers Family*, nos 15, 31, for the Redvers interest and castle at Christchurch. Coins struck at Christchurch in the name of Robert of Gloucester were found in the hoard found at Box near Bath, see below p. 262 note 62.

33. *GS*, c. 29.

34. Herimann, p. 282, wrote in the 1140s when the situation was still uncertain: 'Et futurorum quidem incerti sumus … Angliam … nunc diuturna seditione vastatam et oppressam de pristinis divitiis ad magnam paupertatem devenisse'. Suger, another continental observer, also remarked on the sorry consequences: 'quare perniciosa factio zelo et diversitate baronum, comitum atque optimatum regis taliter terram copiosam et fructiferam a malitia inhabitantium in ea calamitate extinxit ut terram vastitate praeda rapinis homines mortibus fere ad tertiam ut aiunt partem circumquaque per totum regnum exterminavit'. *Vie de Louis Le Gros*, ed. A. Molinier (Paris, 1887), p. 149. The Continuatio Praemonstratensis, begun after 1146, refers to the 'regnum illud quod pre ceteris aliquandiu quietum manserat et opulentium ferro flamma fame misere decerpitur': MGHSS, vi, p. 452. Prémontré's interests in England began with the foundation 1143–46 of the abbey of Newhouse from Licques (diocese of Thérouanne), and Newhouse had provided recruits for the foundation of five more houses before the end of the reign, all in eastern coastal regions, including one in Scotland at Dryburgh. The continental connections of the English Praemonstratensians were not with Normandy but with Stephen's continental domain in Boulogne.

35. *The Peterborough Chronicle*, ed. D. Whitelock (Copenhagen, 1954). G. J. White, 'The Myth of the Anarchy', *ANS*, 22 (1999), pp. 323–37, has recently discussed this passage to good effect.

36. *Chronicle of Hugh Candidus*, ed. W. T. Mellows (Oxford, 1949), pp. 105, 108,

123: the presbytery was built in this period. Stephen made gifts to the monastery and settled pleas in court. There are also seven surviving charters, *RRAN*, iii nos. 655–61. Stephen was at Peterborough on 7 June 1143.

37. *Chronicon abbatiae Ramseiensis*, ed. W. D. Macray, RS, 83 (1886), p. 4; *Cartularium monasterii de Rameseiensis*, ed. W. H. Hart and P. A. Lyon, RS, 79 (1884–93), ii, pp. 273–74, nos 390–91, for the lands and a list of valuable church vestments and ornaments Abbot Walter had disposed of without the consent of the community, *tempore guerrae*, a very similar situation to that of Ely. Both heads of houses may have been in need of money because of the war, but neither community accepted this as sufficient excuse. Ramsey had been seized by Geoffrey de Mandeville and used as his base for some months, 1143–44 and its miseries in this period are duly described by HH, pp. 742–43; LE. pp. 288–94; at Ely some items were pawned to Jews in Cambridge, LE, p. 339.

38. *GS*, c. 96; cp. *The Chronicle of Waltham*, ed. L. Watkiss and M. Chibnall (OMT, 1994), pp. 82-83; JH, p. 331.

39. JH, p. 315.

40. Reginald, *Libellus*, cc. 64, 65, 67; *Miscellanea biographica*, ed. J. Raine Surtees Society, 8 (1838), pp. 33–35; *Coucher Book of Selby*, ed. J. T. Fowler, Yorkshire Archaeological Society, Record Series, 10 (1891), cc. 5, 6, 7, 9, 11–20; *Historians of the Church of York and its Archbishops*, ed. J. Raine, RS, 71 (1879), i, pp. 302–5.

41. *The Pipe Roll of 31 Henry I Michaelmas 1130*, ed. J. Hunter (London, 1833; reprint 1929); J. A. Green, 'Praeclarum et Magnificum Antiquitatis Monumentum:': The Earliest Surviving Pipe Roll', *BIHR*, 55 (1982), pp. 1–17; S. L. Mooers, 'Patronage in the 1130 Pipe Roll' *Speculum*, 59 (1984), pp. 282–307.

42. Continuatio Praemonstratensis refers to Henry I as 'vir in regni sui amministratione singularis severitas atque censurae', where only his manner of discharging his royal office is implied: MGHSS, vi, p. 451.

43. K. Yoshitake, 'The Exchequer in the Reign of Stephen', *EHR*, 103 (1988), pp. 950–59; Warren, *Governance*, pp. 91–94.

44. T. A. M. Bishop, *Scriptores regis* (Oxford, 1961), pp. 10, 13, 25, 30; for exchequer hand, p. 29.

45. *The Great Rolls of the Pipe for the Second, Third and Fourth Years of the Reign of King Henry the Second*, ed. J. Hunter (London, 1844).

46. *RRAN*, ii, nos 963, 1053, 1514, 1538, 1741; compare iii, nos 276, 628, 935, 899. The exchequer is not mentioned by Orderic in his chronicle. Torigni respected Henry I for his riches, because he did not begrudge spending them on churches, but Torigni says nothing about how the riches were amassed or audited. *The Gesta Normannorum Ducum of William of Jumièges, Orderic Vitalis and Robert of Torigni* ed. E. M. C. van Houts (OMT, 1995), ii, pp. 252–61.

47. Richard Fitzneale, *Dialogus de Scaccario*, ed. C. Johnson, F. E. L. Carter, D. E. Greenway (Oxford, 1983), cc. xv, xvi: Henry, bishop of Winchester, is cited as his source of information about Domesday Book; as himself a man of business, Bishop Henry is likely to have taken an interest in exchequer

affairs. For Henry was written a great codex containing nearly two hundred pre-conquest charters, some going back to the seventh century, providing title deeds for the church of Winchester: BL, Add. MS 15350. A. Rumble, 'Codex Wintoniensis', *ANS*, 4 (1981), pp. 153–66; T. Madox, *The History and Antiquities of the Exchequer of the Kings of England* (London, 1711).

48. LE, pp. 314, 321–22, 328, 332–33.

49. B. A. Lees, *Records of the Templars in England in the Twelfth Century: The Inquest of 1185* (London, 1935); J. Walker, 'Alms for the Holy Land: the English Templars' *The Medieval Military Revolution*, ed. A. Ayton and J. L. Price (London, 1995), pp. 63–80.

50. C. Holdsworth, 'The Church', in *The Anarchy*, ed. King, pp. 207–29, calculates that 175 religious houses were founded in England in Stephen's reign, probably a greater number 'than that made in any similar number of years in the Middle Ages', p. 216.

51. *The Chartulary of the High Church of Chichester*, ed. W. D. Peckam, Sussex Record Society, 46 (1946) nos 94, 297, 299, 300, for restitutions or compensation where war is not offerred as the reason for the trouble. Ranulf of Chester similarly paid compensation for injuries he had caused to several churches without referring to acts of war: *The Charters ... of Chester*, nos. 34, 65, 96, 104, 106, 115. *Chronicon Abingdon* ii, pp. 200, 230; *Gesta abbatum*, p. 94; Ramsey, p. 411: Mandeville; for general discussion, T. Callahan, 'Ecclesiastical Reparations and the Soldiers of the Anarchy', *Albion* (1978), pp. 300–18.

52. *Papsturkunden in England*, ed. W. Holtzmann, 3 vols (Göttingen, 1930–56).

53. *Cartae et alia documenta quae ad dominium de Glamorgan pertinent* ed. G. T. Clark (Cardiff, 1910), nos 69, 71, for letters of cardinals to St David's; HP, p. 45: cardinals who claimed family kinship with Stephen presumably acted as his advocates. GF, no. 48 is a letter written to Pullen.

54. The Peterborough Chronicle records the arrival at Whitby of the king of Norway on a pillaging expedition in the time of Abbot Richard, former prior of Peterborough, pp. 121–22; Reginald *Libellus* nos. 29, 32, 52, also reports the damage done by the Norwegians on this occasion and has several other references to the connections between England and Norway in the middle of the century. According to a continuation of the Sigebert of Gembloux Chronicle, the king of Denmark invaded England on hearing of the death of Henry I, claiming a better title to the throne than Stephen. MGHSS, vi, p. 386. Scandinavian contacts in this reign were not all belligerent. Bishop Sigurd of Bergen, who visited England c. 1146 induced English Cistercians to establish daughter houses in Norway, Fountains at Lysa in his own diocese in 1146 and Kirkstead at Hovedo (diocese of Oslo) in 1147: Annales Ryenses, MGHSS, xvi, 401–02; *Memorials of the Abbey of St. Mary of Fountains*, ed. J. R. Walbran, Surtees Society, 42 (1863), pp. xiv, xlvi, 89–90, 97; Thomas de Burton, *Chronica monasterii de Melsa*, ed. E. A. Bond, RS, 43 (1866), i, pp. 74–75.

55. *Papsturkunden;* allusions to troubles of a military nature, i, no. 35; ii, nos 18, 23, 40, 47, 57, 777–8; iii, nos 39, 60, 86.

56. Not all secular intrusions onto church property were consequences of warfare: *Chronicle of Battle Abbey*, ed. E. Searle (Oxford, 1980), pp. 210–13, 224–29. Its very partial evidence betrays the weakness of its legal claims. For the unreliability of the Battle Chronicle: N. Vincent, 'King Henry II and the Monks of Battle', in *Belief and Culture in the Middle Ages*, ed. R. Gameson and H. Leyser (Oxford, 2001), pp. 264–86. See also p. 261 note 51.

57. *EEA*, 4, *Lincoln*, ed. D. M. Smith (1986), no. 200; *EEA*, 5, *York*, ed. J. E. Burton (1988), no. 116; *EEA*, 10, *Bath*, ed. F. M. R. Ramsey (1995) no. 25; Tutbury: *EEA*, 14, *Coventry*, ed. M. J. Franklin (1997) no. 42, pleading damage to get tax excused. Even in Hereford, of 128 documents for the period 1139–54, only twenty-one refer to troubles caused by secular disturbances; A. Saltmann, *Theobald, Archbishop of Canterbury* (London, 1956): of 264 documents for the years 1139–1154, only eight refer to troubles. Norman abbots who visited England in the 1140s include those of Bec, Fécamp, Jumièges, Lire, Lonlay, Mont St-Michel, Savigny, Séez. Episcopal acta which record usurpations of church property do not necessarily imply acts of war: Lincoln, no. 225; Hereford, ed. J. Barrow (1993), nos 21, 40–42; Bath, nos 15, 43, 45.

58. Lateran council on truce of God, canon 12, in J. D. Mansi, *Sacrorum conciliorum nova et amplissima collectio* (Florence and Venice, 1759-), vol 21.

59. HN, pp. 74–75.

60. William of Newburgh, *Historia rerum Anglicarum*, CRSHR, RS, 82, i (1884), p. 69: 'erantque in Anglia quodammodo tot reges, vel potius tyranni, quot domini castellorum, habente singuli percussuram proprii numismatis', developed from JH, p. 324: 'unusquisque enim ad adinventionis suae libitum corrupit monetae et numismatis pretium'. Coins issued in the vicinity of their religious communities included those struck in the names of Earl Henry of Northumberland, Robert de Stuteville and Eustace, see below note 64.

61. M. Blackburn, 'Coinage and Currency', in *The Anarchy*, pp. 146–205; R. F. Mack, 'Mints in Stephen's Reign', *British Numismatic Journal*, 35 (1966), pp. 38–112.

62. *Treasure Trove Reviewing Committee, Annual Report, 1994–95*, nos 17, 18.

63. Torigni, p. 123; B. H. I. H. Stewart, *The Scottish Coinage* (London, 1967), pp. 1–8. David's earliest coins were modelled on Stephen's Type 1 which proves that he did not begin to strike coins on his accession in 1124, but only after 1135.

64. Only two coins are known on which the name Eustace Fitz John has been read. There are about thirty other coins bearing the name Eustace, which for some mysterious reason are also always attributed to Eustace Fitz John. The two Fitz John coins are in a very damaged condition. I have not myself seen these coins, but I have considerable doubts about the reliability of the reading. Even if they were certainly struck by him, they hardly give very substantial evidence of the importance of his mintage. The importance of Eustace of Boulogne at York is attested by John of Hexham.

65. *AM*, i, Margam Annals 1124: 'gens Noricum hyemavit apud Bristolliam'. Bristol also had links with Ireland: HN, pp. 118–19. The forces acquired by the Welsh

prince Cadwalader from Dublin are described as *Germanici* … King Magnus of Norway is also described in this text as *rex Germaniae.*: *Annales Cambriae,* RS, 20, ed. J. Williams ab Ithel (London, 1860), pp. 31, 42.

66. A. Ballard, *The Domesday Boroughs* (Oxford, 1904), p. 76: burgesses of Colchester and Maldon rendered £20 for mint; more often minters personally farmed it.

67. Blackburn in *The Anarchy*, pp. 197–98.

68. Rustics were assumed to have money, even to carry it : *Coucher Book,* nos 11, 17 (p. 38), for stories of ransoms being demanded of a *pelliparius* and a *rusticus*; HN, pp. 70–71: 'vavassores, rusticos quicumque pecuniosi putabantur', from what the editor deems the 'Worcester' version'; GS, c. 29.

69. J. A. Green, 'Financing Stephen's Wars', *ANS,* 14 (1991), pp. 91–114.

70. H. Cam, *The Hundred and the Hundred Rolls* (London, 1930), p. 137, showed that 358 of the 628 English hundreds were in private hands in 1272: well over half. Private hundreds long precede the arrival of the Normans or any 'feudal' system. Miss Cam estimated the number of private hundreds in 1066 as perhaps already one hundred, roughly one sixth. The 1130 pipe roll gives evidence about exemptions from *murdrum* payments for about sixty hundreds. Ten of these seem to have had only one lord; five had two; most made financial allowances for several different lordships, which would presumably have left the hundred court in public hands. This sample suggests that the proportion of private hundreds in 1130 was still about one sixth. Henry I himself had certainly allowed hundreds to pass into private lordship. Stephen did likewise. If the incidence of private hundreds had risen exceptionally under Stephen, Henry II is not known to have taken any steps to recover 'lost' public hundred courts. G. R. J. Hodgett, 'Feudal Wiltshire', *VCH. Wiltshire,* v, ed. R. B. Pugh and E. Crittall (London, 1957), p. 49, estimated that one third of the forty hundreds of Wiltshire were in private hands by 1173. Whatever the reason for this expansion of private lordship of hundreds, Stephen's reign was not anomalous. The earliest continuous records of royal governement show that from Richard I onwards kings continued to make grants of hundreds into private lordship. The 1130 pipe roll which records exemptions from *murdrum* fines in sixty hundreds, shows that in three-quarters of these hundreds, there were many exempt landlords: as many as eight in Cawdon hundred (Wiltshire) and Winfrith hundred (Dorset). It can only be a matter of speculation as to how the properties of so many influental lords in the district affected, even hampered, the effectiveness of the hundred's jurisdiction. Though their number effectively precluded private ownership, the various lords may have been all the more zealous in getting secret slayings reported, if there was a financial bonus for them. In 1272, private hundreds were most common in Devon, Oxfordshire and Somerset, territories where royal supervision may have been most ineffective in Stephen's reign. In those parts of the kingdom where Stephen's kingship had been least contested, only in Sussex were all hundreds in private hands.

71. Attendance at public law courts was an obligation expected of peasantry holding thirty acres of land (virgaters). The peasantry evidently played an even greater role in running local village government. R. Faith, *English Peasantry and the Growth of Lordship* (Leicester, 1997), pp. 222, 256. *The Cartularies of Southwick Priory*, ed. K. A. Hanna, Hampshire Record Series, 9 (1988), nos 120, 121, two chirographs recording complicated exchanges of very small pieces of land awarded by juries of local men selected from both sides in the disputes, early in Henry II's reign. For a hallmoot meeting in the 1140s, Stenton, *First Century*, appendix 42. Stephen attempted to secure the trial in the shire court of Norfolk of men accused of conspiring for his own capture and death, but the abbot of Bury successfully claimed the case because the accused were his men. H. M. Cam, 'An East Englian Shire-Moot of Stephen's Reign', *EHR*, 39 (1924), pp. 568-71; *Chronicon abbatiae Rameseiensis*, p. 274, no. 300, for settlement of any disputes about tenure only at meetings of the shire courts of Bedfordshire and Buckinghamshire; *Chronicon de Abingdon*, ii, p. 230: the abbot offered customary payments of £5 p. a. to the sheriff of Berkshire 'ut abbatiae homines lenius tractaret et eos in placitis et hundredis si quid necesse haberent adjuvaret'. In Henry II's reign a new abbot was able to get out of this obligation when it was established in a public court that such payments had not been made in Henry I's reign.

72. Earl Ranulf had interests in twenty-three shires; Gloucester, in twenty-four; the earls of Huntingdon had major estates in four shires with outposts in seven others.

Notes to Chapter 7: Assigning Blame

1. *Coucher Book*, bk 2, cc. 13, 14, 18-20, for various stories showing that hostages might become victims if the principals refused to pay up ransoms and for false accusations implicating soldiers. It was not only *tempore guerrae* that property might be seized *violenter*; some property was acquired without due process of law in peacetime. W. L. Warren, *The Governance of Norman and Angevin England, 1086-1272* (London, 1987) pp. 94-95, quotes the complaint of the Battle Chronicle that in Stephen's reign, justice was little regarded: *Chronicle of Battle Abbey*, ed. E. Searle (Oxford, 1980), pp. 138-40, 146, 150, 152, 210-12, 222, 224-29, 238. White, 'Myth' notes the Battle Chronicler's inconsistency. Comparably long-drawn out cases occur in the *Chronicon de Abingdon*, ii, pp. 184-85, 201-2.

2. JW, pp. 216-19; *The Peterborough Chronicle*, p. 263.

3. OV, vi, pp. 18 -19 ; cp. Suger, *Louis VI*, pp. 102-3.

4. The pope made no difficulties about confirming episcopal ownership of castles along with other properties: *Papsturkunden*, ii, nos 25, 49, 54, 81.

5. John of Salisbury, *Policraticus*, ed. C. C. J. Webb (Oxford, 1904) lib. vi, c. xviii, pp. 50-53 a particularly vicious attack on Stephen: hominem contemptorem

boni et aequi cuius consilium infatuatum est ab initio, cuius causa in iniquitate et perfidia fundata est.

6. HP, pp. 7, 42: Theobald's exiles.

7. Violence at Fountains: *Memorials of the Abbey of St Mary of Fountains*, ed. J. R. Walbran, Surtees Society, 42 (1863), pp. 101–2; JH, pp. 318–19.

8. GF, letter 26, pp. 60–66; HP, pp. 85–86; *Gesta abbatum S. Albani*, p. 93: Abbot Geoffrey sent Celestine II a chalice and paten worth eight gold marks to buy off his *avaritia* in wanting *ecclesiam hanc app[rop]riare.*

9. JH, p. 315, says that Henry of Winchester, though spurned by Celestine II, recovered the favours of Lucius II.

10. M. Horn, 'Der Kardinalbischof Imar von Tusculum als Legat in England, 1144–45', *Historisches Jahrbuch*, 110 (1990), pp. 429–503. GF, appendix 3, pp. 507–9.

11. M. D. Knowles, 'The Case of St William of York', *Cambridge Historical Journal*, 5 (1935), pp. 162–77, 212–14.

12. Bernard of Clairvaux, *Epistolae*, ed. J. Leclercq, *Opera*, vii–viii (Rome, 1974, 1977), no. 248 on Henry of Winchester, re York election; no. 533 to Stephen.

13. Gervase of Canterbury, i, on the squabbles of the Priors of Christ Church with Archbishop Theobald, pp. 16–28, 143–46, on the archbishop's problems with the abbey of St Augustine's, pp. 74–76, 136, 138–39, 147–48; AM, ii, p. 54, for disputes, not only between Bishop Henry and the abbot of Hyde, but between the same abbot and his own monks. *Chronicle of Battle*, pp. 146–53, for dispute between the monastery and the bishop of Chichester. For the major quarrel between the monks and the secular clergy, 'Un débat sur le sacerdoce', see above p. 249 note 20.

14. Jocelin of Furness, *Vita S. Waldeni*, AASS, August, i, pp. 242–78; D. Baker, 'Legend and Reality: The Case of Waldef of Melrose', Studies in Church History, 12, *Church, Society and Politics* (1975), pp. 59–82. William of Malmesbury, 'Commentary on Lamentations', ed. D. Farmer, *Studia Monastica*, 4 (1962), pp. 283–311, also deplored worldly clergy.

15. *Councils and Synods with Other Documents Relating to the English Church*, ed. D. Whitelock, M. Brett and C. N. L. Brooke, i, part 2, *1066–1204* (Oxford, 1981). Alberic's legatine council of 1138 condemned the arrest of clergy by seculars (10) and forbade clergy to take up arms (13); the London council of 1143 condemned the invasion of church property (1), *indebitas exactiones castellorum* (14) and the saying of mass *in turribus* (16); HH, pp. 742–23 for Henry of Winchester's legatine council at London in 1143; Suger on warfare, PL, 186, ep. 153 does not condemn fighting as such, allowing seculars to fight out their disputes provided they spared church property. Innocent II wrote to Archbishop Hugh of Rouen in July 1131 (Jaffe, no. 7483) about the troubles secular persons in Normandy were making for the clergy. Other papal letters condemn the exercise of secular jurisdiction over clergy: *Papsturkunden* iii, nos 38, 54, 57, 70, 71.

16. *Chronicon de Abingdon*, ii, p. 178

17. HN, pp. 40–41; GS, cc. 78, 80, 85, 96, 104, 112; Simeon, ii, p. 314; *Waltham*

Chronicle, pp. 72–75: a good example of a change in heart in Matthew, an incorrigible scoffer at religion, effected by a miracle.

18. GF, no. 35: 1145; Jaffe, no. 9462: March 1151; Robert Marmion also converted a monastery into a castle: 'monachis avulsis ecclesias dei converteravit in castella', *AM*, ii, p. 230. *GS*, c. 43: 'tam damnosus ... casus ... quia ex quadam ibi ecclesia ... castellum fieri' ; God's punishment on the king for turning a house of prayer into a den of murderers; another instance, GF, no. 5.

19. Newburgh, p. 53.

20. *Chartulary of Chichester* : no. 297, William d'Albini reserved 'his dignities and customs of his ancestors', whatever they were. Secular properties must have remained liable. *Chronicon de Abingdon*, ii, p. 200; *GS*, c. 75; R. Eales, 'Royal Power and Castles in Norman England', *Medieval Knighthood*, 3, ed. C. Harper-Bill and R. Harvey (Woodbridge, 1990), pp. 49–78, esp. p. 60, though Eales doubts whether there was much new castle building in Stephen's reign.

21. *GS*, cc. 94, 66. The shame for a knight in being killed by a man without social status is apparent from the accounts of the deaths of the excommunicate Geoffrey de Mandeville and Robert Marmion, the first by 'quodam pedite vilissimo' and the second, after falling from his horse, by a cobbler (sutor): *AM*, ii. p. 230.

22. *De Expugnatione Lyxbonensi, The Conquest of Lisbon*, ed. C. W. David (New York, 1936; reprinted 1976); the English were such a success in Portugal that the English bishop of Lisbon, Gilbert of Hastings, came to England to recruit more soldiers in 1150, JH, p. 324; *De Expugnatione*, pp. 178–81.

23. 1138 council forbade priests to take up arms; for Cirencester priest who became a soldier and tried to retain his church: *Papsturkunden* iii, nos 39, 73–74.

24. The chroniclers point out that many mercenaries were Bretons or Flemings (possibly recruited through the county of Boulogne): *GS*, cc. 39, 41, 50, 64, 78, 96; HN, pp. 32–33, 62–63, 74–77 ; *Waltham Chronicle*, pp. 80–83; HH, pp. 746–47. The most elaborate description of castle construction 'iuxta morem terrae illius' is provided by the Life of Bishop John of Thérouanne by Gautier of Thérouanne, ed. O. Holder-Egger, MGHSS, xv, 2, pp. 1138–50, c. 12. Had soldiers from that region acquired a particular reputation for their technical experience of that kind of warfare? The Flemish *praetor* of Exeter attracted the amorous interest of a local lady: *EEA, Exeter*, no. 42; for Fitz Hildebrand: *GS*, cc. 74, 77; for Fitz Hubert, *GS*, cc. 43, 50–52; HN, pp. 32–33, 72–73; 76–77, relates the sadistic story of how Fitz Hubert exposed his prisoners naked smeared with honey in the fierce sun so that they could be tormented by stinging insects. This was a form of martyrdom described in Jerome's *Vita Pauli* as occurring under the Emperor Decius. Malmesbury will have been familiar with the summary of Paul's life given by St Aldhelm, the original founder of Malmesbury, in his poetic *De laude virginum*, PL, 89, cc. 237–80, Paul, cc. 252–53 (though without reference to this episode). Jerome's text could nevertheless have been known to Malmesbury. The sufferings of his own times also reminded John of Worcester of the Decian persecutions: JW, pp. 250–51;

Coucher Book, no. xiv, p [39], relates stories showing a soldier washing his hands before meals and others attending mass in the castle chapel. Reginald *Libellus*, no. 71, refers to a man who left his spear outside the church. Just occasionally these clerical writers suggest that soldiers could be polite, considerate and devout.

25. Davis, 'Henry of Blois', p. 302: 'non est mirum si capio ex alieno ad vitam meam et meorum hominum sustendandam'; and the implications of Patterson, *Gloucester Charters*, no. 171, where the castellan of Sherborne was to swear to respect the rights of the bishop of Salisbury and not claim all the rights in the vineyard and mill at the castle foot for himself. *Libellus*, p. 135, c. 67, for the castellan of Nottingham who carried off 'partem maximam armentorum de agris' and c. 65 for a similar raid in search of food supplies; HN, pp. 70–71.

26. Pinkney, *GS*, c. 111; GF, no. 32 asks the bishop of Salisbury to exercise his episcopal authority to restrain John Fitz Gilbert, Angevin castellan of Marlborough and Walter de Pinkney, royal castellan of Malmesbury, on account of the damage their depredations had done to Gloucester abbey's properties. The two castellans may have collaborated to pillage the property or been rival foragers. Foliot was only interested in what his house had suffered. For Fitz Gilbert, see also Crouch, 'From Stenton', pp. 195–96.

27. *GS*, cc. 3, 52, 118, 57: 'a simplici rusticorum plebe in unum se globum in malum illius coniurante'; c. 66: 'in manus rusticorum incidentes, dirissimis flagris atterebantur'. Earl Henry exempted the *homines* of Tynemouth Priory 'de opere Novi Castelli et de opere aliorum castellorum' and allowed that their 'dominici rustici sint quieti ab omni exercitu et equitatu infra comitatum ad defendendum terram meam si eis per breve meum mandavero'. G. W. S. Barrow, *Regesta regum Scottorum*, i (Edinburgh, 1960), nos 28, 43. OV, vi, pp. 526–29, reports the use made by the castellan of Bonneville sur Touques of women and boys to set light to the town while the Angevin occupation forces were asleep.

28. *Chronicon de Abingdon*, ii, p. 213.

29. HN, pp. 128–29.

30. JW, pp. 272–75.

31. Town interests of earls: *Winton Domesday*, pp. 387–92, table 30; The Pipe Roll of Henry I's thirty-first year shows that Robert of Gloucester had urban interests in Winchester, Cambridge, Canterbury, Guildford, Gloucester and Winchcomb. In Southwark, Stephen had held assets in 1130 as count of Mortain, along with Brian Fitz Count, Earl Warenne and the archbishop of Canterbury. Stenton, *First Century*, pp. 238–39, wrote of the 'repugnance of burgesses to a baronial lord', but it is unsafe to take antipathy between the feudal and the urban worlds for granted.

32. *GS*, cc. 37–39, 147, 41, 109, 141, 146, 83, 144, 84, 143; L. W. Marvin, 'Men Famous in Combat and Battle: Common Soldiers and the Siege of Bruges', *JMH*, 24 (1998), pp. 243–58.

33. Robert of Gloucester authorised the customs of Cardiff and Tewkesbury before

1147, *The Earldom of Gloucester Charters*, ed. R. B. Patterson (Oxford, 1973), no. 46, pp. 60–62. Stephen confirmed the customs of Chichester: *RRAN*, no. 181.

34. Stephen sent writs to the citizens or burgesses of Exeter, Lincoln, Oxford, Taunton and York, expecting them to wield executive powers, *RRAN*, iii, nos 286, 472, 637, 993; the burgesses of Colchester were forcing the monks to pay dues, Saltman, *Theobald*, no. 75; the burgesses of Derby made gifts to the church, *EEA*, 14, *Coventry*, no. 19; a dispute was settled *iuxta consuetudinem civitatis EEA*, *Norwich*, no. 153.

35. Stephen was received with solemn procession at Worcester: JW, pp. 266–67; and wore his crown, at Lincoln: HH, pp. 748–49; at London, LE, p. 324.

36. I. J. Sanders, *English Baronies: A Study of their Origin and Descent, 1086–1327* (Oxford, 1960); cp. J. A. Green, *The Aristocracy of Norman England* (Cambridge, 1997). Increasingly, academic historians use 'aristocracy' rather than' baronage' to describe the twelfth-century landlords. This is both anachronistic and misleading since in English 'aristocracy' has an established use in connection with forms of government and society without counterparts in this period. King, 'King Stephen and Aristocracy', pp. 193–94. defends this use of 'aristocracy' by reference to K. B. McFarlane.

37. *Liber Hyda*, pp. 313–21; OV, vi, pp. 16–19, 332–27, 346–57.

38. GS, cc. 66, 94; HN, pp. 84–85, comments on the king's forces at Lincoln in 1141, that at first they thought no more than jousting was in prospect. This might be used by some modern writers to indicate how frivolous they were. Malmesbury probably intended no such slight. The baronial concept of warfare was much less bloodthirsty than is often recognised. They fought less for victory than to show their military prowess and, if necessary were not too ashamed to flee, in order to find later occasions for combat. Gloucester's forces, however, comprised a great number of Welsh mercenaries and an unknown number of 'disinherited'. Did such soldiers have fewer scruples, because they were more desperate for the rewards of victory or booty ? JW uses *dextris datis* to show that men shook hands on agreements.

39. A. Ailes, 'Heraldry in Twelfth-Century England: The Evidence', *England in the Twelfth Century*, ed. D. Williams (Woodbridge, 1990), pp. 1–16 and plates 1–17.

40. D. Crouch, *The Image of Aristocracy in Britain, 1000–1300* (London, 1992), pp. 138, 243: 'It can only be significant that lesser men began to imitate the great seals of kings and magnates around the 1140s ... men identified as lords of only one or two villages, or even part of one. However, since they have themselves depicted on horseback and armed and armoured, they must have considered themselves knights'; T. A. Heslop, 'Seals', *English Romanesque Art* (Arts Council, 1984), pp. 298–320; T. A. Heslop, 'English Seals from the Mid-Ninth Century to 1100', *JBAA*, 133 (1980), pp. 1–16 claims that by 1100 seals had long been in use for sealing letters. W. de Gray Birch, *Seals* (London, 1907); *British Museum Catalogue of Seals*, ii (1892).

41. Reginald, *Libellus*, c. 67: 'omnis pene tyro castelli alicuius donabatur imperio';

Annales Wintonienses, 1138, p. 51: 'non fuit alicujus meriti vel momenti in Anglia qui non faceret aut inforciare munitionem'. The numerous studies of C. A. Coulson have re-examined many basic assumptions about castles and Stephen's reputation in their regard. 'The French Matrix of the Castle Provisions of the Chester-Leicester *Conventio*' *ANS*, 17 (1994), pp. 65–86; 'Freedom to Crenellate by Licence: An Historiographical Revision', *Nottingham Medieval Studies*, 38 (1994), pp. 86–137; 'Cultural Realities and Reappraisal in English Castle Study', *JMH*, 22 (1996) pp. 171–207; Eales, 'Royal Power', pp. 49–78. M. Strickland, 'Securing the North', *ANS*, 12 (1989), pp. 177–98, discusses the military effectiveness of castles; P. Dixon and P. Marshall, 'The Great Tower at Hedingham Castle: A Reassessment', *Fortress*, 18 (1993), pp. 16–23, argue for its ceremonial significance.

42. F. W. Maitand, *Domesday Book and Beyond* (Cambridge, 1897), p. 471, discussing eleventh-century taxation, jovially suggested how problems of assessment may have 'awakened debates in the council of the nation. We may fancy ... the conservatives arguing for the good old rule ... while a party of financial reformers has raised the cry ... [then] pressure was brought to bear in 'influential quarters', and in favour of their own district the witan in the moots jobbed and jerrymandered and rolled the friendly log, for all the world as if they had been mere modern politicians.' Despite his humour, Maitland concluded that 'it is in some conjecture such as this that we may perchance find aid when we are endeavouring to loosen one of Domesday's worst knots'. We have greater chance of penetrating to the heart of the matter if we can find points of contact with the past than if we assume that those who dominated affairs then were like strange monsters.

43. R. H. C. Davis, *King Stephen*, appendix 1 on earls. In 1135 there were seven earls if King David is included; in 1141, there were twice as many again, i.e. twenty-one, but the numbers thereafter fell slightly.

44. *RRAN*, iii, no. 273.

45. The 1166 returns of knights' fees provide a total of 7525, of which 407 are stated to have been of the new enfeoffment since 1135. Of the 313 tenants in chief submitting returns, only twenty-two had created more than five new fees and, of these twenty-two, only nine more than ten fees. These nine were the earls of Norfolk (25), of Gloucester (13), of Essex (11 1/2), Simon de St Liz, heir to the earldom of Northampton (14 +), William d'Albini (13), Henry and Hugh de Lacy (18, 11), Roger de Mowbray (nearly 12), the honour of Totnes (nearly 20). Earl Ferrers came top of the second league with nine and one third new fees. These ten had added nearly 150 fees altogether. *Red Book of the Exchequer*, ed. H. Hall, RS, 99 (1899), i, pp. 186–445: Certificationes factae de feodis militum tempore regis Henrici Secundi.

46. Since the sheriff paid the king an agreed annual farm for the royal estates in his shire, he was entitled to a discount for any royal property the king had independently granted to a third party (*terre date*). The value of such grants recorded in the 1130 audit was barely £40. What survives of the 1155 audit

shows that by then nearly £1000 worth of crown land had been alienated, nearly half of this in Wiltshire alone.; W. L. Warren, pp. 91, 92, 94: decentralisation.

47. Patterson, no. 109, pp. 106–8; *RRAN*, ii, no. 1466.

48. D. Bates, 'The Prosopographical Study of the Anglo-Norman Royal Charter', *Family Trees and the Roots of Politics: Prosopography in Britain and France from the Tenth to the Twelfth Century*, ed. K. S. B. Keats-Rohan (Woodbridge, 1997), pp. 89–102, discusses the difficulties of arguing from charter evidence. D. Crouch 'Earls and Bishops', confidently expects to learn from them something about the 'aristocratic mentality'.

49. HH, pp. 598–99, has the English spokesman deriding the Scots for having no military skills or self-discipline. Similarly, Stephen's supporters were supposedly denounced before the battle of Lincoln for their lasciviousness, perjury, perfidy, drunkenness, boastfulness; some of these sins may have mattered more to Huntingdon than to his baronial mouthpieces.

50. For his action in London, Van Caenegem, *Royal Writs*, Selden Society, p. 84; *The Waltham Chronicle*, ed. L. Watkins and M. Chibnall, OMT (1994), cc. 29–32, pp. 77–83; *GS*, cc. 81–84; HH, pp. 744–47; *Chronicon Abbatiae Rameseiensis*, p. 411, compensation for damage caused, offered by his heir in 1163.

51. J. O. Prestwich, 'The Treason of Geoffrey de Mandeville', *EHR*, 103 (1988), pp. 283–312, 960–67.

52. *The Charters of Chester;* see also A. T. Thacker, *The Earldom of Chester and its Charters: A Tribute to Geoffrey Barraclough*, Chester Archaeological Society (1991).

53. *GS*, c. 103. At Ramsey, comparably, the *barones, milites* and *liberi homines* of Abbot Daniel were upset when the king induced him to renounce the abbey in favour of another: *Chronicon abbatiae Rameseiensis*, nos 408–10, pp. 325–36. General comment by Stenton, *First Century*, pp. 242–43, and King, 'Dispute Settlement', pp. 124–25.

54. Dalton, 'In Neutro Latere'

55. Stenton, *First Century*, p. 217: 'they deserve the hard measure which historians always give them'; Davis, *King Stephen*, p. 111: 'several magnates were prepared to accept any solution which would leave them their hereditary lands'; King, 'Aristocracy', *History* (1974), pp. 185, 192–93: the barons were 'looking for lordship all the time ... they had been tamed; ... they found it difficult to manage without a strong king'; Hollister: in *Anarchy*, p. 64: on magnates 'interested in enjoying the full incomes from their lands ... all were keeping close touch with their profits and losses'; P. Dalton, *Conquest, Anarchy and Lordship, Yorkshire, 1066–1154* (Cambridge, 1994), p. 174: 'pursuit of territorial and jurisdictional ambition in opposition to the king'; p. 178 'if he was to make his authority effective over the countryside, it was essential to dominate his fellow magnates'; Crouch, *Reign*, p. 88: 'As royal interference in the localities had grown in the reigns of the Norman kings, so the local power of the aristocracy would be more likely to be seen as a threat by the centre'; Green,

Aristocracy, p. 318: 'many lords … may have profited by usurping lands and privileges from the crown and from churches and by exploiting the peasantry'. All these historians regard the barons in a negative light as domineering, exploitative, disruptive of royal order and in need of royal discipline to keep them in the place where they belong. They are seen as ambitious for more land, more 'control', more vassals, more prominence, not as supporting family, friends, dependents, or neighbours; their concern to make pacts is judged self-interested. None of them is thought of as indolent, easy going 'aristos', as the king is alleged to be, though even the chroniclers described some of them as indifferent to military reputations and prone to lustful indulgence. The idea that the barons might be almost human is alien to academic historians; the wicked baron of folklore lies behind almost all modern attempts to re-create the baronial profile.

56. *GS*, cc. 35, 81, 101; even Huntingdon granted that the arrests were justified, if not seemly HH, pp. 742–43: 'secundum retributionem nequitie consulis quam secundum ius gentium, magis ex necessitate quam ex honestate'.

57. The conspiracy 'de tradicione et morte regis' plotted at the siege of Bedford 1145–46 involved very minor tenants of the abbot of Bury St Edmund's: see above, p. 264 n. 71.

58. Stephen was suffering from an old wound *c.* 1147, *GS*, c. 104. According to Gervase of Canterbury, i, p. 154, he survived being thrown from his horse three times in 1153.

59. HN, pp. 28–29.

60. When *AM*, ii, p. 55 (from Winchester Annals), refers to Stephen's death and burial at Faversham in the church he had founded and remarks that he had moved on 'ad locum quo eum merita sua ducebant' the meaning could hardly be in doubt. This is interpreted as ironical by Crouch, *Reign*, p. 288.

61. Macbeth Act IV, Scene 3.

62. MGHSS, vi, p. 452, from the Prémontré Continuator of Sigebert of Gembloux. This atrocity is not mentioned in Suger's *Vie de Louis VII*.

63. E. King, 'Dispute Settlement'.

64. *GS*, cc. 39, 78.

65. *GS*, c. 57.

66. *GS*, c. 120; HH, pp. 766–67; Gervase of Canterbury, i, p. 154 puts into the mouth of the earl of Arundel a speech urging reconciliation in 1153 because of the risk of killing relatives if it came to battle, since families were split between supporters of the king and the duke.

Notes to Chapter 8: Endgame

1. H. G. Richardson and G. O. Sayles, *The Governance of Medieval England* (Edinburgh, 1963), pp. 251–64, chapter 14 'Duke and King'; W. L. Warren, *Henry II* (London, 1973), pp. 35–53; J. W. Leedom, 'The English Settlement of 1153', *History*, 65 (1980), pp. 347–64; G. J. White, 'The End of Stephen's Reign', *History*,

75 (1990), pp. 3–22; J. C. Holt, '1153, The Treaty of Winchester', *The Anarchy*, pp. 291–316, esp. p. 312; E. Amt, *The Accession of Henry II in England* (Woodbridge, 1993).

2. HP, pp. 6–8, 10–11, 41–42, 45–49, 51–52, 78–80.

3. GS, c. 113; JH, pp. 324–45 for Chester inviting Henry to get his revenge on Stephen for the attack on him of 1146, wrongly dated by John of Hexham.

4. King, 'Waleran', pp. 173–74.

5. Gervase of Canterbury, i, p. 136; HP, p. 49.

6. HH, pp. 754–55.

7. JH, pp. 322, 325–26, 328–29 The papal curia was at Ferentino, January–June 1151; Easter was 8 April. Further evidence of Murdac's unpopularity comes from Selby, where he tried to despose the abbot: *Coucher Book*, c. 21.

8. HH, pp. 758–59, 760–61; Gervase, i, pp. 151–52.

9. Annales Waverleiensis, *AM*, ii, p. 234; Annales Wintoniae, anno 1152, *Ungedrückte anglo-normannische Geschichtsquellen* (Strassburg, 1879), pp. 56–83. 'Apud Londoniam Eustachio filio regis Stephani fide et jusjurando universi comites atque barones Angliae se subdiderunt.'

10. JH, p. 327.

11. HP, pp. 83–86; *The Letters of John of Salisbury*, ii, ed. W. J. Millor and C. N. L. Brooke (OMT, 1979), no. 136.

12. *Materials for the History of Thomas Becket*, ed. W. Robertson, RS, 67, vi, pp. 57–58. According to HP, p. 44, Cardinal Gilbert of St. Mark (1143–49) had advised Geoffrey of Anjou that 'regna debere non actionibus sed gladiis vendicari', which would explain why the papacy would have preferred not to get involved in the dispute.

13. Henry refers to his hopes of getting his inheritance: *RRAN*, iii, nos 44, 81, 126, but already disposes of the rights of *corona mea* no. 104; he addresses his officials, *ministri, forestarii* (and refers to his *foresta* nos 840, 459), sheriffs and justices, nos 363, 575, 710; he makes gifts from his 'first conquests', no. 582 and obtains money for documents of confirmation, no. 306; he accepts that his grants may not take effect and offers to warrant gifts of comparable value, nos 81, 306, 491–92.

14. *RRAN*, iii, no. 796.

15. HH, pp. 762–63.

16. JH, p. 331 'consenserunt in hoc omnes principes regni humiliatique sunt sub manu regis Stephani qui adversati sunt ei' .

17. Torigni, pp. 171–81, on Henry in England.

18. *RRAN*, iii, no. 438.

19. GS, c. 119.

20. *RRAN*, iii, no. 180; GS, c. 119.

21. BL, Cotton MS Nero C III, fol. 178, first printed by A. Vincent, *A Discoverie of Errours in the First Edition of the Catalogue of Nobility Published by Ralphe Brooke York Herald* (London, 1622), pp. 301–3 because 'it doth lively expresse the calamity of this State under the exorbitant power of the Nobility then,

whereby we may see and thanke God for the felicity we enjoy under the happy monarchy in respect of our Ancestors under so many tyrants' . Vincent's interpretation of the charter has continued to find favour. It is thought that only when the king was powerless would great nobles be driven to settle their differences by themselves. Stenton, *First Century*, pp. 249–55, 285–58; *The Charters of Chester*, no. 110, where it was dated by Barraclough to 1153.

22. T. Callahan, 'Sinners and Saintly Retribution, The Timely Death of Eustace', *Studia monastica*, 17 (1976), pp. 109–17.
23. *RRAN*, iii, no. 81: Bedford canons, a point made by White, 'End', pp. 10–11.
24. HH, pp. 768–69; Torigni, p. 174; GS, c. 119.
25. HH, p. 766: *proceres immo proditores*, a convenient play on words.
26. Davis, *King Stephen*, chapter 10: Magnates' peace; Gervase of Canterbury, i, p. 154; HH, pp. 766–67, 770–71.
27. GS, c. 120.
28. King, 'Dispute Settlement'.
29. *RRAN*, iii, nos 339, 840.
30. HH, pp. 770–71; Leedom, pp. 357, 360.
31. For the meeting of Duke Henry at Colchester 'ubi diem pacis et concordiae cum Gulielmo comite Warenniae filio Stepheni regis, praesente Theobaldo archispicopo Cantuariae et reg' baronibus', William de Vere, *Vita S. Osithae*, *Itinerary of John Leland*, ed. L. Toulmin-Smith (London, 1906–10), v, p. 171.
32. Holt '1153', p. 312; Torigny, p. 177: according to this account, Stephen began by acknowledging Henry's hereditary right to the English crown; cp. *RRAN*, iii, no. 272, where Stephen appoints Henry as his heir; P. R. Hyams, 'Warranty and Good Lordship in Twelfth-Century England', *Law and History Review*, 5 (1987), pp. 437–503, appendix 3, pp. 497–503.
33. Torigni, p. 177; Holt '1153', pp. 304–5: 'We simply do not know how large a tip of how large an iceberg these charters represent'. cp. references to *tempore guerrae* in Certificationes factae, *Red Book of Exchequer*, i, pp. 196, 237, 251, 298, 351, 354, 364, 368, 392, 401, 408–9: about thirty fees in all, compared with over 400 enfeoffments since 1135 (7.5 per cent) and with over 7500 altogether (0.4 per cent of all feeholders).
34. D. J. Cathcart King, *Castellarium Anglicanum* (Millwood, New York, 1983): excluding the border counties, this gives the total number of castles for thirty-two inland English counties as 860 which makes the figure of 1115 adulterine castles destroyed, given by some Torigni manuscripts, look fanciful. King's figures account for all castles known down to 1547 and are not specific to the twelfth century but they serve to control wild guesses. From them the average density of castles can be calculated as one to every forty-eight square miles. Notably higher densities occur in Kent and the Midlands (Buckinghamshire, Leicestershire, Northamptonshire with Rutland, Oxfordshire and Warwickshire).
35. Eales, 'Royal Power', pp. 61, 70–73 ; Coulson rejects the familiar interpretation on other grounds. JH, pp. 331; GS, cc. 104, 117 for Stephen's destruction of

'adulterine' castles; the abbot of St Albans asked the king to destroy the castle of Kingsbury, occupied by *servi* claiming to be the king's *fideles* and keepers of the peace. *Gesta abbatum*, i, p. 122. Stephen's razing of Drax castle is singled out by HH. and William of Newburgh, i, pp. 32, 94, though Philip de Coleville can hardly have been a particularly dangerous baron. Newburgh made the expression *adulterae munitiones* totally familiar to students of English history.

36. HH pp. 772–73: *displicebat* over castles at Dunstable meeting ; Holt, '1153', pp. 307–9; White, 'End', pp. 13–14.

37. *RRAN*, iii, nos 28, 127, 344; Earl Patrick writ in R. Benson and H. Hatcher, *Old and New Sarum, or Salisbury* (London, 1843), p. 32 from a document now lost.

38. *RRAN*, iii, no. 137.

39. The recent issue of coins in 1154 would anyway have diminished the importance of the assay, except possibly in the west, where some coins of lower weight issued in previous years could still have been in circulation.

40. In Surrey the *auxilium* of Guildford and Southwark were the same in 1155 as in 1130; Huntingdon likewise; at Windsor the *firma* in 1130 was £12 3s. 4d.; in 1155 £12 6s. 3d.; in Yorkshire the canons received £18 5s. in both years; in Devon, the canons of Holy Trinity, £25 12s. 6d.; in Hampshire the *telarii* and *fullones* of Winchester both paid £6 or one mark of gold for their guild.

41. *RRAN*, iii, nos 81, 193, 703, 836. R. B. Patterson, 'Robert Fitz Harding of Bristol: Profile of an Early Angevin Burgess-Baron and his Family's Urban Involvement', *HSJ*, 1 (1989), pp. 109–22.

42. In Staffordshire and Shropshire, Robert de Stafford and William Fitz Alan respectively, appear to have assumed the role of earl, if not the title, under Angevin aegis. In 1155 the account for Norfolk and Suffolk was presented by Earl Hugh Bigod though he can hardly have enjoyed in East Anglia authority comparable to that of Matildine earls in the west, granted the evidence for royal sheriffs there. White, 'Continuity' pp. 131–32.

43. Yoshitake, *EHR* (1988), p. 952; *The Great Rolls of the Pipe*, ed. J. Hunter (London, 1844), p. 4: 1156: *in reparatione domorum de Scaccario* 66s. 8d.; since 1130 when the audit was at Winchester, an exchequer house had been built in London and was in need of repair by 1156, possibly from long use, in the absence of information about its actual destruction or dilapidation. *GS*, c. 94, for earl of Chester's failure to render account to fisc: quia regalium fiscorum redditus … reddere negligebat.

44. N. Barratt, 'The Revenues of King John', *EHR*, 111 (1996), pp. 835–55.

45. J. A. Green, 'The Last Century of Danegeld', *EHR*, 96 (1981), pp. 241–58.

46. C. R. Young, *The English Borough and Royal Administration, 1130–1307* (Durham, North Carolina, 1961); J. Tait, 'The *Firma Burgi* and the Commune in England, 1066–1191', *EHR*, 42 (1927), pp. 321–60; Stubbs, *Constitutional History*, p. 363: 'there are not wanting indications that in the town populations, where feudal rule was exercised under more restriction and with less impunity, an important advance towards liberty resulted from the abeyance of government;

or at least that the municipal unity was able so far to hold its own as to prevent disintegration in one of the rising elements of society. But this is an inference from later events rather than a distinctly recorded fact of the reign'.

47. J. K. Hedges, *The History of Wallingford* (London, 1881), pp. 270–73.

48. K. T. Streit, 'The Expansion of the English Jewish Community in the Reign of Stephen', *Albion*, 25 (1993), pp. 177–92.

49. J. M. McCulloch, 'Jewish Ritual Murder: William of Norwich, Thomas of Monmouth and the Early Dissemination of a Myth', *Speculum*, 72 (1997), pp. 698–740.

50. Cade witnessed a document issued in Kent for St Bertin of St-Omer, 1150–53, *CDF*, no. 1327; C. H. Haskins, 'William Cade', *EHR*, 28 (1913), pp. 730–31, commented on Cade's appearance in England in Stephen's reign; this was also discussed by Cronne, *Stephen*, pp. 235–36.

Notes to Chapter 9: Envoi

1. G. J. White, 'The Myth of the Anarchy', *ANS*, 22 (1999), pp. 323–37.

2. Davis, *King Stephen*, p. 124.

3. Crouch, *The Reign of King Stephen*, p. 341.

4. Davis, *King Stephen*, p. 79, where Davis already claimed that Stephen 'had no overall strategy'.

5. T. S. R. Boase, *English Art, 1100–1216* (Oxford, 1953); L. Musset, *L'Angleterre Romane* (Zodiaque, 1983). *Chronicon abbatiae Rameseiensis*, p. 396, for the tower built at the end of Stephen's reign; on the beauty of Waltham, see Laurence of Durham in *The Chronicle of Waltham*, appendix 1, pp. 86–87.

6. For scholarly treatment of the topic, see C. Coulson, 'Cultural Realities and Reappraisal in English Castle Study', *JMH*, 22 (1996), pp. 171–207.

7. Ralph of St. Albans, abbot 1146–51, is described in the *Gesta abbatum* as an Englishman who loved books. C. M. Kauffmann, *English Romanesque Manuscripts, 1066–1190* (London, 1975).

8. D. Crouch, 'From Stenton', discusses the feudal honor, the shire and the neighbourhood as possible focuses for local feelings of community in this period, and the interaction between the king and the communities, esp. pp. 186–197; P. Wormald, 'Charters, Law and the Settlement of Disputes in Anglo-Saxon England', *The Settlement of Disputes in Early Medieval Europe*, ed. W. Davies and P. Fouracre (Cambridge, 1986), pp. 149–68, where the sophistication of English dispute settlement is traced to the ninth century. In the article, emphasis is put elsewhere, but the material discussed illustrates the long established practice of obtaining judgment by local people meeting for formal legal business. Those most concerned with cases of manslaughter, that is family and neighbours, were more interested in reconciling the parties by negotiating terms of settlement, than in enforcement of the criminal law. Royal judges aimed to extend the royal plea of murder to comprise all cases of homicide, a policy much approved by modern historians. The crown refused to draw a

distinction between homicide and murder until the sixteenth century. T.A. Green, *Verdict According to Conscience* (Chicago, 1985).

9. For a more recent exposition of the way Magna Carta may be integrated into the pattern of English legal development in the twelfth century, see P. R. Hyams, 'The Charter as a Source for the Early Common Law', *Journal of Legal History*, 12 (1991), pp. 173–89: p. 174, Magna Carta 'would have been impossible but for the experience of a myriad of private deeds in and around these topics during the preceding century'; p. 178: 'The initial leap forward came under Henry I with the corresponding upsurge in the lay use of charters', where the stress is on the increasing use of written documents, not by the king's administration but by the king's subjects.

Bibliography

Primary Sources

Anglo-Saxon Chronicle, translated G. N. Garmonsway (London, 1953) and M. Swanton (London, 1996).

Annales Cambriae, ed. J. Williams RS, 20 (London, 1860).

Annales monastici, ed. H. R. Luard, RS, 36 (London, 1864–69,), i, *Annales de Margan*, pp. 3–40; ii, *Annales de Waverleia*, pp. 129–411; iv, *Annales de Osneia*, pp. 1–352.

Annales Ryenses ed. J. M. Lappenberg, MGHSS, xvi (Hanover, 1859).

Annales Wintoniae, ed. F. Liebermann, *Ungedrückte anglo-normannische Geschichtsquellen* (Strassburg, 1879), pp. 56–83.

Auctarium Affligense, ed. D. L. C. Bethmann, MGHSS, vi (Hanover, 1844; reprinted 1925), pp. 398–405.

Auctarium Aquicinense, ed. D. L. C. Bethmann, MGHSS, vi (Hanover, 1844; reprinted 1925), pp. 392–98.

The Beauchamp Cartulary Charters, ed. E. Mason, PRS, new series, 43 (1980).

Bernard of Clairvaux, *Epistolae*, ed J. Leclercq, *Opera*, vii–viii (Rome, 1974, 1977).

The Boarstall Cartulary, ed. H. E. Salter, Oxford Historical Society, 88 (1930)

Brut y Tywysogyn, ed. T. Jones (Cardiff, 1952).

Thomas de Burton, *Chronica monasterii de Melsa*, ed. E. A. Bond, RS, 43 (London, 1866).

R. C. van Caenegem, *Royal Writs in England from the Conquest to Glanvill*, Selden Society, 77 (1959).

Calendar of Documents Preserved in France, 918–1206, ed. J. H. Round (London, 1899).

Cartae et alia documenta quae ad dominium de Glamorgan pertinent, ed. G. T. Clark (Cardiff, 1910).

Cartularium monasterii de Rameseiensis, ed. W. H. Hart and P. A. Lyon, RS, 79, ii (London, 1886).

The Cartularies of Southwick Priory, ed. K. A. Hanna, Hampshire Record Series, 9 (1988).

The Cartulary of Worcester Priory, ed. R. Darlington, PRS, new series, 38 (1968).

Certificationes factae de feodis militum tempore regis Henrici Secundi, ed. H. Hall, *Red Book of the Exchequer*, RS, 99, I (London, 1896), pp. 186–445.

Charters of the Anglo-Norman Earls of Chester, c. 1071–1237, ed. G. Barraclough, Record Society of Lancashire and Cheshire (1988).

Charters of the Earldom of Hereford, 1095–1201, ed. D. Walker, Camden Society (1964).

Charters of the Redvers Family and the Earldom of Devon, 1090–1217, ed. R. Bearman, Devon and Cornwall Record Society, new series, 37 (1994).

'Charters of Robert II de Ferrers', ed. M. Jones, *Nottingham Medieval Studies*, 24 (1980), pp. 7–26.

The Chartulary of the High Church of Chichester, ed. W. D. Peckam, Sussex Record Society, 46 (1946).

The Chronicle of Battle Abbey, ed. E. Searle (Oxford, 1980).

Chronicon de Abingdon, ed. J. Stevenson, RS, 2 (London, 1858).

Chronicon abbatiae Rameseiensis, ed. W. Dunn Macray, RS, 83 (London, 1886).

'De compotis diversorum vicecomitum in diversis comitatibus Angliae', ed. H. Hall, *Red Book of the Exchequer*, RS, 99, iii (London, 1896), pp. 648–92.

Continuatio Praemonstratensis, ed. D. L. C. Bethmann, MGHSS, vi (Hanover, 1844), pp. 447–56.

Councils and Synods with Other Documents Relating to the English Church, i, pt 2, 1066–1204, ed. D. Whitelock, M. Brett and C. N. L. Brooke (Oxford 1981).

Coucher Book of Selby, ed. J. T. Fowler, Yorkshire Archaeological Society, Record Series, 10 (1891).

Walter Daniel, *Vita Ailredi*, ed. F. M. Powicke, Nelson Medieval Texts (second edn, Edinburgh, 1978).

'Un débat sur le sacerdoce des moines au XIIe siècle', ed. R. Foreville and J. Leclercq, *Studia Anselmiana*, fasc. 41 (1957), pp. 8–118.

Earldom of Gloucester Charters, ed. R. B. Patterson (Oxford, 1973).

English Episcopal Acta, British Academy (Oxford, 1980–99).

—, Bath and Wells, no. 10, ed. F. M. R. Ramsey (1995):

—, Coventry and Lichfield, no. 14, ed. M. J. Franklin (1997).

—, Exeter, no. 11, ed. F. Barlow (1996).

—, Hereford, no. 7, ed. J. Barrow (1992).

—, Lincoln, no. 1, ed. D. M. Smith (1980).

—, London, no. 15, ed. F. Nenininger (1999).

—, Norwich, no. 6. ed. C. Harper-Bill (1990).

—, Salisbury, no 18, ed. B. R. Kemp (1999).

—, Winchester, no. 8, ed. M. J. Franklin (1993).

—, York, no. 5, ed. J. E. Burton (1988).

English Lawsuits from William I to Richard I, ed. R. C. Van Caenegem, Selden Society, 2 vols (London, 1990, 1991).

De expugnatione Lyxbonensi. The Conquest of Lisbon, ed. C. W. David (New York 1936; reprinted 1976).

Feudal Manuals of English History, ed. T. Wright (London, 1872).

Gautier of Thérouanne, *Vita Johannis Episcopi Morinensis*, ed. O. Holder-Egger, MGHSS, xv, 2, pp. 1138–50.

Geffrei Gaimar, *L'estoire des Engleis*, ed. A. Bell, Anglo-Norman Texts, 14–16 (Oxford, 1960).

Gervase of Canterbury, *Opera historica*, ed. W. Stubbs, RS, 73, i (London, 1879).

Gervase of Tilbury, Otia imperialia, ed. G. G. Leibnitz in *Scriptores rerum Brunswicensium*, i (Hanover, 1707), pp. 881–1006.

Gesta Ambaziensium dominorum, in *Chroniques d'Anjou*, ed. P. Marchegay and A. Salmon, SHF (1856–71).

The Gesta Normannorum Ducum of William of Jumièges, Orderic Vitalis and Robert of Torigni, ii, ed. E. M. C. van Houts (OMT, 1995).

Gesta Stephani, ed. and trans. K. Potter, Nelson Medieval Texts; second edition by R. H. C. Davis (Oxford, 1976).

The Great Rolls of the Pipe for the Second, Third and Fourth Years of the Reign of King Henry the Second, ed. J. Hunter (London, 1844).

Henry of Huntingdon, *Historia Anglorum*, ed. D. Greenway (OMT, 1996).

Herimann of Tournai, *Liber de restauratione monasterii S. Martini Tornacensis*, ed. G. Waitz, MGHSS, xiv (Hanover, 1883), pp. 274–317; translated by L. H. Nelson as *The Restoration of the Monastery of St Martin of Tournai*, Catholic Univeristy of America (1996).

Hildebert of Le Mans, *Epistolae*, PL, 171, cc. 135–312.

Historia et cartularium S. Petri de Gloucestriae, i–iii, ed. W. H. Hart, RS, 33 (London, 1863–65).

Historians of the Church of York and its Archbishops, ed. J. Raine, RS, 71 (London, 1879).

Hugh Candidus, *The Peterborough Chronicle*, ed. W. T. Mellows (Oxford 1949).

P. Jaffe, *Regesta pontificum Romanorum* (Leipzig, 1885–86).

John of Hexham, *Chronicle*, in Symeon of Durham, *Chronicle*, ii, ed. T. Arnold, RS, 75 (London, 1885).

Jocelin of Furness, *Vita*, in 'De S. Waltheno abbate', AASS, August I, pp. 242–78.

John of Marmoutier, 'Historia Gaufredi ducis Normannorum et comitis Andegavorum', *Chroniques d'Anjou*, ed. P. Marchegay and A. Salmon, SHF (1856–71).

John of Salisbury, *Historia pontificalis*, ed. and trans. M. Chibnall (OMT, second edn, 1986).

—, *Policratricus*, ed. C. C. J Webb (Oxford, 1904).

John of Worcester, *Chronicle, 1118–40*, ed. J. R. H. Weaver (Oxford, 1908).

—, *The Chronicle*, iii, ed. P. McGurk (OMT, 1998).

Layamon, *Brut*, ed. F. Madden (London 1847).

The Letters and Charters of Gilbert Foliot, ed. A. Morey and C. N. L. Brooke (Cambridge, 1967).

L'histoire de Guillaume Le Maréchal, ed. P. Meyer, Société de l'Histoire de France, i–iii (Paris, 1891–1901).

Liber monasterii de Hyda, ed. E. Edwards, RS, 45 (London, 1886).

Liber Eliensis, ed. E. O. Blake, Camden Society, 92 (1962)

J. D. Mansi, *Sacrorum conciliorum nova et amplissima collectio* (Florence, 1759-).

Materials for the History of Thomas Becket, ed. W. Robertson, RS, 67 (London, 1875–83).

Matthew Paris, *Historia Anglorum*, ed. F. Madden, RS, 44, i (London, 1866).

—, *Gesta Abbatum*, ed. H. T. Riley, RS, 28 (London, 1867).

Memorials of the Abbey of St Mary of Fountains, ed. J. R. Walbran, SS, 42 (1863).

Miscellanea biographica, ed. J. Raine, SS, 8 (1838).

'The Norman and Wessex Charters of the Roumare Family', ed. F. A. Cazel, *A Medieval Miscellany for Doris Stenton*, ed. P. M. Barnes and C. F. Slade, Pipe Roll Society (1962), pp. 77–88.

Orderic Vitalis, *Ecclesiastical History*, ed. and trans. M. Chibnall, i–vi (OMT, 1969–80).

Papsturkunden in England, i–iii, ed. W. Holtzmann (Göttingen, 1930–52).

The Peterborough Chronicle, ed. D. Whitelock (Copenhagen, 1954).

The Pipe Roll of 31 Henry I, Michaelmas 1130, ed. J. Hunter (London, 1833; reprinted 1929).

Reading Abbey Cartularies, ed. B. R. Kemp, Camden Society, fourth series, 31 and 33 (1986–87).

Records of the Templars in England in the Twelfth Century: The Inquest of 1185, ed. B. A. Lees (London, 1935).

Recueil des actes d'Henri II, ed. L. V. Delisle and E. Berger (Paris, 1916, 1920).

Regesta regum Anglo Normannorum, ii, ed. C. Johnson and H. A. Cronne (Oxford, 1956).

Regesta Anglo-Normannorum regum, iii, iv, ed. H. A. Cronne, and R. H. C. Davis (Oxford, 1968, 1969).

Regesta regum Scottorum, ed. G. W. S. Barrow, i (Edinburgh, 1960).

Reginald of Durham, *Libellus de admirandis beati Cuthberti virtutibus*, ed. J. Raine, SS, 1 (1835).

Richard Fitzneale, *Dialogus de Scaccario*, ed. C. Johnson, F. E. L. Carter and D. E. Greenway (OMT, 1983).

Richard of Hexham, *Chronicle*, ed. R. Howlett, *Chronicles of the Reigns of Stephen, Henry II and Richard I*, RS, 82, iii (London, 1886), pp. 139–78.

Robert of Torigny, *Chronicle*, ed. R. Howlett, *Chronicles of the Reigns of Stephen, Henry II and Richard I*, RS, 82, iv (London, 1889).

'Some Documents of the Anarchy', ed. H. W. C. Davis, *Essays Presented to R. L. Poole*, ed. H. W. C. Davis (Oxford, 1927), pp. 168–89.

Suger, *Epistolae*, PL, 186, cc. 1347–1440.

—, *Vie de Louis Le Gros*, ed. A. Molinier (Paris, 1887).

—, *Vie de Louis VI Le Gros*, ed. H. Waquet (Paris, 1929).

Wace, *Le roman de Brut*, ed. I. Arnold, Société des Anciens Textes Français (Paris, 1938–40); trans. by J. Weiss (Exeter, 1999).

The Book of the Foundation of Walden Monastery, ed. D. E. Greenway and L. Watkiss (OMT, 1999).

The Waltham Chronicle, ed. L. Watkins and M. Chibnall (OMT, 1994).

William of Malmesbury, —, 'Commentary on Lamentations', ed. H. Farmer, *Studia Monastica*, iv (1962), pp. 283–311.

—, *Gesta regum Anglorum*, ed. R. A. B. Mynors, R. M. Thomson and M. Winterbottom (OMT, 1998–99).

—, *Historia novella*, ed. and trans. K. Potter, Nelson Medieval Texts (1955); second edn E. J. King (OMT, 1998).

William of Newburgh, *Historia rerum Anglicarum*, ed. R. Howlett, *Chronicles of the Reigns of Stephen, Henry II and Richard I*, RS, 82, i (London, 1884).

'The Winton Domesday', ed. F. Barlow, *Winchester in the Early Middle Ages*, ed. M. Biddle (Oxford, 1976).

Secondary Works:

A. Ailes, 'Heraldry in Twelfth-Century England: the Evidence', *England in the Twelfth Century*, ed. D. Williams (Woodbridge, 1990), pp. 1–16, plates 1–17.

E. Amt, *The Accession of Henry II in England* (Woodbridge, 1993).

The Anarchy of King Stephen's Reign, ed. E. King (Oxford, 1994).

J. T. Appleby, *The Troubled Reign of King Stephen* (London, 1969).

Ella S. Armitage, *The Childhood of the English Nation* (London, 1877).

D. Baker, 'Legend and Reality: the Case of Waldef of Melrose', Studies in Church History, 12, *Church Society and Politics* (1975), pp. 59–82.

A. Ballard, *The Domesday Boroughs* (Oxford, 1904).

G. Barraclough, 'The Earldom and County Palatine of Chester', *Transactions of the Historic Society of Lancashire and Cheshire*, 103 (1951), pp. 23–57.

N. Barratt, 'The Revenues of King John', *EHR*, 111 (1996), pp. 835–55.

G. W. S. Barrow, 'David I of Scotland (1124–53): The Balance of New and Old' (Reading, 1985).

—, 'King David and the Honour of Lancaster', *EHR*, 70 (1955), pp. 85–89.

—, 'King David I, Earl Henry and Cumbria', *Transactions of the Cumberland and Westmorland Antiquarian and Archaeological Society*, 99 (1999), pp. 117–27.

—, 'The Charters of David I', *ANS*, 14 (1991), pp. 25–37.

—, 'The Pattern of Lordship and Feudal Settlement in Cumbria', *JMH*, 1 (1975), pp. 117–38.

D. Bates, 'The Prosopographical Study of the Anglo-Norman Royal Charters', *Family Trees and the Roots of Politics: Prosopography in Britain and France from the Tenth to the Twelfth Century*, ed. K. S. B. Keats-Rohan (Woodbridge, 1997), pp. 89–102.

R. Bearman, 'Baldwin de Redvers: 'Some Aspects of a Baronial Career in the Reign of King Stephen', *ANS*, 18 (1995), pp. 19–46.

R. Benson and H. Hatcher, *Old and New Sarum, or Salisbury* (London, 1843).

I. Bignamini, 'George Vertue, Art Historian', *Walpole Society*, 54 (1991), pp. 2–18.

W. de Gray Birch, *Catalogue of Seals in the Department of Manuscripts in the British Museum*, ii (London, 1892).

T. A. M. Bishop, *Scriptores regis* (Oxford 1961).

M. Blackburn, 'Coinage and Currency', *The Anarchy*, pp. 145–205.

—, 'Coinage and Currency under Henry I: A Review', *ANS*, 13 (1990), pp. 49–81.

S. Booth, *The Book Called Holinshed's Chronicle: An Account of Its Inception, Purpose, Contributors, Content, Publication, Revision and Influence on William Shakespeare* (San Francisco, 1968).

J. Bradbury, 'Geoffrey V of Anjou, Count and Knight', *The Ideals and Practice of Knighthood*, 3, ed. C. Harper-Bill and R. Harvey (Woodbridge, 1990), pp. 21–38.

—, *Stephen and Matilda* (Stroud, 1996).

R. Brady, *A Complete History of England from the Entrance of the Romans under the Conduct of Julius Caesar unto the End of the Reign of King Henry III* (London, 1685).

M. Brett, *The English Church under Henry I* (Oxford, 1975).

R. Britnell, 'English Markets and Royal Administration before 1200', *Economic History Review*, second series, 31 (1978), pp. 183–96.

C. N. L. Brooke, G. Keir and S. Reynolds, 'Henry I's Charter for London', *Journal of the Society of Archivists*, 4 (1973), pp. 558–78.

Z. N. Brooke, *The English Church and the Papacy* (Cambridge, 1931)

T. Callahan, 'A Revaluation of the Anarchy of Stephen's Reign, 1135–54: The Case of the Black Monks', *Revue Bénédictine*, 84 (1974), pp. 338–51.

—, 'Ecclesiastical Reparations and the Soldiers of the Anarchy', *Albion*, 10 (1978), pp. 300–18.

—, 'Sinners and Saintly Retribution: The Timely Death of Eustace', *Studia Monastica*, 17 (1976), pp. 109–17.

—, 'The Arrest of the Bishops at Stephen's Court: a Reassessment', *HSJ*, 7 (1995), pp. 101–16.

—, 'The Impact of the Anarchy on English Monasticism, 1135–54', *Albion*, 6 (1974), pp. 218–32.

—, 'The Notion of Anarchy in England, 1135–54: A Bibliographical Survey', *British Studies Monitor*, 6 (1976), pp. 23–35.

H. M. Cam, 'An East Anglian Shire Moot of Stephen's Reign', *EHR*, 39 (1924), pp. 568–71.

—, *The Hundred and the Hundred Rolls* (London, 1930).

W. Camden, *Britannia* (London, 1586).

J. Chartrou, *L'Anjou de 1109 à 1151* (Paris, 1928).

M. Chibnall, 'Anglo-French Relations in the Work of Orderic Vitalis', *Documenting the Past: Essays in Medieval History Presented to G. P. Cuttino*, ed. J. S. Hamilton and P. J. Bradley (Woodbridge, 1989), pp. 5–19.

—, *Anglo-Norman England, 1066–1166* (Oxford, 1986).

—, 'Innocent II and the Canterbury Election of 1138', *Medievalia Christiana XI e XII secoli*, ed. C. Viuola (Paris 1989), pp. 237–46.

—, *The Empress Matilda* (Oxford, 1991).

—, 'The Empress Matilda and Bec-Hellouin', *ANS*, 10 (1988), pp. 35–48.

—, 'The Empress Maud and Church Reform', *TRHS*, fifth series, 38 (1988), pp. 107–30.

G. E. Cokayne, *Complete Peerage*, second edn V. Gibbs (London, 1910–59): iv, appendix D: 'Earldoms Created by Stephen and the Empress Maud', pp. 576–79; vii, appendix I: 'Waleran, Count of Meulan, and his Successors', pp. 737–42; x, appendix H: 'The Families of the First and Second Earls of Pembroke', pp. 100–4; appendix J: 'The Early Veres', pp. 110–20; xi, appendix D: 'Henry I's Illegitimate Children', pp. 105–21; appendix F: G. H. White, 'The Earldoms of Wiltshire and Salisbury', pp. 126–32.

B. Coplestone-Crow. 'Payn Fitz John and Ludlow Castle', *Transactions of the Shropshire Archaeological and Historical Society*, 70 (1995), pp. 171–83.

C. Coulson, 'Cultural Realities and Reappraisal in English Castle Study', *JMH*, 22 (1996), pp. 171–207.

—, 'Freedom to Crenellate by Licence: An Historiographical Revision', *NMS*, 38 (1994), pp. 86–137.

—, 'The French Matrix of the Castle Provisions of the Chester-Leicester *Conventio*', *ANS*, 17 (1994), pp. 65–86.

D. Cox, 'Two Unpublished Charters of King Stephen for Wenlock Priory', *Transactions of the Shropshire Archaeological and Historical Society*, 6 (1989), pp. 56–59.

H. A. Cronne, 'Charter Scholarship in England', *University of Birmingham Historical Journal* (1961), pp. 26–61.

—, 'Ranulf de Gernons, Earl of Chester, 1129–53', *TRHS*, fourth series, 20 (1937), pp. 103–34.

—, *The Reign of King Stephen* (London, 1970).

D. Crouch, 'A Norman Conventio and the Bond of Lordship in the Middle Ages', *Law and Government in Medieval England and Normandy: Essays in Honour of Sir James Holt*, ed. G. Garnett and J. Hudson (Cambridge, 1994), pp. 299–324.

—, 'Earl William of Gloucester and the End of the Anarchy', *EHR*, 103 (1988), pp. 69–75.

—, 'Earls and Bishops in Twelfth Century Leicestershire', *NMS*, 37 (1993), pp. 9–20.

—, 'From Stenton to McFarlane: Models of Societies of the Twelfth and Thriteenth Centuries', *TRHS*, sixth series, 5 (1995), pp. 179–200.

—, 'Robert, Earl of Gloucester, and the Daughter of Zelophedad', *JMH*, 11 (1985), pp. 227–43.

—, *The Beaumont Twins* (Cambridge, 1987).

—, 'The Hidden History of the Twelfth Century', *HSJ*, 5 (1993), pp. 111–30.

—, *The Image of Aristocracy in Britain, 1000–1300* (London, 1992).

—, *The Reign of King Stephen, 1135–54* (London, 2000).

—, 'The Slow Death of Kingship in Glamorgan, 1067–1158', *Morgannwy*, 29 (1985), pp. 20–41.

P. Dalton, *Conquest, Anarchy and Lordship* (Cambridge, 1994).

—, 'Eustace Fitz John and the Politics of Anglo-Norman England: The Rise and Survival of a Twelfth-Century Royal Servant', *Speculum*, 71 (1996), pp. 358–83.

—, '*In Neutro Latere*: The Armed Neutrality of Ranulf II Earl of Chester in Stephen's Reign', *ANS*, 14 (1991), pp. 39–59.

—, 'William Earl of York and Yorkshire', *HSJ*, 2 (1990), pp. 155-65.

S. Daniel, *First Part of the Historie of England* (London, 1613); in *Complete Works*, ed. A. B. Grosart, iv (London, 1896).

R. R. Davies, 'Henry I and Wales', *Studies in Medieval History Presented to R. H. C. Davis*, ed. H. M. R. E. Mayr-Harting and R. I. Moore (Oxford, 1985), pp. 133–47.

H. W. C. Davis, 'Henry of Blois and Brian Fitz Count', *EHR*, 25 (1910), pp. 297–303.

R. H. C. Davis, 'Geoffrey de Mandeville Reconsidered', *EHR*, 79 (1964), pp. 299–307.

—, *King Stephen* (London 1967; third edn, 1990).

—, 'King Stephen and the Earl of Chester Revised', *EHR*, 75 (1960), pp. 654–60.

—, 'The Authorship of the Gesta Stephani', *EHR*, 77 (1962), pp. 209–32.

—, 'The College of Saint Martin-le-Grand and the Anarchy, 1135–54', *London Topographical Record*, 23 (1972) pp. 9–26.

C. Dickens, *A Child's History of England* (London, 1853).

J. C. Dickinson, *The Origin of the Austin Canons* (London, 1950).

C. L. Dier, 'The Proper Relationship between Lord and Vassal: Toward a Rationale for Anglo-Norman Litigation', *HSJ*, 6 (1994), pp. 1–12.

P. Dixon and P. Marshall, 'The Great Tower of Hedingham Castle: A Reassessment, *Fortress*, 18 (1993), pp. 16–23.

A. G. Dyson, 'The Monastic Patronage of Bishop Alexander of Lincoln', *Journal of Ecclesiastical History*, 26 (1975), pp. 1–24.

R. Eales, 'Local Loyalties in Norman England: Kent in Stephen's Reign', *ANS*, 8 (1985), pp. 88–108.

—, 'Royal Power and Castles in Norman England', *The Ideals and Practice of Medieval Knighthoood*, 3, ed. C. Harper-Bill and R. Harvey (Woodbridge, 1990), pp. 49–78.

The Earldom of Chester and its Charters: A Tribute to Geoffrey Barraclough, ed. A. T. Thacker, Chester Archeological Society (1991).

R. Faith, *The English Peasantry and the Growth of Lordship* (Leicester, 1997).

W. Farrer, *Honours and Knights' Fees*, i–iii (London, 1923–25).

G. H. Fowler, 'The Shire of Bedford and the Earldom of Huntingdon', *Bedfordshire Historical Society*, 9 (1925), pp. 23–35.

L. Fox, 'The Honour and Earldom of Leicester: Origin and Descent, 1066–1399', *EHR*, 54 (1939), pp. 385–73.

J. Gillingham, 'The Context and Purposes of Geoffrey of Monmouth's *History of the Kings of Britain*', *ANS*, 13 (1992), pp. 99–118.

J. A. Green, 'Financing Stephen's Wars', *ANS*, 14 (1991), pp. 91–114.

—, 'King Henry I and the Aristocracy of Normandy', *Actes du IIIe Congrès National des Sociétés Savantes, Poitiers 1986* (Paris 1988), i pp. 161–73.

—, 'Lords of the Norman Vexin', *War and Government*, ed. J. Gillingham (Woodbridge, 1984), pp. 47–61.

—, 'Praeclarum et Magnificum Antiquitatis Monumentum: The Earliest Surviving Pipe-Roll', *BIHR*, 55 (1982), pp. 1–17.

—, *The Aristocracy of Norman England* (Cambridge, 1997).

—, *The Government of England under Henry I* (Cambridge, 1986).

—, 'The Last Century of Danegeld', *EHR*, 96 (1981), pp. 241–58.

—, 'Unity and Disunity in the Anglo-Norman State', *Historical Research*, 62 (1989), pp. 15–34.

T. A. Green, *Verdict According to Conscience* (Chicago, 1985).

C. H. Haskins, 'William Cade', *EHR*, 28 (1913), pp. 730–31.

J. K. Hedges, *The History of Wallingford* (London, 1881).

R. Helmerich, 'King Stephen's Norman Itinerary 1137', *HSJ*, 5 (1993), pp. 89–98.

T. A. Heslop, 'English Seals from the Mid-Ninth Century to 1100', *JBAA*, 133 (1980), pp. 1–16.

—, 'Seals', *English Romanesque Art* (Arts Council, 1984), pp. 298–320.

R. Hill, 'The Battle of Stockbridge, 1141', *Studies in Medieval History Presented to R. A. Brown*, ed. C. Harper-Bill (Woodbridge, 1989), pp. 173–77.

G. R. J. Hodgett, 'Feudal Wiltshire', *Victoria County History of Wiltshire*, v, ed. R. B. Pugh and E. Crittall (London, 1957), pp. 44–71.

E. Hodnett, *Marcus Gheeraerts the Elder of Bruges, London and Antwerp* (Utrecht, 1971).

C. Holdsworth, 'Peace Making in the Twelfth Century', *ANS*, 19 (1996), pp. 1–17.

—, 'The Church', *The Anarchy*, pp. 207–29.

—, 'War and Peace in the Twelfth Century: The Reign of Stephen Reconsidered', *War and Peace in the Middle Ages*, ed. B. P. McGuire (Copenhagen, 1987), pp. 67–93.

R. Holinshed, *The Laste Volume of the Chronicles of England, Scotlande and Irelande* (London 1577); 6 vols (London, 1807–8).

C. W. Hollister, 'Anglo-Norman Succession Debate of 1126', *JMH*, 1 (1975), pp. 19–41.

—, 'Stephen's Anarchy', *Albion*, 6 (1974), pp. 233–39.

—, 'The Magnates of Stephen's Reign: Reluctant Anarchists', *HSJ*, 5 (1993), pp. 77–88.

—, 'The Misfortunes of the Mandevilles', *History*, 58 (1973), pp. 18–28.

C. W. Hollister and J. W. Baldwin, 'The Rise of Administrative Kingship: Henry I and Philip Augustus', *AHR*, 83 (1978), pp. 867–905.

J. C. Holt, '1153: The Treaty of Winchester', *The Anarchy*, pp. 291–316.

—, 'Politics and Property in Early Medieval England', *Past and Present*, 57 (1972), pp. 3–52.

M. Holmes, 'Some Woodcuts in Holinshed's Chronicle', *JBAA*, third series, 15 (1952), pp. 30–34, plates xxi–xxiii.

M. Horn, 'Der Kardinal Bischof Imar von Tusculum als Legat in England, 1144–45', *Historisches Jahrbuch*, 110 (1990), pp. 492–503.

J. Hudson, *The Formation of the English Common Law* (London, 1996).

R. Hüls, *Kardinäle, Klerus and Kirchen Roms, 1049–1130* (Tübingen, 1977).

D. Hume, *The History of England from the Invasion of Julius Caesar to the Accession of Henry VII*, 2 vols (London, 1762).

P. R. Hyams, 'The Charter as a Source of Early Common Law', *Journal of Legal History*, 12 (1991), pp. 173–89.

—, 'Warranty and Good Lordship in Twelfth-Century England', *Law and History Review*, 5 (1987), pp. 437–503.

W. Janssen, *Der päpstlichen Legaten in Frankreich vom Schisma Anaklets II bis zum Tode Coelestins III (1130–98)* (Köln, 1961).

A. Jessop and M. R. James, *Saint William of Norwich* (Cambridge 1896).

E. J. Kealey, 'King Stephen, Government and Anarchy', *Albion*, 6 (1974), pp. 200–17.

—, *Roger of Salisbury, Viceroy of England* (Los Angeles, 1972).

K. S. B. Keats-Rohan, 'The Bretons and Normans of England 1066–1154: The Family, the Fief and the Feudal Monarchy', *Nottingham Medieval Studies*, 36 (1992), pp. 42–78.

—, 'The Devolution of the Honour of Wallingford, 1066–1148', *Oxoniensia*, 54 (1989), pp. 311–18.

—, 'The Making of Henry of Oxford: Englishmen in a Norman World', *Oxoniensia*, 54 (1989), pp. 287–309.

T. Keefe, 'Geoffrey Plantagenet's Will and the Angevin Succession', *Albion*, 6 (1974), pp. 266–74.

D. C. King, *Castellarium Anglicanum* (Millwood, New York, 1983).

E. King, 'Dispute Settlement in Anglo-Norman England', *ANS* 14 (1992), pp. 115–130.

—, 'King Stephen and the Anglo-Norman Aristocracy', *History*, 59 (1974), pp. 180–94.

—, 'Mountsorrel and its Region in King Stephen's Reign', *Huntington Library Quarterly*, 44 (1980), pp. 1–10.

—, 'The Foundation Pipewell Abbey Northamptonshire', *HSJ*, 2 (1990) pp. 167-77.

—, 'The Anarchy of King Stephen's Reign', *TRHS*, fifth series, 34 (1984), pp. 133–53.

—, 'Waleran, Count of Meulan, Earl of Worcester, 1104–66', *Tradition and Change*, ed. D. Greenway (Cambridge, 1985), pp. 165–81.

M. D. Knowles, 'The Case of St William of York', *Cambridge Historical Journal*, 5 (1936), pp. 162–77, 212–14.

—, *The Monastic Order in England* (Cambridge, 1940).

P. Latimer, 'Grants of *Totus Comitatus*', *BIHR*, 59 (1986), pp. 137–45.

J. W. Leedom, 'The English Settlement of 1153', *History*, 65 (1980), pp. 347–64.

—, 'William of Malmesbury and Robert of Gloucester Reconsidered', *Albion*, 6 (1974), pp. 251–63.

Leland, John, *Itinerary of John Leland*, ed. L. Toulmin-Smith (London, 1906–10).

J. Le Patourel, 'What Did Not Happen in Stephen's Reign', *History*, 58 (1973), pp. 1–17.

K. Leyser, 'The Anglo-Norman Succession, 1120–25', *ANS*, 13 (1991), pp. 233–39.

J. Lingard, *A History of England from the First Invasion by the Romans to the Accession of Henry VIII* (London, 1819).

V. D. Lipman, *The Jews of Medieval Norwich* (London, 1961).

K. A. LoPrete, 'The Anglo-Norman Card of Adela of Blois', *Albion*, 22 (1990), pp. 177–92.

F. Lot, *Etudes critiques sur l'abbaye de St-Wandrille* (Paris, 1913).

B. Lyon: 'Henry II: A Non-Victorian Interpretation', *Documenting the Past: Essays in Medieval History Presented to G. B. Cuttino*, ed. J. S. Hamilton and P. J. Bradley (Woodbridge, 1989), pp. 21–31.

R. P. Mack, 'Mints in Stephen's Reign', *British Numismatic Journal*, 35 (1966), pp. 38–112.

T. Madox, *History of the Exchequer* (London, 1711).

F. W. Maitland, *Domesday Book and Beyond* (Cambridge, 1897).

J. Martindale, 'His Special Friend? The Settlement of Disputes and Political Power in the Kingdom of France (Tenth to Mid-Twelfth Century)', *TRHS*, sixth series, 5 (1995), pp. 21–57.

—, 'Succession and Politics in the Romance-Speaking World', *England and Her Neighbours*, ed. M. Jones and M. Vale (London, 1989), pp. 19–41.

L. W. Marvin, 'Men Famous in Combat and Battle: Common Soldiers and the Siege of Bruges', *JMH*, 24 (1998), pp. 243–58.

J. M. McCulloh, 'Jewish Ritual Murder: William of Norwich, Thomas of Monmouth and the Early Dissemination of Myth', *Speculum*, 72 (1997), pp. 698–740.

I. Megaw, 'The Ecclesiastical Policy of Stephen, 1135–39: A Reinterpretation', *Essays on British-Irish History in Honour of J. E. Todd*, ed. H. A. Cronne (London, 1949), pp. 24–45.

S. L. Mooers Christlelow, 'A Moveable Feast: The Itinerary of Henry I', *Albion*, 28 (1996), pp. 187–228.

—, 'A Revaluation of Royal Justice under Henry I of England', *AHR*, 93 (1988), pp. 340–58.

—, 'Patronage in the Pipe Roll of 1130', *Speculum*, 59 (1984), pp. 282–307.

—, 'The Royal Love in Anglo-Norman England: Fiscal or Courtly Concept?', *HSJ*, 8 (1996), pp. 27–42.

A. Morey and C. N. L. Brooke, *Gilbert Foliot and his Letters* (Cambridge, 1965).

C. Newman, *The Anglo-Norman Nobility in the Reign of Henry I* (Philadelphia, 1988).

D. Nicholl, *Thurstan, Archbishop of York, 1114–40* (York, 1964).

K. Norgate, *England under the Angevin Kings* (London, 1887).

R. B. Patterson, 'An Unedited Charter of Henry Fitz Empress and Earl William of Gloucester's Comital Status', *EHR*, 87 (1974), pp. 189–200.

—, 'Bristol as Angevin Baronial Capital under Royal Siege', HSJ 3 (1991), pp. 171–82.

—, 'Robert Fitz Harding of Bristol: Profile of an Early Angevin Burgess Baron Patrician and his Family's Urban Involvement', HSJ, 1 (1989), pp. 109–22.

—, 'The Ducal and Royal *Acta* of Henry Fitz-Empress in Berkeley Castle', *TBGAS*, 109 (1991), pp. 117–37.

—, 'William of Malmesbury's Robert of Gloucester: A Revaluation of the *Historia Novella*', *AHR*, 70 (1965), pp. 983–97.

D. Postles, 'The Austin Canons in English Towns, 1100–1350', *Historical Research*, 66 (1993), pp. 1–20.

D. J. Power, 'What Did the Frontier of Angevin Normandy Comprise?', *ANS*, 17 (1994), pp. 181–201.

J. O. Prestwich, 'The Treason of Geoffrey de Mandeville', *EHR* (198), pp. 283–312, 960–7, and reply by R. H. C. Davis pp. 313–17, 967–68.

Paul Rapin de Thoyras, *The History of England*; second edition with illustrations, translated and edited by N. Tindal (London, 1732).

H. G. Richardson and G. O. Saylers, *The Governance of Mediaeval England* (Edinburgh, 1963).

J. H. Round, *Geoffrey de Mandeville: A Study of the Anarchy* (London, 1892).

—, 'King Stephen and Ranulf Earl of Chester', *EHR*, 10 (1895), pp. 87–91.

—, *The Coming Terror* (Brighton, 1881).

—, 'The Counts of Boulogne as English Lords', *Studies in Peerage and Family History* (London, 1901), pp. 147–80.

A. Rumble, 'Codex Wintoniensis', *ANS*, 4 (1981), pp. 153–66.

A. Saltman, *Theobald, Archbishop of Canterbury* (London, 1956).

I. Sanders, *English Baronies, a Study of their Origin and Descent, 1086–1327* (Oxford, 1960).

K. Schnith, 'Regni et pacis inquietatrix, *JMH*, 2 (1976), pp. 135–57.

—, 'Zur Vorgeschichte der Anarchie', *Historisches Jahrbuch*, 95 (1975), pp. 68–87.

J. B. Smith and T. B. Pugh, 'The Lordship of Gower and Kilvey', *Glamorgan County History*, iii, *The Middle Ages*, ed. T. B. Pugh (Cardiff, 1971), pp. 205–83.

R. W. Southern, *Medieval Humanism and Other Studies* (Oxford, 1976).

—, 'The Place of Henry I in English History', *Proceedings of the British Academy*, 48 (1962), pp. 127–69.

J. Speed, *History of Great Britaine* (London, 1611).

M. Spurrell, 'Containing Wallingford Castle, 1146–53', *Oxoniensia*, 60 (1995), pp. 257–70.

F. M. Stenton, *First Century of English Feudalism, 1066–1166* (Oxford, 1932; second edn, 1961).

B. H. I. H. Stewart, *The Scottish Coinage* (London, 1967).

K. T. Streit, 'The Expansion of the English Jewish Community in the Reign of King Stephen', *Albion*, 25 (1993), pp. 177–92.

M. Strickland, 'Securing the North', *ANS*, 12 (1989), pp. 177–98.

M. Stroll, *The Jewish Pope* (Leiden, 1987).

W. Stubbs, *The Constitutional History of England* (sixth edn, Oxford, 1897).

H. Summerson, *Medieval Carlisle*, Cumberland and Westmorland Antiquarian and Archaeological Society (1993).

J. Tait, 'The *Firma Burgi* and the Commune in England, 1066–1191', *EHR*, 42 (1927), pp. 321–60.

C. H. Talbot, 'New Documents in the Case of St William of York', *Cambridge Historical Journal*, 10 (1950), pp. 1–15.

Polydore Vergil, *Historia Anglicana*, 26 books (Basel, 1534).

A. Vincent, *A Discoverie of Errours in the First Edition of the Catalogue of Nobility Published by Ralphe Brooke York Herald* (London, 1622)

N. Vincent, 'King Henry II and the Monks of Battle: the Battle Chronicle Unmasked', in *Belief and Culture in the Middle Ages*, ed. R. Gameson and H. Leyser (Oxford, 2001) pp. 264-86.

—, 'New Charters of King Stephen with Some Reflections upon the Royal Forest during the Anarchy', *EHR*, 114 (1999), pp. 899–928.

D. Walker, 'Miles of Gloucester, Earl of Hereford', *TBGAS*, 77 (1958), pp. 64–84.

—, 'Ralph, Son of Richard', *BIHR*, 33 (1960), pp. 195–202.

—, 'The 'Honours' of the Earl of Hereford in the Twelfth Century', *TBGAS*, 79 (1960), pp. 174–211.

J. Walker, 'Alms for the Holy Land: The English Templars', *The Medieval Military Revolution*, ed. A. Ayton and J. L. Price (London 1995), pp. 63–80.

A. Wareham, 'The Motives and Politics of the Bigod Family, *c.* 1066–1177', *ANS*, 17 (1994), pp. 223–42.

W. L. Warren, *Henry II* (London, 1973).

—, *The Governance of Norman and Angevin England, 1086–1272* (London, 1987).

L. Wertheimer, 'Adeliza of Louvain: Anglo-Norman Queenship', *HSJ*, 7 (1995) pp. 101–16.

G. H. White, 'King Stephen's Earldoms', *TRHS*, fourth series, 13 (1930), pp. 51–82.

—, 'The Career of Waleran Count of Meulan and Earl of Worcester, 1104–66', *TRHS*, fourth series, 17 (1934), pp. 19–48.

G. J. White, 'Continuity in Government' *The Anarchy*, pp. 117–43.

—, 'King Stephen, Duke Henry and Ranulf de Gernons, Earl of Chester', *EHR* (1976), pp. 555–65.

—, 'The End of Stephen's Reign', *History*, 75 (1990), pp. 3–22.

—, 'The Myth of the Anarchy', *ANS*, 22 (1999), pp. 323–37.

—, 'Were the Midlands Wasted during Stephen's Reign?', *Midland History*, 10 (1985), pp. 26–46.

P. Wormald, 'Charters, Law and the Settlement of Disputes in Anglo-Saxon Eng-
    land', *The Settlement of Disputes in Early Medieval Europe*, ed. W. Davies and
    P. Fouracre (Cambridge, 1986), pp. 149–68.
K. Yoshitake, 'The Arrest of the Bishops in 1139 and its Consequences', *JMH*, 14
    (1988), pp. 97–114.
—, 'The Exchequer in the Reign of Stephen', *EHR*, 103 (1988), pp. 950–59.
A. Young, 'William Cumin: Border Politics and the Bishopric of Durham', *Borthwick
    Papers*, 54 (1978).
C. R. Young, *The English Borough and Royal Administration, 1130–1307* (Durham,
    North Carolina, 1961).

Index

Denmark, king, 261 n. 54; Danes, 48
Derby, 268 n. 34
Devizes, castle, 90, 98, 114, 118, 124,
126, 163, 207, 258 n. 21
Devon, 119–20, 263 n. 70, 274 n. 40;
earl Baldwin de Redvers, 2, 74, 94,
120–21, 126, 164, 181, 217,
257 n. 13, 259 n. 32
Dickens, Charles, 26
disinherited, 61, 173–74, 214, 268 n. 38
disorder, 60, 75–76, 80, 98–99, 101,
120–22, 127, 130–34, 137, 149, 180,
202, 230, 238, 251 n. 1
documents, study, 29–31, 133–35,
138–40, 208
Domesday Book, 35, 82, 133, 145, 170,
172–73, 260 n. 47
Domfront, 75
Dorset, 121, 138
Dover, 66, 80, 145
Drax, 214, 274 n. 35
Drincourt, 117
Dryburgh abbey, 259 n. 34
Dublin, 263 n. 65
Dunstanvilla, Robert de, 257 n. 7
Dunster, castle, 97
Durham, 65, 81–82, 107, 114, 128, 131,
200, 234, 256 n. 27; peace of, 81, 89

earls, 97, 107–8, 114, 119–20, 122, 126,
134–35, 144–45, 148, 167, 180, 203,
217–18, 221–22, 257 n. 11, 267 n. 31,
269 n. 43; military duties, 177–79,
182; comital rank, 124, 177
East Anglia, 166, 210, 264 n. 71,
274 n. 42
Edmund, king and martyr, 237
Ely, 99, 234, 256 n. 27; bishops,
Hervey, 136; Nigel, 2, 67, 91–92, 99,
102, 136–37, 139, 216, 218–19;
castle, 128, 136
England, monarchy, 11–12; kings,
Aethelred II, 61; Canute, 50, 172;
Charles I, 20; Charles II, 228, 243;

Edward the Confessor, 59; Henry III,
73; Henry VII, 15; Henry VIII, 15,
17, 235; John, 219, 227, 233; Richard
I, 223, 243, 263 n. 70; William I, 23,
43, 50, 59, 61, 67, 83, 97, 134,
171–72, 185, 193, 254 n. 1; William
II, 21, 23, 40–42, 44, 47, 59–60, 69,
72, 81; William III, 22; queens of,
Adeliza of Louvain, second wife of
Henry I, 2, 52, 94–95, 247 n. 4,
248 n. 4, 251 n. 17, 257 n. 8; Eleanor
of Aquitaine, wife of Henry II, 11,
15, 46, 76, 205–6, 212; Elizabeth I,
18; Matilda of Boulogne, wife of
King Stephen, 1, 3, 16, 56, 80–81, 89,
105–6, 108, 110; Matilda of Scotland,
first wife of Henry I, 37, 43, 51–52,
88; see also Henry I, Henry II,
Stephen
English, sins of, 99, 151
Essex, 66, 108, 138, 216, 273 n. 34; earl
Geoffrey de Mandeville, 28, 107–8,
144, 157, 178–79, 181–82, 187, 223,
259 n. 30, 260 n. 37, 266 n. 21,
269 n. 45; Henry of, 221
exchequer, 85, 107, 133–36, 147,
216–19, 224, 233, 256 n. 1, 260 nn.
46–47, 266 n. 24, 268 n. 34, 274 n. 43
Exeter, 2, 74, 143, 164, 181, 266 n. 24;
bishop Robert, 120–22
Exmes, 75–76
Eye, honour, 67

Falaise, 116
Faringdon, 123, 129, 165, 184
Faversham, 10, 234, 271 n. 60
fealty, 51, 53, 70–71, 95, 105, 203
Fécamp abbey, 139, 262 n. 57
Ferrers, earl Robert, 137, 177–79, 209,
269 n. 45
feudalism, 16, 21, 24, 26–27, 29–31,
149, 152, 169, 177, 182, 185, 191,
218, 230
Fitz Alan, William, 80, 217, 274 n. 42

Warwickshire, 138, 273 n. 34

Waverley, abbey, 138

Wenlock, 257 n. 8

Westminster abbey, 1, 59; abbot
Gervase, 66

Whitby, 261 n. 54

William Aetheling, son of Henry I, 1,
51–52, 56, 71, 89, 203

William Clito, son of Duke Robert of
Normandy, 39, 46, 51–52, 54–55,
count of Flanders, 52, 56, 99

William Flandrensis, soldier, 117

Wilton, 120, 170, 191

Wiltshire, 97, 99, 120–21, 130, 137,
147, 257 n. 14, 263 n. 70, 270 n. 46;
earl Patrick of Salisbury, 120, 215,
217, 274 n. 37

Winchcombe, abbey, 267 n. 31

Winchester, 3, 15, 19, 34, 68, 90, 105,
108–9, 114, 170, 181, 184, 212–13,
234, 250 n. 25, 267 n. 31, 274 nn. 40,
43; council, 105–6, 109; diocese, 114;
bishop Henry, favoured by Henry I,
56; relations with Stephen, 3, 16, 67,
85, 90; as reformer, 40, 156;
management, 88, 260 n. 47;

negotiator, 76, 96, 212; patron, 236;
relations with papacy, 85–86, 202,
265 n. 9; as papal legate, 86–88,
92–93, 101–2, 105–11, 122, 155, 198,
254 n. 7

Windsor, 274 n. 40

Worcester, 21, 88, 97, 101, 114, 121,
170, 178, 201, 257 n. 11, 268 n. 35;
bishops, Simon, 114; John of
Pagham, 202; John of, chronicler, 39,
51, 53, 60, 66, 101, 244, 256 n. 26,
266 n. 24

wreck, rights of, 150

Wycombe, 32

York, 48, 114, 131, 144–45, 170, 201,
268 n. 34; ecclesiastical province, 69,
155; archbishops, Thurstan, 67, 79,
107, 127, 156, 198–99; William Fitz
Herbert, 16, 131, 156, 198; Henry
Murdac, 16, 131, 144, 156, 198–99,
201–3, 272 n. 7; Roger of Pont
L'Evêque, 198; earl, William of
Aumâle, 144, 178, 183

Yorkshire, 79–82, 125, 138, 274 n. 40

Ypres, William of, 167